Gender and Transitional Justice

'This book offers not only a rich and detailed account of transitional justice in East Timor over the last decade but also an important theoretical framework to understand the complexities of women's lives after conflict.'

Professor Hilary Charlesworth, *Australian National University*

'A must read for all who want to know and importantly understand the role and standing of women regarding transitional justice as it unfolds in Timor-Leste. Dr Harris Rimmer's account brings to bear both an engaged and an academic perspective that makes it a singularly unique contribution.'

Janelle Saffin, Australian Member of Parliament:
former advisor to Dr José Ramos-Horta

'Harris Rimmer's *Gender and Transitional Justice* offers a rare blend of theory and empirical inquiry. It makes a well-founded critique of the debates over punishment versus reconciliation in the transitional justice field while addressing its political realities in an exceptionally nuanced and creative way.'

Ruti Teitel, Ernst C. Stiefel, Professor of
Comparative Law, *New York Law School*

Gender and Transitional Justice provides the first comprehensive feminist analysis of the role of international law in formal transitional justice mechanisms. Using East Timor as a case study, it offers reflections on transitional justice administered by a UN transitional administration. Often presented as a UN success story, the author demonstrates that, in spite of women and children's rights programmes of the UN and other donors, justice for women has deteriorated in post-conflict Timor, and violence has remained a constant in their lives.

This book provides a gendered analysis of transitional justice as a discipline. It is also one of the first studies to offer a comprehensive case study of how women engaged in the whole range of transitional mechanisms in a post-conflict state, that is domestic trials, internationalised trials and truth commissions. The book reveals the political dynamics in a post-conflict setting around gender and questions of justice, and reframes the meanings of success and failure of international interventions in the light of them.

Susan Harris Rimmer is a Research Fellow at the Centre for International Governance and Justice, Regulatory Institutions Network, Australian National University.

Routledge Contemporary Southeast Asia Series

Land Tenure, Conservation and Development in Southeast Asia
Peter Eaton

The Politics of Indonesia–Malaysia Relations
One kin, two nations
Joseph Chinyong Liow

Governance and Civil Society in Myanmar
Education, Health and Environment
Helen James

Regionalism in Post-Suharto Indonesia
Edited by Maribeth Erb, Priyambudi Sulistiyanto and Carole Faucher

Living with Transition in Laos
Market integration in Southeast Asia
Jonathan Rigg

Christianity, Islam and Nationalism in Indonesia
Charles E. Farhadian

Violent Conflicts in Indonesia
Analysis, representation, resolution
Edited by Charles A. Coppel

Revolution, Reform and Regionalism in Southeast Asia
Cambodia, Laos and Vietnam
Ronald Bruce St John

Cambodia, Laos and Vietnam
Ronald Bruce St John

The Politics of Tyranny in Singapore and Burma
Aristotle and the rhetoric of benevolent despotism
Stephen McCarthy

Ageing in Singapore
Service needs and the state
Peggy Teo, Kalyani Mehta, Leng Leng Thang and Angelique Chan

Security and Sustainable Development in Myanmar
Helen James

Expressions of Cambodia
The politics of tradition, identity and change
Edited by Leakthina Chau-Pech Ollier and Tim Winter

Financial Fragility and Instability in Indonesia
Yasuyuki Matsumoto

The Revival of Tradition in Indonesian Politics
The deployment of adat from colonialism to indigenism
Edited by Jamie S. Davidson and David Henley

Communal Violence and Democratization in Indonesia
Small town wars
Gerry van Klinken

Singapore in the Global System
Relationship, structure and change
Peter Preston

Chinese Big Business in Indonesia
The state of the Capital
Christian Chua

Ethno-religious Violence in Indonesia
From soil to God
Chris Wilson

Ethnic Politics in Burma
States of conflict
Ashley South

Democratization in Post-Suharto Indonesia
Edited by Marco Bünte and Andreas Ufen

Party Politics and Democratization in Indonesia
Golkar in the Post-Suharto era
Dirk Tomsa

Community, Environment and Local Governance in Indonesia
Locating the Commonweal
Edited by Carol Warren and John F. McCarthy

Rebellion and Reform in Indonesia
Jakarta's security and autonomy polices in Aceh
Michelle Ann Miller

Hadrami Arabs in Present-day Indonesia
An Indonesia-oriented group with an Arab signature
Frode F. Jacobsen

Vietnam's Political Process
How education shapes political decision making
Casey Lucius

Muslims in Singapore
Piety, politics and policies
Kamaludeen Mohamed Nasir, Alexius A. Pereira and Bryan S. Turner

Timor Leste
Politics, history and culture
Andrea Katalin Molnar

Gender and Transitional Justice
The women of East Timor
Susan Harris Rimmer

Gender and Transitional Justice

The women of East Timor

Susan Harris Rimmer

Routledge
Taylor & Francis Group
LONDON AND NEW YORK

First published 2010
by Routledge
2 Park Square, Milton Park, Abingdon, Oxon OX14 4RN

Simultaneously published in the USA and Canada
by Routledge
711 Third Avenue, New York, NY 10017

Routledge is an imprint of the Taylor & Francis Group, an informa business

Typeset in Times New Roman 10pt by GreenGate Publishing Services,
Tonbridge, Kent

British Library Cataloguing in Publication Data
A catalogue record for this book is available from the British Library

Library of Congress Cataloging in Publication Data
Rimmer, Susan Harris.
Gender and transitional justice : the women of East Timor / Susan Harris Rimmer.
p. cm. – (Routledge contemporary Southeast Asia series)
Simultaneously published in the USA and Canada.
Includes bibliographical references and index.
1. Women – Legal status, laws, etc. – East Timor. 2. Justice, Administration of – East Timor. I. Title.
KNW5007.3.W65R56 2010
342.598708'78 – dc22
2009030543

ISBN10: 0-415-56118-3 (hbk)
ISBN10: 0-203-86004-7 (ebk)

ISBN13: 978-0-415-56118-1 (hbk)
ISBN13: 978-0-203-86004-5 (ebk)
ISBN13: 978-0-415-62622-4 (pbk)

To Marina Rae and Joshua Finn Rimmer
and to past and present survivors of conflict in Timor Leste

War, which produces large-scale destruction of visible objects, does so even more with humans. Only some individuals, and only gradually, become aware of this type of destruction. It takes off from our faces the last mask of humanity, turns us inside out and brings to the surface some unexpected qualities, radically different from what others believed us to be and what we believed we were. Moreover, it transforms the family system and produces changes of the sanctified rules and relations, including those deemed eternal and immutable, such as gender relations.

Ivo Andrić, 'Destruction', 1948

Contents

Acknowledgements

This book builds upon a doctoral thesis undertaken at the Australian National University College of Law, Canberra. Some additional primary materials and references can be found in the thesis, available at http://cigj.anu.edu.au/cigj/people/staff/harris_rimmer.php.

I am very grateful to my supervisory panel, Professor Penelope Mathew, Professor William Maley, Professor Hilary Charlesworth and Professor Andrew Byrnes. I am especially grateful for the unfailing generosity and talent of primary supervisor Professor Penelope Mathew. To me, these individuals represent the embodiment of academic excellence combined with dedication to human rights.

I am grateful for the assistance of style editor *par excellence* Ria van der Zandt and the team at Routledge, especially Dorothea Schaefter. Thank you to Karina Pelling for an excellent map. I am grateful for the comments and camaraderie of fellow academics over the course of this work, especially at the ANU College of Law. Many thanks to all those dedicated people who assisted with the Timor fieldwork and since in various ways, especially Sieneke Martin, Kieran Dwyer, Caitlin Reiger, Pat Walsh, Mark Byrne, Janet Hunt, John Scott Murphy, James Dunn, Nathan Laws, Galuh Wandita, Carolyn Graydon, Martin Clutterbuck, Lia Kent, Janelle Saffin, Helen Donovan, Jennifer Drysdale, Adérito Soares, Daniel Fitzpatrick and the past and present staff of the Australian Council for International Development, the East Timor NGO Forum, FOKUPERS and the Judicial System Monitoring Programme. Their collective dedication to the people of East Timor is truly inspiring.

My deep gratitude to the Vincent Fairfax Fellowship for allowing me to visit East Timor in 2002, and to the Bernard and Audre Rapoport Center for Human Rights and Justice at the University of Texas School of Law for timely encouragement.

Special thanks to the immeasurable support I received from Dr Sue Rimmer in all aspects of my work/life/thesis/sanity balance. Many thanks also for the support I received from Professor Peter Rimmer, Karen Fainges, Jean Poole, Joane Ford and my parents Peter Harris and Heather and Noel Woo. Thank you to all the exceptional teachers I have encountered so far, especially Pauline Cain, who first set me on this path of higher learning.

Finally, my deepest gratitude to my husband and extraordinary academic Dr Matthew Rimmer, who makes all things possible.

Early versions of this material have appeared in the following book chapters and journal articles: 'Untold Numbers: East Timorese Women and Transitional Justice'. Sharon Pickering and Caroline Lambert (eds), *Global Issues, Women and Justice.* Sydney: Federation Press, 2004: 335–66; 'The Roman Catholic Church and the Rights of East Timorese Women'. Carolyn Evans and Amanda Whiting (eds). *Mixed Blessings: Laws, Religions and Women's Rights in the Asia-Pacific Region*, The Hague: Brill, 2006: 654–701; 'Orphans or Veterans? Justice for Children Born of War in East Timor' in *Born of War: Protecting Children Born to Sexual Violence; Survivors in Conflict Zones*, R. Charli Carpenter (ed.), Bloomfield CT: Kumarian Press, 2007: 53–75; '"Orphans" or Veterans?: Justice for Children Born of War in East Timor' *Texas International Law Journal* 42.2 (2007): 323–44; 'Beloved Madam: Gender Issues at the Indonesian ad hoc Human Rights Court' *Timor-Leste: Challenges for Justice and Human Rights in the Shadow of the Past.* William Binchy (ed.). Dublin: Clarus Press, 2009: 427–74.

Permission has kindly been granted by Picture Media Australia to use in the concluding chapter the photo of 'East Timorese President Xanana Gusmão meets Indonesian Presidential candidate former General Wiranto in Badung Bali on 29 May 2004', taken by Dadang Tri for Reuters.

The map is supplied by the Geospatial and Cartographic Services Research School of Pacific and Asian Studies College of Asia and the Pacific, The Australian National University.

Abbreviations

AIHRC Afghanistan Independent Human Rights Commission
BPU Border Patrol Unit
CAT Convention Against Torture
CAVR Comissão de Acolhimento, Verdade e Reconciliação de Timor Leste (Commission for Reception, Truth, and Reconciliation, East Timor)
CIVPOL Civilian Police
CRP Community Reconciliation Process
CTF Commission of Truth and Friendship
DAC Development Assistance Committee
DAW Division for the Advancement of Women
DDR Disarmament, Demobilisation and Reintegration
DPR Dewan Perwakilan Rakyat (People's Representative Assembly, Indonesia)
ETDF East Timor Defence Force
FALINTIL Forças Armadas de Libertação Nacional de Timor Leste (Armed Forces for the National Liberation of East Timor)
F-FDTL FALINTIL Forças Armadas de Defesa de Timor Leste
FOKUPERS Forum Komunikasi Untuk Perempuan Loro Sae' (East Timorese Women's Communication Forum)
FRETILIN Frente Revolucionária do Timor Leste Independente (Revolutionary Front for an Independent East Timor)
ICC International Criminal Court
ICIET International Commission of Inquiry on East Timor (UN)
ICTJ International Center for Transitional Justice
ICTR International Criminal Tribunal for Rwanda
ICTY International Criminal Tribunal for the Former Yugoslavia
IDP Internally displaced person
IHL International humanitarian law
IMET International Military Education and Training
INTERFET International Force for East Timor
IRC International Rescue Committee
JSMP Judicial System Monitoring Programme
KKR Komisi Kebenaran dan Rekonsiliasi (Indonesian Truth Commission)

Komnas HAM Komisi Nasional Hak Asasi Manusia (National Human Rights Commission Indonesia)
Kopassus Indonesian Army Special Forces
KPP HAM Komisi Penyelidik Pelanggaran Hak Asasi Manusia di Timor Timur (Commission of Inquiry on East Timor)
KUHP Kitab Undang-Undang Hukum Pidana (Indonesian Criminal Code)
NGO Non-governmental organisation
OPMT Organização Popular da Mulher Timor (The Popular Organisation of East Timorese Women)
PDO Public Defenders Office
PKF United Nations Peacekeeping Force
PNTL Polícia Nacional de Timor Leste
POLRI Indonesian National Police
SCIU Serious Crimes Investigation Unit
SPSC Special Panels for Serious Crimes
SRSG Special Representative of the Secretary-General
TNI Indonesian National Army
TRCA Indonesian Truth and Reconciliation Commission Act
UNAMET United Nations Mission in East Timor
UNCHR United Nations Commission on Human Rights
UNHCR United Nations High Commissioner for Refugees
UNMISET United Nations Mission of Support in East Timor
UNMIT United Nations Integrated Mission in Timor Leste
UNOTIL United Nations Office in Timor Leste
UNPOL United Nations Police
UNTAET United Nations Transitional Administration in East Timor

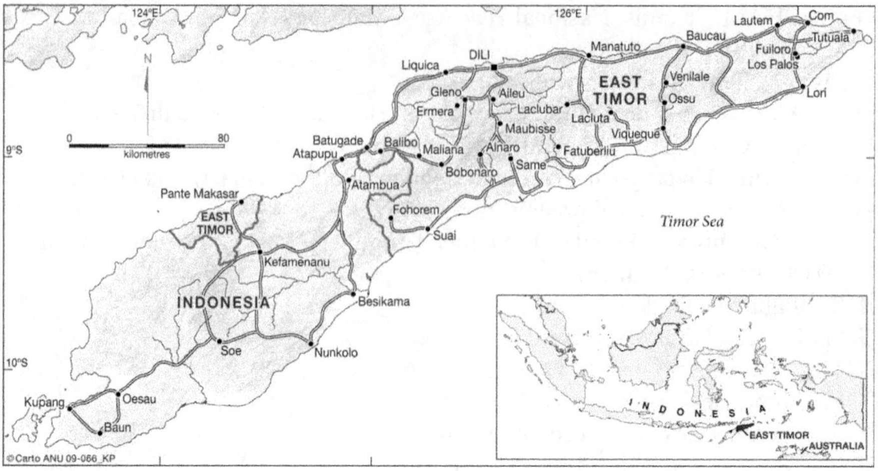

Figure 1 Map of East Timor (Source: Geospatial and Cartographic Services Research School of Pacific and Asian Studies College of Asia and the Pacific, The Australian National University).

1 Introduction: *A luta continua!* (The fight continues!)

One of the bravest but least known acts during the East Timorese[1] resistance to Indonesian occupation occurred in November 1998 when over 20 Timorese women told their stories of surviving sexual violence[2] to crowds of hundreds at a public meeting in Dili. The stories were collated into an English language book called *Buibere*,[3] which means 'woman' in Mumbai, the second most common Timorese language after Tetum. It was written only in English, published in Australia, and intended as an advocacy document for the international community. Between 1975 and 1999, there had only been four short but searing reports from international non-governmental organisations (NGOs) about gender-based persecution of women in East Timor, and no official United Nations (UN) comment.[4] But the persecution, as described first-hand in these collected testimonies, was intense, and included rape, torture and other inhumane acts.

In November 2001, in an independent East Timor, the local women's rights NGO FOKUPERS[5] released a second version of *Buibere* in Tetum at a public event, with many of the women who contributed stories to the book present. The second edition is intended to formally respect and honour the contribution of East Timorese women to independence and the high price they paid during the Indonesian occupation.

Some of the problems that continue to face the women of East Timor were graphically outlined by advocate Sister Maria de Lourdes Martins Cruz at the launch:

> 'A luta continua!' she said, and described how the women of East Timor were still second-class citizens in their own land. 'A luta continua!' and she described how girls still don't receive the same educational or employment opportunities as men. 'A luta continua!' and she told of domestic violence still rampant, women still serving as slaves in their own homes, women bought and sold like commodities under the tradition of bride price, and men leaders still unwilling to accept East Timorese women as equals. Ovation after ovation shook the hall.[6]

Given the serious nature of the crimes outlined in *Buibere*, Sister Maria's speech is striking in that in the eyes of those survivors present that day, independence did not necessarily mark the end of violence against women, just a new manifestation of violence and subordination. There appeared to be a clear linkage between the gender-based political persecution and violence by invading forces, understood as the burden of the feminine face of resistance, and endemic gender-based violence and inequality experienced by women as citizens in the transitional Timorese society.

ARGUMENT

This book seeks to answer the question of what role international law has played in relation to East Timorese women engaged with transitional justice processes from 1999 to 2009. Despite the placement of women in some key decision-making positions within the transitional justice mechanisms,[7] I argue that women in East Timor generally did not receive tangible and satisfactory results from the justice system in the post-independence period. I assess what women can demand and expect from transitional justice processes, and how transitional justice models can be revised to achieve these results.

I focus on a feminist examination of the role of international law within the overall framework of transitional justice interventions designed for the violations of human rights in East Timor. I limit my inquiry to an analysis of the treatment of gender-based violence[8] experienced by East Timorese women in the period from 1975 to October 2007 as highlighted within the formal transitional justice processes that occurred between 1999 and 2009.

My analysis shows there are still gaps and silences in the categorisation and prosecution of gender-based violence under international law as experienced in Timor. The question is whether feminist analysis needs to question the obligation to prosecute imposed by international law, especially the imperative to immediately hold criminal trials.

Reopening debate about the timing and manner of trials in a post-conflict state is important because I contend that Sister Maria was correct in stating that the problems facing Timorese women in the independence period are linked to the problems women faced during the occupation. Recognition and redress under the law for gender-based violence in war is linked to recognition and redress for domestic violence and socio-economic rights in 'peace'.[9] The claims made for the transitional justice mechanisms chosen for Timor were that they would contribute to building the rule of law in both Timor and Indonesia. Women in Timor generally lack political power and representation in comparison to men,[10] and possess the worst socio-economic indicators of the Timorese population.[11] One can assume that the strength or weakness of the rule of law in a new state will have a gendered impact.[12]

The vulnerable situation of women in East Timor in the post-independence period has several implications. There is a growing consensus in donor countries that international interventions should seek to at least do no harm, a proposition derived from the Hippocratic oath and increasingly applied to humanitarian interventions.[13] Put simply, transitional justice interventions should seek to be inclusive of women's experiences of the conflict and post-conflict periods and not undermine any progress for women. If this cannot be achieved at the outset of the post-conflict period, I argue that other strategies should be pursued to gain material benefits for women, even if the goal of combating impunity can eventually be met in substance by holding gender-sensitive trials.

Even if perfect trials and truth commissions were held which achieved all the traditional goals of transitional justice mechanisms, there may be limitations on what law, especially international law, can achieve to benefit women. Katherine M. Franke argues that transitional justice outcomes for women should be judged on whether they provide *recognition* and *redistribution*.[14] Recognition deals with establishing facts and identities, such as who are the victims and perpetrators of criminal practices. Redistribution deals with redistributing money and land, but also shame or symbolic and cultural resources.[15]

Where women have been recognised at all in legal processes in Timor, there is a danger that it has only led to marginalisation and stigmatisation of survivors of sexual violence. Trials have not contributed to a material rise to the basic living standards and status of women. There may also be negative consequences for survivors of domestic violence if there is no confidence in the judicial sector to acknowledge and protect women. I therefore propose one alternative way of addressing the situation of women. By moving beyond ideas of women as victims or even survivors, by redefining what it is to be a 'veteran', progress could be made as veterans receive both maintenance and status in the new state. East Timorese women themselves have continuously stressed the need for justice to encompass their ongoing economic and social rights.[16]

The danger for East Timorese women now is what I term the 'changing the curtains' phenomena – that fundamental changes in the sovereignty of the state in the form of independence may mean that the basic conditions of women's lives, or their potential to claim their legal rights, does not change in any meaningful sense, as described in the call to arms by Sister Maria. Despite some important efforts to include women and their experiences in the justice mechanisms established in East Timor since 1999, Timorese women such as Sister Maria may indeed have cause to be disenchanted.

1.1 Parameters

The scope of the book is bounded by several factors. The most important limitation is that I try to measure the impact of international law on the women of East Timor, which can only be a partial and contested enterprise. In analysing the impact of international law on Timorese women, I am cognisant of my own writing position as an Australian academic, and the immense diversity of the female population of Timor.[17] The aim of the book is to be exploratory and ask the question 'where are the women'[18] in the transitional justice processes for Timor.[19] The quotation by Ivo Andrić prefacing the book invites us to think more broadly about masks of humanity ripped away from survivors of armed conflict and see the reality or complexity of what might be exposed underneath.[20] It also asks us to think about men and women wearing different masks, as fighters, victims, survivors, citizens, veterans.[21]

The evidence about women and transitional justice is therefore impressionistic because comprehensive data about Timorese women's attitudes towards transitional justice issues does not yet, and may not ever exist. Nevertheless, Timorese women's voices are foregrounded wherever possible. Key documents produced by Timorese women's groups containing their positions and voices on justice issues, such as the Women's Charter of Rights adopted in 2000, are fundamental to this book.[22]

Another limitation is that research about the transitional justice mechanisms in East Timor and Indonesia is heavily reliant on translated primary materials such as indictments, judgments and court observations by NGOs such as the Judicial Systems Monitoring Programme (JSMP) and the Berkeley War Crimes Studies Center, as well as translated Indonesian and Timor press articles.[23] The lack of access to the primary materials is important in itself because access to the law is a key indicator to denote the existence of the rule of law.

A final limitation is that I focus only on the formal transitional justice mechanisms. The impact of informal mechanisms; such as traditional justice, non-state actors on justice outcomes for women including the Catholic Church,[24] civil society groups,[25] and cultural/artistic programmes;[26] plus economic actors, such as donor governments, the World Bank, International Monetary Fund, corporations and development NGOs[27] are very important and deserve further research but are outside the bounds of the book.

FEMINIST CRITIQUES OF TRANSITIONAL JUSTICE MECHANISMS IN EAST TIMOR

This book aims to provide the first comprehensive feminist analysis of the role of international law in the formal transitional justice mechanisms that relate to East Timor.[28] As such, I survey the current literature in relation to general transitional justice debates and theory that deal with the role of international law or transition to the rule of law, with an emphasis on literature that has concentrated on East Timor as a case study. I have further assessed the literature dealing with gender and transitional justice, and gender issues in occupied Timor and post-conflict Timor.

1.2 Transitional justice debates

Transitional justice is a relatively young but burgeoning area of research, which has rapidly gathered momentum in the post-Cold War period. It began with work in the 1980s and 1990s, mainly produced by US political scientists and economists in relation to post-conflict states in Latin America and Eastern Europe.[29] Transitional justice scholars focus on what it means for a nation to come to terms with a violent past and what to do with the perpetrators of the violence. This is usually done by analysing accountability mechanisms at a point of transition for those accused of having committed human rights violations during the prior regime.[30] Analysis is heavily focused on institutions and institution-building. Accountability options include the following mechanisms; (a) international prosecutions; (b) international and national investigatory commissions; (c) truth commissions; (d) national prosecutions; (e) national lustration mechanisms; (f) civil remedies and (g) mechanisms for the reparation for victims.[31] Recent scholarship is moving to a more organic consideration of transitional justice from the point of view of the community, or 'from below',[32] and is also refining new methods of empirical research in the area.[33]

Theoretical debates in the political science field focus on the balance to be achieved in transitional societies between 'truth' and 'reconciliation';[34] 'peace' and 'justice'; 'amnesty' and 'punishment'; and the contested nature of these terms..[35] For example, Michael Ignatieff, in his seminal piece 'Articles of Faith', analyses the claims often made in transitional justice rhetoric and notes the implicit assumptions: 'that a nation has one psyche, not many; that the truth is one, not many; that the truth is certain, not contestable; and that when it is known by all, it has the capacity to heal and reconcile.'[36]

Chilean playwright Ariel Dorfman has articulated these dilemmas with particular eloquence:

> How can those who tortured and those who were tortured coexist in the same land? How to heal a country that has been traumatised by repression if the fear to speak out is still omnipresent everywhere? And how do you reach the truth if lying has become a habit? How do we keep the past alive without becoming its prisoner? Is it legitimate to sacrifice the truth to ensure peace? And what are the consequences of suppressing that past and the truth it is whispering or howling to us? Are people free to search for justice and equality if the threat of a military intervention haunts them? And given these circumstances, can violence be avoided? And how guilty are we all of what happened to those who suffered most? And perhaps the greatest dilemma of them all: how to confront these issues without destroying the national consensus which creates democratic stability?[37]

1.3 Legal scholarship

Analysis relating to transitional justice studies from the perspective of international law has, in the main, been limited to those conflicts where international criminal trials have been held.[38] For example, the Nuremberg and Tokyo trials held after the Second World War, and the ad hoc tribunals set up by the UN Security Council to deal with international crimes committed in the former Yugoslavia and Rwanda have been closely examined.[39]

The scholarship tends to deal with the conduct of the trials, the development of jurisprudence or the content of international criminal law, and the creation of the International Criminal Court.[40] In other words, legal scholarship in the transitional justice field has been almost exclusively trials-focused. The overwhelming majority of international law academics advocate the holding of trials as the preferred accountability option for post-conflict settings.[41] This is also the stated view of the United Nations secretariat.[42] Where legal scholarship is critical, it tends to focus on the question of whether amnesties given in relation to truth commissions are compliant with international law;[43] or whether trials are better than truth commission processes or no process at all.[44]

Legal scholarship in this context often focuses on three trends: attempts to move focus from the state to a more victim-centred conception of justice;[45] attempts to complement the operation of trials with truth commissions; and reframing the goal of transitional justice mechanisms from punishment of individual criminals to rebuilding the rule of law.[46] Louise Arbour observes that transitional justice is 'out-growing' its intellectual and political origins as a sub-discipline of law.[47] She refers to efforts to establish a common base of human rights for the future political and social order for all members of society, including perpetrators, victims and bystanders.[48]

Recent legal scholarship has encompassed wider examinations of the concept of the term 'justice' employed in theoretical debates on transitional justice. Rama Mani advocates three categories of justice: legal justice, rectifying justice and social justice.[49] Mani defines *rectificatory justice* as rectifying the injustices that are direct consequences of conflict, such as abuses committed against civilian noncombatants.[50] *Legal justice* is defined as addressing the breakdown of the rule of law, the political manipulation of the legal system, the corruption of law makers, law enforcers and judges, and the consequent lack of legal redress for injustices and grievances experienced by the population.[51] *Distributive justice* refers to redressing the structural and systemic injustices and distributive inequalities that frequently underlie the causes of conflict.[52]

Within the idea of rectificatory justice, the concepts of 'restorative' and 'retributive' justice recur in the literature.[53] Debates over the nature of restorative and retributive justice predominate in domestic criminal contexts[54] and are beginning to influence the international arena. Briefly, restorative justice can be defined as the idea that harm to another requires a healing response or creative restitution that punishment by a court alone is inadequate to provide. The focus is on the well-being of the victim. It predicates that the community, the offender and the victim are all key stakeholders in the outcome of the justice process.[55] The concept of restorative justice has had a significant impact on discussions of how to improve the manner in which war crimes trials are conducted, as can be observed in the discourse of therapeutic jurisprudence,[56] and in broadening the goals that transitional justice mechanisms should strive to achieve, such as the way in which truth commissions can complement trials.

Retributive justice is predicated on the idea that justice equates to punishment of the perpetrator by the state under the law. The two concepts can reside in the same legal mechanism, such as the International Criminal Court.[57] The UN General Assembly emphasised the importance of both ideas when it adopted resolution 60/147 of 16 December 2005 on the *Basic Principles and Guidelines on the Right to a Remedy and Reparation for Victims of Gross Violations of International Human Rights Law and Serious Violations of International Humanitarian Law*.[58]

Rama Mani's thesis is that 'addressing rectificatory justice while paying only nominal attention to the parallel need to restore legal justice (rule of law) and distributive justice means that the task remains incomplete and inadequate'.[59] It is now said almost by rote in the literature that transitional justice mechanisms should support the rule of law in post-conflict states. This is because the task of transitional justice is in part forward-looking, to ensure that 'never again' will violations reoccur in the society.[60]

The reason for this support for the dual role of law in a post-conflict state is a belief in the transformative value of transitional justice processes. For example, the leading academic in transitional justice studies, Ruti Teitel states that transitional criminal justice 'does not simply advance the conventional purposes of punishment in a rule-of-law state' but that the law in a transitional period holds an 'independent potential for effecting transformative politics' and 'liberalising' change.[61] She suggests that there is no universal norm but rather that transitional justice measures may be 'partial, contextual and multiple'.[62] In other words, trials can and should assist the efforts to restore the justice sector to a society where the rule of law has broken down or weakened as a result of conflict.[63]

Teitel proposes a spectrum of transitional justice options. These range from mechanisms critical of the prior regime, to those that maintain the pre-existing legal order. Each should be tailored to the legacy of the injustice, the legal culture, the dynamics of the transition and the expectations of the affected people.[64] What Teitel is suggesting is that the outcomes of transitional justice should be judged by how much they contribute, not to peace or justice however defined, but to building the rule of law and democratic participation.

Teitel's spectrum is still usually turned into a hierarchy by international lawyers in relation to Timor. International trials are at the apex on a ladder of possible options, which would place a truth commission somewhere in the middle, and the state or international community doing nothing at all at the other end.[65] The legal literature on Timor tends to focus on the Special Panels as an example of a hybrid tribunal, or the CAVR as an example of restorative justice processes. There is also a range of international NGO and UN reports assessing the processes in Timor against the goal of combating impunity for violations of international law and arguing for an international tribunal.[66] There has also been some focus on challenges to building the rule of law in East Timor.[67]

In contrast, academic literature assessing the transitional justice processes in East Timor from a political science perspective tends to focus on institution-building,[68] especially as an example of UN transitional administrations,[69] and explores the idea of the balance struck between peace and justice.[70]

This book is informed by developments in the international relations field into theories and practice of transitional justice, but will also involve a gendered analysis of these questions in relation to the case study of East Timor – something that has not been undertaken in a sustained fashion before.[71]

1.4 Gender and transitional justice scholarship

Gender and international law,[72] and gender persecution within the framework of international law,[73] are well-trodden paths of analysis. However, there has not yet been a systematic investigation of gender and transitional justice in relation to a particular country.[74] In a groundbreaking article, Christine Bell and Catherine O'Rourke ask whether feminism even needs a theory of transitional justice.[75]

There is, however, general feminist scholarship that has informed this book. Important scholarship has focused on women's experiences in armed conflict,[76] and the interplay of gender and militarism.[77] There has been a focus on women's roles in post-conflict reconstruction and peace-building,[78] centred on Security Council Resolution 1325 to promote the role of women in conflict and conflict-resolution, calling for 'all actors involved, when negotiating and implementing peace agreements, to adopt a gender perspective'.[79]

Feminist legal scholarship has mainly focused on the categorisation and prosecution of crimes against women as they have featured in international criminal trials,[80]especially the International Tribunal for the Former Yugoslavia (ICTY).[81] Galvanised by the fact that there had been no historic prosecutions of gender violence in armed conflict and the framework of international humanitarian law still referred to rape as a crime against 'honour', the aim of feminist scholars has therefore been the global acceptance of gender-persecution in armed conflict as crimes under international humanitarian law. As Kelly Dawn Askin states '[r]eviewing the totality of international humanitarian law instruments establishes that museums, paintings, buildings and armed combatants have been provided far more protections over the years than have female civilians'.[82] This is a project which many feminist scholars now consider finished with the advances made by the Rome Statute.[83]

There has been some feminist analysis of prosecution strategies, also. Motivated by concepts of restorative justice, within the field of therapeutic jurisprudence there is an increasing body of writing on how trials may need to be improved to meet the needs of women. For example, many have explained that under the right conditions, the provision of testimony by survivors of sexual violence can assist in the healing and recovery process.[84] In relation to prosecution strategies at the current tribunals, the focus has been primarily on the inclusion of women in judicial institutions,[85] investigating, bringing indictments and bringing to trials those alleged to have committed gender persecution, and protection of witnesses.[86] Much of the literature focuses on the ad hoc international tribunals and the International Criminal Court.[87]

This has led some scholars to begin significant inquiry into the role of women in anti-impunity alternatives such as truth commission processes,[88] alternative tribunals,[89] and traditional justice processes,[90] as well as social and cultural rights issues in the transitional justice context, particularly in relation to reparations.[91]

1.5 Feminist counter-narratives

Generally speaking then, the theoretical framework of transitional justice – outside of the focus on the prosecution of sexual violence in criminal trials – has so far proven resistant to feminist analysis or has perhaps seemed benign and gender neutral. However, there have been some important insights. One feminist counter-narrative to the obligation to punish under international law, states that law is so resistant to women's lived experiences as to make trials not worth pursuing.[92] This is partly because it is flawed in recognising the full experience of gender-based violence and because it does not 'redistribute' shame or any type of tangible benefit.[93] Even if improvements were made on current practice in trials, scholars such as Karen Engle and Julie Mertus argue that better prosecution strategies may not solve the inherent problems facing women involved in international trials,[94] and we should be critical of claims that international adjudication of wartime rape cases necessarily advances the interests of female survivors.[95]

The second important feminist counter-narrative I adopt relates to the categorisation function of international law. Judith Gardam argues that the project of categorisation of crimes should not be considered closed, that international humanitarian law does not adequately address the protection needs of women in armed conflict as it currently stands despite the admitted advances made,[96] and violations must be perceived as sufficiently serious to constitute an international crime.[97] This legal gap is explored in the area of forced maternity and post-conflict domestic violence in Chapter Six, along with the general lack of acknowledgment of economic, social and cultural rights.

The third important counter-narrative focuses on outcomes for women. Christine Bell and Catherine O'Rourke propose that feminist theorists should focus on how transitional justice debates help or hinder broader projects of securing material gains for women through transition.[98] Similarly, Katherine M. Franke argues that transitional justice outcomes for women should be judged on whether they provide *recognition* and *redistribution,* as mentioned above.[99] While transitional justice mechanisms can do both, Franke decides that they are mostly engaged with recognition-based justice projects and that this has come at a cost to the individual women involved, while the limited script offered to women casts them only as victims of sexual violence.[100]

Fionnuala Ni Aolain and Michael Hamilton suggest that what may appear to be a moment of opportunity in transitional societies can become what they term 'a moment of retrenchment'. They argue that despite substantive advances in dismantling the public/private divide in many Western societies, those same Western states through 'rule-of-law proselytizing' can entrench the operation of this divide in transitional states.[101] Ni Aolain further explores this role of international masculinities, and the 'patriarchy that is imported with international oversight of transitional societies'.[102]

This book therefore explores the broader question as to why and how these limitations in the legal and social outcomes for women have occurred; are the deficiencies due to gaps in the law or are they structurally embedded – 'hard-wired' – in the law itself? What if international law is not as relevant to transitional justice processes as international lawyers think it is?[103]

CHAPTER OUTLINE

Chapter Two examines theoretical questions about whether there is a role for international law at all in transitional justice choices for modern post-conflict states, and if so, what might be its impact on women involved in the relevant transitional justice processes.

I posit that international law impacts on transitional justice mechanisms in three primary ways. The first impact is normative, in that international law seeks to *categorise* what behaviour can be considered a crime under international law.

The second impact, consequent on the categorisation of certain behaviours into crimes, is that international law places an *obligation to prosecute* and punish certain crimes and designates individual responsibility for those crimes, although the obligation falls both on the violating state and the international community. The third impact, again consequential, is that the categorisation of offences influences what is tried and with what priority, termed *prosecution strategies*.

I set out the 'legalist' versus 'realist' arguments over the obligation to punish in international law. Most international lawyers believe international law is central to the project of transitional justice because it imposes an obligation on states to punish individuals guilty of the most serious violations of international law, and this determines that trials must be among the mechanisms chosen (the 'legalist' approach). The counterpoint to this position posed by 'realist' political scientists is that these choices should be left entirely to the post-conflict state concerned in the interests of democracy and stability. I argue that both theoretical positions are based on the absence and silence of women. A third-way counter-narrative to both positions is examined – that so-called 'realist' international relations theorists focus only on elite men as the subject of discourse and do not describe the reality of women's lives or the complexity of gender roles,[104] but for much the same reasons the gendered nature of international law means that it too will be resistant to the lived experience of women.[105]

In Chapter Three, I provide a brief background on the historical backdrop of East Timor from 1975 to 1999, including the situation of women. I then outline the transitional justice choices made by the UN in East Timor and Indonesia after 1999 to 2007, and their basis in international law.

This chapter also presents the evidence that the cultural and political realities of women in East Timor were and remain extremely complex and fluid. Timorese women play multiple roles, including in government, politics and transitional justice systems, which will be outlined in detail in relation to the different mechanisms. Women played an active role in the liberation movement (*Buibere* paints only one portrait),[106] and at times were armed fighters in the guerrilla movement and are therefore also potential perpetrators of international crimes. The equality of women occupied a central place in the liberation ideology of FRETILIN,[107] and continued to be one of the party's key platforms when it gained a parliamentary majority in the 2001 elections.[108] This is reflected in the Timorese Constitution, as will be examined.[109]

Despite this complexity, Timorese women's groups have identified some general problems for women in the post-conflict period, which include: the failure of domestic and international law to adequately address gender-based persecution experienced during the Indonesian occupation from 1975 to the present; the impact of poor economic and social conditions, including bars to property ownership; the failure of policy or law to provide acknowledgment or compensation for survivors of gender-based persecution or the children born of rape; the failure of domestic law to protect women from the escalation of domestic violence post-independence; obstacles to participation in pre- and post-independence decision-making, including representation in formal elections; and obstacles to participation in key decisions about transitional justice mechanisms, such as amnesties.[110]

In Chapters Four to Six, I consider how this theoretical examination plays out in relation to the case study of East Timor, focusing on the UN trials in Dili, the Jakarta trials and the truth commissions. The transitional justice choices in East Timor were novel and informed by previous experiences of the UN in other countries. Secretary-General Kofi Annan went so far as to call Timor a 'child of the international community'.[111] Moreover, crucial precedents have been set regarding the definition and prosecution of gender-based violence under international criminal law. There have been breakthroughs in the area of state obligations to punish violations, such as the establishment of the ICC and the doctrine of complementarity. But these global developments have not yet translated into local gains for Timorese women. I examine reasons why international lawyers may have misunderstood the nature of the role that international law plays in post-conflict states.

Chapters Four and Five deal with the Jakarta and Dili trials, assessing the operations of the trials, specific cases and jurisprudence produced by the courts and the overall experience of women complainants. Notably, the operation of the trials is contrasted with the aims of transitional justice theory outlined in Chapter Two, and the reality of the experience of women outlined in Chapter Three, to see if the design and results of the mechanism met the experience of gender persecution, and fulfilled the existing requirements of international law.

The effectiveness of the mechanisms is judged according to four main criteria as applied to women. The first criterion is whether victims of serious violations and their relatives obtain any measure of restorative justice. For example, do they receive reparations, including compensation, restitution, rehabilitation, satisfaction and guarantees of non-repetition? Second, in the wider interests of reconciliation and ending impunity, does the process provide a full and truthful account of the events that took place in East Timor from 1975 to 1999? Third, are perpetrators of serious crimes, including crimes against humanity, held to account for their actions in accordance with international law according to the principles of retributive justice? Finally, is there an effective justice process that contributes to preventing such crimes from occurring in the future?

Chapter Six focuses on gender issues in the operation and outcomes of the Commission for Reception, Truth and Reconciliation process in East Timor ('the CAVR'). The Final Report entitled *Chega!* ('No more, stop, enough!' in Portuguese) was released in late 2005 and details gender-persecution in East Timor from 1975 to the present. The Report did not win full acceptance by the Timorese Government, mainly due to controversial recommendations about national and international reparations.

The chapter focuses on two particular issues raised in the *Chega! Report* which are of enormous importance to women in post-independence East Timor: the experience of forced maternity and raising children born of rape; and the sharp increase in domestic violence and its relationship to the years of armed conflict. These issues are entirely absent in the prosecution-based transitional justice processes. As well as a special session dedicated to women and mandated participation of women, the CAVR introduced a novel programme of urgent reparations which has some important potential for addressing the post-conflict needs of survivors of gender-violence. However, any assessment of the CAVR also illustrates the limits of a purely restorative justice approach. Another such mechanism, the Joint Truth and Friendship Commission between East Timor and Indonesia, officially presented its final report *From Memory to Hope* to the presidents of the two countries on 15 July 2008 in Bali. The JTFC has produced a much more credible report than expected,[112] but also disappointed Timorese women stakeholders in many respects.[113]

CONCLUSION

This book attempts to explain why, even if formal justice outcomes are lacking for all Timorese, women in that society may generally receive no overall benefit from transitional justice outcomes compared to men, despite their contribution to achieving independence. This then raises the crucial question – transitional justice rests on the assumption that there has been a transition from a state of conflict to a state of peace, however uneasy. If women are still experiencing serious levels of domestic violence and economic deprivation, commensurate with their experience of violence during the proclaimed conflict, have they entered a state of transition at all? If we ask the question – transition to what? – then the next logical question is therefore – justice for whom? These questions may hold implications for women's participation in rebuilding the rule of law in East Timor.

The strategies of improving trials and their alternatives are valuable but I argue that feminist advocates need to be more creative about possible options which go to the structural nature of gender discrimination in both war and peacetime, and are capable of making tangible improvements to women's enjoyment of rights, especially economic, social and cultural rights. The case study of Timor also highlights that future justice interventions will need to be more informed by and responsive to challenges to a legalist approach from 'realist' conceptions of international relations, so that transitional justice strategies are not pursued without political will and resources to match. Focusing on the Timor experience shows us that the most fundamental impact of international law within the emerging field of transitional justice studies, the obligation to punish, is in need of feminist analysis and reinvention.

Xanana Gusmão (then President, now Prime Minister) stated in 2002 that '[w]e must do our best to eradicate all sentiments of hatred, of revenge. If you still feel like this, then you are living with the ghosts of the past.'[114] Bishop Belo countered: 'I hear the voices of widows, the complaints of raped women, of orphans. They don't like to live together and meet in the street their perpetrators.'[115] The 'ghosts of the past' for many women are living threats. These contrasting attitudes, State versus Church, male versus female, capture neatly one of the key dilemmas of transitional justice – who is to bear the cost of the compromises made for peace?

It is easy to empathise with Gusmão in his publicly articulated dilemmas over pursuing the best future for his country. East Timor is poor, with a giant, hostile neighbour and vulnerable borders. Within Timor, peace is fragile, as shown by the April–May 2006 Dili riots and 2007 election violence. On 11 February 2008, President José Ramos-Horta was injured when he was shot during an assassination attempt.

However, the question of compromise for peace cannot be answered by a democratic society, or a society that hopes to become democratic, without properly considering the perspective of women. The society and the international community must in the first instance know what those costs have been for the women of Timor and the contribution women made to independence. Even where gender persecution is acknowledged, there are two contrasting narratives – one of victims or even scapegoats, and one of survivors and fighters in the independence struggle, which have different consequences for the status and redress of women.

Ultimately, women should be able to negotiate any compromises to be made for peace, not have compromise thrust upon them. South African poet and journalist Antjie Krog reflected on her experience covering the South African Truth and Reconciliation Commission for national radio in the following bittersweet terms:

> The word 'reconciliation' is my daily bread. Compromise, accommodate, provide, make space for. Understand. Tolerate. Empathise. Endure…without it, no relationship, no work, no progress is possible. Yes, piece by piece, we die into reconciliation.[116]

The message Krog sends us is that the price of transitional justice may be a heavy price to be paid by women, not the coveted prize often presented by international lawyers.

2 Sexing the subject of transitional justice

> Our argument is...that international law does not provide even momentary distance from subjectivity. It is intertwined with a sexed and gendered subjectivity, and reinforces a system of male power. Until international law focuses on all people and peoples, not just a powerful few, it will always be subject to geopolitical agendas inimical to genuine security...[1]

Martin Luther King Junior in his celebrated letter from Birmingham Jail on 16 April 1963 differentiated between those who prefer 'a negative peace which is the absence of tension' to 'a positive peace which is the presence of justice'.[2] In Dili in 1999, Maria Dominggas Alves of the Timorese women's NGO Fokupers demanded 'Why is it that men who are tortured by the military forces are seen as heroes, whereas women who are tortured (including rape) are seen as traitors?'[3] This chapter seeks to examine what effect international law has had for Timorese women involved in transitional justice processes by linking the two ideas above.

Transitional justice processes often claim as an ultimate objective not just the alleviation of tension but the positive 'presence' of justice. Scholars in the transitional justice field are currently considering whether the aims of the mechanisms should therefore be more linked to broader and longer-term human rights issues, such as economic justice.[4] The Norwegian philosopher, Johan Galtung, has developed the notion of structural violence, which highlights causes other than warfare, for example poverty, as the major cause of death and suffering.[5] Some scholars identify the interconnections of poverty, environmental degradation, discrimination, exploitation, militarisation and violence as the causes of insecurity.[6] Even when these broader themes are considered, this objective of transitional justice and the audience who will one day feel this presence of justice are often presumed to be gender neutral.

The first part of this chapter sets out two types of argument about the obligation to punish in international law, which I term 'realist' and 'legalist'. Most international lawyers believe international law is central to the project of transitional justice because it imposes an obligation on states to punish individuals guilty of the most serious violations of international law, and this determines that trials must be among the mechanisms chosen. The counterpoint to this position posed by realist political scientists is that these choices should be left entirely to the post-conflict state concerned in the interests of democracy and stability.

The second part of the chapter sets out feminist theoretical contributions to this realist/legalist debate. If international law has the central role ascribed to it by legalists, what might we expect to be its impact on women involved in the relevant transitional justice processes? Is international law detrimental or beneficial in its impact on women in an immediate post-conflict setting? As noted, the project of most feminist international lawyers has been to extend the obligation to punish to the category of crimes committed against women in armed conflict so that the rule of law will be equally applied to women and men, which has meant the adoption of a legalist position.[7]

If instead the realist position has more explanatory power in the case of East Timor, what would we expect the outcomes to be for women? Or are both theoretical positions based on the absence and silence of women? A feminist critique of both positions is that so-called 'realist' international relations theorists focus only on elite men as the subject of discourse and do not describe the reality of women's lives or the complexity of gender roles,[8] but for much the same reasons the gendered nature of international law means that it too will be resistant to the lived experience of women.[9]

I argue that embedded within accepted transitional justice discourse are some gendered assumptions that affect the choices made by the UN and emerging states in setting up their new legal systems. Key terms used in the literature – transitional justice, retributive justice, restorative justice, reconciliation and truth-telling – must be subjected to sustained feminist analysis. Concerns raised by this counterpoint feminist legal theory, such as the gendered subjectivity of international law and the representation of women in transitional processes, are deployed in this section to assess how the mechanisms relating to East Timor could be evaluated in terms of their impact on women. This forms the basis of my critical analysis of the formal legal mechanisms in the following substantive chapters.

My analysis confirms Dianne Otto's claims that the 'international struggle for the full inclusion of women in the paradigm of universal human rights has reached a point where it needs reinvention'.[10] In light of this, in the third part of the chapter, I consider ideas which could 'reinvent' approaches to transitional justice. If transitional justice interventions cannot be inclusive of women's experiences of the conflict and post-conflict periods, then it may be a more strategic approach to pursue other non-legal strategies against impunity. One such idea is a reinvention (or subversion) of the concept of a war veteran, to give women and children the legal status and benefits of a veteran in the same manner as a combatant if their suffering has contributed to or been a consequence of the struggle for independence.

LEGALIST VERSUS REALIST ARGUMENTS OVER THE ROLE OF INTERNATIONAL LAW IN TRANSITIONAL JUSTICE PROCESSES

This section addresses arguments about whether there is a role for international law in transitional justice choices for modern post-conflict states, and if so, how international law should be incorporated into transitional justice processes. The arguments focus on the imposition of an obligation on states under international law to punish individuals guilty of the most serious violations of international law.

International law plays three possible theoretical roles in transitional justice processes. International law *categorises* what behaviour can be considered a crime under international humanitarian law or human rights law. For example, international law states when an act of murder should be considered an act of genocide[11] or a crime against humanity[12] that rises above the jurisdiction of domestic criminal law.

International law also categorises the types of situations where particular international legal rules will become relevant, such as when peacetime becomes a state of emergency,[13] or an internal armed conflict,[14] or an international armed conflict.[15] This categorisation of the situation often feeds into the response of the international community, for example, in the deliberations of the Security Council in deciding whether a particular situation constitutes a risk to global peace and security under Chapter VII of the UN Charter.[16]

The second impact, consequent on the categorisation of certain behaviours into crimes, is that international law imposes an *obligation to prosecute* and punish certain crimes and designates individual criminal responsibility for those crimes. The obligation lies on the state, and then, if the state is unwilling or unable, on the international community as a whole.[17]

The third impact is that the categorisation of offences influences who is considered most responsible, what violations are tried and with what priority, or prosecution strategies.[18] This is reflected in the practice of the *ad hoc* tribunals for Yugoslavia and Rwanda and the International Criminal Court, domestic prosecutions of war crimes, treaty interpretation and a growing body of 'soft' international law,[19] in particular the UN General Assembly resolution on the *Basic Principles and Guidelines on the Right to a Remedy and Reparation for Gross Violations of International Human Rights Law and Serious Violations of International Humanitarian Law*[20] and the UN Commission on Human Rights (now the Human Rights Council), *Updated set of principles for the protection and promotion of human rights through action to combat impunity.*[21]

2.1 The legalist approach: the obligation to punish

The impact of international law that causes the most friction in transitional justice debates is the imposition on a state of the obligation to punish, because this necessarily limits the options a new state has at its disposal to deal with past violations, including the option of doing nothing.[22] Calls for an international tribunal for East Timor are based on the legalist view that the crimes committed in East Timor were not only crimes against the East Timorese population, but crimes against international law and against the UN itself. As Mary Robinson, then UN High Commissioner for Human Rights, stated in September 1999, 'There has to be accountability for this level of savage terror'.[23] East Timor's civil society has been united in calling for an international tribunal since 1999 on this basis: 'Demands for an international tribunal inform the responsibility of the international community, in particular the UN, as the chain of crimes that occurred in East Timor form crimes that threaten human dignity and values throughout the world'.[24]

The legalist position is based on the characterisation of international crimes as *jus cogens* norms of international law; peremptory and non-derogable norms which are fundamental to the interests of the international community.[25] All states have a joint legal interest in the protection of *jus cogens* norms (i.e. they are applied *erga omnes*), because they are crimes that *threaten the peace and security* of humankind and *shock the conscience of humanity*.[26] Protection under international humanitarian law (IHL), including the primary instruments of the 1949 Geneva Conventions, is firmly based on three rules which acknowledge this *jus cogens* basis: (a) IHL is not subject to reciprocity; (b) victims cannot give up or waive their rights to protection; and (c) IHL is consistent, and does not discriminate.[27]

M. Cherif Bassiouni argues that, despite the clear obligation to prosecute certain crimes under international law, the current paradigm is that of unfettered 'tradeability' around transitional justice decisions. Bassiouni and other legal experts such as Diane Orentlicher instead favour a legalist or 'minimum accountability' approach to transitional justice, which posits that accountability should never be bartered in a *Realpolitik* fashion in order to arrive at 'peace', however defined. Certain parameters are set by international law on what options a state can take in a post-conflict setting, such as identifying and prosecuting individuals with criminal responsibility.[28] War crimes, as well as torture, genocide, and crimes against humanity in both times of war and times of peace, are international crimes that have risen to the level of *jus cogens*, and there therefore exists a non-derogable obligation to prosecute or extradite the individuals responsible. No amnesties can be given.[29]

International law has thus been considered chiefly as effecting punishment or retributive justice only, in classic Nuremberg style.[30] Exponents of the minimum accountability position make several claims for trials and retributive justice within the framework of transitional justice that go beyond the minimum requirements of prosecution; including that trials are the 'most effective insurance against future repression',[31] bring solace to victims,[32] serve as an education in the rule of law,[33] and bring about what Martin Luther King Junior would call the 'presence' of justice to a torn society.[34]

As described in the introduction to this book, this legalist approach is beginning to embrace processes complementary to trials such as truth commissions, restorative justice elements within trials, interplay with traditional justice systems and a focus on longer-term issues such as the establishment of the rule of law.[35] Overall though, according to the legalist view, the role of international law in any transitional justice process is to impose an obligation to punish. International law demands that certain crimes be punished and prescribes how this is to be done.

2.2 The realist challenge

The counter-narrative to the legalist approach comes from political realist opposition who see justice as an impediment to peace, of use only as a bargaining chip to be bartered away for a better settlement.[36] There are three key realist arguments against the legalist approach. First, a realist would argue that the notion of legal accountability itself is fanciful and irrelevant. A pragmatist believes that the international community's decision-making with respect to the nature and extent of post-conflict justice needs is governed more often by geopolitical considerations than by notions of international law, ethics or morals. This belief is often part of a broader theoretical position which claims that international law has no impact or place in international relations.[37] But second, even if it was relevant, the realist argues that the legalist approach is destabilising and undemocratic. A realist favours the role of the elected leader in deciding transitional justice issues, unfettered by any supranational considerations.[38] Finally, realists argue that the legalist approach is applied selectively and usually only to assuage Western guilt, rather than in any consistent or objective manner.

The best-known exponent of the realist position in relation to the first critique of legalism is American academic Samuel Huntington. He derides the idea that international law has made any contribution to transitional justice decisions.

> In actual practice, what happened was little affected by moral and legal considerations. It was shaped almost exclusively by politics, by the nature of the democratisation process, and by the distribution of political power during and after the transition.[39]

This is borne out to some extent by what little research data exists in the area of transitional justice. In a study of war crime trials, truth commissions, and amnesties pursued in civil wars that have ended since 1989, Jack Snyder and Leslie Vinjamuri find that states have tended to follow the dictates of pragmatism while paying lip service to legalist arguments for justice. They also find that throughout the post-Cold War era, powerful states have been effective at pushing the development of the norm in directions that reinforce the authority of states and especially of liberal states.[40]

That is not only how it is, according to pragmatists, but how it should be, which constitutes the second realist critique of the legalist approach. Deals may need to be done to establish a lasting peace. A leader may need to give amnesties to promote security and should be able to do so based on the democratic mandate the leader has. As the former president of Uruguay, Julio M. Sanguinetti once stated, in relation to calls for justice for past atrocities in his country: 'What is more just, to consolidate the peace of a country where human rights are guaranteed today or to seek retroactive justice that could compromise that peace?'[41]

The third type of realist critique of the legalist approach does not negate the obligation to punish itself but criticises the implementation of the doctrine in practice such as weaknesses in trials; that they are slow and expensive, selective and political. For example, rather than spending millions to prosecute 12 individuals in the *ad hoc* International Criminal Tribunal for Rwanda, the same money could have been used more productively to rebuild the Rwandan national justice system and to encourage the development of a culture of compliance there.[42] This critique can also take the form of arguing that every conflict is different and should be treated differently, which means that there are no agreed guidelines as to minimum measures to be taken to avoid impunity.

For example, Neil J Kritz advances the idea of primary and secondary audiences of transitional justice processes such as international tribunals. He asserts that international efforts can often be more reflective of Western guilt over tragic failures to intervene, such as the Rwanda tribunal – located in Arusha but administered by The Hague – than efforts that will reconstruct the rule of law in that state as well as avoid impunity.[43] He notes that the primary audience should be the people of the society, who lived through and suffered in the conflict: victims, bystanders and perpetrators. The international community should be only a secondary audience, who might hope for jurisprudence, deterrence value and a better understanding of the conflict, which will aid early warning systems.[44]

The realist view of international law therefore is that it is irrelevant or a veneer for political concerns, but in a transitional justice context any insistence on the obligation to prosecute is anti-democratic and could also be destabilising to the new society. The important challenge to legalist thinking from the realist school relevant to this examination of Timor is threefold. What if the leadership of the new democracy is not committed to the obligation to punish? What if the geopolitical considerations are not sufficient for holding trials or the dynamic changes part way through the process? What if the trials are nothing more than a veneer? Impunity can still be the outcome of holding trials – if they are sufficiently flawed. The jurisdiction of the Rome Statute is triggered by a situation where a state is unwilling or unable to hold fair trials for violations of international law. But what happens when it is the UN itself who cannot guarantee fair trials?

2.3 New interdisciplinary approaches to transitional justice

The legalist and realist approaches are for the most part mutually exclusive. However, Jack Snyder and Leslie Vinjamuri have identified a stream of 'strategic legalism' in the work of theorist Carlos Santiago Nino.[45] Nino was highly critical of Argentine human rights groups, who he says 'held a Kantian view of punishment; even if society were on the verge of dissolution, it had the duty to punish the last offender'.[46] But he also found that in relation to Argentina, trials could be 'great occasions for social deliberation and for collective examination of the moral values underlying public institutions', which can help break that power structure and invent a new, democratic society.[47] In other words, trials might just be one more tool in a transitional justice toolkit, to be chosen only if the trials would promote some other type of social objective, not just the punishment of an individual criminal.

Strategic legalists might re-imagine the concept of impunity measures as consisting of immediate and mandatory trials, accept the limitations of law, and critique the idea of *erga omnes* and *jus cogens* norms themselves. New interdisciplinary studies of transitional justice challenge the normative basis of the obligation to punish, by asking whether or not courts actually help post-atrocity societies to move beyond the multiple traumas inflicted during the era of atrocities and build a new society in which the violence of the past is not iterated.[48] The argument is that trials of a few do not recognise that the scope of these crimes could not have been as large without the harnessing and the transformation of key societal institutions. In order to address the situation fully and provide a level of stability and order for the future of the society, these institutions, and thereby the parameters within which the crimes occurred, need to be addressed. For example, trials cannot deal with unindicted perpetrators, states outside the area of conflict that may have contributed to the violence, or bystanders.[49] This goes to the very heart of the legitimacy for creating individual responsibility for war crimes.[50] It assumes that wartime atrocities or 'extraordinary evil' can be dealt with by the methods we use to deal with 'ordinary' crime.[51]

Laurel Fletcher and Harvey M. Weinstein interviewed Bosnian judges and prosecutors and conclude that people's attitudes to accountability mechanisms are deeply affected by their proximity to the violence and their personalised experience of conflict.[52] They conclude that a more 'ecological' response to social repair is necessary, addressing the damage mass violence causes at the community level.[53] Some examples of ecological responses include truth commissions and traditional rituals, which have recently become sites of feminist examination.[54] This idea is considered further in relation to reconceptualising the concept of a veteran.

The underlying debate is over what is the proper role of law, that is, is political change a precondition to development of the rule of law or vice versa?[55] This dissertation argues for a new category of 'feminist strategic legalism' for those who are against *Realpolitik* impunity but are also sceptical of the claims made about criminal trials in a post-conflict setting in relation to gender concerns.

FEMINIST CRITIQUES OF THE ROLE OF INTERNATIONAL LAW IN TRANSITIONAL JUSTICE PROCESSES

Thinking about gender and transitional justice yields some immediate questions. The research suggests that violence continues against women regardless of political context, in other words, that women may not experience a transition to non-violence because an end to formal hostilities is called.[56] Gender-based violence may get ignored or devalued because it is privatised.[57] For example, sexual violence in armed conflict is conceived of as motivated by personal 'needs' of soldiers, unrelated to the conflict, even if perpetrated in places of public detention,[58] or because it occurs in the private sphere such as domestic violence or home-based sexual slavery.[59]

The focus in international law on sexual violence seems to have blocked any consideration of other gender-based violations committed in wartime. For example, the dramatically increased levels of domestic violence that occurs in conflict; the failure to provide civilians with adequate access to shelter or protective equipment; the suffering of refugees and displaced persons who are forced to flee their communities; the lack of access to reproductive health assistance, and other socio-economic harms have all been substantially overlooked.[60]

This section focuses on the work feminist theory has done in bettering the understanding of women's experience of armed conflict, resulting in critiques of both the legalist and realist positions. It is clear though that most feminist approaches to the impact of international law in transitional justice processes have usually adopted the legalist approach advocating minimum accountability without further examination, and sought to make any trials resulting from the obligation to punish gender-inclusive.[61]

The prominence given to prosecutorial remedies for gender violations of international humanitarian and human rights law is reproduced in the accountability provisions of UN Security Council Resolution 1325 (2000) on Women, Peace and Security.[62] In addition to calling for an exclusion of amnesties, these provisions emphasise the responsibility of states to prosecute those responsible 'for genocide, crimes against humanity, and war crimes including those relating to sexual and other violence against women and girls', yet are silent on complementary forms of redress.[63]

Similarly, the Secretary-General's 2002 study on Women, Peace and Security[64] and the Independent Experts' Assessment on the Impact of Armed Conflict on Women and Women's Role in Peace-building[65] place greater emphasis on criminal prosecution than truth commissions, reparations or other forms of justice.
The legalist approach assumes *jus cogens* norms are universal and gender-neutral, and therefore powerful advocacy tools for women.[66] However, universality cannot be assumed.[67] Rather, international law norms tend to have a primarily Western audience. Universality of *jus cogens* norms has also been questioned by feminist theorists who ask whether international criminal law has been 'transformed' to meet the reality of women's experience of armed conflict, or only the experience of Western women,[68] or is still fundamentally limited to the experience of elite men.[69]

One feminist reading of the legalist position could say that limiting the 'tradeability' of trials for a new state works in favour of women, who might be in a weak position as citizens after a conflict to 'trade' politically for a justice outcome. An example of this would be amnesty deals for ex-military struck at a peace negotiation where no women are present as leaders of the factions. International law is understood in this sense as a method of controlling the use and abuse of power.[70]

Realists could argue that international law is irrelevant and merely a rhetorical device, so that focusing on trials would be a waste of feminist energy and resources. Alternatively, realists could argue that a decision by a new state to prosecute crimes, even including gender-based violence, may be destabilising to the fragile state. Women might then be the most vulnerable to any recurrence of violence. Neither view takes into account the idea of 'changing the curtains' expressed in the introductory chapter, that in fact women might still be experiencing a continuum of violence and not be in a position to 'trade' – all they have traded is one set of curtains for another.[71] So a feminist strategic legalist view might see value in not trading trials for some other benefit in a post-conflict setting, but accept that there are gendered holes in the legalist view too.

The legalist position does not necessarily benefit women for three main reasons: lack of representation of women in decision-making structures within transitional justice mechanisms (or what Christine Bell and Catherine O'Rourke term 'visible exclusions');[72] the incomplete categorisation of acts that affect women as international crimes; and flawed prosecution strategies (which Bell and O'Rourke term 'conceptual exclusions').[73] These criticisms are predicated on making the legalist approach work better for women. However, Bell and O'Rourke also identify a 'growing feminist unease' with the question of 'where is the feminism in transitional justice discourse?'[74] I argue the unease stems from acknowledging that the legalist approach might be insufficient to assist the attainment of material benefits for women in post-conflict settings. New and creative strategies are required.

2.4 Representation of women in transitional justice processes

Although the obligation to punish is non-discriminatory, it does not rely on democratic acceptance and does not address proactively the issue of representation of women in transitional justice mechanisms.[75] Women are unlikely to be represented in transitional justice mechanisms if there is little 'gender-mapping' of the conflict and women are excluded from the peace negotiations and agreements.[76] Even democratic means might not automatically mean that women represent other women or that all women's views are well represented.[77]

The term 'gender-mapping' a conflict refers to assessment and documentation of gender-based violations during a conflict.[78] Lack of documentation of gender-based violations has consequences for the proper prosecution of those offences. An all-female team of investigators conducted the first rape investigation in time of conflict for the Independent Commission for Former Yugoslavia (ICTY), and the evidence was provided to the Office of the Prosecutor of the ICTY.[79] It is no surprise that the first rape prosecution in history resulted from subsequent trials using this testimony.

Christine Chinkin argues that 'mapping' a conflict is crucial to drafting an effective peace agreement.[80] It is important in its own right, and also crucial to establish factual bases for any proposed humanitarian intervention by the international community, to provide objective evidence of the role and status of women and any changes in that society. Moreover, transitional justice outcomes that benefit women are impossible unless the full realities of their lives before and after the conflict are understood.

In the Timorese context, the UN accountability mechanisms for human rights violations did not, perhaps could not, adequately monitor, document or serve as a check on Indonesian actions during the period of occupation.[81] As Mario Carrascalão, former Governor of East Timor expressed: 'Timor Leste was a closed land…it was a place of lies and falsities…the people that came here could do anything. It was a secret'.[82]

Almost all violations in East Timor were documented and brought to the attention of the international community by the work of NGOs.[83] It was not until the

Santa Cruz massacre that the UN bodies began to use stronger language, and even then, it was under the auspices of Special Rapporteurs rather than the Commission on Human Rights where the most useful work was conducted.[84]

This silence both reflects and helps perpetuate a situation in which women are not being consulted or participating adequately in transitional justice processes. The requirement for the equal representation of women in public life is based on the principle of non-discrimination in human rights law and the idea that politics is constitutive for the processes of society as a whole and not simply a mechanical 'reflection' of social and economic interests.[85] Therefore, the exclusion of women and non-integration of a gender perspective in transitional justice processes perpetuates existing power asymmetries between women and men and therefore these processes are less likely to contribute to sustainable peace-building.[86]

Part of the answer is to pursue strategies which facilitate the participation of women to mechanisms designed around the obligation to punish, and also to those designed to promote truth-telling. This can inadvertently lead to an 'add women and stir' approach.[87] For example, in a truth commission context, women often tell men's stories of violations (their husbands or sons) to commission hearings rather than their own.[88] The most visible female activists in transitional contexts have often been mothers of disappeared, or widows.[89] It follows that truth commissions may portray the violations experienced by women as a relatively small percentage of the total violations reported to the commission.

Gender bias has been identified in the truth-telling function of truth commissions. First, a gender dimension is lacking when examining the range of harms in a conflict;[90] second, there is a focus only on sexual violence when harms against women are considered;[91] and third, 'ordinary' or routine violence is omitted, especially socio-economic harm experienced by women in conflict due to their gendered roles.[92] The failure of truth commissions to fully integrate women's experiences is troubling on a practical level as it may restrict women's entitlement to additional forms of legal redress,[93] but also on a symbolic level because it leads to a distorted historical record of 'truth'.[94] These ideas are central to the discussion of the truth commissions dealing with events in Timor set out in Chapter Six.

2.5 Categorisation of crimes: exceptionalism or revolution?

Jan Jindy Pettman asked in 1996: '[w]hat has it meant to displace sex onto women, and to see sex as not political?'[95] Chilla Bulbeck replied '[i]t has meant drawing a sharp line of visibility and invisibility between military violence and domestic violence, thus obscuring useful ways to understand intra-state or intermediate forms of patterned sexual violence, for example, war rape'.[96]

There have now been significant achievements by feminist lawyers in the project of categorising gendered behaviour in conflict as an international crime.[97] Feminists have concentrated on this strategy because the categorisation of behaviour into international crimes has a critical influence on Security Council decisions to intervene, the triggering of the obligation to punish, and the resulting prosecution strategy.

On this point of recognising patterned sexual violence, there has been considerable progress. Article 7(g) of the Rome Statute explicitly enumerates rape as a crime against humanity. A unanimous Security Council Resolution 1325 (2000) was passed on the topic of 'Women, Peace and Security' urging the Secretary-General to carry out a study on the impact of armed conflict on women and girls, and the role of women in peace-building. Prosecutions for gender-related crimes in international criminal law have also been hailed as revolutionary. The ad hoc tribunals for both Yugoslavia and Rwanda have successfully indicted, prosecuted and convicted defendants for gender-based crimes for the first time in history, including rape as a crime against humanity and an element of genocide in the *Akayesu* case before the ICTR,[98] and the *Celebici, Furundzija* and *Kunarac* cases relating to rape as torture, sexual slavery and sexual acts as inhumane treatment before the ICTY.[99] There have been significant decisions by regional human rights courts, such as *Mejia Egocheaga v. Peru* in the Inter-American Commission of Human Rights, which accepted rape as torture.[100] It is these developments to which Charlesworth and Chinkin refer when they state 'the silence about the suffering of women in all forms of conflict has been broken'.[101] This shattering of the silence is a triumph indeed.

Why then do expert commentators Hilary Charlesworth and Christine Chinkin argue that law, including international law, is gendered and has been resistant to attempts to transform it into a legal system that can properly deal with women's experience?[102] Feminist lawyers claim that generally the law of armed conflict has historically set up the male combatant's experience in conflict as the standard and thereby has misunderstood or left women's experience of conflict unregulated in the 'private' sphere.[103] In this light, the breakthroughs above could be seen as exceptionalism and not revolutionary – much of the progress in the feminist categorisation project has been made by reinterpreting existing international violations through a gendered lens.[104] For example, domestic violence can be prosecuted as torture or rape as a crime against humanity[105] as opposed to transcending or reinventing the existing template of male experience.

I agree that there are still significant gender gaps in international humanitarian law and corresponding gaps in gender theory, which affect transitional justice mechanisms. For example, the issues of forced maternity and domestic violence explored in Chapter Six in my view are key transitional justice issues that raise important gender questions, but there is little recognition of either of these problems in their own right[106] under international law. Theoretical explanations of their impact on women in a post-conflict setting are also thin. Forced maternity is a particularly complex phenomenon, perhaps because it straddles states of war and peace, and there is no parallel offence that can happen to a man.[107] Forced maternity raises forcibly the constant question in feminist strategy of whether to emphasise the 'sameness' or 'difference' of women's experience to men's.[108]

The continuance of the categorisation project therefore has merit, but Judith Gardam has cogently argued that the project of moving crimes which happen to women in war into the public sphere may not rectify the limitations of the law.[109] One important limitation, as noted in relation to truth commissions above, is that international law tends to emphasise women's sexual and reproductive identities and harms inflicted by opposing forces.[110] The International Committee of the Red Cross (ICRC) also made this point when it released a comprehensive study in 2001 titled 'Women Facing War'.[111] The ICRC found that women are not innately vulnerable, but can be made vulnerable since they are seen as 'symbolic' bearers of their racial, cultural or religious identity, as well as being the producers of future generations.[112] Other factors that render women vulnerable are specific skills, social status and economic situation, an intersection of distinguishing features.

However, women are not, if they ever were, exclusively the victims, the caregivers or the passive supporters of men in times of armed conflict.[113] The reality of modern conflict is that women's roles also include being involved as members in armed forces and perpetrators of various forms of violence. It is this sort of complexity and recognition of intersectionality in gender identity that should be reflected in legal responses and the categorisation of crimes. I conclude that recognition of rape as a war crime has been welcome but exceptional, and the broader issue of gender justice after an armed conflict has been largely ignored.

2.6 Prosecution strategies and problems: wholesale justice

In this section I set out feminist challenges to the third impact of international law, the prosecution of international crimes. Even if women are represented in a meaningful way, or if international law itself can be made inclusive of women's experiences, it does not follow automatically that the implementation of the law will be gender-sensitive, or pursued 'with the same fervour as are the war crimes which happen routinely to men'.[114]

Due to the precedents such as *Akayesu* or the ICTY cases, feminist lawyers assume that progress in jurisprudence will be retained: that each time, trials will be proceeding from a better base of gender-sensitive legislation, procedural rules and jurisprudence. This assumption may be ill-founded. For example, crimes against humanity are required to be widespread and systematic, and as Charlesworth and Chinkin point out,

> although the rapes and sexual violence in the former Yugoslavia have been perceived in such terms, this may not always be the case. There is a tendency to regard the sexual abuse in the former Yugoslavia as exceptional and not as a regularly occurring part of armed conflict.[115]

They note that the UN's 'fact-finding' in Rwanda in 1994 did not detect systematic sexual violence against women until nine months after the genocide, 'when women began to give birth in unprecedented numbers'.[116]

There may be hierarchies of 'seriousness' within the prosecution of serious crimes.[117] For example, although difficult to prove, it is possible that if men as combatants are more likely to be killed, and women may be tortured, raped but often live, could a focus on deaths as the most serious violation under international law therefore lead to a gendered view of war crimes? For instance, the Serious

Crimes Unit in Dili focused mainly on murder indictments, with gender persecution investigated only incidentally.

There are a series of practical problems with prosecution strategies in attempts to achieving justice for women. First, successful prosecutions require witnesses. A recurring problem for transitional justice processes is significant under-reporting of gender-persecution. Due to the trauma of the victim, the social stigma attached to rape and the fear of ostracism from her family and inadequate concern of authorities, women are less likely to seek redress by reporting rape to the authorities, increasing the likelihood of impunity for a persecutor.[118] Many serious acts of gender-based violence, including domestic violence, can have the psychological effect of torture. Torture, as a crime, has a lasting effect on its victims, that of silencing and alienating them from communal support. The psychological impunity created by torture can have disproportionately negative effects on women, already disadvantaged in power structures.[119]

The purpose of a criminal trial in a transitional justice context is to prosecute and punish the major war criminals for violations of international law. Consequently, a war crimes trial can 'only do so much'.[120] The second practical problem with trials is that the process of giving testimony in trials or to a lesser extent other types of public proceedings may only serve to re-traumatise women. Nicola Henry has analysed the experience of women giving evidence of gender-based violence in international war crimes trials. Henry notes that war crimes trials might have an 'inherently counter-narrative effect',[121] despite the best efforts of investigators and prosecutors.[122] The physical and psychological wounds as a consequence of rape and sexual abuse are often not part of accepted rape testimonies, as emotions have no place in the courtroom.[123] That is, if prosecutors or judges want to deal with sexual violence issues at all.[124]

The nature of defence strategy is to discredit the evidence of the witness or prove consent, which may exacerbate the devaluation of raped women who have come to testify. The possibility of re-traumatisation is a highly likely response within this context. Inevitably, the reconstruction of the story will entail reliving of the traumatic event and may induce re-traumatisation.[125]

Third, a war crimes trial may not in fact be the appropriate context for sexual violence survivors to reconstruct their stories and thus recover from their traumatic experiences. Even if not re-traumatised, victims of sexual violence, if they are actually chosen to give testimony at a trial, only get to tell a piece of their story. Further, those experiences remain cloaked in secrecy given that, out of necessity for protection and safety, the court sessions are often in private. There is no necessary link between publicity per se and healing. There have also been reports of the ostracism of women on their return to their communities.[126]

Healing may not then be the result of a trial process. On the other hand, testifying at public proceedings such as a trial is potentially an empowering process for survivors given that it constitutes a measure of justice due to the legal weight given to their words.[127] This may be an advantage of truth commissions, although Ni Aolain and Turner warn that the informality and flexibility of the truth commission mechanism may make them more susceptible to discriminatory factors, not less.[128] In my opinion, based on experience at the Yugoslav tribunal, even in the rare case where every care is taken of the witness, progress in jurisprudence comes at a great personal cost to the women involved. As Franke puts it, war crimes trials operate best on the 'wholesale' not 'retail' level.[129]

Fourth, material benefits in the form of financial compensation for women who participate in trials and truth commissions may not be forthcoming. The legal consequences of the supranational criminal law system (sentencing and reparations) are increasingly being examined with the situation of survivors of gender-based violence in mind which is a welcome development,[130] but there is still a lack of long-term financial assistance available through the trial process. These four problems would confirm Fletcher and Weinstein's argument that trials may not promote social repair, even for the individual women directly involved.

2.7 Feminist strategic legalism

Each of the four problems outlined above point to the question 'where is the feminism in transitional justice'?[131] There are cogent arguments to address the above three concerns with the minimum accountability model. Trials can be made better. The participation and representation of women in transitional justice mechanisms could be mandated beyond the token gesture. Gaps in international criminal law with issues such as forced maternity could be successfully filled and implemented in the same manner as the issue of rape as a war crime. I believe these strategies should be pursued vigorously by feminist legal scholars and practitioners,[132] but that they are ultimately insufficient strategies.[133]

My argument rests on different concerns. Transitional justice as a discipline causes feminist unease because the issue of whether trials really achieve social repair is harder to address.[134]

Bell and O'Rourke describe this unease as being about 'what exactly transitional justice is transiting "from" and "to"',[135] and categorise conceptions of transitional justice as ordinary, liberalising or restorative justice.[136] They argue that feminist theory should focus on a 'larger dream' of substantive and material justice for women,[137] and I concur. If the violations against women in armed conflict arise from structural inequalities experienced in peacetime, then processes are required which address structural discrimination in the society. Can individual criminal trials, or even communal truth commissions, separately or in combination contribute to this end-game?

Part of the question is whether violence against women in armed conflict is ordinary violence writ large or 'extraordinary' violence. For example, does war interrupt the 'unthinkableness' of rape?[138] On this point the literature is complex and inconclusive.

Feminist commentators have suggested at least three explanations of the common rape of women in war. First is the booty principle, where women are seen as spoils of war when victory is declared. Second, while rape serves to humiliate enemy women, the target is also the masculinity of the enemy men.[139] The third explanation is male bonding theory: that rape, particularly gang rape and systematic rape, is given as a privilege to soldiers by officers because it promotes soldierly solidarity.[140] These ideas are picked up by the UN and NGO literature. A UNIFEM expert report commissioned by Kofi Annan entitled 'Women, War and Peace' ('UNIFEM report'), agreed that violence against women is not an accident of war but a strategy used in warfare.[141] The *raison d'être* is to spread terror; destabilise society and break its resistance; reward soldiers; and extract information.[142]

While these ideas are a distinct improvement on the belief that gender violence is private by-product of armed conflict, all posit the male as the object of the perpetrator's gaze, even while the woman is the victim. The fourth explanation is that women are often agents in conflict themselves, and are targets because of their own political or strategic importance, but their punishment is often gendered to punish them in the most effective and demeaning way the enemy can imagine.[143]

Cynthia Cockburn states that the violence against women in war is different to violence perpetrated against men, even though men experience gendered harms:

> And it is perhaps in brutality to the body in wars that the most marked sex difference occurs. Men and women often die different deaths and are tortured and abused in different ways, both because of physical differences between the sexes and because of the different meanings culturally ascribed to the male and female body...
>
> [T]he instruments with which the body is abused in order to break the spirit, tend to be gender-differentiated, and in the case of women, to be sexualized. Political violence and armed conflict are not distinct{--}one spills into the other. Nor is it necessarily helpful to identify discrete moments like 'before', 'during' and 'after' conflict. Violence flows through all of them, and peace processes may be present at all moments too.[144]

The question is whether this violence in armed conflict represents extraordinary violence. UNIFEM found that the extreme sexual and physical violence women suffer in times of war does not solely arise out of wartime conditions, but is an escalation of the violence that exist in times of peace.[145] In times of warfare women's bodies serve as barter systems in the form of sex work or to exchange sex for basic needs such as food and shelter,[146] but this is an extension of what happens in peacetime economies as well.

If the experience of women in armed conflict is seen only as 'extraordinary' sexual violence to be dealt with by an individual criminal trial or truth commission hearing, is this of benefit to women in transitional societies dealing with 'ordinary' violence? It may not be to the woman whose experience is the subject of the trial, other than in a symbolic sense, depending on the conditions of the trial as explained above. Is the message sent to society by the trial enough? Is the message received only by the international community, rather than the transitional state? Dealing with communal structures which engender violence is important when considering the transition from gender-persecution within a conflict zone to post-conflict justice. The sexual stereotyping of women in transitional justice processes has even been linked to the increased vulnerability of women in transitional societies to sexual trafficking and slavery.[147] This also has ramifications for 'post-conflict' economic policies:

> ...not only is 'post-conflict' a misnomer for women, so too may be reconstruction, reintegration and rehabilitation. These concepts all assume an element of going back, restoring people to a position or capacity that previously existed. But this is not necessarily what women seek. The goal is rather societal transformation, that is, not restored dependence and subordination but rather an enhanced social position that accords full citizenship, social justice and empowerment based upon respect for standards of women's human dignity and human rights that may never have previously existed. On the other hand, going back may be precisely what is wanted and it should not be assumed that because women have been subordinated by conflict that they have no agency or are unable to formulate their own agendas.[148]

Women may be experiencing a mere changing of the curtains from transitional justice processes, and the curtain may even be cut from the same cloth. Katherine M. Franke has argued that the most useful theoretical framework for addressing the benefits of transitional justice for women is that which considers both recognition of individual experience and redistribution of shame and the benefits of peace.[149] Even where recognition is achieved (or partially achieved for the reasons noted above) by the obligation to punish, redistribution of shame and basic livelihoods affected by conflict has not been achieved.[150]

Alternative measures to trials such as truth commissions, unofficial tribunals and traditional justice practices deserve further attention. As was noted in the arguments about representation presented in this chapter, the participation of women in the less formal mechanisms is still partial and may still be predicated on the same problematic foundations as trials, such as the 'truth' being what happened to men, and the only truth about women being their experience of sexual violence.[151] I argue that moving gender issues from the private to the public sphere may not lead to a material benefit for survivors of gender violence from a transitional justice process, even those which focus on restorative justice measures. In other words, breaking down the public/private distinction may not be a sufficient strategy.

On the other hand, due to their mandate to present an overall narrative of the conflict, truth commissions may be better at finding patterns and structural gender problems. The Sierra Leone Truth Commission sought to answer the question in its final report as to 'why extraordinary violence was perpetrated against women?'[152] It found that the low status of women, their lack of economic self-sufficiency and the belief of men that women were their property were all part of the answer.[153]

This is valuable, but truth commissions do not address impunity directly, and this may be important to women in transitional justice settings being asked to live with the perpetrators of crimes against them. Much depends on how the final report and recommendations are dealt with by the particular society, and how the process is complementary to any serious crimes process. Truth commissions may not provide any material benefit to women's lives.

POSSIBILITIES FOR REINVENTION: WOMEN AS VETERANS

For feminist international lawyers like myself who accept a role for international law in post-conflict societies, there is a need to move beyond improving the content and application of international criminal law in trials to a broader quest for justice for women in post-conflict states. The development of jurisprudence is an important endeavour, but it should not be the sole or even the primary endeavour, particularly in a context where the trials themselves are badly designed or executed. To this end, this section poses what Cynthia Enloe terms the radical feminist question 'what if?'[154] What if lawyers were more focused on the right political conditions to hold trials? What would need to happen for the curtains to be ripped down and a new view of the world exposed?

As a bare minimum, any international interventions in transitional justice decisions, such as the setting up of hybrid tribunals or truth commissions, should at least seek to do no harm to women. The international community should seek to be inclusive of women's experiences of the conflict and post-conflict periods in anything it funds or recommends in a transitional society. In relation to the transitional justice processes in East Timor, I suggest that it might have been better to pursue non-legal methods of attaining material benefit than to encourage women to participate in flawed trials in a post-conflict transitional period.

This is an area where the realist arguments expounded in the first section of the paper deserve to be engaged with. Narrow legalist scholarship in the area may be leading to failures of imagination in responding to the complexities of transitional justice processes. While I reject the realist acceptance of impunity for political expediency, international lawyers cannot afford to ignore the political pressures new states face when making transitional justice decisions. Feminist lawyers cannot ignore the possibility that trials can do damage, or just change the curtains. International lawyers need to move beyond the concept of 'trial as end-game', and be more responsive to both the political realities faced by a new state and the situation of women in that state when advocating and designing particular mechanisms. Legalist scholarship has centred on the appropriate forum for prosecuting war criminals and the implications of war crime tribunals for the further development of international humanitarian law and, more generally, of the international criminal justice system. The risk is that if the trials are not well designed and well executed, they may fail and undermine the establishment of the rule of law in the longer peace-building effort.

Much depends on the right conditions for holding trials. If those hearings may serve only to construct women as victims of sexual violence, re-traumatise them and further stigmatise them at a time when it is most important that women build trust in the rule of law to protect them, then the time may have come to rethink trials from first principles. Truth commissions and other ritualised processes may do better at providing some sort of ecological social repair for communities. Then there may need to be additional measures to ensure women's long-term economic rights and protections are addressed.

First, as stated, the mounting evidence is that women in armed conflict, (and certainly women in East Timor) experience violence as a continuum, from peace to war. Although the acts of persecution may move from the public to private realms of the state, and from the mandate of international to national law, the experience of violence may remain a constant. Evidence suggests that reports of domestic violence increase after the end of conflict,[155] which is certainly the case in East Timor. Women's experience of domestic violence should be seen as relevant to the proper evaluation of their needs in a post-conflict situation. This was a key recommendation of the Independent Expert Assessment Report, *Women, War, Peace*.[156] Domestic violence in a post-conflict state deserves to be considered a transitional justice issue.

Even taking into account realist challenges, the minimum accountability model is currently presented or assumed to be gender-neutral in its effects. One of the aims of this book is to show that such assumptions are incorrect, at least in the case of East Timor. Pursuing legal responses in the wrong circumstances may be worse for women than doing nothing at all in the early periods of transition. In the absence of the requisite political will at both the domestic and international level, transitional justice mechanisms can be manipulated or rendered impotent, whilst creating false expectations,[157] waylaying the efforts of human rights advocates and costing millions of precious donor dollars.[158]

A feminist strategic legalist approach would focus on gaining the full participation of women in peace negotiations and key decisions about transitional justice processes and the development of a justice sector, and preserving evidence and acquiring data in relation to international and domestic gender crimes for the day when fair trials can be held. The obvious starting point in East Timor would be to assist the implementation of the National Action Plan 2005–8 formulated at the Second National East Timorese Women's Congress 27–31 July 2004. The Plan includes a proposal for a special women's tribunal, similar to the Tokyo Women's Tribunal dealing with justice for comfort women held in 2000.[159]

Efforts could be focused on keeping women safe from post-conflict spikes in domestic violence and improving basic standards of living through interventions based on a rights-based approach to development.[160] Advocacy for access to a victims fund or reparations that did not rely on a lengthy legal process could be beneficial. But as well as these defensive manoeuvres, feminist theory should try to imagine some creative alternatives that seek to provide justice for both the individual and communal harms women experienced in war and peace, to fulfil the call for Timor's women to be treated as heroes.[161]

2.8 Women become veterans

Female non-combatant survivors of armed conflicts should be accorded veteran status. Improving the material position of women and pursuing strategies that make trials better will not rectify the core problem of providing material long-term assistance to survivors of the conflict and improving their status in society. A perennial question facing feminists is how to recognise the scope in reality of the harms visited upon women without characterising them as victims.[162] In particular, women in a transitional justice process need to be offered a script which does not cast them only as victims of sexual violence.[163]

Franke's conception is that in the first dynamic stages of transition, different narratives of the past are battling for dominance, including masculinised and feminised narratives of the conflict and the future. She presents the idea that the deaths or absence of many men can create a feminised society which then can be confronted by a strong 'remasculinisation' of culture, of which domestic violence is a part.[164] As Sheila Meintjes has expressed:

> …women do gain from the shifts in gender relations during the war, they may lose their wartime gains in the cusp, in the period between war and peace. Thus the transition from war to peace emerges as a critical moment in the shifting terrain of gender power.[165]

Fionnuala Ni Aolain and Michael Hamilton suggest exactly the opposite, that what may appear to be a moment of opportunity in transitional societies can become what they term 'a moment of retrenchment', partly due to Western interventions which entrench the operation of the public/private divide in transitional states.[166]

In this light, perhaps much more creative ideas about women in transitional societies need to be entertained, such as the controversial concept of according female non-combatants the status of veterans. Such a move would take away an exclusive focus on sexual harms, and refocus attention on violations of women's economic social and cultural rights during and after armed conflict.[167]

The second benefit is such a measure might focus on patterns of behaviour that surface the gendered dimensions of violence occurring to men in armed conflict, especially non-combatant men.[168] As Franke puts it: 'The reduction of gender to the sexual and the ignorance of how men can suffer gendered violence is, to be most generous, a form of overcompensation for the years of ignoring women's place in humanitarian law.'[169] Since the World Wars the concept of a veteran has come to mean many different things in different contexts,[170] but at the core of the term it has three benefits. A veteran receives maintenance and entitlements from the state, for life. The veteran has a certain status and standing when it comes to transitional justice decisions. If not always consulted, veterans are at least considered central to the process. Society is called upon to reflect on the contribution to the overall welfare of society that a veteran has made.[171] Article 11 of the Timorese Constitution is entitled 'Valorisation of Resistance' and guarantees 'special protection to the war-disabled, orphans, and other dependents of those who dedicated their lives to the struggle for independence and national sovereignty, and protect all those who participated in the resistance against the foreign occupation'. The idea of veteran as fighter could be displaced and replaced with the idea of veteran as survivor.

Feminist international relations scholars alert us to a possible fourth benefit of thinking of women survivors as veterans as a transitional justice process. In a post-conflict context, the historical record of the conflict produced by trials and truth commissions is also a nationalist narrative, which employs deeply gendered discourse. Pettman notes that the nation 'is often called up in familial language – motherland, kin, blood, home – language that is strangely different from the Realist representations of power politics and rational self-interest. In a complex play, the state is often gendered male and the nation female'.[172] The nation is often represented as a woman under threat of violation;[173] and sexual harms can be directed at eliminating the integrity of the individual woman's community.[174] The 'complex politics between actual women's bodies and the dangers they experience in wars and identity conflicts on the one hand, and nationalist discourses using representations of women's bodies to mark national or communal bodies on the other'[175] is made very clear when I examine the Jakarta trials in Chapter Four.

Policy proposals that would construct women as wartime veterans might therefore have the effect of redistributing shame and changing the nationalist discourse. It may at least provide a language and a framework – a new script – which may be validating to the survivors themselves. In addition, a step such as this would go a long way towards meeting some of the economic, as well as social needs of women and their children. It may also focus attention on women as development actors. This is explored in Chapter Six in relation to the female survivors of armed conflict in Timor, particularly those who bore children from forced maternity. Money from the international community earmarked for victim funds could become veterans' programmes.[176]

CONCLUSION

To examine the impact of international law on Timorese women involved in transitional justice processes, this chapter first sets out debates over the role for international law in transitional justice choices for modern post-conflict states. I then focused on the effect of international law on women involved in relevant transitional justice processes from a feminist perspective.

The debate could be taken further by asking the women involved in a post-conflict state what they expect and require from transitional justice processes. As Catharine MacKinnon states:

> Behind all law is someone's story – someone whose blood, if you read closely, leaks through the lines. Text does not beget text; life does. The question – a question of politics and history and therefore law – is whose experience grounds what law?[177]

The benefit of the legalist model of transitional justice for women lies in the fact that a new state or the UN cannot 'trade' the rights of the least powerful for the benefit of the most powerful or vocal in the new state. However this model runs the risk of being imposed without any consultation with the affected community, including women, thus limiting the possibilities of democratic participation or the incorporation of indigenous justice mechanisms.

At the same time, claims for truth commissions or informal justice mechanisms may be oversold, as will be made clear in the chapter on the CAVR where women's experiences were very narrowly described.[178] Legal responses per se need to be carefully and modestly evaluated for their capacity to deal with the intense dislocation, the complete destruction, that conflict inflicts on humanity.[179]

Echoing the idea of Martin Luther King Junior, the formal ending of violence does not necessarily mean the achievement of peace, rather it provides a 'new set of opportunities that can be grasped or thrown away'.[180] Law in a transitional period might hold an 'independent potential for effecting transformative politics' and 'liberalising' change.[181]

On the other hand, in the context of the societal breakdown caused by armed conflict, feminist scholars may be asking international law to engage in too much 'heavy-lifting'.[182] If transitional justice represents theory and praxis in a liminal zone between international relations and international law, both of which have proved resistant to feminist analysis, why are many feminists so certain that transitional justice represents an opportunity for transformative change? This may be an 'article of faith' held by feminist lawyers which needs to be revisited, or it might even represent a distraction from the main game of achieving justice for women in a broader sense.

The concept that international law should be 'transformative' is central to a feminist methodology and is applied in this book to the case study of East Timor, but in the full acknowledgement of the limitations and problems of law in this context, and in pursuit of the 'larger dream' of gender justice.[183] For the international lawyer, modesty about what the law can accomplish is an important virtue.[184]

3 Cecelia Soares recalls

East Timor as case study

On UN Human Rights Day, 10 December 2005, Cecelia Soares related her memories of the Indonesian invasion to the Inter-Press Service. On 7 December, 1975, she had been married for a year, and three months earlier had given birth to a baby girl. Soares observed:

> I used to live near the Dili port and on that day I saw planes dropping Indonesian paratroopers. And that was the day my life was shattered forever…
>
> The next thing I knew there were battleships firing shells. It was frightening. I ran home, grabbed my baby, and then just ran to the hills. I tried looking for my husband, but he was nowhere to be seen.[1]

Soares further relates how for four years, she and her daughter lived with the Falintil resistance in the hills, until they were captured by Indonesian troops and sent to prison on Atauro Island, 22 kilometres north of Dili: 'It was hell there. There wasn't enough food; we were tortured; and my girl who was now about four died of hunger.'[2] Soares said she once tried to commit suicide but was saved by a priest who told her that Timor would be free someday and all the suffering would end. In an independent East Timor in 2005, she was washing clothes for foreign aid workers staying in a local hotel.

Soares' story is illustrative of the occupation of East Timor. A brief history of Timor is presented, so the reader understands the choice of case study in this book and its key features. The evidence of gender-based violence during the occupation is also presented. An introduction to the judicial and non-judicial transitional justice mechanisms employed in relation to the Timor conflict is then set out.

HISTORY OF THE CONFLICT

East Timor became a Portuguese colony in the sixteenth century. In 1960 it was deemed by the UN General Assembly a 'non-self governing territory'.[3] In 1974 the colonial power Portugal withdrew from East Timor and a brief civil war followed. After achieving nine days of independence, declared by the Revolutionary

Front for an Independent East Timor (*Frente Revolucionária de Timor Leste Independente*, or Fretilin) on 28 November 1975, Indonesian forces occupied and annexed East Timor.[4]

An estimated 20,000 Indonesian troops were deployed to the region by the end of 1975. While casualty estimates vary, anywhere from 60,000–100,000 Timorese were probably killed in the first year after the violence began in 1975.[5] Timor was declared the 27th province of Indonesia on 31 May 1976. Indonesia's claim over Timor was never accepted by the UN, and was only unilaterally accepted by one nation, Australia.[6]

In 1979 the US Agency for International Development estimated that 300,000 East Timorese (nearly half the population) had been uprooted and moved into camps controlled by Indonesian armed forces.[7] During the 25 year occupation of Indonesia, the UN documented a series of massacres including in Kraras (August 1983), Santa Cruz (2 November 1991), Maubara and Liquiça (4–6 April 1999) and Dili (17 April 1999).[8]

The exact number of Timorese deaths at the hands of Indonesian military is not definitively known, with estimates ranging from 120,000 to 230,000.[9] On 12 November 12 1979, Indonesia's foreign minister, Mochtar Kusumaatmadja, estimated that 120,000 people had died in East Timor since 1975.[10] Amnesty International estimates that 200,000 died from military action, starvation or disease from 1975–99.[11] A genocide expert Ben Kiernan has noted that the deaths must also be seen in the context of the total original population base of just 700,000 people.[12]

The Final Report entitled *Chega!* ('Enough' in Portuguese) by Timor's Commission for Reception, Truth and Reconciliation (CAVR) released in 2006 says that an upper estimate of 183,000 died as a result of both killings and deaths due to privation.[13] CAVR's estimate of the minimum total number of conflict-related deaths is 102,800 (plus or minus 12,000). The report finds that 18,600 non-combatant East Timorese were killed or disappeared and at least 84,000 more died as a direct result of displacement policies during Indonesia's occupation.[14]

Ongoing and systematic violations were prevalent in all areas of East Timor life, specifically targeting the civilian population, and included loss of employment and livelihood; repression of cultural traditions, including language and religion; lack of access to basic needs including health care; loss of home and property, and forced displacement.[15] The UN Commission on Human Rights condemned the imprisonment of thousands of activists (most notably Xanana Gusmão in 1992), the exile of thousands more and incidences of torture, assault and inhumane treatment against Timorese resistance and civilians; including systematic gender persecution outlined below.[16]

Contemporaneously within Indonesia a political transition began in 1998 after 33 years of widespread human rights abuses committed by the armed forces and other groups under the 'New Order' regime led by General Suharto.[17] In January 1999, against a backdrop of economic crisis, Indonesian President Habibie unexpectedly announced that the East Timorese would be allowed a referendum to decide between greater autonomy within Indonesia or a transition to independence. A formal agreement between Indonesia, Portugal and the UN was reached on 5 May 1999 which established the United Nations Mission in East Timor (UNAMET) to organise a referendum. According to the agreement, Indonesia was to provide the security for the ballot.[18] Voter registration began on 16 July 1999, with teams of independent observers reporting serious accounts of political violence by the Indonesian military (*Tentara Nasional Indonesia*, or TNI) and paramilitary groups, designed to intimidate voters.[19]

A popular consultation was held on 30 August 1999. On 4 September 1999, it was announced that 78.5 per cent of the population had voted against East Timor remaining as part of Indonesia, and therefore independence would be granted to the territory.[20] The announcement of the ballot result on 4 September 1999 resulted in immediate acts of violence, a scorched earth policy, looting, massive evacuations and forced deportation of the population. In the months surrounding the 1999 vote, pro-Jakarta militias killed an estimated 1,400 people, burned towns to the ground, destroyed 80 per cent of the territory's infrastructure and forced or led more than a quarter of a million villagers into Indonesian-ruled West Timor.[21] There were also concerns about the possibility of genocide raised by members of the international community observing the referendum violence.[22]

3.1 Situation of women 1975–1999

Prior to 1975, information on the situation of Timorese women is sparse. Timor is described as a heavily patriarchal society, influenced by layers of indigenous beliefs and Portuguese colonialism and Catholicism, where most women are illiterate subsistence farmers.[23] An ethnographic study into fertility and gender in East Timor by David Hicks made several observations about gender relations: including that masculine is considered superior to feminine as the adult (father) is superior to the child.[24] Unverified numbers of Timorese women were also kept as 'comfort women' during the Japanese occupation of Timor in the Second World War from 1942 to 1945, with two Timorese women testifying at the Women's International War Crimes Tribunal in Tokyo in 2000.[25]

Most of the scarce available information about Timorese women from 1975 to 1999 concerns their experience of sexual violence. During the occupation from 1975 to 1999, an unverifiable number of Timorese women were abducted, raped and impregnated by Indonesian solders, often kept captive under slavery-like conditions, and later rejected by their families. A more acute form of gender-based violence occurred during the post-referendum violence in 1999: the systematic rape of East Timorese women in the context of the forced deportation of over 250,000 people into camps in West Timor.[26]

There are no accurate statistics on sexual violence during the occupation until 1999 and consequently during the period of forced deportation and internment in West Timor. However, a wealth of anecdotal evidence shows that gender-based international crimes in Timor have been widespread since 1975, and were rife during the 1999 violence. Testimonies to this effect have been collected by the United Nations,[27] human rights NGOs such as Amnesty International,[28] the

Indonesian Human Rights Commission KPP HAM,[29] Australian journalists,[30] and most importantly, East Timorese NGOs themselves.[31]

The most comprehensive overview of sexual violence in Timor appears in Chapter 7.7 of the report by the CAVR entitled *Chega!*[32] The CAVR recorded 853 cases of sexual violence but concluded:

> [t]he Commission notes the inevitable conclusion that many victims of sexual violations did not come forward to report them to the Commission. Reasons for under-reporting include death of victims and witnesses (especially for earlier periods of the conflict), victims who may be outside Timor-Leste (especially in West Timor), the painful and very personal nature of the experiences, and the fear of social or family humiliation or rejection if their experiences are known publicly. These strong reasons for under-reporting and the fact that 853 cases of rape and sexual slavery, along with evidence from about another 200 interviews were recorded lead the Commission to the finding that the total number of sexual violations is likely to be several times higher than the number of cases reported. The Commission estimates that the number of women who were subjected to serious sexual violations by members of the Indonesian security forces numbers in the thousands, rather than hundreds.[33]

In a 2004 study of 288 women, one in four East Timorese women reported being exposed to violence during 1999.[34] Leading Timorese women's NGO FOKUPERS has documented 46 cases of rape during the 1999 violence: nine of them by Indonesian soldiers, 28 by pro-Jakarta militias, and nine of them joint attacks by militias and soldiers. Eighteen were categorised as mass rapes. 'Many of these crimes were carried out with planning, organisation and coordination,' a FOKUPERS report states. 'Soldiers and militias kidnapped women together and shared their victims.'[35]

In the camps in West Timor where tens of thousands of women were forcibly deported, a fact-finding team in one study alone found 163 different cases of violence against 119 women, and noted serious impacts of sexual violence on women's health.[36] There is still a serious campaign by activists, including the then First Lady of East Timor, Australian Kirsty Sword Gusmão, to obtain the release of several young women in the refugee camps of West Timor who are thought to be held against their will as 'war trophies' by militia leaders.[37]

The Special Rapporteur on Violence against Women, during a joint fact-finding mission in November 1999 together with the Special Rapporteur on extrajudicial, summary or arbitrary executions and the Special Rapporteur on the question of torture, found evidence of widespread violence against women in East Timor during the period [from January 1999]. They concluded that 'the highest level of the military command in East Timor knew, or had reason to know, that there was widespread violence against women in East Timor.'[38] The Rapporteurs reported that:

> Rape was used by the military as a form of revenge, or to force the relatives out of hiding. Much of the violence against women in East Timor was

> perpetrated in the context of these areas being treated as military zones... rape by soldiers in these areas is tried in military tribunals, and not before an ordinary court of law. Under Indonesian law, for a rape to be prosecuted it required corroboration – including the testimony of two witnesses. Women lived in a realm of private terror, for any victims or witnesses who dared to take action were intimidated with death threats.[39]

An article titled 'Raping the Future' concurred that:

> Since their homeland was invaded in 1975, the women of East Timor have felt the brunt of some of the Indonesian military's most egregious human-rights violations: They have been raped in the presence of family members, forced to marry Indonesian soldiers, subjected to torture by electric shock, sexually abused, and forcibly sterilized. East Timorese women have been forced to bear much of the load of what many believe is an Indonesian government plan to eliminate the East Timorese culture.[40]

Miranda Sissons wrote a careful examination of human rights abuses perpetrated through the implementation of the Indonesian national population control programme, *Program Keluarga Berencana* (the 'KB program') in 1997. Her report alleged that the Indonesian government targeted indigenous Timorese in particular for 'reproductive oppression', and that these practices might constitute a breach of the Convention on the Prevention and Punishment of the Crime of Genocide, which prohibits intentional limitation of births within a specific national, ethnic, religious or racial group.[41]

The report states that the first phase began from the time of the Indonesian invasion and extended through the mid-1980s. The report alleges that Indonesian soldiers raped and impregnated East Timorese women and girls, mutilated pregnant women, and covertly sterilised them. The second phase, which extended to the late 1990s, saw further covert sterilisation and coerced contraception of East Timorese women through the World Bank-funded population control KB programme.[42]

3.2 Post-conflict Timor

In late 1999, Security Council Resolution 1264 approved the immediate dispatch of the Australian-led, International Force for East Timor (INTERFET), and expressed concern at 'reports indicating that systematic, widespread and flagrant violations of international humanitarian and human rights law have been committed in East Timor' and stressed individual responsibility for these acts.[43]

UNTAET was established under UN Security Council Resolution 1272 of 25 October 1999. It was the executive and legislative authority from 25 October 1999 until East Timor became independent on 20 May 2002. The UN Special Representative to East Timor, Sergio de Mello (the transitional administrator) became the executive and law making authority for East Timor on 25 October 1999.

The resolution also condemned all acts of violence in the Indonesian claimed province of East Timor, demanded that those responsible be brought to justice and called for all parties to cooperate with investigations into reports of systematic, widespread and flagrant violations of international humanitarian law and human rights law.[44]

Investigations into the post-ballot violence were carried out by special UN teams, in particular the International Commission of Inquiry on East Timor (ICIET),[45] and by the National Human Rights Commission (*Komisi Nasional Hak Asasi Manusia*, or Komnas HAM) in late 1999.[46] Komnas HAM used its powers under a government regulation expressly issued for the purpose to set up a special team, the National Commission of Inquiry on Human Rights Violations in East Timor (*Komisi Penyelidik Pelanggaran HAM di Timor Timur*, or KPP HAM), to investigate human rights abuses in East Timor during the period from 1 January to 25 October 1999.

In a letter of 31 January 2000 accompanying the International Commission of Inquiry (ICIET) report, Kofi Annan wrote of the violence in 1999:

> …[T]he actions violating human rights and international humanitarian law were directed against a decision of the Security Council and were contrary to the agreements reached by Indonesia with the United Nations to carry out the decision of the Security Council. This fact reinforces the need to hold the perpetrators accountable for their actions…The International Commission of Inquiry found that the United Nations and the international community had a particular responsibility to the people of East Timor in connection with investigating the violations, establishing responsibilities, punishing those responsible and promoting reconciliation. I believe the United Nations has an important role to play in this process in order to help safeguard the rights of the people of East Timor, promote reconciliation, ensure future social and political stability and protect the integrity of Security Council actions.[47]

As a result of the recommendations of these investigations, three main transitional justice mechanisms were established to address the crimes. First, in East Timor the UN set up the Serious Crimes Unit and Special Panels of the Dili District Court and the Commission for Reception, Truth and Reconciliation (CAVR).

In Indonesia the chosen transitional justice mechanism was the East Timor trials at the Indonesian ad hoc Human Rights Court in Jakarta, as well as a proposed truth commission (KKR). In 2005, East Timor and Indonesia agreed to set up a Joint Truth and Friendship Commission, which would offer a full amnesty to all who participated in violations in return for their cooperation.

At the same time, developments in governance and moves to independence were as follows. The UN Mission of Support in East Timor (UNMISET) was to withdraw from East Timor entirely in May 2004, but the Secretary-General announced the Mission would stay for another year but be dramatically reduced from almost 3,000 civilian and military personnel to 700 while the country becomes self-sufficient. In May 2004, roughly 1,650 peacekeeping troops, 300 civilian police and 1,000 civilian personnel were deployed in East Timor.[48]

In 2005, another extension was granted. The United Nations Office in Timor Leste (UNOTIL) was established by Resolution 1599 (2005) adopted by the Security Council on 28 April 2005, with effect from 21 May 2005. UNOTIL was mandated to support the development of critical state institutions by providing up to 45 civilian advisers; support further development of the police through the provision of up to 40 police advisers and support the development of the Border Patrol Unit (BPU), by providing up to 35 additional advisers, ten of whom may be military advisers; provide training in observance of democratic governance and human rights by providing up to ten human rights officers; and review progress in all those tasks.[49]

Post-independence, there have been episodes of serious internal conflict in Timor. Violence in the Timorese capital Dili in April and May between police, the military and youths resulted in at least 37 persons killed, more than 150 injured and some 150,000 persons displaced, as well as arbitrary arrests and detention by the armed forces. There was significant damage to property, particularly looting and burning of houses in Dili.

In mid-July 2006, 72,000 internally displaced persons were receiving food aid in 62 makeshift camps scattered throughout Dili, while up to 80,000 people had fled to the countryside where they were sheltered by host families and in a very small number of camps.[50]

In late June 2006 the United Nations High Commissioner for Human Rights, on the request of the UN Secretary-General established a Special Independent Commission of Inquiry for Timor Leste which reported on 17 October 2006. The Commission found that 'failures of the rule of law and accountability were at the heart of the events in April and May'.[51]

After the Dili riots in April/May 2006, the United Nations Integrated Mission in Timor Leste (UNMIT) was established, on 25 August 2006 by Security Council Resolution 1704 with the priority of restoring public security (and replacing UNOTIL). At full strength it included some 1,608 UN Police (UNPol) as well as 34 military liaison and staff officers. UNPol will provide support to the Timorese police force (PNTL) while it is being reconstituted, plus provide interim law enforcement. It had an initial six-month mandate.

There has been considerable unrest across East Timor in relation to the Presidential and Parliamentary elections in mid-2007. José Ramos-Horta and Xanana Gusmão effectively swapped roles as Prime Minister and President. An estimated 600 houses and confirmed 142 were allegedly burnt by pro-FRETILIN supporters in villages between Viqueque and Baucau. In August, violence occurred in several places, including Dili and Metinaro, with two people reported as killed in Ermera. On 10 August 2007, a convent in Baucau was attacked and damaged, and a number of female students at the convent were said to have been raped.[52]

On 11 February 2008, a group of rebels led by Alfredo Reinado attacked President Ramos-Horta and Prime Minister Gusmão. Ramos-Horta and one of his guards were badly wounded, and Reinado and another rebel were killed. A joint F-FDTL and PNTL command was established to pursue the surviving rebels.[53] Resolution 1802 of 25 February 2008 was adopted directly after these attacks. The Security Council requested UNMIT to assist the Timor Government to thwart all attempts to destabilise the country. This mandate lasts until 26 February 2010 (SC/RES/1867 (2009). The current Special Representative of the Secretary-General is Atul Khare of India.[54]

As of 31 March 2009, Timor Leste hosts 1,485 total uniformed personnel, including 1,452 police and 33 military liaison officers; 371 international civilian staff; 908 local civilian personnel; and 128 UN Volunteers. The UNMIT budget for 1 July 2008 to 30 June 2009 is $180.84 million (A/C.5/62/30).[55]

3.3 Women in post-conflict Timor

As of June 2009, East Timor is the poorest country in Asia.[56] According to a United Nations Development Programme report on East Timor released in January 2006, 90 out of 1,000 children die before their first birthday, half the population is illiterate, 64 per cent suffer from food insecurity, half lack access to safe drinking water, and 40 per cent live below the official poverty line, defined by an income of 55 cents a day.[57]

New figures produced by the World Health Organisation in early 2002 show that twice as many women die in childbirth in East Timor as anywhere else in East Asia or the Western Pacific.[58] According to the WHO, there are only 196 midwives available for a population of 800,000, and less than a quarter of East Timor's women have ready access to a health facility or a qualified midwife. The WHO says these figures represent 'an absolute tragedy'.[59]

As of January 2004, domestic violence in East Timor accounted for some 45 per cent of all crime cases in the young country and made up 67 per cent of the cases reported to the police. Over half (51 per cent) of married East-Timorese women say they feel unsafe in their relationship. An estimated 95,000 women had received sterilising injections since 1975; and over half of women in East Timor are illiterate.[60]

The Dili riots in 2006 again underscored the vulnerability of women in present-day Timor.[61] The UN Secretary-General stated:

> The mass displacement of people that resulted from the crisis has had particularly adverse effects on women and children, including premature labour and vulnerability to sexual abuse in overcrowded camps. The ongoing humanitarian response should thus address the security and protection needs of women and children and involve them in the planning, management and delivery of humanitarian assistance and psychosocial support to heal their trauma.[62]

The last remaining camp began emptying in June 2009, more than three years after unrest drove an estimated 100,000 people from their homes.[63]

OVERVIEW OF TRANSITIONAL JUSTICE MECHANISMS

Since 1945 there have been some 250 conflicts all over the globe, which have caused between 70 and 170 million casualties.[64] Only a handful of people have been prosecuted, but recent research shows that since 1982 one-third of conflicts have utilised some kind of legal transitional justice mechanism in the post-conflict period.[65]

In 1992, the Security Council established the Commission of Experts to investigate crimes arising out of the conflict in the former Yugoslavia, headed by expert M. Cherif Bassiouni. This was the first truly international effort to investigate with the intent to prosecute international crimes, based on similar commissions established by the Allies during the First and Second World Wars. After that, the International Tribunals for the Former Yugoslavia and Rwanda were established, and then the International Criminal Court in 2002, along with a plethora of tribunals and truth commissions around the globe.

3.4 Judicial mechanisms relating to East Timor

The serious crimes process

The preferred transitional justice mechanism for human rights advocates is usually an international criminal tribunal.[66] There have been several key precedents set in the past 20 years relating to international prosecutions and reparation for victims in particular, with the apogee being the International Criminal Court. The International Criminal Court is unable to deal with the crimes committed in East Timor because the court cannot hear cases of crimes that were committed before its inception, and the Rome Statute entered into force in July 2002.

The UN Security Council can establish an ad hoc international criminal tribunal mechanism in the interests of global peace and security under Chapter VII of the Charter. The Council delegates the court with powers to compel the support of Indonesia and other affected countries. Criminal tribunals have been established in Yugoslavia (the ICTY) and Rwanda (the ICTR) by Security Council Resolutions, making them subsidiary bodies of the Security Council.

There are several advantages to an international tribunal. Being part of the Security Council gives an ad hoc tribunal financial security as they are funded through assessed funds rather than voluntary contributions. This allows for a longer time frame in which to run trials. The use of international tribunals underscores the international nature of the crimes committed in that it acknowledges that all people and states have a responsibility to ensure justice is served for such crimes, rather than just the state in which they were committed. An international tribunal can therefore avoid the appearance of victor's justice.

However, such a tribunal would only deal with the 'authors' of war crimes and crimes against humanity: those who planned and prepared the violence. In the Timorese context, these authors are generally senior Indonesian military officials. This means that Indonesian cooperation is required for their prosecution. The political and diplomatic weight of the Security Council may be the only way to pressure a state to hand over senior indicted officials. Threat of an international tribunal can also pressure a state into holding their own trials, an issue which is explored at length in Chapter Four in relation to the setting up of the Jakarta ad hoc Human Rights Court.

Finally, an international tribunal can take pressure for justice issues off fragile states. As then President Gusmão enunciated:

> What is the mandate of an international tribunal? It is to punish and to prevent atrocities. I say, don't force East Timor to punish. Have an international tribunal. The international community should deal with punishment of crimes, not East Timor. We also committed crimes before 1975; if we wanted to start to punish ourselves, we wouldn't exist as a community. If we talk about prevention: Indonesia will not invade us again. Also, there was a process of justice in Indonesia. Look at its size and population and how many challenges they have to face today. We ask ourselves to be patient with us and with Indonesia. They are dealing with their past. We don't want to undermine the democratization process in Indonesia in which they do very well.[67]

Instead of an international tribunal, the UN chose a 'hybrid' tribunal for East Timor.[68] A 'hybrid' court utilises domestic and international judges and considers international (and occasionally some national) laws. A post-conflict state can request support of donor countries for assistance with the prosecution of specific crimes. This could include providing evidence to a court for a specific case, or providing financial or other contributions to assist with the prosecution of a particular case.

The advantages of a hybrid tribunal are development of local judges, infrastructure and access by citizens to the proceedings. The downside is that non-international efforts can be impeded by lack of ongoing funds, or stymied by the violating parties still within the country until international interest dies away. Again, a state such as East Timor is reliant on Indonesian cooperation for providing indicted persons for trial.

The Special Panels within Dili District Court were set up by UNTAET by Regulation 2000/15.[69] The Panels had exclusive jurisdiction over genocide, crimes against humanity, war crimes wherever and whenever they occurred; and over murder, sexual offences and torture that occurred in Timor Leste between 1 January and 25 October 1999. The UN was set to withdraw its support for the serious crimes process in May 2005 in the context of its overall withdrawal from Timor, but has a renewed mandate to assist as part of the UNOTIL mission.

The broad aim of the serious crimes process was to ensure that those responsible for serious crimes committed in 1999 were brought to justice. This was reiterated by the UN Secretary-General in his report to the Security Council dated 29 April 2004 noting that '[i]n its resolution 1410 (2002), the Security Council stressed the critical importance of cooperation between Indonesia and East Timor, and with UNMISET, to ensure that those responsible for serious crimes committed in 1999 are brought to justice'. The call for justice has since been reiterated by the Security Council in resolutions 1319 (2000), 1338 (2001), 1410 (2002), 1543 (2004) and 1599 (2005), 1677 (2006), 1690 (2006), 1703 (2006) and 1704 (2006).

The Transitional Administrator decided for purely practical reasons that Indonesian law would apply in East Timor, and therefore to the mandate of the serious crimes process 'insofar as [it] conformed with internationally recognized human rights standards and did not conflict with the Security Council's mandate to each mission or any subsequent regulation promulgated by the mission'.[70] Certain Indonesian laws particularly obnoxious to international human rights standards were declared not to apply and, in case of doubt as to its legality, capital punishment was specifically abolished.

Due to lack of cooperation from Indonesia in handing over suspects still in Indonesian territory, both the Special Panels and the CAVR were focused on Timorese nationals who participated in violent acts, either as guerrillas in Falintil or as collaborators with the Indonesian forces.

The Jakarta trials

A post-conflict state often holds its own domestic trials. Under international law, including the Rome Statute, responsibility for providing justice for serious crimes falls upon the state first and then the international community only if the state is unwilling or unable to provide fair trials. In a weak democracy with little or no judicial infrastructure, holding trials can be a significant problem, as Gusmão's words above attest. More importantly, the key violators of international law were Indonesian, thus it is important to examine the attempts to deal with violence in East Timor by Indonesian institutions.

In Indonesia, Law 26/2000 on Human Rights Courts was adopted by the Indonesian legislature in November 2000. The law provided for the establishment of four permanent Human Rights Courts and, for cases which took place prior to the adoption of the legislation, the possibility of establishing ad hoc Human Rights Courts. The new courts were to have jurisdiction over crimes against humanity and genocide, crimes which until then had not been included in Indonesian domestic law. Presidential Decree No. 96/2001 was issued by the newly installed President Megawati Sukarnoputri in August 2001 establishing an ad hoc Human Rights Court on East Timor. The jurisdiction was limited to only those crimes occurring in the districts of Liquiça, Dili and Suai in the two months of April and September 1999. The trials were completed in 2004, and are examined in Chapter Four.

Lustration and Alien Torts Claims

The other judicial mechanism relevant to the Timor violence was the practice of third states using universal jurisdiction to try international crimes if a person is in their jurisdiction, as explored below in relation to the United States.[71] According to the universal jurisdiction principle, certain crimes – such as war crimes which are classified as grave breaches and torture – are regarded as so abhorrent that they are categorised as international crimes. Universal jurisdiction allows the national courts of any state to try people accused of such crimes, regardless of the nationality of the alleged perpetrators or victims and regardless of where the crimes were committed. Universal jurisdiction grants a right to apprehend (if a perpetrator enters voluntarily a third state) and the right to extradite.[72]

In certain states, civil trials can be held, most notably in the United States under the *Alien Tort Claims Act of 1789*, which allows non-citizens to sue for acts committed outside the United States 'in violation of the law of nations or a treaty of the United States'.[73] The 1991 *Torture Victim Protection Act* reaffirms the 1789 law and gives US courts jurisdiction over claims by citizens involving torture and extra-judicial killing occurring anywhere. Lawsuits can only go forward if the defendant is served legal papers while in the US.

In 2000, US Federal Court Judge Alan Kay held General Lumintang liable, on the basis of command responsibility, for $66 million for his role in systematic human rights violations.[74] Lumintang was personally served notice of the civil suit on March 30, 2000, while visiting the Washington, DC area.[75] In 1999, Lumintang, as vice chief of staff, was second in command of the Indonesian army. He chose not to defend himself in court. The six plaintiffs or their estates were granted $10 million each in punitive damages. Compensatory damages ranged from $750,000 to $1.75 million each. Lt. Gen. Lumintang has subsequently held the post of secretary general of the Ministry of Defence in Indonesia.

In 1994, a judgment for $14 million was issued in a similar case against General Sintong Panjaitan for his involvement in the Santa Cruz massacre of over 270 East Timorese on 12 November 1991. He was sued while residing in Boston where he was sent in 1992 to pursue a business school education.[76] US District Court Judge Patti Saris ordered the general to pay $4 million in compensatory damages and $10 million in punitive damages to Helen Todd, the mother of 19 year-old Kamal Bamadhaj, the only non-East Timorese killed that day.[77] Panjaitan has subsequently been an adviser in the Indonesian Ministry of Industry and Technology in Jakarta. The judgments are unenforceable while the defendants remain outside the US.

On 5 February 2007, the NSW Coroner's Court in Australia began an inquest into the death of Brian Peters, one of several Australian journalists killed in Timor in 1975, known as the 'Balibo Five'.[78] Even if the Deputy Coroner refers the matter to the Director of Public Prosecutions, again, any defendant would have to present themselves in the Australian jurisdiction. Measures such as this and Interpol monitoring of the Special Panel arrest warrants do serve to put diplomatic pressure on a state, however, and prevent the movement of the possible defendants, which may be seen as a form of lustration to a limited extent. On the other hand, although General Wiranto was the subject of an arrest warrant, most of the world's heads of state formally announced they would work with Wiranto if he were to be elected President of Indonesia when he campaigned in 2004.[79] He again stood in the 2009 election.

Perhaps the single most important bargaining tool that an individual state has at its disposal to influence Indonesia's choices on matters of justice is America and its decision to withdraw military funding. This is explored in Chapter Four as the political backdrop to the Indonesian ad hoc Human Rights Court. All military ties were suspended in 1999 after the referendum violence, and were restored in November 2005.

3.5 Non-judicial mechanisms – truth commissions

Truth commissions have been a growth industry in the last few decades. Priscilla Hayner surveyed 21 official truth commissions established between 1974 and 1999, noting at the time that as many as 16 other jurisdictions were contemplating the creation of a truth commission.[80]

Truth commissions have emerged as an accepted alternative, or with increasing frequency as a complementary accountability mechanism, to criminal prosecution. Many commissions will attempt to achieve a number or all of the following goals: giving meaning to the voice of individual victims; making historical corrections according to incidents of gross human rights violations; providing public education and awareness; investigating the systematic violation of human rights, leading to institutional reform; providing an assessment of the effect of human rights violations on victims; and confirming the responsibility of the perpetrator.[81]

The CAVR (Timor truth commission)

The Commission for Reception, Truth and Reconciliation (CAVR) was established by UNTAET Regulation No. 2001/10 as an independent statutory authority that will inquire into human rights violations committed on all sides, between April 1974 and October 1999, and facilitate community reconciliation with justice for those who committed less serious offences. The Commission cannot grant amnesty and is meant to refer 'serious crimes' as defined to the Serious Crimes Unit. The CAVR delivered its final report to Parliament in November 2005 but it was not publicly disseminated within Timor until June 2006.

The CAVR's mandate included: establishing the truth regarding the human rights violations that occurred in the context of political conflicts in East Timor between 1974 and October 25, 1999; assisting in restoring the dignity of victims; promoting reconciliation, and supporting the reintegration of individuals who committed harmful acts through community-based reconciliation mechanisms; identifying practices and policies that should be addressed to prevent future human rights violations and to promote human rights; and referring human rights violations to the Office of the General Prosecutor with recommendations for prosecution.[82]

The mechanism of a truth commission is a traditional response for a society that has experienced a civil, rather than an international conflict. It is an unusual choice for Timor due to the nature of the international armed conflict from 1975 to 1999, except for the backdrop of the civil conflict in 1975 prior to the occupation and the militias controlled by the Indonesian military. One question particularly relevant to East Timor is what a society should do to deal with collaborators, especially those whose collaboration may not have been freely chosen.

Another important aspect of the CAVR is its incorporation of indigenous justice processes.[83] 'Tetum speakers have a word for reconciliation: 'Nahe Biti' literally meaning 'stretching the mat'; this stretching of the traditional grass mat and opening it out makes space for others to sit on the mat and so tell their sides of the story too'.[84]

In this spirit, Community Reconciliation Processes (CRP) were set up under the auspices of the CAVR. A total of 1,400 CRPs were held between August 2000 and November 2005. The process involved the perpetrator going to the village where the crime occurred, meeting relatives of victims and offering an apology.[85] The Timorese version of a truth commission in the CAVR did not offer an official amnesty. Gusmão did table draft amnesty legislation on his first day in office but all debate on the draft in Parliament stopped after 20 May 2004 when the end of the serious crimes process seemed imminent. By contrast, the Joint Truth and Friendship Commission agreed to between Timor and Indonesia in 2005 contained the possibility of a full amnesty.

The CAVR final report is called *Chega!* ('Enough!' in Portuguese). The 2500 page report was handed to the President on 31 October 2005, and tabled in the East Timorese Parliament for consideration on 28 November 2005. President Xanana Gusmão handed the report to UN Secretary-General Kofi Annan on 20 January 2006. Upon receipt, the Secretary-General referred the report to the Security Council, General Assembly, the Special Committee on Decolonization, and the UN Commission on Human Rights.

The KKR (Indonesian Truth Commission)

The Indonesian Truth and Reconciliation Commission Act (TRCA) provided the framework for the establishment of the *Komisi Kebenaran dan Rekonsiliasi* (KKR) to provide truth, accountability and compensation for past abuse in Indonesia prior to the establishment of the Human Rights Courts.[86] Proposals for a national truth commission circulated in Indonesia shortly after the fall of Suharto in 1998, but implementing legislation was not passed until 2004.

The Commission received sustained criticism from Timorese and Indonesian NGOs that it would be a 'whitewash machine'.[87] Six Indonesian human rights and victims groups brought legal challenges against two provisions, one granting the TRC the power to award amnesties to perpetrators of past crimes and barring victims from taking any future legal action against them; and the second which made the provision of reparations to victims contingent upon the signing of a formal statement exonerating their perpetrators.

After months of deliberation, the Constitutional Court declared that provisions of the TRC law violate Indonesia's obligations under international law, the Indonesian Bill of Rights and domestic human rights laws, and struck the whole law down.[88] This was greeted as a positive development by some activists but others felt that compensation for victims of the New Order violence would be further delayed and eroded.[89] There have been no further developments with a new KKR law reported as of June 2009.

Joint Truth and Friendship Commission

On 14 December 2004, then Presidents Gusmão and Yudhoyono declared their intention to create a commission of truth and friendship (JTFC) presumably to pre-empt any chance that the UN may yet entertain the idea of an international tribunal as a result of the Experts' report described below.

On 9 March 2005, the two Presidents agreed on the terms of reference of the JTFC, and a memorandum of understanding was signed on 11 August 2005 on its establishment. The JTFC was composed of ten Commissioners, five from Indonesia and five from Timor Leste, as well as six alternates, three from Indonesia and three from Timor Leste. It was led by two co-chairs, from Indonesia and Timor Leste, elected by the Commissioners. The Joint Secretariat of CTF was located in Denpasar, Indonesia.

The commission could recommend amnesty for those involved, but its findings explicitly 'will not lead to prosecution'. It could 'emphasize institutional responsibilities' rather than identifying and assigning blame. It was be able to recommend rehabilitation for those 'wrongly accused', but had no power to propose rehabilitation or reparations for victims.[90] On 30 November 2006, the JTFC announced it would invite parties such as General Wiranto to answer questions in January 2007, and then announced it would recommend amnesties for people who cooperated with the Commission.[91] This announcement was publicly denounced by Timor MPs Cipriana Pereira (Fretilin) and Maria Paixão (PSD).[92] Hearings were held from January to September 2007,[93] and an ongoing extension of the JTFC mandate was granted.

The report was finally handed to Indonesian President Susilo Bambang Yudhoyono and Timorese President José Ramos-Horta at a ceremony on Bali, Indonesia on 15 July 2008. The report, *From Remembering Comes Hope*, concludes that the Indonesian military, police and civilian government bear institutional responsibility for widespread and systematic gross violations of human rights, including crimes against humanity.[94] The final report does not recommend amnesties. The recommendations on military reform were the most controversial but have yet to be followed up.[95]

UN efforts: The Commission of Experts

A Commission of Experts was appointed by Kofi Annan in January 2005 to investigate why a 1999 Security Council resolution calling for the trial of those accused of atrocities in Timor during its independence referendum had not been implemented. The three experts, Justice Prafullachandra Bhagwati of India, Professor Yozo Yokota of Japan and Shaista Shameem of Fiji, visited Indonesia and East Timor in early 2005.

The UN Security Council, as mentioned in Resolution 1599 (2005), called on all parties (including Indonesia) to cooperate fully with the work of the Commission of Experts. Despite this, in May 2005 Indonesia initially refused their visas. The Experts' 160-page report to UN Secretary-General Kofi Annan debated in the Security Council found that Indonesia should retry accused war criminals acquitted by a special court in Jakarta because the process was a sham.[96] The report says the trials were 'manifestly inadequate' with 'scant respect for relevant international standards'. Prosecutors were 'not committed to justice', and the court had been hostile to defence witnesses but lenient on the accused.[97]

The report recommended that Indonesia be given six months to prepare credible trials. If it does not comply, the experts argued, the UN should invoke its charter to set up an international war crimes court for East Timor. Such action has not yet been taken by the UN as of June 2009.

The Security Council asked the Secretary-General to make recommendations on the Experts Report which he did on 26 July 2006.[98] He recommended the establishment of an experienced investigation team, led by an international serious crimes investigator, with sufficient resources to resume the investigative functions of the Serious Crimes Unit and complete investigations into outstanding serious crimes cases of 1999 in a timely fashion. As a result, among UNMIT's other priorities are assisting the Office of the Prosecutor General in resuming investigative functions of the former Serious Crimes Unit in order to complete investigations into the serious human rights violations of 1999.

On Human Rights Day 2005, Cecelia Soares summed up what she wanted from the transitional justice process in the following words:

> My whole life was ruined by the 1975 invasion and I want the world to acknowledge that. The outside world stood by while my people were being slaughtered by the Indonesians.[99]

It is clear that the situation in East Timor has provided a wealth of material and incidents for the transitional justice scholar to examine.

4 Beloved madam

The Indonesian ad hoc Human Rights Court

Dominggas dos Santos Mouzinho was a survivor of the Suai massacre[1] who testified on 28 May 2002 in the trial of Lieutenant Colonel Herman Sedyono and four others in the Suai case. During cross-examination by the defence counsel she was subjected to a diatribe couched in elaborate courtesy:

> Thank you, if you don't want to respond, I won't force you. But follow the conscience of your heart, my most beloved madam, were your daughters raped or about to be raped or wanting to be raped (diperkosa atau mau diperkosa). It's up to you if you don't want to answer, I am only talking about the pure inner self. Beloved madam.

Dominggas dos Santos Mouzinho was questioned in a similar manner for five hours without a break—she was not even offered a glass of water.[2]

Trials dealing with the international crimes committed in East Timor were held concurrently in East Timor and in Indonesia. In Indonesia, Law 26/2000 on Human Rights Courts was adopted by the Indonesian legislature in November 2000. The law provided for the establishment of four permanent Human Rights Courts and, for cases which took place prior to the adoption of the legislation, the possibility of establishing ad hoc Human Rights Courts and a truth commission. The new courts were to have jurisdiction over crimes against humanity and genocide, crimes which until then had not been included in Indonesian domestic law.[3]

Presidential Decree No. 96/2001 was issued by the newly installed President Megawati Sukarnoputri in August 2001 establishing an ad hoc Human Rights Court on East Timor. The jurisdiction was limited to only those crimes occurring in the districts of Liquiça, Dili and Suai, and only within the two months of April and September 1999. The trials were completed in 2004, and the appeal process in May 2006.

This chapter will provide a gender analysis of the role, operation and jurisprudence of the Jakarta Court, the most controversial of the transitional justice mechanisms established to date to deal with international crimes in East Timor. I argue that the experience of women was almost completely excluded, and further that masculinist, nationalist, militaristic discourse seen in the trials has been allowed to subjugate feminised international justice.

The first section presents an analysis of the political circumstances in which the Court came to be established. I aim to illustrate that the obligation to punish under international law may be realised in such a fashion as to render it meaningless. Theoretical debates discussed in Chapter Two between legalist versus realist approaches to transitional justice can be seen clashing in the foundations of the trials. What happens when a trial process is set up to fail and no international tribunal will be forthcoming?

Analysis of the trials raises many questions about the domestic prosecution of war crimes, but none more pertinent to a global legal system which now features the International Criminal Court (ICC) than this: how exactly will the ICC determine when a state is 'unwilling or unable' to prosecute international crimes (Article 17)? What criteria will be applied where trials have been held that are perceived to be inadequate?[4] Will this criterion be applied in a manner that does not acknowledge gender?

The second section provides an overview of the investigation process, legislative framework, and funding and staffing issues of the Court, the indictments issued by the Court, and the eventual results and convictions. I then note the report of the UN Commission of Experts in 2005 and the resulting move on the part of the governments of Indonesia and East Timor to set up a Joint Truth and Friendship Commission.

In the third section I ask, as have many other legal commentators, whether the trials were a sham, and what the consequences were for women.[5] The overall failure of the process has overshadowed the detrimental consequences for women, yet these are significant, especially in terms of silencing what happened to women in the conflict. As Cynthia Enloe writes:

> ...assignments of significance or triviality—that is, visibility or invisibility—are typically based on the gendered presumption that what men did must have been more important than what women did in determining how the war was fought, how it ended, and what its impact is on postwar society.[6]

The Commission of Experts identified inherent procedural flaws in the legislative foundation of the Court; possible conspiracy between the prosecution and the military; and the lack of training of prosecutors and judges.[7] The cumulative effect of these factors was that the Court was unable to provide even the basic measure of justice in the cases before it.[8] A gendered analysis brings into focus the official silence in the indictments on gender-persecution, the intimidating courtroom atmosphere, ill-treatment of female witnesses and judges, and the reaction of Timorese women's groups to the trials.

The implications of the Law on Human Rights Courts for the project of building the rule of law in Indonesia goes far beyond the Timor trials. As an International Crisis Group Report on Indonesia noted, gross violations in Indonesia have taken many different forms and affected different parts of society:

> ...communists and communist sympathisers who were massacred or imprisoned in large numbers at the beginning of the New Order era in 1965–66;

> Muslim political opponents imprisoned in their hundreds in the 1980s; Muslim protestors at Tanjung Priok (Jakarta) in 1984 and Lampung in 1989 who were killed by government forces; and thousands of petty criminals who were systematically murdered during the early 1980s. Gross violations occurred during military operations in provinces where separatist or independence movements are or were active, including Aceh and Irian Jaya, as well as the special case of East Timor.[9]

Therefore, I argue that the examination of these trials has import for justice for Indonesian women as well.[10] As Fionnuala D. Ni Aolain states:

> Compounded patriarchies may ultimately threaten the viability of transition to a liberal and inclusive political state that works for women and stands as a powerful example of the extent to which the transitional project can threaten not just to silence women's particular experience of the previous regime or conflict but actually operate to thwart the broader liberal project of equality for women in transitional societies.[11]

FOUNDATIONS: THE OBLIGATION TO PUNISH

The UN Security Council found that prosecutions were warranted as a result of the investigations into the 1999 violence.[12] Once the UN had reached this conclusion, the pressing issue was where and how the trials would take place.

Indonesia's opposition to an international tribunal was clear from the outset. Dr Alwi Shihab, the then Indonesian Foreign Minister, stated to the Parliamentary Defence and Foreign Affairs Commission, 'We will try not to deliver the generals to an international tribunal'.[13] The *Indonesia Observer* reported that on 19 January 2000, Shihab met UN Secretary-General Kofi Annan and explained Indonesia's opposition to an international tribunal on East Timor. He told Annan that the KPP HAM must be given the authority with no interference from any institutions, 'including the UN', to handle the question of accountability for the crimes committed in East Timor.[14]

At the UN Headquarters in New York, Shihab also met with several members of the Security Council and UN representatives of some 20 members, including China, Russia, Portugal, Middle East and Asian countries. He then stated publicly that '[w]e are trying to halt the international tribunal at all costs because it will lead to a bad name for Indonesia' and stated that there was a secret agreement among members of the UN Security Council to give Indonesia a chance to settle the case in Indonesia. He added that 'If there is voting we will win a veto'.[15]

Finally, in a letter to the UN Secretary-General dated 26 January 2000, Dr Shihab confirmed Indonesia's rejection of the recommendation of the ICIET for an international tribunal. He insisted that 'Indonesian laws are the only applicable laws to those violations and the Indonesian judicial mechanism is the exclusive mechanism for bringing the perpetrators of the violations of human rights to justice'.[16]

However, it was clear the international threat of a tribunal had an effect on Indonesia. Several confidence-building measures were taken to allay the concerns of the international community. In January 2000 the Indonesian investigation was turned over to Attorney-General Marzuki Darusman, the former head of the Indonesian Human Rights Commission, Komnas HAM.[17] Most importantly, President Abdurrahman Wahid suspended General Wiranto from his post of Security and Political Affairs Minister in February 2000, against muttered threats of a military coup reported in the press.

The then Secretary-General Kofi Annan visited Indonesia in mid-February 2000 to assess the prospect of a credible domestic response from Indonesia firsthand. He said:

> And I am personally very pleased that the Indonesian government has taken on the responsibility of ensuring that those responsible for the atrocities in East Timor will be made accountable and will be brought to trial.[18]

CNN reported that Annan, upon meeting with Indonesia's Attorney-General, then investigating Wiranto, said again only a credible effort by the Indonesian government would stop the establishment of an international tribunal. The criteria for a 'credible effort' were obviously a source of tension and confusion from the outset. According to CNN, the Secretary-General 'bristled' when the Attorney-General asked for his definition of justice, and replied 'What is yours?'[19]

Foreign Minister Alwi Shihab, at the time of the February 2000 visit, urged the Komnas HAM as well as the Attorney General's office to perform well in handling post-ballot atrocities in East Timor. He stated clearly that Indonesia's measures were designed to avoid a tribunal:

> Those institutions have to show the international community that Indonesia is able to set up a credible and transparent trial, so that there is no need for an international tribunal…If those parties do not seem serious in carrying out their duties, the Security Council could actually favour an international tribunal to settle the case.[20]

Annan then visited Dili and told thousands of East Timorese at a news conference that an international court could be established if Indonesia failed to prosecute those responsible for the mass violence in the region in 1999. He said:

> If the trial does not go forward as planned, they (the UN Security Council) may revert to an international tribunal…It is essential that those who committed the atrocities be brought to justice.…We will also never forget the extreme violence that erupted. I wish we could have prevented or contained it.[21]

The US ambassador at the UN, Richard Holbrooke, said he expected pressure for an international tribunal would 'continually and dramatically increase' if the Indonesian Government did not produce what the UN expected of it.[22]

Despite these remarks by the UN and international community, it was widely reported at the time, confirming the Foreign Minister Shihab's secret veto comments, that the Security Council – especially China and Russia – would not sanction an international tribunal because of the precedent it could set for conflicts with certain similarities such as Chechnya or Tibet.[23]

Leading NGO commentators were sceptical about the prospects of successful domestic trials. Sidney Jones, at that time the head of UNTAET'S human rights division and now with the International Crisis Group, said 'I am worried that waiting for Indonesian justice to run its course may mean waiting for something to happen, that may never happen'.[24] Sonia Picado, leader of the UN International Commission of Inquiry, said that holding trials before an Indonesian court would 'simply amount to the denial of justice'.[25]

I have set out the political context of the foundations of the Court in detail as it is pertinent to the quality of trials the UN was able to demand of Indonesia. If we try to locate the response in the spectrum of theoretical positions on transitional justice, the UN was clearly motivated by the legalist notion that international crimes must be prosecuted because they constituted breaches of *jus cogens* norms. In contrast, the Republic of Indonesia was clearly stating the realist view that states should have the right as part of their sovereignty to determine their response to crimes committed in what was then their territory. Under international law East Timor was not Indonesian territory. But even so, this view holds little value given that it is not Indonesians who have to live with their 'justice' but the East Timorese. One might think that the eventual Indonesian decision to hold trials therefore constituted a win for the legalist position, but the reality of the trials was to prove otherwise. An analysis of the international relations factors at play in the debate is critical to understanding why the Jakarta trials were destined to fail. Nevertheless, the impact of international law in imposing an obligation to punish is clearly demonstrated in the political debate.

THE ROLE AND OPERATION OF THE COURT

The previous section outlined the significance of the Indonesian lack of political will in the kind of trials that were instigated. This section details how lack of political will infected the investigation process, legislative framework, and funding and staffing issues. The prosecution strategy and indictments are presented in brief, as well as the eventual outcomes of the trials.

4.1 Investigations

The first and most successful step was investigations. On 22 September 1999, along with the decree setting up the ad hoc human rights court for East Timor, the Habibie Government gave approval to Komnas HAM to form a Commission of Inquiry into Human Rights Violations in East Timor (KPP HAM)[26] to investigate crimes committed between January and October 1999. This Commission consisted of five members of Komnas HAM and four independent human rights advocates.

The terms of reference of KPP HAM included a specific focus on 'crimes against women'.[27] The Commission was mandated to assemble information and search for evidence in relation to violations of human rights that occurred in East Timor from January 1999 until the People's Consultative Assembly issued a decree in October 1999 recognising the ballot results, with special attention to gross violations of human rights such as genocide, massacre, torture, enforced displacement, crimes against women and children and scorched earth policies; investigate the level of involvement by the apparatus of state and/or other bodies, national and international, in these crimes; and formulate the results as basis for prosecutions in the Human Rights Court.[28]

A few days later a resolution was adopted by a special session of the UN's Commission on Human Rights (UNCHR) to set up an international commission of inquiry (ICIET) into the referendum violence beginning 30 August 1999.[29] As a compromise with Indonesia, the UNCHR resolution stipulated that the international commission of inquiry should work 'in cooperation with the Indonesian National Commission on Human Rights...to gather and compile systematically information on possible violations of human rights and acts which may constitute breaches of international humanitarian law committed in East Timor since... January 1999'.[30] The resolution also affirmed that 'the primary responsibility for bringing perpetrators to justice rests with national judicial systems'.[31] The scene was thus set for two parallel investigations, one domestic and one international.

The UN's commission of inquiry came into being in late October, with a mandate to investigate human rights violations in East Timor since the beginning of 1999 and to complete its work and report to the UN Secretary-General by 31 December 1999. The five-member commission headed by Sonia Picado of Costa Rica, with members from Nigeria, India, Papua New Guinea and Germany, visited East Timor for two weeks in late November and early December.[32] Both the ICIET and the KPP HAM reports were handed down on 31 January 2000 after consultation with each other.

The UNCHR resolution also provided for three UN Special Rapporteurs – dealing with extra-judicial killings, torture and violence against women – and the UN Working Group on Disappearances to conduct investigations in East Timor. Indonesia denied the Rapporteurs entry to West Timor. Their report was handed down in December 2000.[33]

The ICIET Report of January 2000 recommended that the UN should form an international human rights tribunal.[34] The UN Commission on Human Rights Special Rapporteurs also concluded in their December 1999 report that:

> [u]nless, in a matter of months, the steps taken by the Government of Indonesia to investigate TNI involvement in the past year's atrocities bear fruit...the Security Council should consider the establishment of an international criminal tribunal for the purpose...This should preferably be done with the consent of the Government, but such consent should not be a prerequisite.[35]

KPP HAM found that the army, police and civilian government in East Timor had provided pro-Indonesian militia with arms, finance and training.[36] It stated that individual TNI personnel had been implicated directly or indirectly in the mass killing, torture, disappearances, forced evacuations and destruction that followed the 4th September announcement of the ballot result supporting East Timor independence. Finally, it recommended that the Attorney commence a formal investigation of at least 33 people, and named some of the highest ranking generals in Indonesia as responsible, including Wiranto, who was interviewed by a KPP HAM team for three hours on 24 December 1999.[37] The report was initially secret but was obtained by the Australian newspaper *Sydney Morning Herald* and published on its website on 30 April 2001.[38]

The processes had other benefits as well in preventing impunity. UK-based NGO Tapol reported the impact of the KPP HAM investigations within Indonesia:

> When three army generals were publicly grilled in November by members of Indonesia's newly elected Parliament, the DPR, about atrocities in Aceh, the whole nation was transfixed by the three hour spectacle on their television screens. Now, at last, after more than three decades of impunity, men with the blood of many victims on their hands were being called to account. Then on 24 December, General Wiranto, former commander-in-chief of the Indonesian armed forces, TNI, was summoned to appear before a civilian commission investigating crimes against humanity in East Timor. That he agreed to appear signalled that the once all-powerful armed forces have been forced to acknowledge that they will have to account for their crimes to civilian authorities. They can no longer hide behind the smokescreen of 'officer honour councils' to exonerate the top brass as they did in 1992 following the Santa Cruz Massacre in East Timor in November 1991, or military courts to hand down derisory sentences to low-ranking officers.
>
> However, the senior officers have treated the commission with contempt; they have used their appearances before the commission to spin lies, refute irrefutable evidence and prolong the commission's proceedings. They have shown that they will do everything in their power to protect themselves from possible prosecution.[39]

Tapol also reported that top generals attempted to discredit the activities of KPP HAM, accusing it of pursuing an anti-Indonesia agenda, of being funded by money from abroad and of basing its evidence on information from INTERFET – '[t] hey are seeking to portray KPP HAM as serving foreign interests. Some of its members have even been threatened with physical violence'.[40] General Wiranto, the highest ranking public figure implicated by the KPP HAM report, said it was biased, and did not constitute an accusation: '[the report] was raw material which should be evaluated by the Attorney-General judiciously'.[41]

These reports and the investigative process formed a solid basis for prosecutions. All three reports contained hard-hitting evidence of systematic sexual violence, as noted in Chapter Three.[42] The KPP HAM report found: 'Cases of violence towards women identified by the Investigative Commission included torture and public sexual humiliation by the militia and the TNI, forcing under age females to serve the sexual needs of the militia, enforced prostitution and rape.'[43] The report went on to outline three specific cases of sexual enslavement. A list of perpetrators was also prepared and handed to the Attorney-General's office.

The ICIET report concluded:

> Because the men fled to the mountains, the women were targeted for sexual assault in a cruel and systematic way.
>
> There is evidence of actual sexual abuse and rape of women. While in general, the militia refrained from killing women, they were subjected to humiliation and different forms of harassment that includes stripping and sexual slavery. Women and children were also victims of force displacement into exile.[44]

4.2 Legislative framework

The investigations made it clear that prosecutions had a good chance of success. The legislative framework for the trials therefore became politicised and had a torturous road to fruition. Indonesia's criminal code (KUHP – *Kitab Undang-Undang Hukum Pidana*) covers such crimes as murder, assault, torture, kidnapping, rape and destruction of property. Gross human rights offences can technically be prosecuted under this code. However, as confirmed by the Serious Crimes Unit's early experiences in Dili, the code has a number of inadequacies for dealing with gross human rights offences, especially in relation to dealing with those who plan the systematic nature of crimes and military personnel acting under orders.[45] Legislation to deal with human rights violations had been put in train by the Indonesian Government before the referendum violence in Timor. It was accelerated dramatically as a result of international pressure.

An ad hoc Human Rights Court can be established by a presidential decree on the recommendation of the lower house of parliament, the People's Representative Assembly (*Dewan Perwakilan Rakyat*—DPR). President Habibie issued a Presidential decree in September 1999 (Perpu 1/1999) providing for the creation of a human rights court to be considered by the Parliament, just days before the UN Commission on Human Rights met in special session to discuss East Timor. In the case of East Timor, the DPR recommended the establishment of such a court.[46] After eleven drafts, Law 26/2000 on Human Rights Courts was adopted by the Indonesian legislature on 23 November 2000.[47] The law provided for the establishment of four permanent Human Rights Courts and, for cases which took place prior to the adoption of the legislation, the possibility of establishing ad hoc Human Rights Courts. The new courts were to have jurisdiction over crimes against humanity and genocide, crimes which until then had not been included in Indonesian domestic law. Crucially, neither war crimes nor torture are included in the jurisdiction of the Human Rights Courts.[48]

The new law also introduced the concept of 'crime of omission' alongside 'crime of commission'. The law specifically made military commanders responsible for gross violations committed by their troops where they knew 'or under the prevailing circumstances ought to have known' that they were perpetrating or had recently perpetrated gross violations of human rights and where they failed to take action to prevent or stop such actions. Police and civil leaders were also made responsible for failure to control subordinates.[49]

The provision for retrospective application of the new law on human rights courts proved to be very controversial, which explains why the East Timor trials were undertaken before an ad hoc rather than a permanent court.[50] Retroactive prosecution conflicts with Indonesian statutes (Clause 1 of the Criminal Code stating that an offence can be tried only if illegal at the time of the crime, and Clauses 4 and 18 of the Law on Human Rights adopted in 1999), as well as general principles of the rule of law.[51] The final version of Law 26/2000 reflects compromise on this issue and was unanimously adopted. It provides for special ad hoc human rights courts to try gross violations of human rights that occurred before the new law came into force. As a safeguard, such courts can only be established to try specific cases (such as those determined for Timor) through a special procedure. The procedure is as follows: the president may establish an ad hoc court by decree only on the explicit recommendation of the DPR (clause 43). Provision is also made for the resolution of gross violations before this date through a Truth and Reconciliation Commission (KKR) to be established by a later law (clause 47).[52]

This compromise on retrospectivity was quickly overtaken by a constitutional amendment in August 2000. An Ad Hoc Committee of the MPR's Working Committee had been preparing a detailed set of alternative amendments to the chapter of the constitution dealing with human rights. Among the 26 sub-clauses on human rights that were eventually adopted unanimously by the MPR, the new Clause 28, paragraph (i) read:

> The right to life, the right not to be tortured, the right to freedom of thought and conscience, the right to religion, the right not to be enslaved, the right to be recognised as a person before the law, and the right not to be prosecuted on the basis of a retroactive law are human rights that cannot be diminished under any circumstances.

The MPR claimed not to have been aware of the possible implications for the Timor trials, especially of the last right relating to retrospectivity, but the Minister of Foreign Affairs, Alwi Shihab, stated that 'The Ministry of Foreign Affairs will certainly find it very difficult to explain the article to the world in the midst of our effort to avoid an international tribunal'.[53]

Further, serious geographic and temporal restraints were placed on the East Timor trials. The then President, Abdurrahman Wahid, decreed in Presidential Decree 53/2001 that strict limits should be placed on its jurisdiction – specifically that it could only hear cases of violations that took place in the period after the 30 August 1999 referendum, thus excluding many hundreds of crimes committed throughout the year and through the years of occupation since 1975.

After strong protests the jurisdiction was later extended by a second decree, Presidential Decree No. 96/2001, issued by the newly installed President

Megawati Sukarnoputri in August 2001. Nevertheless, the jurisdiction remained unacceptably limited. In contrast to the mandate of the KPP HAM which covered the whole of East Timor for the period from 1 January to 25 October 1999, the ad hoc Human Rights Court on East Timor was authorised only to hear cases that took place in April and September 1999. The jurisdiction was also further limited on the basis of locality, so that only cases that occurred within three of Timor's 13 districts would be heard. Thus, all prosecutions were based on events occurring only in the districts of Liquiça, Dili and Suai in the two months of April and September 1999.

Limiting the temporal and geographical jurisdiction of the Court in this way made it unlikely that the trials would uncover the full extent of human rights violations in East Timor in 1999 (let alone 1975 to 1999), or the full extent of the involvement of military, police and government officials. As with the temporal limitations imposed on the Dili trials, the obligation to prosecute under international law was severely undermined.

The inadequacy of the foundational legislation was the first warning given to the international community that the process was under pressure. Turning to the conduct of the trials, the roles of defence and prosecution counsel and the selection of judges all proved controversial.

4.3 The Defence

The conduct of the trials can be contrasted with the Dili trials analysed in Chapter Five in that there was considerable fire-power on the defence team. The team of defence lawyers was led by Adnan Buyung Nasution, a well-known human rights lawyer. Former justice minister Professor Muladi was the defence team's senior legal adviser. Their defence strategy was simple and never wavered throughout the trials. The defence alleged that the human rights violations in the aftermath of the ballot 'were a manifestation of society's disappointment with the conduct of the ballot which had been unfair and dishonest'.[54] It was also alleged and continually repeated that INTERFET, the international peacekeeping force that took control of security in East Timor on 20 September, had itself been responsible for 20 killings.[55]

4.4 The Prosecution

By contrast to the defence, a report released in late 2004 titled *Unfulfilled Promises: Justice in East Timor* by the Justice Initiative and the Coalition for International Justice confirmed the general view of court observers that the Attorney General's office exerted 'little capacity and political will to pursue prosecutions vigorously'.[56]

Despite the promise shown by the investigations, the indictments process was not transparent and the lack of indictments of nearly half the senior figures identified was not explained. KPP HAM publicly identified 32 persons who fell into one of three categories of perpetrators: those responsible for specific crimes of violence on the ground; those with field responsibility for such crimes; and those with ultimate command responsibility. It recommended that these categories of perpetrators should be charged with a far broader range of crimes against humanity than the two, murder (Article 9(a)) and persecution or assault (Article 9(h)), that formed the basis of the charges in the Indonesian indictments.[57]

Despite the results of the official KPP HAM investigation, the official indictments issued by the Attorney-General were against only 18 people – ten military and five police officers, two civilian government officials and a militia leader. The most senior official to be indicted was the Regional Military Commander, Major-General Adam Damiri. The Indonesian authorities never explained why others named in the KPP HAM report were not indicted.[58]

Excluded were some of the higher ranking members of the armed forces that KPP HAM had recommended should be investigated. Among them were the most senior military officials of the time, including General Wiranto (former Commander of the Armed Forces and Defence Minister) and Major-General Zacky Anwar Makarim (the Security Advisor to the Indonesian Task Force for the Implementation of the Popular Consultation on the Special Autonomy on East Timor). As already noted, both have since been indicted by East Timor's General Prosecutor.[59]

By focusing primarily on what can be described as middle-level perpetrators with operational responsibilities and by drafting the indictments in terms that omit any charges that the accused themselves were responsible for acts of violence committed in East Timor in 1999, the prosecutors created for themselves multiple burdens of proof: that there was a chain of command linking the accused to certain persons who committed crimes; that those persons committed crimes against humanity; and that the accused were criminally responsible for failing to exercise proper command responsibility of those subordinates. None of the defendants were accused of planning or ordering the alleged crimes to be committed. Nor were they accused of any form of direct participation, even by way of aiding and abetting. Rather, the indictments alleged that the defendants were either accomplices to the commission of such crimes committed by others or, on the basis of command responsibility, had failed to prevent, stop or take steps to investigate and prosecute the commission of crimes against humanity committed by persons under their command or authority.[60]

This inadequacy in the indictments was borne out by the findings of the Commission of Experts in 2005. The Commission of Experts report gives the example of the Suai indictment, where although it was alleged that the regent and district military commander had created, funded and trained militia groups, the defendants were not charged for this form of participation. In its report, KPP HAM alleged that one of the accused in the Suai case, Lt Sugito, participated in the burning and pillaging and that the attack by the militias, TNI and police on the Suai church was directly led by Herman Sudyono and Lt Sugito. They were not charged for this form of participation either. Instead, the indictments were predicated on the omission of the accused in failing to prevent, suppress or punish.[61]

The consensus from experts was that the indictments and evidence introduced at trial revealed that the prosecutors were either 'unfamiliar with – or else wilfully disregarded – basic international law concepts that are essential to proving a case of crimes against humanity',[62] even taking into account the jurisdictional and temporal limits upon the charges. Prosecutors were similarly not only unfamiliar with but also reluctant to pursue individual and superior responsibility for the crimes, expressed by judicial reform expert Greg Churchill as a 'resistance to concepts of command responsibility'.[63] This was linked to a fundamental lack of political will by the Attorney General's office to charge high-level military officers.

There is some evidence that the prosecution faced genuine difficulties in building a case. Ketut Murtika, Abilio Soares' prosecutor and the Indonesian Attorney General's director of human rights says the 'big fish' like General Wiranto and the then chief of territorial affairs, Susilo Bambang Yudhoyono were not prosecuted, because not a single witness could be found to testify against them.

> When we investigated these defendants, the witnesses seemed to have their mouths locked. No one was willing to say who was behind the violence. They weren't prepared to go any further than the regional commander...[i]f there's sufficient evidence from the regional commander and his subordinates pointing the finger at these people, suggesting they were involved as planners, then of course we would want to look again at this matter.'[64]

As H.S. Dillon, a former member of Komnas HAM, put it: 'When you are a prosecutor, why would you really want to prosecute the army generals? The only thing you might get is a bullet in your head.'[65]

The Justice Initiative report also identified as a problem the lack of trial skills and preparation on the part of the lawyers, including those who argued the cases at trial. This was acknowledged as a problem that pervades the Indonesian court system generally, but was an acute problem in these difficult cases based on new laws.[66]

This failure at the indictment stage was the second and clear sign that the trials would be flawed. It was also at this point that it should have been clear to the international community that the trials would ignore completely the findings on gender violence contained in the UN and KPP HAM reports, because the indictments were completely silent on the issue.

4.5 The Judges

Judicial appointments also presented problems in this new field of law for Indonesia. Law 26/2000 on Human Rights Courts provides that the human rights courts are to consist of five judges, two of whom will be career judges and three of whom will be ad hoc judges drawn from outside the present judiciary and appointed for five-year terms. In January 2002, Presidential Decree No. 6/2002 appointed 18 judges for the ad hoc human rights tribunal dealing with East Timor in 1999 and the Tanjung Priok riot in 1984. All 18 judges appointed by the President were recommended by the Supreme Court. Twelve judges served as trial judges and six others served as appeals judges. They received a salary of 1 million rupia per month (about US$100) in addition to a fee of 4 million rupia for every case they handled. The 18 AD hoc judges worked together with 12 career judges appointed by Chief Justice Bagir Manan in December 2001.[67]

There were three female First Degree Justice Non-Career Ad Hoc Judges: Seyfulina Faruddin (retired judge of the Jakarta State Administrative Court (PT TUN); Komariah Emong Sapardjaja (academic) and Sanwani Nasution (academic). There were two women appointed as Appeal Court judges: Marni Emmy (Central Jakarta District Court) and Adriani Nurdin (Cibinong District Court). The lack of participation of women in the trial process in any capacity created an extremely masculine and aggressive atmosphere in the courtroom.[68]

Concerns were expressed at the appointment of the judges by rights activists, doubting the credibility and capability of the judges for the ad hoc tribunal. Caretaker of the Indonesian Legal Aid Institute Foundation (YLBHI), Irianto Subiyakto, said it would be hard to put faith in the judges because their recruitment itself was not transparent, but 'considering that the ad hoc judges have solid academic qualifications, we expect them to produce credible rulings'.[69] Legal expert Achmad Ali of the Hasanuddin University in Makassar, South Sulawesi also doubted whether 'The judges have the courage to try those powerful persons who can control many things, including law'.[70]

The promulgation of Law 26/2000 setting up Human Rights Tribunals, which provides also for Ad Hoc Tribunals to take up cases occurring in the past, the appointment of the judges and of the prosecutors, and generally, the organisation of the trials, were all done in a situation where there was no experience or precedent. The Law 26/2000 is largely modelled on the Rome Statute, which was then yet to be implemented. The ICTY and ICTR experience showed the complications and considerable resources needed to carry out the investigations and trials. There was – and still is – no other similar court at the national level in any other country. It could be argued then that the international community singularly failed to give the trials in Jakarta the practical support they required to make the novel court work, although how welcome the support would have been if requested is a moot point.

Unlike the ICTR, the ICTY and the ICC, the Indonesian Human Rights Tribunal does not have its own Rules of Evidence and Procedure, but applies the Code of Criminal Procedure used in ordinary criminal trials. Thus, among other differences with the international tribunals, there is no provision for pre-trial procedures, putting the judges in a situation of 'fait accompli' in regard to the indictments that they have to test. Regulation 2/2002, providing for witness protection, is no substitute for the arrangements for Victim and Witness Protection provided in the international tribunals. These, and other considerations, reduced the scope of the trials considerably, since they affect the availability of witnesses, their testimony, and generally, the validity of the process. The judges lacked the most basic court management techniques and did not have independent court security. It is these practical aspects that affected the conduct of the trials.

The Commission of Experts described the jurisprudence produced by the Court in the following terms.

> [I]nconsistent verdicts and factual findings of the Ad Hoc Court resulted directly from the application of diverging judicial techniques, differing legal interpretations of identical subject-matter and the lack of willingness

> or otherwise to utilize international jurisprudence and practices and proficiency in analytical evaluation of the facts and law.[71]

It should be noted that the International Criminal Tribunal for Rwanda (ICTR) faces similar allegations of bias and mismanagement,[72] as did the Yugoslavia tribunal (ICTY) to a lesser extent.[73] Prosecutor Mohammed Yusuf has defended the Court's record and pleaded for patience: 'This is a new area for prosecutors and judges in Indonesia. We have never had a Human Rights Court before.'[74] There is evidence that international opinion has had an effect on some judges – Judge Roky Panjaitans has been quoted as being 'embarrassed' over the public criticism of earlier acquittals of soldiers and police.[75]

Ifdhal Kasim of the Institute for Policy Research and Advocacy (ELSAM) has acknowledged that poorly trained judges and prosecutors made for very poor performance.

> The judges and prosecutors are not even given appropriate literature to learn about other human rights cases in other countries, although the information is very important to help them to take action. So only the creative prosecutors or judges, who will spend extra time and money to get the information can understand human rights.[76]

ELSAM has noted that:

> The judges restricted themselves to the weak charges built by prosecutors who perceived the East Timor mayhem as a mere communal conflict. The court has allowed anyone connected to a state institution to be exonerated and cleared of any involvement.[77]

ELSAM went on to state:

> Most of the prosecution witnesses who testified in these trials were indictees, individuals affiliated to the TNI and government officials. The prosecution did not make substantial use of available documentary evidence and witnesses statements gathered by KPP HAM and the Serious Crimes Unit investigators. Significantly, investigations and prosecutions were undertaken at a time when there was an evident lack of political will to prosecute the defendants and lack of material and moral support for these investigations.[78]

4.6 Outcomes of the trials

In total, six out of the 18 defendants brought before the ad hoc Human Rights Court were found guilty of crimes against humanity. Those convicted and sentenced to three years' imprisonment were the Regional Military Commander, Major General Adam Damiri, the former Governor, Abilio José Osorio Soares, and the former Police Chief for Dili District, Lieutenant Colonel Hulman Gultom. The

Military Commander for East Timor, Brigadier General Mohammad Noer Muis and the District Military Commander for Dili, Lieutenant Colonel Soedjarwo, were sentenced to five years' imprisonment each. Eurico Guterres, the Deputy Commander of the PPI and commander of the Aitarak militia received the longest sentence of ten years.

All but Eurico Guterres were sentenced to terms of imprisonment below the specified minimum legal limit for these crimes – both the articles under Law 26/2000 with which all the defendants were charged, murder as a crime against humanity (Article 9a) and assault/persecution as a crime against humanity (Article 9h), carry a minimum prison sentence of ten years. It is unclear on what legal basis the judges were able to ignore these provisions.[79]

After appeals regarding his sentence finally failed in May 2006, Timorese militia leader Eurico Guterres became the only person, from the 18 individuals indicted by the Indonesian authorities for acts of violence committed in East Timor in 1999, whose trial ended in a conviction.[80] Six police and military officers were acquitted on charges similar to those faced by Guterres relating to the Carrascalão massacre.[81] Guterres was imprisoned in Cipinang prison centre in Jakarta on 4 May 2006.[82] Former Governor of East Timor, Timorese civilian Abilio Soares received a jail term of five years for crimes against humanity and entered Cipinang prison in August 2004 where he spent only a few weeks before being released on appeal.[83]

On 29 November 2004, the tribunal acquitted four military and police officers being tried for crimes against humanity, bringing the number of officers found not guilty in the case to nine. A panel of five judges from Indonesia's Human Rights Court dismissed all charges against Liquiça's army commander Lieutenant Colonel Asep Kuswandi, its police chief, Lieutenant Colonel Adios Salova and Mr Martins of the same offence in connection with a massacre of up to 60 people in the Liquiça church on 6 April 1999. Prosecutors put the death toll at 22.[84] 'It is true there have been human rights abuses but they were carried out by the Red and White Iron group, which has no relation with the defendants,' Chief Judge Sutiarso said.[85]

Others cleared included the former provincial police chief, Brigadier-General Timbul Silaen, as well as eight military personnel including the former district chief, Colonel Herman Sedyono, charged over the specific case of the Suai church ground massacre of 6 September 1999. Lieutenant-Colonel Endar Priyanto, the former military commander in the capital Dili who is a member of the army's Kopassus special forces, was acquitted of charges that he failed to intervene to prevent the Carrascalão massacre.

In March 2005, the Supreme Court upheld the acquittal by the human rights tribunal of Brigadier General Tono Suratman, who was the chief of the now defunct Wiradharma military command in Dili. The team of prosecutors led by Gabrial Simangunsong had asked for a ten-year sentence but then failed to submit legal arguments to the Supreme Court within the two-year deadline. Human rights advocates in Indonesia said the Attorney-General's Office should explain their negligence and called on the new President Susilo Bambang Yudhoyono to summon Attorney General Abdul Rahman Saleh for an explanation.[86] None was forthcoming. However, Saleh had stated in November 2004 that there was still a chance that prosecutors could build new cases and name new suspects for crimes against humanity in East Timor.[87]

All those convicted remained at liberty pending the outcome of their appeals. In some cases, including that of Major General Adam Damiri, the defendants remained in active service in the military or police. Some TNI officers named in the KPP HAM report or acquitted in the trials have been promoted. Major General Sjafrie Sjamsoeddin was appointed as the chief military spokesman. Brigadier General Mahidin Simbolon was the chief of staff of the Udayana regional command in Bali, which oversaw the military operations in Timor. Simbolon has subsequently been promoted to the rank of Major General and is now the military commander for Papua. Timbul Silaen, who was acquitted of crimes against humanity, is now the Security Assistant, Inspector General to the National Police Chief, Da'i Bachtiar.[88]

After the acquittals, the Court was then at the point where the UN should have resumed responsibility for justice because the trials were clearly not credible.

4.7 Reactions to the acquittals

Reactions to the verdict from various sources offer evidence that the outcome of Guterres trial, coupled with the acquittal of senior military figures did not satisfy the basic expectations of stakeholders – the defendant himself, the victim, the Timorese government, Indonesian civil society or international public opinion.

At the political level within Timor, East Timor's then foreign minister, now President, José Ramos-Horta, reacted angrily. He described the acquittal of the former Indonesian military commander in Dili, Lieutenant-Colonel Endar Priyanto as 'scandalous'. He also said that Eurico Guterres 'deserved the maximum penalty [death] both under Timorese law and Indonesian law'.[89] However, the jailing (albeit only briefly) of Abilio Soares went against the express wishes of the Timorese Government.[90]

Mario Carrascalão, father of murdered Manuel Carrascalão, who now heads East Timor's Social Democracy Party, was asked whether the verdict had restored credibility to the Court. He responded that Guterres should 'stay in jail forever' and said:

> We really don't trust it. We don't believe that the court is serious. This is just something to show to the international community that they did something. Justice should be equal to everybody whether he is East Timorese or he is Indonesian, he's military or he's a civilian. It should be the same for everybody. But this is not the case you know. For me, this is normal, it is normal, this happens in Indonesia, it is normal.[91]

Despite this anger, the leadership of the National Resistance Council of East Timor (CNRT) made clear that it will not press for a thorough investigation, trial and punishment of the Indonesian generals.

José Ramos-Horta, now President of East Timor, reaffirmed his opposition to an international rights tribunal, telling Parliament that the country's economic future depended on good relations with its former occupier.

> Almost everything for our daily needs comes from Indonesia. Therefore, if we have a bad relationship with Indonesia it will effect the living standard of the people of East Timor. The past is history now…the future is more important.[92]

This made it clear to Timorese civil society that any push for a tribunal would not be supported by the country's leadership. Within Indonesia, NGOs and international media correspondents in Jakarta judged the Court harshly. Their reaction makes it clear that the proper operation of the Court is as significant to Indonesian civil society as to Timorese victims. Hendardi, an Indonesian human rights activist, told Associated Press on 28 November 2002 that Guterres had been 'sacrificed' to protect the top military. 'They are untouchable by law'.[93]

International opinion was mostly negative. Adam Ereli, deputy spokesman for the US State Department stated after the November 2004 acquittals:

> We are dismayed by this decision, and we are profoundly disappointed with the performance and record of the Indonesian ad hoc tribunal. In our view, as a result of this appeals decision, only two of the 18 defendants have been convicted, and both individuals are ethnic Timorese and received sentences below the ten-year minimum set by law. We think that the overall process was seriously flawed and lacked credibility.[94]

The European Union, in a Declaration by the Presidency, stated that the trials 'have failed to deliver justice and did not result in a substantiated account of the violence'.[95]

The response from Indonesia to critics was fierce – acting senior security minister Hari Sabarno said '[t]his is a court verdict…America should better take care of its own self'.[96] Justice Minister Yusril Ihza Mahendra added:

> We are not satisfied with America's actions in Vietnam, which have yet to be investigated…[97] If we are talking about dissatisfaction, I am also not satisfied with what America is doing and its invasion of Iraq, but we are powerless against America.[98]

The response that Indonesia cared most about was the response of the UN Security Council. Presumably it had already judged that there was not the requisite will at this point (if there ever was) to set up an international tribunal. This gamble proved correct.[99] The UN's reaction was to appoint a Commission of Experts in January 2005 to investigate why a 1999 Security Council resolution calling for the trial of those accused of atrocities in Timor during its independence referendum had not been implemented.

The Experts' 160-page report to UN Secretary-General Kofi Annan which was debated in the Security Council found that Indonesia should retry accused war criminals acquitted by a special court in Jakarta because the process was a sham. It says the trials were 'manifestly inadequate' with 'scant respect for relevant international standards'.[100] Prosecutors were 'not committed to justice', and the Court had been hostile to defence witnesses but lenient on the accused.[101]

The report briefly notes that the indictments completely leave out sexual violence but inserts a footnote stating that many of those crimes were pursued by the serious crimes process in Dili.[102] The report recommended that Indonesia be given six months to prepare credible trials. If it did not comply, the experts argued, the UN should invoke its charter to set up an international war crimes court for East Timor. In direct response, in March 2005 the Governments of Indonesia and East Timor agreed to establish a bilateral Truth and Friendship Commission (CTF), set up to 'resolve once and for all the events of 1999'.[103] The process will not lead to prosecutions and appears to be aimed at preventing all future national investigations and prosecution of senior Indonesian officials alleged to bear primary responsibility for the crimes against humanity committed in East Timor before and during 1999.

The six-month deadline given by the UN Commission of Experts expired in early 2006. The Security Council considered the report on 28 September 2005, then promptly asked for a further report from the Secretary-General on justice and reconciliation efforts in the light of the CTF. This was delivered on July 2006, but was overtaken by the new focus on the riots.[104] On 28 August 2006, disillusioned human rights groups within Indonesia called for the Commission to be disbanded, fearing that the CTF's ability to 'rehabilitate reputations' may actually prove a setback in their attempts to make the military more accountable.[105]

GENDER ANALYSIS OF THE TRIALS

It seems clear that on most traditional measures of a fair trial, the trials were a failure.[106] The then UN High Commissioner for Human Rights Sergio de Mello listed problems including inherent procedural flaws in the legislative foundation of the Court; intimidation of the judges and witnesses; possible conspiracy between the prosecution and the military, and the lack of training of prosecutors and judges.[107] A more difficult question is whether they were a sham from the beginning, and whether the reasons for the failure can be pinpointed to a conspiracy or basic inadequacy. An even more difficult question is the responsibility the UN, representing the will of the international community, bears for the failure of the trials and what the consequences of the failure will be for the building of the rule of law in Indonesia. The question that has not even been asked is whether, given the complete absence of any prosecution of sexual violence or offences against women, the trials should have been considered fair or adequate even if more convictions had been recorded?

4.8 The obligation to punish: flaws in the legislative foundations

It is of particular concern that no cases of rape and other crimes of sexual violence were brought to trial in Jakarta despite the findings of the KPP HAM and UN reports discussed above. The trials focused only on some events linked to the 1999 referendum violence. This is a particularly important context because at the time the Jakarta trials were commencing, the UN serious crimes process in Dili had singularly failed to provide justice for women who had been forcibly deported to West Timor as will be explained in Chapter Five. While the investigations process was happening, according to Bernard Kerblat, the UNHCR chief in East Timor: '100,000-plus are there in a hostage-like situation, where there is no longer an international presence to monitor what is happening.'[108] Moreover, the temporal limit completely ignored the long history of abuse of Timorese women from 1975 until the referendum. Indonesia's record on addressing allegations of abuse of women has been poor, not only in East Timor, but also in other areas where military operations have taken place, notably in the provinces of Nanggroe Aceh Darussalam and Papua.

The Jakarta trials were the only real chance to put the suffering of Timorese women on the record, even if only in indictment form, in the only jurisdiction which mattered. Why did the UN not insist on the inclusion of such offences at the beginning when it clearly had influence over Indonesia's response? The indictments of the Jakarta trials are the clearest indication that silence about sexual violence in armed conflict is still tolerated by the international community.

4.9 Gendered discourse in the Jakarta trials

Military figures routinely turned up in court to intimidate the judges and witnesses, often wearing matching t-shirts which read in Bahasa 'Victims of UN Deception'. More than 30 supporters of Timbul Silaen stood silently outside the courtroom during his trial with placards which read 'Don't Make Us Angry'.[109] The threat was quite real – the original chair of the committee charged with setting up the Court, Judge Syafuiuddin Kartasasmita, was gunned down in daylight in late July 2001 by unknown assassins.[110] The independence of the Indonesian ad hoc judges must therefore be at least questionable. The atmosphere for female judges and witnesses, as well as non-military men, must have been frightening.

The Jakarta trials are therefore a good example of what Hilary Charlesworth describes as gendered discourse.[111] For example, Charlesworth cites rhetoric surrounding the Iraq War – urging tough leadership, taking action and military security – as coded 'masculine' traits. In contrast conciliation, negotiation and human security, associated with 'feminine traits', are seen as weak, and belittled.[112] Gendered discourse has been defined as 'the phenomenon of symbolically organizing the world in these gender-associated opposites' or binary oppositions.[113]

The trials showcased the military, masculine voice shouting down feminised justice, women victims and the UN (which is also feminised). This is a broader issue for Indonesian society, as evidenced by writings by Indonesian feminists about the militarisation, nationalism and its impact on Indonesian civil society in post-colonial times.[114] It also serves as a potent illustration of Jan Jindy Pettman's analysis of masculine voices drowning everything and everyone else out in the area of international relations.[115]

4.10 Treatment of female witnesses

There was a lack of testimony from East Timorese witnesses due to the inability of the Court to reassure witnesses of their safety. NGOs Amnesty International and the Judicial System Monitoring Programme (JSMP) highlighted the situation for female witnesses, noting 'the exposed position they found themselves in as a result of imperfect arrangements'.[116] In the report *Justice for Timor-Leste*, the NGOs list the lack of security at airports; lack of secure accommodation; and lack of security in and around the Central Jakarta District Court as serious breaches of witness protection:

> Witnesses were forced to walk through public areas to enter the courtroom. Witness waiting areas were also insecure enabling members of the public, members of the defence teams and, on one occasion, the defendant and former militia leader Eurico Guterres himself to enter unchallenged. The witnesses from Timor Leste were also subjected to intimidating and at times humiliating treatment by the Court.[117]

The Commission of Experts report noted that government regulation on witness protection had not been elaborated in legislative form and had not been incorporated into the laws of Indonesia (such as the Code of Criminal Procedure).[118]

The Experts also comment on the lack of a witness protection unit in POLRI and judge the system for witness protection as 'haphazard and unprofessional'.

> For instance, a witness safe house bore a sign outside declaring it to be so. There was also cause for witnesses to fear for their security, for instance as members of the militia group BMP (Besih Merah Putih) and TNI soldiers, wearing uniforms and sometimes carrying weapons, were permitted to attend court proceedings in large numbers.[119]

This was the fate of all witnesses, but it had a particularly intimidating effect on the few female witnesses who testified at the trials. Amnesty and JSMP chronicle the treatment of one female witness in particular, based on unofficial transcripts compiled by a JSMP trial observer, which is also picked up by the Commission of Experts. Dominggas dos Santos Mouzinho, a survivor of the Suai massacre, and an uneducated villager from a remote part of Timor Leste, testified on 28 May 2002 in the trial of Lieutenant Colonel Herman Sedyono and four others in the Suai case. Before the start of proceedings, she had asked the prosecution through UNTAET not to have to testify in the presence of the accused, as provided for under Section III, Article 5 of the Government Regulation on Victim and Witness Protection. It appears that this request was not conveyed to the Court.[120]

Amnesty and JSMP comment that it quickly became apparent that Dominggas dos Santos Mouzinho was far from fluent in Bahasa Indonesia and was unable to understand many of the questions.[121] The NGOs report that

> [the] combined effect of the intimidating manner in which questions were asked and her inability to fully understand what was being said was to undermine the credibility of the witnesses who often remained silent or gave confused and contradictory answers to questions.[122]

The prosecution, who had called her as a witness, did not at any point raise an objection with the judge about the lack of interpretation. Nor did the prosecution object to what the NGOs termed the 'intimidating and frequently mocking manner' in which she was questioned by lawyers for the defence.[123] The judges also failed to exercise their responsibilities under Article 153 of KUHAP which requires them to 'to see that nothing shall be done or that no question shall be asked that will cause the defendant or witness not to be free in giving his answer'. The following exchange is cited as 'typical' between the defence counsel and Dominggas dos Santos Mouzinho:

Q: Your children, did they actively follow as officials in the Referendum, were there children of yours who followed?

A: Followed.

Q: Oo, so your children were with UNAMET? True madam? True madam, yes your children were chummy with UNAMET?

A: No answer

Q: Fatimah was working when you were examined two years ago, or before you became a witness? Do you remember before you became a witness or after you became a witness, do your remember madam? Witness first or Fatimah worked first?

A: No answer

Q: Madam can choose not to reply. This really is a 'sham court' [pengadilan abu abu], political court. False testimony, madam, in Indonesia, is punishable by seven years, to give false testimony. Sorry, but this concerns four TNI officers and police, their fate is to be accused. Beloved madam, I beg your honesty, Fatimah worked before you became a witness or after you became a witness? Don't look at the bule [white foreigner] on your right, I know he has been coaching you, don't look. Look at me if you need to, look at the judge, just listen no need for coaching. Beloved madam, was Fatimah working after you became a witness or before you became a witness?

A: No answer

Q: Thank you, if you don't want to respond, I won't force you. But follow the conscience of your heart, my most beloved madam, were your daughters raped or about to be raped or wanting to be raped (*diperkosa atau mau diperkosa*). It's up to you if you don't want to answer, I am only talking about the pure inner self. Beloved madam.

Dominggas dos Santos Mouzinho was questioned in a similar manner for five hours without a break or any refreshment.[124] The intimidation of witnesses and the gendered language is clear even from the extract in translation.

This is a classic example of the concerns feminist scholars have over the high price women can pay as individuals seeking justice in a courtroom. The 'wanting to be raped' quotation is a clear example of what Alison Young calls the 'insinuation strategy' (although it could also be termed plain lying).[125] She states that the suffering produced by the examination of the witness comes from 'the process of law's storytelling itself' because the 'implication of the victim in the defence narrative works by challenging the very foundation of the victim's narrative':

> It is not enough for the victim to be vilified according to received ideas about dress or drink, she must also be made to rub up against the fantasy that informs the defence account, made to perform as a character in a narrative.[126]

In a transitional justice context, this idea has special significance. If we consider the ways in which East Timor and the UN themselves are feminised, the question arises as to whether the overall strategy of the trials was to insinuate and implicate Timor itself into the Indonesian military's narrative, that of mere bystanders unable to stop Timorese savagery. In other words, the insinuation strategy was working on both an individual and national level in that trial. This tactic goes to the heart of the stated aim of transitional justice mechanisms to bring out the truth of historical events.

The Jakarta trials seemed to make women's groups within Timor even more adamant about the need for an international tribunal. An East Timorese widows' organisation Liquiça named *Rate Laek* (Tetum for 'without graves') met with the UN High Commissioner for Human Rights Mary Robinson in mid-2002 and made this plea to her:

> We are women who have been interrogated and violated, women who have lost our family members, and women who carry great burdens from the loss of our husbands who were killed and disappeared. We are still waiting to know when will we see justice? At times, 'justice' seems to be moving farther and farther away from us and we wonder what can help us heal from our deep wounds.
>
> The Ad Hoc Tribunal in Jakarta has not given us anything; in fact, it has only increased our suffering. We feel sick to hear that military and police officers who were part of the planning and even directly involved in killing our family members are free without any sentence and without any accountability. From the beginning, we rejected the establishment of the Indonesian Ad Hoc Tribunal because we knew that the decision would not give justice or truth to us, victims and families of victims. For 25 years, we have experienced the Indonesian justice system, and we do not believe that the Indonesian tribunal is credible unless there is a complete reformation.
>
> We continue to be committed to our demand for an international tribunal.[127]

The experience of women in the Jakarta trials also hardened feelings of disappointment towards the serious crimes process in Dili. The National Commission on Violence Against Women in Indonesia (Komnas Perempuan), founded in 1998, was also disappointed as it had set out to ensure that the enforcement of Law 26/2000 addressed cases of gender-based violence.[128]

CONCLUSION

Topo Susanto of the University of Indonesia stated that the implementation of the Law No. 26/1999 on Human Rights Tribunal has so far reflected the 'brotherhood among security personnel and the courts', instead of efforts to uphold human rights, and added that any effort to review the law in the current political climate would be fruitless.[129] The trials also serve as an example of the security personnel deliberately 'feminising' justice.

Were the trials worth holding in light of the clear evidence that political will was weak? The joint Amnesty and JSMP report on justice for East Timor decides with considerable insight that the Indonesian court process was significant for two key reasons:

> First, the trials in Indonesia, however imperfect, represent a first attempt by the Indonesian authorities in what is intended to be an ongoing process of bringing to trial persons charged with crimes against humanity in a range of different cases. Second, the shortcomings of the process in Indonesia to bring to account those regarded as bearing final responsibility for crimes committed in Timor Leste during 1999, together with the uncertainties surrounding the future of the process in Timor Leste, throw the spotlight back on the international community and its responsibilities in such situations.[130]

The most thorough examination of the Jakarta trials has been undertaken by Professor David Cohen in late 2003 on behalf of the International Centre for Transitional Justice entitled provocatively *Intended to Fail*.[131] Ian Martin in his preface to this excellent analysis summarises Cohen's conclusions in the following manner:

> The inescapable conclusion of this report is that the trials as a whole must be regarded as a failure on every level, from technical competence to institutional integrity and political will. Some may point to the fact that six individuals, including high-ranking officials, have been convicted. However, the report shows that this is more due to the notable bravery of a few individual judges than to a credible system of justice.[132]

While I agree whole-heartedly with Cohen's conclusions about the complete trials and the reasons for their failure, and even the premise that the Jakarta trials were intended to fail by the Indonesian authorities, I do not accept that this failure was inevitable. International pressure from the UN and international community was the first condition necessary to produce the political imperative for a fair and full investigation of the violence by KPP HAM. It was clear from the beginning what it would entail to produce fair trials, and that level of international pressure was noticeably absent thereafter. What seemed like a victory for legalism and the fight against impunity was distorted by the trials into not only impunity for the actions of the senior military figures but reward.[133]

There are two issues here – the first is that knowing how likely it was even in 1999 that the trials would fail, was it right for the UN to allow Indonesia to proceed with domestic prosecutions? There may not have been any real political alternative given the likelihood of a veto in the Security Council, but without this *Realpolitik* consideration, was it legally and ethically correct given the suffering of the East Timorese? The very hard answer in my opinion is yes – even the slightest chance that Indonesia might itself move to limit the impunity of its military through the rule of law was a chance that had to be taken, for the sake of the future of both countries.

The question is what the UN had up its sleeve if the gamble failed and what resources it had to help Indonesia with a difficult process. This was a judgment call that had to be made fairly and wisely by the UN. As Cohen notes, it would not be fair to conduct a 'trial of the trials' in Jakarta, without taking the totality of an extremely complicated process into account, and without comparison to the inordinately difficult task of transitional justice in other jurisdictions – Yugoslavia, Rwanda, Sierra Leone, Cambodia to name a few.[134] Numbers of convictions are not a proper guide, just as indictments do not give a proper picture of the trials in Dili. The core issue is justice for the wrongs that have been committed in East Timor. The substantive problem is that the international political process has led to a mixed approach consisting of entrusting the justice process to two national jurisdictions, neither of which had the slightest chance of carrying out their mandate for a myriad of reasons, of which most were foreseeable.

The Indonesian ad hoc Human Rights Court as a mechanism may not be completely ill-conceived and may still hold some value for the future. Certainly Indonesia should be encouraged by the international community to try their own violators of human rights. Under international law a sovereign nation must be given the opportunity to demonstrate accountability in its own courts before any international war crimes tribunal may be convened. But trials with the results of the Timor trials are counterproductive, in terms of producing justice in the individual case or building support for the rule of law.

There are some positive aspects to the trials. The KPP HAM investigations and report were excellent both as blueprints for prosecutions and as a historical record. The recommendations for indictment included senior military figures up to General Wiranto and Damiri themselves. The report dealt thoroughly with systematic gender persecution, as well as displaying a good analysis of apportioning accountability for the violence in accordance with international law. Some of the judges in the trials showed bravery and a commitment to humanitarian law that is to be commended in a fledgling institution, given the levels of intimidation in the court. Finally the facts that there were indictments of senior military figures at all, and that Wiranto was initially forced to step aside is a breakthrough that should not be underestimated given Indonesia's history. The indictment and judgment of Damiri was extremely significant in this light.

However, these small gains pale next to the serious inadequacies of the trials and the legacy the Court has left. There was no reflection of sexual offences in the indictments at all, and there was serious harassment of female witnesses and judges. The overall court environment was extremely distressing to all but military participants. Like the serious crimes process in Dili, basic fair trial standards were not met, but this time the weakness lay squarely with the prosecution. Despite the investigations, coupled with the convictions in the Dili court, the trials have confirmed on the public record the military's distorted view that the Timorese themselves was responsible for the atrocities while the Indonesian army entrusted with security were entirely unable to prevent their civil savagery, and that the UN and INTERFET were the real villains of the piece.[135] What was at stake in these trials is not only justice in individual cases but also the rewriting of history, at least for the Indonesian audience.[136]

What was also at stake was the perception of impunity of the Indonesian military actors for crimes with Indonesian territory, such as violations of women's rights in the May 1998 riots (which led to the establishment of Komnas Perempuan, the National Commission on Violence against Women), or Papua, or Aceh. As Enloe again states:

> ...women...face a critical postwar choice...they can collectively push for a genuinely demilitarized society in which neither military needs nor masculinized presumptions determine historical memories, current job opportunities, or long-term public status.[137]

The East Timorese Government has been placed in an extraordinarily difficult diplomatic position as a result of the trials, and arguably it has simply not been in a strong position to criticise the outcomes as seen by the changing reaction to trial outcomes over time. This has led to the weakening of public support towards its leadership on questions of justice by Timorese citizens, as well as undermining the faith of Timorese civil society in the UN. The UN is also a victim of these trials, both in terms of its credibility within Indonesia and the proper record of the role it played in East Timor, but also because of its inability to set clear standards for when the trials would be considered a failure. This is one reason the UN refused to participate in the Joint Truth and Friendship Commission. The lack of a definite and credible threat to Indonesia posed by an international tribunal at the outset, a threat which only dwindled as time went on, meant that the failure of the trials was in some ways predetermined.

In the wake of the 'war against terrorism' declared in 2001, the US has restored the International Military Education and Training (IMET) programme for TNI officers, which had been suspended following a series of rights violations blamed on the military in East Timor. The US revived military ties with Indonesia on the grounds that it needs local military partners to fight terrorism. Sidney Jones said the chances of the Congress rejecting renewed IMET funding are now fairly slim. 'I think there will be a collective shrugging of shoulders.'[138] The coded message is that the masculinist, nationalist, militaristic discourse has been allowed to subjugate feminised international justice.

As a post-script, in March 2008 the Indonesian Supreme Court overturned the conviction of Eurico Guterres (Decision No. 34 PK/PID.HAM.AD HOC/2007).[139] With the reversal of the conviction, all 18 people indicted by the Indonesian Ad Hoc Human Rights Court on East Timor have been acquitted.

In the final analysis, the UN took on the responsibility to push for justice for such blatant human rights violations in Timor, and it has not yet fulfilled that responsibility. International law was pushed to the margins and distorted during the trials, and in the rush to judgment opportunities to promote justice in the longer term for women were lost.

5 Wearing his jacket

The serious crimes process

> In the Serious Crimes Unit, we punish some militias who are stupid enough to come back. I also think that the UN is spending too much money on the Serious Crimes Unit. The lawyers there earn more than I earn as President. And there is no infrastructure for the judicial system in East Timor. We need a working competent, free and functioning judicial system, not only in Dili, but also in the country. I think the SCIU can be there for 100 years for all the stupid to come back across the border. In practical terms we don't see any benefit from this.[1]

In June 2005, United States Judge Phillip Rapoza reflected on his two years of service on the Special Panels for Serious Crimes in Dili. He expressed particular regret about the situation of a woman he met in Maliana. Rapoza recounted that the woman said she often saw the two men who killed her husband when she went to the local market. What bothered her more was that one man wore her late husband's jacket. Judge Rapoza stated 'They knew that she knows that they will never be prosecuted'.[2]

The aim of this chapter is to examine the role, operation and jurisprudence of the serious crimes process in Dili. I focus on whether it delivered 'justice' for women, and whether it did justice to the experience of women in armed conflict, according to the criterion set out in my Introduction. As noted in Chapter Two, Christine Bell and Catherine O'Rourke propose that feminist theorists should focus on how transitional justice debates help or hinder broader projects of securing material gains for women through transition.[3] Similarly, Katherine M. Franke argues that transitional justice outcomes for women should be judged on whether they provide *recognition* and *redistribution*.[4] Recognition deals with establishing facts and identities, such as who are the victims and perpetrators of criminal practices. Redistribution deals with redistributing money and land, but also shame or symbolic and cultural resources.[5] While transitional justice mechanisms can do both, Franke decides that they are mostly engaged with recognition-based justice projects and that this has come at a cost to the individual women involved, while the limited script offered to women casts them only as victims of sexual violence.[6] Did the serious crimes process fit this general description?

I ask further what 'justice judgments' the Timorese community have made about the trials, meaning whether the court's processes were accepted and understood in the general population.[7] This examination sheds some light on the benefits, if any, that the existing framework of international law has for women engaged with this transitional justice process. My assessment in Chapter Six looks at the impact of the trials on women experiencing 'ordinary' violence in the new formal legal sector.

The first section of the chapter provides an overview of the establishment of the serious crimes process that operated from 6 June 2000 until 20 May 2005. I then introduce the function and legislative basis of the Special Panels and Court of Appeal, the Serious Crimes Investigation Unit and the Public Defenders Office, as well as relevant funding and staffing issues including gender composition, and the general prosecution strategy. The second section focuses on jurisprudence regarding gender-based violence produced from the trials, with in-depth analysis of the *Leonardus Kasa* and *Lolotoe* trials. The third section provides a critique of the overall serious crimes process.

That the United Nations was duty-bound to hold trials as soon as it took control of East Timor is assumed by international lawyers. A few basic expectations or hopes are held at the outset of the serious crimes process in Timor as part of the legalist approach. Trials may contribute to leaving an accurate historic record. Successful prosecutions may lead to the removal of a perpetrator from where he or she could access the victim again, provide a form of punishment in the form of detention, and rehabilitate the perpetrator so that the perpetrator may not commit the offence again.[8] In other words, at least trials might stop the perpetrator from wearing the jacket of the deceased husband.

The Dili court was the one 'internationalised' process dealing with the violence in East Timor, if within a very limited time frame. The Dili court is the first clear example of a 'hybrid tribunal', a system that shares judicial accountability jointly between the state in which it functions and the United Nations.[9] The role of the East Timorese judges in the court was very important. As Suzannah Linton notes:

> The entire process is historic, for despite international domination of the process, never before have East Timorese judges sat in judgment over their fellow people, and never before have East Timorese prosecutors and defence lawyers appeared as legal professionals in their own land.[10]

A legalist would hope that trials might also contribute to the building of the rule of law in East Timor. The express aim of setting up a 'hybrid' tribunal in Timor was so that the formal legal sector could receive both international assistance and role models. The Special Panels were unique because they were given jurisdiction over both international crimes and 'ordinary' murder and sexual offences in the independence period. I argue that the promotion of the rule of law and the infrastructure of a justice system can be especially important to women suffering post-conflict spikes in domestic violence.

A final hope might be that the trials fulfil some kind of healing or truth-telling purpose on a communal level, contributing to social repair.[11] Exponents of the legalist position make several claims for trials and retributive justice within the framework of transitional justice that go beyond the minimum requirements of prosecution. Theodor Meron has argued '[t]he great hope of tribunal advocates was that the individualization and decollectivization of guilt…would help bring about peace and reconciliation.'[12] Even if successful prosecutions cannot be said to have the communal healing effect often asserted by international lawyers, such trials may be important in their own right to the victims, and their families, such as the woman in Maliana. Linton states:

> The stakes are very high in East Timor. A dissatisfied and disappointed society is more likely to turn to vengeance if the courts do not satisfy its need to see justice and accountability for gross violations of fundamental rights. A key question is whether a half-hearted effort at bringing justice will in the long term have a detrimental effect on the aims of peace and reconciliation.[13]

The realist school of thought would pick up on this idea of vengeance and expect the trials to be a destabilising influence that threatened Timor's fragile peace, or else a façade, with the politics behind the scenes rendering the proceedings symbolic only.

A feminist strategic legalist might look for the participation of women in the system and look for new international criminal jurisprudence or the application of novel precedents on gender violence in a different context. The Timor process had global significance because the UNTAET Regulations adopted the offences of the Rome Statute of the International Criminal Court[14] (hereafter 'Rome Statute') and the trials can therefore be considered the first state application of the new global provisions, particularly crime against humanity. Moreover, as noted, it is the first clear example of a 'hybrid tribunal'.[15] The Dili process is judged then, by what impact it has on the recognition of women's experiences and the redistribution of material benefit and shame from survivors to perpetrators.[16]

FOUNDATIONS OF THE SERIOUS CRIMES PROCESS: BEGINNING AT SUB-ZERO

It is crucial to understand the starting point for the court. Hansjorg Strohmeyer, the United Nations official in charge of the Judicial Affairs Unit of UNTAET until 2000 noted that the United Nations was working literally from scratch:

> How can a justice system be administered when there is no system left to be administered; when the personnel needed to carry out judicial tasks have departed or are tainted by their perceived affiliation with the previous regime; when the courthouses and related facilities have been destroyed, looted, or even mined; and when the laws to be applied are politically charged and no longer acceptable to the population and the new political classes?[17]

The term commonly used in the literature is that the United Nations was beginning at 'ground zero' in East Timor.[18] Given the negative experience of the Timorese with the legal sector in the past, the starting point may actually have been below zero. As the United Nations Development Programme notes '[t]he Indonesian government suborned the legal system to its own ends and corrupted both courts and the judiciary in East Timor—effectively turning the legal system into a servile extension of the executive.'[19] The justice sector in Indonesia itself was and remains in a parlous state.[20] However, this view of the formal legal sector meant that traditional legal systems in Timor were ignored.[21]

An International Commission of Inquiry established to investigate the crimes in East Timor (ICIET) recommended that the United Nations 'should establish an international human rights tribunal consisting of judges appointed by the United Nations, preferably with the participation of members from East Timor and Indonesia'.[22] The report stated:

It is fundamental to the social and political future of East Timor that the truth be established and that those responsible for the crimes committed be brought to court. All efforts must be made to compensate the victims appropriately as only this can open the way to real reconciliation.[23]

The ICIET felt that this was important in light of the fact that United Nations Security Council Resolution 1264 of 1999 had been breached:

> The actions violating human rights and international humanitarian law in East Timor were directed against a decision of the United Nations Security Council acting under Chapter VII of the charter and were contrary to agreements reached by Indonesia with the United Nations to carry out that Security Council Decision.
>
> Under Article 25 of the Charter, Member States agree to accept and carry out decisions of the Security Council. The organised opposition in East Timor to the Security Council decision requires specific international attention and response. The United Nations, as an organisation, has a vested interest in participating in the entire process of investigation, establishing responsibility and punishing those responsible and in promoting reconciliation. Effectively dealing with this issue will be important for ensuring that future Security Council decisions are respected.[24]

The same recommendations were made by the Special Rapporteurs on extra-judicial, summary, or arbitrary executions, on torture and on violence against women,[25] as well as Indonesian's own Human Rights Commission report by Komnas HAM.[26]

When the United Nations Secretary-General Kofi Annan delivered the report of ICIET in January 2000 to the United Nations Security Council and General Assembly, he stated that he would 'closely monitor progress' of the response to the crimes in East Timor in order to see that it was a 'credible response in accordance with international human rights principles'.[27] Specific criteria for what would denote a 'credible response' were not enumerated. At no time was the Timorese population consulted about the establishment or the discontinuation of the serious crimes process.[28] Security Council Resolution 1264 of 1999 in relation to East Timor calls for 'those responsible for these acts to be brought to court'.[29] Notably the term used is specifically 'court', not the broader term 'justice'.

The foundations of the Dili trials therefore reflect clearly the legalist approach that there is a duty on the international community to punish perpetrators of international crimes. The decision to punish is not subject to any democratic processes. There was no consultation with the Timorese leadership by the United Nations about the decision to set up a Serious Crimes process, let alone the wider populace,[30] although there was some limited consultation over the Commission for Truth, Reception and Reconciliation (CAVR).[31]

5.1 The Special Panels for Serious Crimes

The Special Panels for Serious Crimes (the Special Panels) were established, within the District Court in Dili, pursuant to Section 10 of UNTAET Regulation No. 2000/11. The Transitional Administrator, in consultation with the Court Presidency, was empowered to appoint panels of judges to the District Court of Dili, composed of both East Timorese and international judges. Regulation 2000/15 on the Establishment of Panels with Jurisdiction over Serious Criminal Offences, 6 June 2000[32] established the framework for the process, including a prosecution service for East Timor. Regulation 2000/16 set up the Serious Crimes Investigation Unit (SCIU) within the Office of the Deputy General Prosecutor to conduct investigations and prosecutions of serious crimes. At the same time, a national justice system was also being established by UNTAET for ordinary crimes, other than murder and sexual offences.

The Special Panel must be comprised of two international judges and one East Timorese judge. Judicial appointments created difficulties in convening the Court. The departure of Judge Benfeito Mosso Ramos (Cape Verde) in April 2003 meant that the Special Panel for Serious Crimes was unable to convene a full panel of the Court and conduct hearings, as Judge Sylver Ntukamazina (Burundi) was the sole remaining international judge. This problem was remedied with the swearing in of three new international judges to the Panel in late 2003, these being: Judge Francisco Florit (Italy), Judge Siegfried Blunk (Germany) and Judge Dora Martins de Morais (Brazil). In 2004, Coordinating Judge Phillip Rapoza, Oscar Gomes and Brigitte Schmid joined the bench.

The Special Panels were directed to apply three sources of law.[33] The first was UNTAET Regulations and directives. The second was applicable treaties and recognised principles and norms of international law, including the established principles of the international law of armed conflict. The third source was the law validly applied in East Timor prior to 25 October 1999, until replaced by UNTAET Regulations or subsequent legislation, insofar as they did not conflict with either the internationally recognised human rights standards; the fulfilment of the mandate given to UNTAET under the Security Council Resolution 1272 (1999); or UNTAET Regulations or directives.[34] Controversy erupted over what the applicable law was before 1999.[35] After a series of cases,[36] the National Parliament finally resolved the issue by the adoption of a law stating that applicable law in East Timor was law promulgated by East Timor after its independence, UNTAET regulations and, in the absence of either, Indonesian law on 8 October 2003.[37] The question still remains as to whether crimes committed before 1999 could have been adjudicated by the Special Panel. All Serious Crime Unit updates state that the Special Panel's temporal jurisdiction is limited to crimes committed in 1999.[38]

The Special Panels exercised exclusive jurisdiction with respect to the following serious criminal offences: genocide, war crimes, crimes against humanity, murder, sexual offences and torture, as specified in Sections 4 to 9 of UNTAET Regulation 2000/15 (collectively known as 'serious crimes'). The definition of international crimes is taken almost verbatim from the subject matter jurisdiction of the Rome Statute.[39] Section 4 contains the definition of genocide from the Genocide Convention,[40] which includes preventing births and forcible transfer of children to another group.[41] Section 5 enumerates 'rape, sexual slavery, enforced prostitution, forced pregnancy (defined in Section 5.2(e)), enforced sterilisation, or any other form of sexual violence of comparable gravity' as a crime against humanity within the context of a widespread or systematic attack and directed against a civilian population.[42] Under Section 6 on war crimes, acts designated as a violation of the laws and customs of war,[43] include '(xxii) rape, sexual slavery, enforced prostitution, forced pregnancy as defined in Section 5.2(e), enforced sterilization, or any other form of sexual violence constituting a grave breach of the Geneva Conventions'.[44] Section 5.2(e) reflects precisely the definition of forced pregnancy in the Rome Statute meaning:

> the unlawful confinement of a woman forcibly made pregnant, with the intent of affecting the ethnic composition of any population or carrying out other grave violations of international law. This definition shall not in any way be interpreted as affecting national laws relating to pregnancy.[45]

Section 7 adopts the definition of the crime of torture[46] contained in the United Nations Convention against Torture and Other Cruel, Inhuman or Degrading Treatment or Punishment (CAT).[47]

The term 'serious crimes' draws upon the distinction in the Indonesian Penal Code between felonies and misdemeanours. The Special Panels are explicitly stated to have universal jurisdiction for these international crimes, but not universal jurisdiction with regard to murder or sexual offences done between 1 January and 25 October 1999, which must be prosecuted under the Indonesian Penal Code.[48] The sexual offences in the Penal Code are contained in the section 'Crimes Against Decency'.

The United Nations therefore gives the Special Panels jurisdiction over two categories of crimes, international and domestic, with both categories of crimes dealing with sexual offences against women. There are two important things to note here. The first is that there is no explicit delineation in Regulation 2000/15 as to when a sexual assault might fall under the Penal Code or when it becomes an element of one of the serious crimes as defined. The second is that as a 'hybrid' tribunal, one of the claimed advantages of the Dili process was that it would assist in the creation of the formal legal sector in Timor. The mandate of the Special Panels goes beyond providing a role model. The Dili court assumed sole responsibility for murder and sexual offences in the post-conflict state.

5.2 The Serious Crimes Investigation Unit

After East Timor's independence on 20 May 2002, the SCIU worked under the legal authority of the Prosecutor General of East Timor. The SCIU was headed by the Deputy General Prosecutor for Serious Crimes (DPSG) who reported functionally to the Prosecutor-General and was responsible for managing the investigations and prosecutions of the SCIU. Under UNTAET's various successor missions, the most important being the United Nations Mission of Support in East Timor (UNMISET), the SCIU was mandated to assist the authorities in East Timor in the conduct of serious crimes investigations and proceedings. In reality, the lack of resources, capacity and expertise in East Timor meant that the work of the SCIU and Special Panels remained heavily dependent on United Nations staff and United Nations and other international funding.

The SCIU was divided into four Regional teams comprised of United Nations prosecutors, case managers, investigators and trainee staff with separate forensic investigation, evidence management and witness support teams. The Regional Investigation and Prosecution teams covered all 13 districts of East Timor with Regional investigation teams operating from offices in Dili, Maliana and Manufahi. The SCIU Office in Oecussi was closed in early 2004. By mid-2004, the SCIU had 110 staff members including 37 United Nations international civilian staff including prosecutors, investigators, forensic specialists and translators as well as eight United Nations Police investigators and 34 United Nations national staff including translators and mortuary staff. In addition, 12 East Timorese trainee staff worked with the SCIU including prosecutors, ITU and evidence management staff funded by the Norwegian Government. A total of 17 East Timorese Police (PNTL) investigators underwent practical training in SCIU district investigation teams with United Nations investigators and United Nations police trainers, and two PNTL officers worked in the SCIU witness management team. Low Timorese national staffing levels can be explained by the fact that according to the United Nations, in late 1999 there were about 100 East Timorese qualified in law of whom about 70 were in East Timor; however, few of these had actually practiced law prior to 2000,[49] and none had ever served as a judge or prosecutor.[50]

Prosecution strategy

Using the findings of the ICIET,[51] the SCIU initially identified ten priority cases relating to specific incidents raised in the report, most of which involve mass killings, although there were also incidental cases of sexual violence.[52] The ten cases were: the Liquiça church massacre on 6 April 1999; the Los Palos case, 21 April to 25 September 1999; the Lolotoe case, 2 May to 16 September 1999;

the murders at the house of Manuel Carrascalão on 17 April 1999; the Kailako and Maliana Police Station killings, April/September 1999; the Suai church massacre on 6 September 1999; the attacks on Bishop Belo's compound and the Dili Diocese on 6 September 1999; the Passabe and Makaleb massacres, September to October 1999; the TNI Battalion 745 case, April to September 1999; and cases of sexual violence from various districts, March to September 1999.[53]

A decision was made that the focus of the investigations and prosecutions should be those cases involving murder (there were approximately 1,400 such cases).[54] Some cases of rape and torture were investigated, particularly when associated with murders, but cases that, for example, only concerned forcible transfer across the border to West Timor, even when this potentially constituted a crime against humanity, were not pursued.[55] According to DPSG Carl de Faria, torture cases were not prioritised, while deportation and destruction of property cases were not investigated thoroughly.[56]

Several of the later indictments were particularly significant because they named as suspects a number of high-ranking Indonesian officials, including military commanders, as well as militia leaders, only some of whom were put on trial in Indonesia. Importantly, the later indictments also address the institutional responsibility of the Indonesian security forces for the violence.[57] A number of military commanders are specifically charged with participating in the establishment of militia by cooperating on a policy of funding, arming, training and directing the militia. They are accused of having had effective control over militias operating in East Timor and responsibility for crimes they committed. The commanders are also accused of command responsibility for the acts or omissions of their subordinates in the Indonesian military due to their failure to take reasonable measures to prevent crimes or punish the perpetrators.[58]

Among those named in an indictment issued in February 2003 are two of the most senior Indonesian military officials at the time: the then Indonesian Defence Minister and Commander of the Armed Forces, General Wiranto; and Major General Zacky Anwar Makarim who was a member of the Task Force for the Popular Consultation in East Timor. Both men were publicly named as suspects in the inquiry initiated in 1999 by Komnas HAM, but were never charged in Indonesia. Wiranto and Makarim were indicted for 280 alleged murders, based on more than 1,500 witness statements.[59] These indictments were immediately opposed publicly by the then President of East Timor Xanana Gusmão and then Foreign Minister José Ramos-Horta for fear of damaging the political relationship with Indonesia.[60] Other persons who have been indicted include 15 of the 18 individuals who were brought to trial in the Jakarta ad hoc Human Rights Court, which was discussed in Chapter Four.

5.3 The Public Defender's Office

No legislation for a Public Defenders' Office was passed by UNTAET. It was not until 2004 that the Public Defenders Office (PDO) Law was drafted. As of September 2009, it was still in the process of being put to Parliament. Defence lawyers continued to work under the Indonesian legislation, which remained in effect in East Timor throughout the transition period. During the summer of 2002, there were just two international Public Defenders, one paid by the United Nations as a judicial affairs officer 'on loan', and the other funded by the organisation 'No Peace Without Justice'. The United Nations Development Programme funded one additional lawyer to work primarily as a mentor to East Timorese public defenders involved with ordinary crimes. With the exception of these three lawyers, the Public Defenders' Office was staffed and funded entirely by East Timorese.[61] In 2003 there were ten Public Defenders for the whole of East Timor. The PDO was and continues to be responsible for both serious and ordinary crimes, and has had great difficulty securing adequate resources to properly fulfil its role.[62]

In September 2008, the private lawyers' statute was passed by Timor-Leste's National Parliament, creating a new regulatory framework for the governance of the legal profession. Under the new law, a process of formal accreditation is established, in line with a regime of practical training and an enforceable code of conduct. Most interestingly, lawyers are required to collaborate toward the betterment of the legal system, and to protest human rights violations and other miscarriages of justice.

5.4 The Court of Appeal

The Court of Appeal was established under UNTAET regulation 2000/11 and began to hear appeals from the Special Panels for Serious Crimes in July 2000. Section 40 of UNTAET Regulation 2001/25 established that the Court has jurisdiction to hear appeals of decisions rendered by any district court in East Timor, and such other matters as are provided for by legislation.

The Court of Appeal is designed to function as the highest court of law and the guarantor of a uniform enforcement of the law, and has jurisdiction throughout all the national territory. It operates as the court of last instance for all legal matters and administers justice on matters of a legal, constitutional and electoral nature until the Supreme Court is constituted as provided by the Constitution. However, from November 2001 until July 2003, the Court was non-operational due to the lack of proper judicial appointments. The Court of Appeal has four judges, namely the Chief Judge and three other judges, of whom two are internationals. The first Judges appointed to the Court were the President, the Honourable Claudio Ximenes de Jesus (an East Timorese judge with Portuguese citizenship), the Honourable Jacinta Correia da Costa (East Timorese) and the Honourable Frederick Egonde-Entende (Uganda).[63]

There followed an exceptionally high turnover of international judges, resulting in the Court being properly constituted for a period of one month from April to May 2002.[64] The importance of the right to an appeal under international law was a point lost on even some of the judges of the Court. The only female Judge Jacinta Correia da Costa at one stage was forced to state: 'For me, the important thing is how we are working to build this judicial system for the East Timorese. If there is no Court of Appeal it's a big problem.'[65] The problem was finally resolved with the appointment of Judge José Maria Calvário Antunes (Portugal) in July 2003.[66] The International Crisis Group observed rather tartly that any further appointments of international judges should be on grounds of international judicial experience and human rights expertise rather than the ability to speak Portuguese.[67] In March 2009, JSMP criticised the Timorese Government for leaving the President of the Court of Appeal vacant for over a year.[68]

5.5 Overall budget

Funding figures for the serious crimes process are not publicly available on an annual basis. David Cohen reported, based on personal interviews undertaken in 2001 and 2002, that the tribunal had a $6.3 million US dollar budget in 2001–2. $6 million was spent on the prosecution and the remainder mainly on judges' salaries. Cohen was unable to determine what the budget of the Public Defender's Office was.[69]

In the 2002–3 period, the Dili-based NGO Judicial System Monitoring Programme (JSMP) reported that the SCIU operated on a budget of US$5 million employing 111 staff, this figure being based on a radio transcript.[70] For the period 2003–5, the United Nations Commission of Experts reported that total operating cost of the SCU and Special Panels was US$14,358,600, or around 5 per cent of the overall assessed contribution to UNMISET, which amounted to approximately $296,557,000.[71] The voluntary contributions amounted roughly to US$120,000.[72] By contrast, the ICTY and ICTR have annual budgets of about $100 million, and the Sierra Leone tribunal has a budget of about $20 million.

GENDER ANALYSIS OF THE SERIOUS CRIMES PROCESS

5.6 Representation of women

The gender composition of the legal sector in East Timor is concerning. Feminist scholars have consistently pushed for equal representation of female judges and counsel, especially in trials relating to sexual violence in armed conflict.[73] In August 2004, the tiny legal and judicial sector in East Timor had only a smattering of women, but there was considerable success in securing judicial positions for women. In the Court of Appeal there was one female judge out of three. In the Special Panel there were three female judges (out of a total of six judges). One female judge had unique insight into the 1999 violence. Justice Perreira, appointed to the Court at age 31, had lost her home to arson, was threatened with death by armed men and was deported, with her five children, into a militia-controlled camp in West Timor.[74]

In the Dili District Court there were two female judges and in Baucau District Court there were also two female judges. Of the 15 prosecutors in East Timor, two are female. Of the seven Public Defenders, three are female. There are only two female private lawyers out of a total of at least 20. At present there appears to be no formal Government or United Nations programme to encourage women entering into the legal sector. Despite a commitment to 'gender mainstreaming', where appointments have been made by the United Nations, gender composition has been even worse.[75] While two of the three Timorese judges have been women, only one of the 11 international judges has been female.

In contrast to the Dili trials, Article 36(8)(a)(iii) of the Rome Statute for the International Criminal Court (ICC) requires that the need for a 'fair representation of female and male judges' be taken into account in the selection process.[76] The same provision applies to the selection of staff in the Office of the Prosecutor and in all other organs of the Court. Further, the statute requires that, in the selection of judges, prosecutors and other staff, the need for legal expertise on violence against women or children must be taken into account (Articles 44(2) and 36(8)). Finally, the Prosecutor is required to appoint advisers with legal expertise on specific issues, including sexual and gender violence (Article 42(9)). In the next section, I examine the jurisprudence on gender-based violence that was produced by the serious crimes process, questioning whether the outcomes were affected by this lack of representation of women.

5.7 Jurisprudence on gender persecution from the serious crimes process

The International Center for Transitional Justice (ICTJ) in their report *Justice Abandoned?* acknowledge that 'very few' gender crimes were indicted by the SCIU.[77] The ICTJ point out that progress was made only when a female Deputy Prosecutor was appointed, although a special gender investigation team composed of three women was established to investigate rapes and other sexual violations. However, Frigaard has stated that the reluctance of female victims to testify in open court prevented the SCIU from proceeding with many gender crime prosecutions.[78]

The only three cases which were decided by the serious crimes process represent a series of steps: one, a serious step back (the *Leonardus Kasa* rape case[79]); two, a limited step forward (the *Lolotoe* rape as a crime against humanity case[80]); and three, some useful obiter regarding rape within marriage (the *Soares* rape case[81]), which represents marking time. Other indictments issued by the Prosecutor, discussed briefly below, give some indication of systemic gender persecution but the accused remain at large in Indonesia. The question therefore needs to be asked – did women receive any material benefit from the trials?

The Leonardus Kasa case: a step backwards

The case of *The Prosecutor v. Leonardus Kasa*[82] (the *Kasa case*) was decided by the Special Panel for Serious Crimes in May 2001. The *Kasa* case has been chosen for analysis because it illuminates three key challenges to the realisation of justice for women in East Timor. First, the case illustrates that no knowledge of the international advances in the prosecution of gender-based crimes was displayed or applied in the judgment. Second, the trial proceeded without any reference to the context of systematic gender-based violence in West Timor. Third, the outcome for the alleged victim has actually deteriorated, rather than improved, as a result of the case.

The facts of the case are straightforward. Leonardus Kasa was an alleged member of Laksaur militia from Covalima district. He was arrested and detained by the Civilian Police (CIVPOL), pursuant to the Indonesian Criminal Procedure Code. The Public Prosecutor, Raimund Sauter indicted him in December 2000 with one charge of rape of a woman in Betun village, West Timor, in September 1999. At the preliminary hearing in February 2001 the defence claimed the Special Panel lacked jurisdiction to hear the case as the alleged rape occurred outside the territory of East Timor, and that as the sex was consensual, it should be classified as adultery, which is not a serious crime.[83]

On 9 May 2001 the Special Panel declared that it had no jurisdiction in the case.[84] The defendant had already been released from detention in February 2001 but had been prevented from approaching the victim's home. Immediately after the judgment was given, the Special Panel announced that such restrictions on the defendant no longer applied. An appeal was filed by the Prosecution on 11 October 2001 and withdrawn on 5 April 2004.

The judges of the Special Panel were Luca L. Ferrero (Presiding Judge, Italy), Maria Natercia Gusmao Pereira (Judge Rapporteur, East Timor) and Sylver Ntukamazina (Burundi). The judges stated that the same charges might be raised before courts in Indonesia, or in East Timorese courts if jurisdictional issues were clarified by way of amendment to the regulations, which seemed to influence their judgment. The Special Panel also emphasised that it made no finding as to the defendant's innocence or guilt on the charge of rape.

Disturbingly, the Special Panel makes no reference to the background to this case. The alleged victim in this case, Maria da Costa and her two children were displaced on 5 September 1999 from East Timor and brought to a refugee camp located in the warehouse of Betun in West Timor. This was a week after the popular consultation, where militias, organised and supported by the Indonesian military, were forcibly removing up to 250,000 Timorese into camps in West Timor and wreaking widespread and systematic violence on those perceived to be pro-independence supporters and their property in the process.

The indictment does not refer to this context at all, and the context changes the nature of the offence that should have been charged in the indictment. The mass deportation and rape of women in East Timor is an absent fact in the case. The defendant claimed not to be aware of the chaos around him. The *New York Times* reported in early 2001:

> In an interview at the Dili courthouse, Mr. Casa put forward a defense that… he knew his victim. She belonged to him. The sex was consensual. Beyond that, Mr. Casa said, he knew less than just about anybody else in East Timor about the violence occurring around him. 'I never saw any massacre or any destruction,' he said. 'I never even left my house.'[85]

The consequence of this lack of context is that the Prosecutor charged Kasa with the crime of rape in violation of Section 9 of UNTAET Regulation 2000/15 and Article 285 of the Penal Code of Indonesia. Section 9 'Sexual offences' merely states that the provision of the applicable Penal Code in East Timor shall, as appropriate, apply. As noted above, the Special Panels exercise exclusive jurisdiction with respect to the following serious criminal offences: genocide, war crimes, crimes against humanity, murder, sexual offences and torture, as specified in Sections 4 to 9 of UNTAET Regulation 2000/15 (collectively known as 'serious crimes'), but not universal jurisdiction with regard to 'ordinary' murder or sexual offences between 1 January 1999 and 25 October 1999, which must be prosecuted under the Indonesian Penal Code.[86] The sexual offences in the Penal Code are contained in the section 'Crimes against Decency'. Adultery is a criminal offence under Article 284(1), and the definition of rape is 'any person who… forces a woman to have sexual intercourse with him out of marriage' (Article 285).[87] This dissonance between the context of the offence and what was charged created jurisdictional problems for the Special Panel to resolve.

The Special Panel cited the arguments from the Prosecutor regarding jurisdiction (who was aware of potential problems from the indictment stage). His motion read:

> Since the crime (of rape) was committed outside East Timor and since it does not belong to the crimes listed under Sect. 10.1 (a), (b), (c) and (f) of U.R. 2000/11 as specified in Sect. 4 to 7 of U.R. 2000/15 for which the Special Panel of the District Court of Dili shall have 'universal jurisdiction' the jurisdiction of the Special Panel might be questionable.[88]

The Prosecutor instead based his case on the extraterritorial provisions in the Indonesian Criminal Code which he argued should be applied *mutates mutandis*[89] to this situation.

It was undisputed that the crime occurred outside the East Timorese territory. The Special Panel worked through the criteria used to determine the applicability of national criminal law to crimes that occurred out of the country: (a) universality (or total extraterritoriality), (b) territoriality, (c) active personality (or nationality, or personal status) of the perpetrator and (d) the defence or security principle. They noted: 'Modern states usually don't adopt a single principle. They rather choose a combination between territoriality and other principles. It can be said that the kind of combination depends on the international relations of the state.'[90] The Special Panel decided that the United Nations transitional administration had chosen to adopt the principle of territoriality with very few exceptions:

> This choice could be said mandatory for a transitional administration empowered by the United Nations Security Council, which has also the mandate of administration of justice. How could such a temporary and 'neutral' administration have jurisdiction for crimes committed out of the territory administrated?[91]

The judges relied on Section 5 of UNTAET Regulation 2000/11, which provides that:

> …in exercising jurisdiction, the courts in East Timor shall apply the law of East Timor as promulgated by Section 3.1 of UNTAET Regulation 1999/1. Courts shall have jurisdiction in respect of crimes committed in East Timor prior to 25 October 1999 only insofar as the law on which the offence is based is consistent with Sect. 3.1 of UNTAET Regulation 1999/1 or any other UNTAET regulations.

The alleged rape occurred in September 1999.

The Panel decided that the only exception to the principle set out in Section 5 of UNTAET Regulation 2000/11 is contained in Section 2.2 of UNTAET Regulation 2000/15, which grants the Panel universal jurisdiction for the crimes of genocide, war crimes, crimes against humanity and torture. The Special Panel noted that serious crimes 'deserve universal jurisdiction due international customary laws and (more recently) international laws. That means that the aforementioned Indonesian rules are no longer applicable because they are not consistent with UNTAET Regulation and the principles of the United Nations mandate.'[92] The Special Panel therefore did not accept the Prosecutor's argument and did accept the idea of universal jurisdiction for international crimes happening in West Timor.

However, because the charge brought was rape under domestic law rather than rape in the context of a crime against humanity, the Special Panel found it had no jurisdiction. The Special Panel deemed the applicable criminal law to be Section 9 of UNTAET Regulation 2000/15 and Article 285 of the Indonesian Penal Code, and therefore held that only Indonesia has the jurisdiction on the case. This meant that the East Timorese courts and the Special Panel of Dili District Court itself did not have jurisdiction over a crime of rape committed in West Timor before 25 October 1999. '[N]o East Timorese Court, according to the laws in force at the present time, could try this case.'[93]

The Judicial System Monitoring Programme (JSMP) in East Timor speculated that the judgment was designed to increase pressure on Indonesia to prosecute:

> According to the Special Panel, the universal jurisdiction they have over the international crimes of genocide, war crimes, crimes against humanity and torture, does not extend to individual cases of murder and sexual offences, including rape.
>
> Although rape and murder committed between 1 January and 25 October 1999 are considered 'serious crimes' by UNTAET, yesterday's decision means that no suspected perpetrators of such crimes, if committed in West Timor, can be tried by the Special Panel of the East Timorese courts unless the crimes can be categorised as any of the international crimes over which the court enjoys universal jurisdiction.[94]

In my view, the Special Panel erred in its failure to consider the principle of active personality (or nationality) of the perpetrator as a basis of jurisdiction. Universal jurisdiction is generally only relied upon where the crime is a gross human rights violation; and there is no link with the territory where the crime took place, the offender or the victim.[95] There was no impediment to assessing the other grounds of jurisdiction under customary international law, especially the nationality principle, even if universal jurisdiction in this case was found not to exist due to the judicial interpretation of Regulation 2000/11. The Special Panel is able to apply 'recognised principles and norms of international law'[96] and it is unquestionable that the extra-territorial application of criminal jurisdiction in certain circumstances, for example, on the ground of the nationality principle is one of these norms.

It was also open to the Court to ask the Prosecution to justify why this act of rape was an 'ordinary' crime, opportunistic only, or else reframe the charge.[97] Had the Prosecutor charged the case as an international crime, the jurisdictional arguments could have been handled quite differently. Both the Prosecutor and the Special Panel seemed to completely fail to entertain the idea that a single rape by a militia leader could have been characterised as a crime against humanity if part of a 'widespread and systematic attack' as envisioned by Section 5.1(g); a war crime under Section 6.1(b)(xxii) in an international armed conflict or Section 6.1(e)(vi) in a non-international armed conflict; or an act of torture under Section 7.1.

The Special Panel is directed to apply 'established principles of international law of armed conflict',[98] but fails to mention that the *Furundzija* case in the International Criminal Tribunal for the Former Yugoslavia (ICTY) decided that the rape of a single victim is a crime serious enough to warrant prosecution by an international war crimes tribunal. The defendant in that case was charged and convicted with rape and torture as war crimes.[99] This oversight can only be explained by speculating that either the Panel or Prosecutor or both lacked sufficient knowledge of recent precedent in international criminal law.[100] The Panel's inattention to international criminal jurisprudence is not limited to the *Kasa* case. The JSMP trial report of the first Serious Crimes Court convictions in the *Los Palos* case[101] noted that 'it is surprising that the Panel's arguments seem not to be based on international jurisprudence', noting that the Panel did not mention the *Tadic* case when assessing the elements of an armed conflict.[102] Suzannah Linton has argued cogently that the first two initial decisions handed down by the Special Panel in the cases of Joao and Julio Fernandes[103] should have been deal with as international crimes rather than a violation of domestic law.[104] In that case, the authors of the Maliana POLRES massacre,[105] one of the SCIU's top ten priority investigations, were charged and subsequently convicted not with crimes against humanity but with murder.[106] Timorese civil society treated the decision with scorn.[107] In an unreported dissenting judgment, the only Timorese judge, Maria Natercia Gusmao Pereira J questioned how the practice of prosecuting acts such as these as a domestic crime 'could bring justice to a people who had suffered so much during the many years of occupation'.[108]

But the *Kasa* judgment could also be read as the participants having insufficient insight into the crime of rape during armed conflict. In Chapter Two, I outlined the long struggle by feminist legalists to have rape considered as a weapon of war, not a private, unavoidable circumstance unconnected to the conflict. The legal errors above could be illustrative of a type of gender-blindness. For example, Hilary Charlesworth and Christine Chinkin ask: '[w]hy is extra-territorial jurisdiction traditionally involved against violations of monopoly and competition law but only rarely in cases of trafficking of women and children?'[109]

The Lolotoe trials: rape as a crime against humanity

Criticism of the *Kasa* case had an influence on the Lolotoe crimes against humanity trials,[110]which were decided before a Special Panel for Serious Crimes in 2000. The *Lolotoe* case was the second of ten priority cases to be tried by the Special Panels, and the first crimes against humanity case in East Timor to include charges of rape and charges against superiors based on the actions of their subordinates.[111] Section 26.2 of UNTAET Regulation 25/2001 clearly states that the record of criminal proceedings 'shall be made available to the public'. The indictment and judgment have been made available by the Berkeley War Crimes Centre and JSMP. A JSMP report *The Lolotoe Case: A Small Step Forward* from July 2004, contains unofficial transcripts of the hearings taken by JSMP observers beginning with the first preliminary hearing on 6 April 2001.[112]

The three defendants in the *Lolotoe* case—*Kaer Metin Merah Putih* (KMMP) militia commanders José Cardoso Ferreira and João França da Silva and former Guda village chief Sabino Gouveia Leite – were accused of waging a terror campaign in the Lolotoe area of Bobonaro district during the months surrounding the 1999 Popular Consultation on the future of East Timor.[113] The three defendants were arrested and detained separately in the period from 19 May 2000 to 5 February 2001.

The two KMMP commanders were accused of illegal imprisonment, murder, torture, rape, persecution and inhumane treatment of civilians in Lolotoe subdistrict, near the border with West Timor, Indonesia. Gouveia Leite was accused of being an accomplice in the offences allegedly committed by the KMMP and members of the Indonesian Armed Forces (TNI). The original indictment filed on 6 February 2001 charged 5 co-accused with various counts of crimes against humanity: murder, serious maltreatment, unlawful deprivation of liberty of persons and rape. Two defendants, 2nd Lt Bambang Indra (sub-district commander (DANRAMIL) of the TNI forces in Lolotoe, with alleged de facto control of the KMMP militia), and Francisco Noronha (an East Timorese member of the KMMP), were severed from the original indictment as they were still at large, presumed to be in Indonesia. The Court issued an Interpol arrest warrant on 6 April 2001 which has so far not been complied with.[114]

An important aspect of the case was the maintenance by the accused of a 'rape house' where three women suspected of being related to Falintil guerrillas were raped repeatedly from May to July 1999. According to the indictment,[115] sometime in May 1999, José Cardoso, about 50 KMMP militia and a few TNI soldiers, armed with automatic weapons, grenades, machetes and knives went to Guda and gave a speech to the villagers. Acting on the information of Sabino Leite, they named Mariana Da Cunha, Victim A, Victim B and Victim C as FALINTIL supporters. They claimed these four women were supplying FALINTIL with food and were in relationships with its members. At different times, these four women were taken to Lolotoe and detained in Sabino Leite's house. From there, Victims A, B and C were taken to Jhoni Franca's house and then to a hotel in Atambua on 27 June. At this stage the three women had been detained for a number of weeks. At Atambua, it was stated that José Cardoso would have intercourse with Victim A, Bambang Indra with Victim B and Francisco Noronha with Victim C. On various nights in late June, the three women were injected with medicine they were told would prevent them from getting pregnant. The three victims were then sexually penetrated by the men, with José Cardoso also raping Victim B. The women were threatened that if they did not obey the men they would be killed.

This was a prime opportunity for the Special Panel to apply the jurisprudence of the *Akayesu* case in the ICTR and the *Kunarac* case in the ICTY, where rape was determined to be a crime against humanity. The *Kunarac* case is based on a fact situation in the town of Foca in Bosnia involving a 'rape hotel', which was comparable to the Lolotoe 'rape house' and also examines the issue of enslavement.[116]

The indictment in the case was filed on 25 May 2001 and the accused had already been in detention at that stage for more than two years.[117] The trial ran from 5 March 2002 until 5 April 2003, with numerous delays.[118] In October 2002, Jhoni Franca pleaded guilty to one count of torture and four counts of imprisonment and was sentenced to five years' imprisonment. In November 2002, Sabino Leite pleaded guilty and received three years' imprisonment and was conditionally released by the Special Panel.[119] On 5 April 2003, José Cardoso Fereira was sentenced to 12 years' prison for crimes against humanity.[120] The judgment is not available but NGO transcripts of the court hearings attest to a much stronger reliance on international law and recent jurisprudence on gender-based persecution than the *Kasa* decision.[121]

The breakthrough in the *Lolotoe* judgment was the fact that the Court considered relevant jurisprudence from the ICTR and ICTY and also looked to the Rome Statute of the International Criminal Court for the first time to consider gender persecution. The relevant international jurisprudence was raised comprehensively in the Final Statement of the Prosecutor.[122]

The Court relied on jurist M. Cherif Bassiouni to make a finding that the crime of rape was a part of customary international law:

> Rape and other forms of sexual violence were not explicitly listed as crimes against humanity in Article 6(c) of the London Charter nor in Article 5(c) of the Tokyo Charter. However, both charters contained the term 'other inhumane acts', and rape and other forms of sexual violence clearly constitute other inhumane acts, under general principle of law16. Rape and sexual violence is included in article 5 of the ICTY Statute, Article 3 of the ICTR Statute and Article 7 of the ICC Statute. It is therefore clear that rape is part of customary international law.[123]

However, the Court managed to come to some of its findings without applying international jurisprudence to the facts of the case before it, especially in the areas of consent and aiding and abetting. The Special Panels made a single statement that they particularly relied on the ICTY decision in *Kunarac*[124] and noted that: 'this Court considers as persuasive the absence of consent as the central element of the definition of the crime of rape'.[125]

The international jurisprudence does state that wartime conditions such as the breakdown of law and order can be taken into account when determining consent issues,[126] but the fact of an armed conflict does not mean consent issues do not have to be examined at all. The Court relied on the definition of rape as established under the Rome Statute, as the offence is not defined in the UNTAET Regulation. The Rome Statute definition of rape in Article 7 notes the absence of consent as a crucial element of the offence.

José Cardoso claimed that he committed the rape only due to superior orders and that one of the victims allegedly consented to the intercourse. The Court did not address Cardoso's claim of consent directly. According to the Judicial Systems Monitoring Programme (JSMP) report on the trial, the Special Panels turned to evidentiary provisions in UNTAET Regulation 2000/15 that relate to sexual assault cases to determine what circumstances negate consent. Section 34.3(b) of UNTAET Regulation 2000/15 disallows consent as a defence to sexual assault if the victim: (1) has been subjected with or has had reason to fear violence, duress, detention or psychological oppression, or (2) reasonably believed that if the victim did not submit, another person might be so subjected, threatened or put in fear. The Court used the circumstances in this provision, which related to consent as a defence, as general examples of situations which negate consent in the execution of rape as a crime against humanity. JSMP criticises the fact that the Court held that José Cardoso personally raped Victim A and B without systematically applying the definition of rape to the facts of the case, especially the aspects of consent and superior orders raised in defence. The opportunity was lost to make it clear that the existence of superior orders is not a defence to a rape charge, rather than ignoring the claim. While JSMP does not find fault with the decision, they find the reasoning behind the decision inadequate.[127]

The Court further analysed the role of José Cardoso in aiding and abetting the rape of Victims B and C by the two Indonesians severed from the original indictment by reference to the ICTY trial case of *Furundzija*[128] and both the trial and appeal judgments of *Aleksovski.*[129] The Court accepted the facts that José Cardoso threatened the victims that they would be killed if they did not have sexual intercourse and took the victims to the rooms where they were raped by the Indonesian men. The Court referred to the ICTR judgment of *Akayesu*:

> The accused having had reason to know that sexual violence was occurring, aided and abetted acts of sexual violence by allowing them to take place on or near the premises of the bureau communal and by facilitating the commission of such sexual violence through his words of encouragement or in other acts of sexual violence which, by virtue of his authority, sent a clear signal of official tolerance for sexual violence, without which these acts would not have taken place.[130]

Accordingly, the Court held that José Cardoso aided and abetted the rape of Victims B and C. Under section 15 of UNTAET Regulation 2000/15, aiding and abetting the commission of a crime results in individual criminal responsibility. Applying this provision, José Cardoso was convicted of the rape of all three victims. Was this a fair outcome?

The fairness of the trial is relevant to whether the quest for gender justice has been realised on a deeper level than merely gaining a judgment. Unless the process can be seen as fair, the aim of transitional justice in promoting the rule of law is diminished with consequences that may be severe for women in post-conflict societies. There is a question as to whether the trial met basic standards of fairness to the defence. JSMP note that in this case there were lengthy delays that created long periods of pre-trial detention, as well as problems in achieving 'equality of arms' before the Special Panel. Cardoso had five lawyers represent him throughout the trial at various times, and the defence generally had far fewer resources than the prosecution.[131] JSMP also note continuing problems with interpreters, uncertainty over plea bargaining processes and admissions of guilt, and lack of access to court transcripts.[132]

The charge of selectivity can also be made of the judgment, that the Court was being too hard on the 'small fish' in custody despite the more severe guilt of the defendants at large in Indonesia.[133] Defence counsel emphasised the relatively minor role the defendant had as commander of the KMMP militia in their closing statement:

> Where are the perpetrators – hiding in West Timor. I want to warn the court away from the temptation of convicting the accused. I know the burden is heavy and because witnesses came that lost their husbands, fathers who lost their sons. It does not necessarily mean that because the accused is the one in charge, he is the one to pay for their losses.[134]

As 2nd Lt Bambang Indra did not face trial, the role of the TNI in the Lolotoe attacks was not heavily scrutinised, although it was an important factor. Therefore, the judgment does not address the systematic nature of the crimes or the culpability of the people who organised the attacks. However, the logic does not follow that, because access to the main perpetrators is denied, the defendants proven to have raped women as a crime against humanity should walk free. Overall, the outcome of the trial was fair.

The manner in which the trial was conducted has ramifications for gender justice. Admirably, the Special Panels granted protection orders for Victims A, B and C (with some debate over whether it was prejudicial to label them 'Victim' instead of 'Witness').[135] These protection orders were therefore granted to protect the rape victims from any intimidation, harassment or interference by the accused or their family members. Specifically, the protection orders stipulated that documentary evidence related to protected witnesses should only be shown to the prosecution, defence and defendants; no identifying information should be given to a third party, the public or the media; and any person acting on behalf of the witness should not contact the witnesses or their families without the consent of the prosecutor or a judge.[136]

The Court accepted the affidavit of a Serious Crimes Unit investigator which stated the protection orders were required due to the situation of the victims:

> The kidnapping and rape have traumatized the victims. Their mistrust and emotional breakdowns in the presence of investigators attempting to pursue finer details from them demonstrate this. The victims live in remote villages, and have limited knowledge of the legal system. Any attempt to force the victims to testify in public would exacerbate the trauma they have suffered. They have shown a reluctance to speak any further about the matters, unless it is to see justice being done.[137]

When Victims A, B and C did actually give testimony, the Court was completely closed to the public, including JSMP monitors, which JSMP protested against.[138] JSMP reports that despite the protective measures put in place, Victims A, B and C informed the prosecution that they were yelled at by the accused's family on court premises after the close of proceedings. The prosecution requested the Court take action as these witnesses did not feel safe in the courtroom due to the presence of family members of the accused. Upholding the importance of a public trial and the need for the accused to have moral support from their family, the Court permitted the family members to stay providing they did not speak to or have direct contact with the three witnesses. A similar request was made from the defence counsel of José Cardoso, in response to which the Court banned family members of the witnesses from intimidating or harassing the accused.[139]

The *Lolotoe* trials set an important jurisprudential precedent and were the high-water mark of the Dili trials for gender justice, notwithstanding some concerns about the conduct and fairness of the trial and its selective nature, as examined above. However, that high-water mark was set very low in Timor compared to the international tribunals. As Alexander Zahar comments, the part of the judgment dealing with rape was better written and reasoned relative to the rest of the judgment, which he describes as 'tedious', 'behind its times, obviously produced on a shoestring judgment' and 'far from being integrated with the world of international criminal justice'.[140]

The Soares case: rape as 'ordinary' crime

In September 2002, the Special Panel handed down its first and only conviction for rape. Francisco Soares, a former militia commander was sentenced to four years jail for raping a woman taken from the TNI 744 base in Becora in September 1999 (Case Number: 14/2001). The maximum penalty was 12 years.

The Panel found Soares guilty under section 285 of the Indonesian Penal Code, which states that: 'Whosoever uses force or the threat of force to coerce a woman who is not his wife to have sexual relations with him is liable to imprisonment of 12 years'. One member of the three-judge panel dissented on whether not being married to the victim remained an element of the crime of rape under East Timorese law,[141] given that Indonesian law continued to prevail in East Timor only to the extent that it is compatible with international human rights law.[142] Once again in this case, the rape was portrayed as an 'ordinary crime' despite the context of conflict in 1999, but at least the defendant was arrested in the jurisdiction and jailed.

Other indictments involving gender persecution

From the inauspicious beginnings of the *Kasa* decision, the Special Panels and the SCIU appeared to be making progress in applying their mandate of international criminal law to the investigation and prosecution of gender-based persecution, and breaches of international humanitarian law generally when the process finished in 2005. All other indictments dealing with gender persecution were left hanging when the SCIU closed, as the indicted perpetrators were at large in Indonesia. The aspects of the indictments relating to gender violence are outlined below in chronological order.

In the *Atabae* case,[143] three militia members were charged with 13 counts of crimes against humanity that include multiple rapes and torture between April 1999 and late September 1999 that took place in Atabae sub-district, Bobonaro district. The offences include claims that several women, who along with their families were suspected to be pro-independence, were repeatedly targeted and subjected to sexual violence by the militia. The leader, Joao Tavares, died in June 2009 in West Timor.

On 5 April 2003, the same day as the *Lolotoe* judgment was handed down, the Serious Crimes Unit issued an indictment for the arrest of five accused TNI soldiers in West Timor who allegedly raped a number of women from the Cailaco Sub-District of Bobonaro District for an extended period of time (Case Number: 15/2003). The five accused TNI soldiers allegedly 'used intimidation, threats of force or actual force to elicit compliance and subservience from the victims'.[144] For some women, the rapes continued after the victims were forcibly deported to West Timor following the announcement of the result of the popular consultation in September 1999.

The *Laksaur* militia case (Case Number: 9/2003) concerned charges of 51 counts of crimes against humanity against a total of 11 accused. The accused were each members of the Laksaur militia which operated in Covalima District and around Suai near the border with Indonesian West Timor. The charges include multiple counts of murder, enforced disappearance, persecution, torture, rape, other inhumane acts directed against the civilian population of Covalima District, and the summary execution of many persons suspected to be supporters of the East Timorese independence movement. They also include the forced deportation of civilians to West Timor.

An important gender aspect of this indictment concerned the case of Juliana dos Santos. The crimes alleged against Vice Commander of the Laksaur militia group, Egidio Manek include participation by the Laksaur militia in the Suai Church Massacre of 6 September 1999 which resulted in the death of three priests and an estimated 200 civilians. Her family alleges that then 15-year-old Juliana dos Santos watched as her brother was murdered by Manek during the massacre, before being taken by Manek and his militia men across the border into West Timor. After being paraded as a war trophy, she was repeatedly raped and became pregnant. She gave birth to a son, Carlos, on 27 November 2000.[145]

Juliana was held by Manek in Rai Henek Ho'an, West Timor, from where he led the activities of pro-Indonesian militias under his command. He was arrested in July 2001 by Indonesian authorities and is being held on corruption charges in spite of the fact that he is wanted for crimes against humanity in East Timor.[146] The Indonesian Government consented to two family visits to West Timor to visit Juliana but at rare sightings Juliana has expressed her consent to be with Manek. The voluntariness of that 'consent' and her continued presence in Indonesia is the subject of debate. Due to a campaign by Kirsty Sword Gusmão, Juliana dos Santos became the public face of the women trapped in West Timor.[147]

The *Covalima* indictment filed 6 December 2004, charges Mahidi militia members Domingos Mau Buti and Adriano Nascimento with crimes against humanity including murder, attempted murder and rape (case 8/2004). The *Ermera* indictment filed on 15 December 2004 alleges facts relating to the rape and murder of a prominent female CNRT member and UNAMET staff member by Indonesian military (case 12/2004).

These cases represent only a tiny snapshot of the violence against women in East Timor from 1975 until 1999, as is clear when we examine the CAVR in Chapter Six. From a feminist viewpoint, the prosecution strategy did not prioritise violence against women. Even where some measure of formal justice was obtained in these cases, there were limitations. There was generally no subsequent material benefit to the victims involved, or their surviving families. Although the definition of international crimes in Timor's domestic jurisdiction of the Special Panels is taken almost verbatim from the subject matter jurisdiction of the Rome Statute, the compensation provisions were not included. The limited transcripts available chronicle the horrors of the victims' experiences but none of their heroism and resistance.

In the next section I demonstrate that overall the serious crimes process failed not just due to the lack of cooperation by Indonesia but also within the limited political confines allowed it. Where the United Nations administers a territory, the duty to prosecute violations of international law must be meaningful, not token. Part of the role of the United Nations is to create the political circumstances in which fair trials can be held but it failed to do so. I set out the key criticisms and assess them in relation to gender justice concerns.

THE 'NOT SO SERIOUS' CRIMES PROCESS

This section critiques the overall serious crimes process, beginning with the failure of the United Nations to properly resource the process. The Special Panels can be judged first on their results, and second on the selectivity of these results, and they are of course interrelated. There were three key problems that could not have been resolved by the addition of adequate human and financial resources. These were the continued lack of cooperation by Indonesia in securing perpetrators; the inequity of outcome with convictions of only low-level Timorese militia; and the uncertainty of future funding or commitment to the serious crimes process once the United Nations withdrew.

5.8 Outcomes of the serious crimes process

International observers often note with approval the SCIU had filed 95 indictments with the Special Panels.[148] By the time the serious crimes process was concluded on 20 May 2005 in accordance with Security Council resolution 1543 (2004), the SCIU had recorded reports of 1,339 murders committed in East Timor in 1999. The Unit completed investigations that resulted in the indictment of 391 persons in relation to 684 murders, for which SCIU requested and obtained 285 arrest warrants. The Special Panels for Serious Crimes, consisting of both international and Timorese judges, conducted 55 trials involving 87 defendants, of whom 85 were found guilty. However, the number of murders for which indictments have been issued represents only about two-fifths of the number of killings committed in 1999. In addition, the 87 defendants tried before the Special Panels represent only a fraction of the number of individuals indicted, 303 of whom live in Indonesia and are therefore outside the territorial jurisdiction of Timor-Leste.[149]

JSMP notes that in comparison, by September 2003, ICTR had indicted 81 persons while in January 2004, the ICTY had indicted around 140 persons. This is despite a far greater amount of funding and time than the SCIU, and noting that while the SCIU has around 15 lawyers in total, the ICTY has approximately eight lawyers per case.[150] These numerical results give the impression of efficiency, but could equally tell another story, on closer reflection, about quality and time pressures. Given the issues with defence and appeals, the quality of the process overall in comparison to the international tribunals is very troubling, seen for example in poor reasoning in judgments, lack of reference to applicable law and correspondingly few examples of persuasive jurisprudence.

Overall, there remain outstanding 186 murder cases which have been investigated but for which no one has been indicted, and 469 additional murder cases for which investigations could not be conducted owing to the closure of the investigative arm of SCIU six months prior to the termination of the Unit as a whole.[151] Of these, there are 60 alleged cases of rape or gender-based crimes.[152]

Following the closure of the serious crimes process, the Government of East Timor has made further efforts to prosecute individuals indicted by SCIU but not tried. A number of suspects, including former militia members, have been arrested and charged for crimes alleged to have been committed in 1999, the most prominent being Manuel Maia in April 2006. Some Interpol processes are also continuing.[153]

These outcomes of the process require deeper examination. I argue below that the withdrawal of the United Nations backing for the serious crimes process represents the breaking of a promise for justice to these victims and their families.

5.9 The struggle for resources: the story behind the results

The Special Panel faced significant administrative and substantive difficulties until its closure.[154] It was not resourced properly by the United Nations. The task of setting up any kind of justice mechanism in East Timor was admittedly enormous. Infrastructure, including courthouses, had for the most part been burnt or otherwise destroyed. The court administration had collapsed and there were few Timorese with any professional experience to take on the roles of judges, prosecutors, defence counsel, court administrators and other positions necessary to the functioning of a judicial system. Seth Mydans of the *New York Times* described the 'modest beginnings' of the Dili District Court in 2001:

> And so the tiny courthouse in Dili – with its ill-prepared staff, its shortage of translators, its missing records, its lack of a court reporter or copy machine, its confused schedule and its inadequate budget – is for the moment the sole venue for justice for this ravaged country. Prosecutors misplace their indictments, the police misplace defendants who are free on bail and cases recess in midstream when foreign judges break for vacations.[155]

Even taking this into account, the operation of the SCIU and Special Panels were extremely disappointing until late 2003, with some serious injustices to defendants arising from the maladministration of the court procedures. Resource issues did not ease and there was continued uncertainty about the future of the SCIU and the Special Panels. For the first two years of operation, trials were subject to lengthy delays resulting from lack of capacity, poor administration and lack of organisational planning in the allocation of cases. During 2003 many of these difficulties were resolved, but then the United Nations cut back resources in May 2004 and withdrew in 2005.[156]

The United Nations budget provided for two Special Panels and the first began operating in January 2001. The initial delays arose in large part because the second Panel was not operational until November 2001 due to problems recruiting international judges. It appears to have been difficult to attract international judges with relevant legal background and experience to East Timor to sit on the Special Panels and in some case judges were employed who had only limited expertise or experience in the relevant fields of law.[157] The shortage of international judges – each Panel is comprised of one local and two international judges – meant that during 2002 the two Special Panels could not sit simultaneously. It was only in mid-2003 that the full complement of four internationally appointed judges was in place and both Panels were able to sit at the same time with the result that trials proceeded in a more timely fashion.[158]

The most crucial problem in terms of the overall justness of the trials was the parlous state of the Public Defenders Unit. The PDU did not have its own library, translators, investigators or budget for witness expenses such as travel and protection programmes. The Unit was so under-funded and inexperienced that it did not call a single witness in any of the first 14 trials.[159]

The lowest point for the serious crimes process appeared to be in 2001 when it was reported in the press that the SCIU was 'on the point of collapse'.[160] In January 2001, the United Nations sent a senior official from the International Criminal Tribunal in The Hague, Mary Fisk, to report on problems at the task force, dubbed by its own staff the 'not so serious crimes unit'.[161] Within a period of a fortnight in May 2001 there were three resignations including two senior investigators. There was no forensic pathologist for some months. One Australian Federal Police officer working at the unit was investigating on his own more than 300 individual homicides that occurred in Bobonaro and Ermera districts, including the murders of United Nations staff.[162]

Blame was laid on the Norwegian head of the unit, Mr Oyvind Olsen on the grounds that he had little understanding of the situation that existed in 1999 and was tardy in his support of prompt investigations of major crime scenes. Mr Olsen then resigned in 2001. His replacement, Norwegian prosecutor Siri Frigaard started with a negative opinion of the prospects of the trials. She said bluntly upon her arrival that there would be no international criminal tribunal and most of those indicted [before the Special Panels] would not turn up.[163]

In April 2003, Ms Frigaard finished her contract and left East Timor, telling the press:

> How many people were killed…the list is not 100% but we still have a list of 1310 people being killed. And so far we have only investigated only 40% of those. They will not have enough skills and enough people to take over the process. So I am worried about what is going to happen. I think in June 2004, I think that is a concern, and one internationals should look into because they [East Timor] need help.[164]

On 14 May 2004, the Security Council voted to extend the United Nations Mission in East Timor for six months, with another six-month extension after that, unanimously adopting Resolution 1543 (2004). The mandate of UNMISET was meant to concentrate on:

(i) support for the public administration and justice system of East Timor and for justice in the area of serious crimes;
(ii) support to the development of law enforcement in East Timor; and
(iii) support for the security and stability of East Timor.

Immediately prior to the United Nations' decision, Timorese civil society expressed concerns that the withdrawal of the United Nations as planned in May 2004 would have been, in JSMP's words, 'catastrophic' for the serious crimes process and would also jeopardise the reconciliation process in East Timor.[165]

Even with the United Nations' decision to postpone its withdrawal to 2005, those concerns remained. JSMP reported that the number of UNPOL investigators at the SCIU was scaled down from 23 to only eight investigators in December 2003 and United Nations Investigators were reduced from 13 to nine. Although the Deputy General Prosecutor for Serious Crimes stated that investigations were continuing and new cases were to be investigated, the investigation process was necessarily affected by the reduction in international staff, the complete closure of an SCIU office and the lack of trained Timorese staff to replace the scaled down international contingent.[166]

The question that lingers is why did the United Nations undertake the serious crimes process in East Timor with such obviously inadequate resources for so long? In 2001, Linton noted that 'Sadly, the weak and under-supported institutions are unable to meet such demands or guarantee the international standards that one would expect from a United Nations enterprise'.[167] In 2002, David Cohen wrote forcefully that the 'deeply flawed process' in East Timor made it clear that the United Nations 'should not proceed "on the cheap" so as to avoid the excessive expenditure of the ICTR and ICTY'. He asks the hard question whether a 'minimally credible tribunal' is better than none at all.[168] It is also debatable whether the expenses of the ICTY and ICTR are excessive, given the requirements of providing a fair trial. A former senior staff member, one of those staff who resigned in 2001, was quoted as saying that 'There is no doubt, in my mind, that we were not properly funded because they [the United Nations] did not want results'.[169] But why would the United Nations not want results? Suzannah Linton proposes one theory as to the poor resourcing and narrow decisions of the Court was that 'the Serious Crimes venture exists simply to be used as political leverage in dealing with Indonesia'.[170] If so, it did not work.

5.10 Indonesia's refusal to cooperate

The chances under the current Indonesian government of the indictees facing trial in East Timor in the foreseeable future were remote even in August 2003, according to the Office of the Deputy General Prosecutor for Serious Crimes.[171] The Indonesian government had publicly said that it would not cooperate with the Timorese government in bringing to trial persons against whom indictments have been presented to the Special Panels, specifically with regard to the seven military officers and one civilian official charged with senior command responsibility for crimes against humanity in the indictment for Deputy General Prosecutor for Serious Crimes Against Wiranto, Zacky Anwar Makarim, Kiki Syahnakri, Adam Rachmat Damiri, Suhartono Suratman, Mohammad Noer Muis, Yayat Sudrajat and Abilio José Osorio Soares, issued in February 2003. The Indonesian Foreign Minister, Dr Hassan Wirajuda, said that his government would 'simply ignore' the indictments, on the grounds that the United Nations had no mandate to try Indonesian citizens in East Timor.[172]

These comments reflect a longer standing reluctance by Indonesia to cooperate with the serious crimes process in East Timor. Prosecutors from Indonesia's Attorney General's Office travelled to East Timor several times and UNTAET investigators shared information with their Indonesian counterparts in accordance with the terms of the Memorandum of Understanding on legal cooperation signed with Indonesia's Attorney General in April 2000. Although the parties had agreed to provide legislative backing to the commitments they had made in the Memorandum of Understanding as necessary, vociferous challenges to the validity of the agreement by members of the TNI and nationalist politicians and lawyers in Indonesia limited its long-term usefulness, and the cooperation offered by UNTAET was never reciprocated. Indonesia has repudiated the Memorandum of Understanding on judicial cooperation signed with UNTAET in January 2000, on the grounds that it is not binding without ratification by the Indonesian parliament.[173] Letters rogatory issued by the SCIU were ignored.[174]

To date Indonesia has also been reluctant to respond to arrest warrants issued by Interpol against suspects indicted by the Prosecutor General in East Timor. As of the beginning of 2006, Interpol Red Notices had been obtained in relation to more than 40 individuals believed to be residing in Indonesia. Indonesia is a member of Interpol, but has no extradition treaty with or other effective cooperation on mutual legal assistance agreement with East Timor.[175] The Joint Truth and Friendship Commission final report recommends a number of measures, including an acknowledgement and an apology, but does not recommend handing over perpetrators to Timorese courts.[176]

5.11 Inequity of outcome with Indonesian perpetrators

Indonesia's refusal to cooperate meant that the serious crimes process was faced with the clear prospect of results open to criticism of selectivity. The inequity involved in bringing low-level, mainly illiterate militia members to trial in East Timor, while their commanders and high-level civilian and military officials have been acquitted in Indonesia, is clear and palpable. Perceptions of injustice or imperfect justice are reinforced by the disparities between the sentences handed down in Indonesia and those in East Timor. Suspects found guilty by the Special Panels in East Timor, most of whom are uneducated, low-level militia, have been sentenced to terms of imprisonment of up to 33 years and four months. In Indonesia, where officials and militia leaders widely regarded as bearing significant responsibility for orchestrating the crimes in East Timor were tried, the longest sentence handed down was ten years, but the actual time served was only four months.

The *Lolotoe* judgment represents the only real contribution to international jurisprudence on gender persecution from the East Timor processes, but even here JSMP was concerned:

> If the broad social purpose of the Lolotoe trial was to bring those primarily responsible to justice, then it has failed. Although Jhoni Franca, Sabino Leite and José Cardoso were rightly convicted of crimes against humanity, they were low level East Timorese perpetrators and were influenced by the highly coercive environment created by the Indonesian authorities. It seems an affront to common notions of justice that these low level perpetrators serve time while those most responsible avoid an impartial judicial process and live in impunity. Overall, it appears beneficial for victims and families that the three defendants have been punished for the crimes they committed in Lolotoe. Yet justice in the broader sense can only be served when people

such as 2nd Lt Bambang Indra and his superiors face an independent, impartial trial. Unless this occurs, accountability for the Lolotoe crimes cannot be fully established.[177]

5.12 Contribution of serious crimes process to the rule of law in East Timor

Due to the rigorous investigation of the root causes of the riots in Dili in mid-2006 by the Special Independent Commission of Inquiry for Timor-Leste, the United Nations itself has done some rare soul-searching and reflection on their efforts to restore the rule of law.[178] On 28 and 30 May 2006, the Office of the Prosecutor-General of Timor-Leste, which holds original serious crimes records and electronic servers, was ransacked in the course of general civil unrest in Dili.[179] As a result, among the priorities of the new 2006 UNMIT mission was assisting the Office of the Prosecutor General in resuming investigative functions of the former Serious Crimes Investigative Unit – the aim being to complete investigations into the serious human rights violations of 1999.[180]

Despite there never having been a proper consultative process on the serious crimes process, there is some evidence that victims' groups and Timorese NGOs consider the continued work of the SCIU vital to the reconciliation process and the future of East Timor. A crucial aspect of reconciliation in their view is determining the truth of the alleged crimes through an impartial judicial process. As one victim explained:

> How will the crimes against humanity and other crimes committed in 99 be figured out properly if the Serious Crimes Unit has to stop…[t]he closure of the Serious Crimes Unit means that no one, even East Timorese themselves, will ever know exactly the number of people [who] died as result of the 99 violence.[181]

Victims felt that a failure to investigate and prosecute alleged perpetrators, including those identified as low-level militia members, would possibly lead to revenge attacks, which may threaten the stability of the nation, the exact reversal of the realist 'destabilisation' argument against international law:

> Although they are just small fishes, it is important to know that letting them live together with the victims and their families who are still seeking justice is a danger as the community is still traumatized by the past atrocities.[182]

There are already signs that the lack of an effective mechanism to procure accused persons may be leading to vigilantism. According to the 2003 US Government *Country Reports on Human Rights Practices*, on 19 September 2003, an officer from the Border Protection Unit shot and killed a fugitive militia leader, Francisco Vegas Bili Atu, as he crossed into East Timor from West Timor.[183] While security forces claimed that the shooting was in self-defence, there were credible reports that excessive force may have been used. The SCIU had indicted Atu in February on seven counts of crimes against humanity, including three counts of murder, for his role in the 1999 conflict.

The necessity of continuing the serious crimes process has so far been rejected by the Timorese leadership. East Timor's Justice Minister, Domingos Maria Sarmento stated clearly that as East Timor has not got the money to continue the process in the absence of an international tribunal:

> I think to start the work of the Serious Crimes Unit, personally I think it will be difficult. The first thing is when UNMISET leaves East Timor, those international judges will be gone, and East Timor won't have the budget to recruit new international judges to replace them. And the second thing is there needs to be a special tribunal to proceed with all of the cases, all of the crimes that have been committed.[184]

Furthermore, in May 2008, the President commuted the sentences of and pardoned 94 persons by Presidential Decree 53 of 2008. The pardons and commutations were granted without any formal evaluation of the beneficiaries' conduct in prison or ability to reintegrate into society. Nine of these persons included SCIU cases such as militia commander Joni Marques and others responsible for Lospalos clergy killings in 1999, as well as those convicted for their role in the Passabe massacre. Some politicians and NGOs challenged the constitutionality and other legality of the president's actions.[185]

The decision to withdraw from the serious crimes process prematurely seemed to break the trust of Timorese citizens in the United Nations itself. Nelson Belo from JSMP makes this point clearly: 'We lose trust for the UN. When the campaign for the referendum UNAMET say that whatever going to happen in East Timor, UNAMET is not going to leave but in reality UNAMET left. And this one is going through the same things…'[186] This sentiment was reflected in statements by the departing Deputy Prosecutor Siri Frigaard that the United Nations should take responsibility for following the process through to its conclusion.

> Then of course the questions we are getting is but my husband was killed he is not on your victim list. Why haven't you indicted his killer. So people are still very occupied about it and they are telling their stories again and again like it was yesterday. So this is strong strong feeling among the people that they want the justice to be done. So I think somebody has to take that responsibility and do it.[187]

The relationship between the SCIU and the CAVR truth commission process was also left hanging at the closure of the SCIU. The CAVR Community Reconciliation Process was able to deal with the rehabilitation of people who had committed minor offences, but those who had committed serious crimes had to be referred to the SCIU. Those files are in limbo.

Conclusion

The Serious Crimes United Nations experiment in East Timor was largely a failure. There was a complex mixture of reasons for that failure, of which only the most pressing have been presented. Suzanne Katzenstein concludes that the weaknesses can:

> partly but not solely be attributed to inadequate resources and early policy decisions about staffing. A more complete explanation would need to account for, at a minimum, the failures of the capacity-building program and the barriers potentially arising from domestic politics and the UN.[188]

There are at least three complex consequences of such failure. The first most direct effect may be the loss of confidence of the Timorese people in the rule of law, as can be distilled from Xanana Gusmão's frustrated comments that opened this chapter. The second effect may be the distortion of the historical record of what happened in East Timor and who was responsible. The indictments of the SCIU set certain incidents on the record, and this has been an important contribution, but the judgments recorded will show a distorted view due to the inability to obtain any perpetrators in command responsibility roles.

The third effect may be the diminution of the credibility of United Nations transitional administrations and their ability to cope with the legal sector implementation issues.[189] As Strohmeyer has noted:

> The enormous difficulties encountered in Kosovo and East Timor in this respect have shown that the United Nations and the international community at large must enhance their rapid-response and coordination capacities so that the necessary attention and resources can be directed to this key area of civil administration.[190]

Strohmeyer has suggested some practical changes the United Nations should consider in missions subsequent to Timor, recommending six key prescriptions.[191] The prescriptions include the establishment of judicial ad hoc arrangements to facilitate the detention and subsequent judicial hearings on individuals who are apprehended on criminal charges by the quick deployment of units of military lawyers, as part of either a United Nations peacekeeping force or a regional military arrangement such as INTERFET, to fill the vacuum until the United Nations is staffed and able to take over.[192] A recommendation for interim justice systems is also made by the UNIFEM Expert Report.[193] This seems a sensible approach to rectify some of the delays that proved so difficult for the serious crimes process in Dili.

Strohmeyer advocates the need to establish adequate arrangements for the prosecution and trial of individuals involved in serious violations of international humanitarian and human rights law, which must be given due consideration in the planning and set-up phase of an operation, especially in post-conflict situations where the international community's initial involvement was governed by human rights concerns. He notes that adequate funding for these pivotal activities cannot be left to occasional voluntary contributions, but needs to be included in the regular mission budget.[194] These are all suggestions a strategic legal feminist should welcome.

The most striking thing about these recommendations is that the layperson might have imagined naively that these fundamentals would already be in place in a United Nations Mission of the kind in East Timor.[195] Yet the United Nations did not give the judicial sector the priority and resources it required to deal with the post-conflict situation. It also overlooks any traditional justice systems that may already be in place, therefore conceiving of only very thin conceptions of the rule of law.[196] Finally, the United Nations approach in Timor did not acknowledge that while establishing a legal sector might be an immediate priority, establishing a serious crimes process without proper political will, resources, consultation and planning may not be.

The special crimes process was therefore hamstrung from the outset. Suzanne Katzenstein has written that the hybrid model ‘endeavors to combine the strengths of the ad hoc tribunals with the benefits of local prosecutions’,[197] but its greatest risk is that it ‘may reflect the worst of both’ in the sense that limited resources and lack of expertise will produce flawed trials.[198] She concludes that while the model of a hybrid tribunal may eventually work, the risk has not paid off in East Timor and the country is currently ‘paying a high price for the possibility of improving justice elsewhere’, in future conflicts.[199]

Were the trials worth holding? The one jurisprudential breakthrough of rape as a crime against humanity does not outweigh the overall failure of the serious crimes process to acknowledge the needs of female survivors more generally. The narrative of trials such as the *Kasa* case does not do justice in any way to the suffering of Timorese women under the occupation and withdrawal of Indonesia, and did not meet expectations of feminist international lawyers hoping for progress in gender jurisprudence. In terms of their impact on women, the answer must be that the trials were mostly irrelevant to women. Even in this internationalised process, run by the United Nations, international law was actually rendered extremely marginal to the experience of gender violence in Timor. The two men will go on wearing the dead husband’s jacket in Maliana.

6 Women cut in half

The Commission for Reception, Truth-seeking and Reconciliation and the limits of restorative justice

> Yes, you in the back there, who are laughing and judging me. You who call me 'whore' behind my back. Today I will speak about what happened to me and maybe you will stop judging me.[1]

BEATRIZ GUTERRES SPEAKS – WOMEN AND THE CAVR

Beatriz Guterres was one of 14 East Timorese women invited to Dili by the Commission for Reception, Truth-seeking, and Reconciliation (Comissão de Acolhimento, Verdade e Reconciliação de Timor Leste or CAVR) to participate in the Commission's third national public hearing held on 28–29 April 2003 on the theme of Women and Conflict. The proceedings were broadcast on radio throughout the territory and published.[2] Beatriz told the nation her story:

> In 1991 [a] Kopassus soldier, Prada M, had duty in Lalerek Mutin. When my friends and I were in the rice field he shot in our direction. My friends pressured me so that I would become his wife in order to save myself. Because I was ashamed I stood and said, 'OK. I'll cut myself in half. The lower half I'll give to him, but the upper half is for my land, the land of Timor.' They said to me, 'Don't be afraid, don't run. You probably must suffer like this because your husband was murdered, whereas you are still alive...Our lives are the same.' Then Prada M. walked with me and I answered each of his questions only with, 'Ya'...I was just resigned to my fate. We lived as husband and wife and I had a child.[3]

Beatriz's story contains many common elements to other women's experiences of gender-based persecution during the Indonesian occupation of East Timor from 1975 to 1999. She was targeted by the Indonesian military due to her husband's political activities and interrogated. Her husband was murdered. Her child died due to illness and she was forced into 'marriage' and sexual servitude to three Indonesian soldiers over the following decade. She had two children and a miscarriage as a result and was abandoned by the soldiers. In an independent East Timor, Beatriz was then stigmatised by her own family and village, and her children were not accepted.[4]

Building on the discussion of theoretical frameworks for transitional justice regarding the limitations of international law in relation to transitional justice mechanisms, this chapter seeks to evaluate the CAVR overall, and address two particular issues which have critical implications for the rights and well-being of Timorese women in the newly independent state. One is the situation of women who bore children out of rape or sexual slavery during the occupation (defined here as forced maternity). Another is the drastic situation of domestic violence and assaults against women in Timorese society since 1999.

Neither of these phenomena received any attention as transitional justice issues in the mechanisms designed around the obligation to punish impose by international law. In this chapter, I argue that these factual situations show the importance of breaking down the public/private distinction in legal thought, and the need for evidence and documentation to break legal silences in transitional justice processes. The *Chega! Report* has been successful in acknowledging these issues in a transitional justice context. The Report is an important historical document which fulfils the truth-telling aim of transitional justice mechanisms.[5]

Is the mechanism of a truth commission better able to deliver a material benefit to women in a post-conflict society? In this chapter, I move beyond the impact of international law in the form of transitional justice trials to examine the more diffuse impact of international law norms upon truth commissions. In Chapter Three I introduced the establishment and operations of the Timorese truth commission, the CAVR. Restorative justice is designed to be victim-focused, and the CAVR was more successful than any other mechanism in Timor in involving, recognising and telling the truth about women as victims, mostly because women were better represented in its processes, and women with significant expertise in gender issues were in important leading roles. The CAVR's Community Reconciliation Process and Urgent Reparations programme were both innovative and important for the women it reached, as set out in Part One.

However, as presented in the second part, the CAVR faced some serious challenges from political factors outside its control, such as the tardy acceptance of the final report by the Timorese Government, and the failure of the concurrent UN serious crimes process and Jakarta trials. I also conclude that the obligation to punish gender-based crimes was in part 'traded' for the political outcome of encouraging militia to return from West Timor. Proper exclusion interviews were never conducted under the 1951 Refugee Convention by the UN refugee agency UNHCR,[6] which may have prevented those individuals who had committed war crimes from being considered refugees deserving of protection in West Timor at all. This is only barely acknowledged in the *Acolhimento* section of the *Chega! Report* (roughly translated as 'reception'). The realist view of transitional justice, that law has no place or is mere puffery is important to consider in this section. The chapter also highlights some of the problems faced by women due to the design of complementary mechanisms to prosecution strategies to comply with international law.

Some of the theoretical ideas about 'representation' of women are highlighted in the third section. The *Chega! Report* succeeds in showing some gender-dimensions of the violence, and presents evidence of forced maternity in East Timor, and what has happened to women in this situation in the independence era. Instead of heroes, the report shows that women like Beatriz are treated as collaborators with the Indonesians.

However, although the report as a whole dealt very well with issues of economic social and cultural rights, the role of women is seen primarily through the lens of victims of sexual violence. Forced maternity is treated as a consequence of the crime of rape or sexual slavery, not as a crime in its own right. The status of forced maternity under international law is examined in this section, in its own right and as a component of genocide. I argue that it is important to treat forced maternity as *sui generis*, different to genocide. The evidence suggests that the categorisation function of international law has so far failed in relation to forced maternity.

Finally, the *Chega! Report* makes special mention of domestic violence in relation to Recommendation 4 on women, linking the issue in post-conflict Timor to gender persecution during the occupation. The fourth section considers the evidence of 'ordinary' domestic violence in Timor, and the CAVR acknowledgement of this violence as a transitional justice issue. The case of Dr Sergio Lobo is given as an illustration of a conflict between the needs of elite men in a newly independent state and justice for women. The status of domestic violence under international law is examined in this section. There is no existing evidence about whether recognition of the issue under the CAVR process contributed to the prevention of domestic violence. Generally though, the poor treatment of women in the formal justice sector since independence is evidence of the 'changing the curtains' phenomenon.

6.1 Gender issues in the *Chega! Report*

Vasuki Nesiah reports on a survey of truth commissions that the 'truth' they tell about legacies of human rights abuse suggests that 'truth *is* gendered; in terms of the truth that it describes, the truth telling process it sets up, the truth tellers who come forward'.[7] Feminist theorists have noted the difficulty of women telling truth commissions about their own stories. Fionnuala Ni Aolain and Catherine Turner identify three serious gender biases in the truth-telling function of truth commissions: first, the general lack of a gender dimension in examining the range of harms in a conflict;[8] second, a focus only on sexual violence when harms against women are considered;[9] and third, the omission of 'ordinary' or routine violence, especially socio-economic harm experienced by women in conflict due to their gendered roles.[10] The failure of truth commissions to fully integrate women's experiences is troubling on a practical level as it may restrict women's entitlement to additional forms of legal redress[11] but also on a symbolic level because it leads to a distorted historical record of 'truth'.[12] Some of these problems have been avoided by the CAVR process due to conscious inclusion of gender in its mandate, but some evidence of these gender biases can be observed.

UNTAET Regulation 2001/10 established the Commission as an independent authority with a mandate to investigate violations of international law from 1974 to 1999. The CAVR had three core programmes: truth-seeking, community reconciliation, and reception and victim support. Annexe A to Chapter Two on the mandate of the Commission clearly sets out the international law principles the CAVR relied upon in dealing with violations of women's rights with special reference to sexual slavery.[13] The sources of international law relied on for this interpretation includes international human rights treaties; jurisprudence, especially from the ICTY; and General Comments from the Human Rights Committee.[14] Rape is expressly listed as a possible basis for crimes against humanity, as a form of torture and a war crime.[15]

Accordingly, the Chega! Report has succeeded in documenting important aspects of the involvement of women in the East Timor conflict, by focusing on human rights violations against women during and after the conflict period that have implications for transitional justice outcomes and the way in which the gendered experience of women in conflict is acknowledged (or not). The special hearing on 'Women and Conflict' and the resulting Chapter 7.7 of the report focusing exclusively on the experience of gender-based persecution make important contributions to knowledge about women's experience of armed conflict. In one of its key findings, the Report claims: 'Rape, sexual slavery and sexual violence were tools used as part of the campaign designed to inflict a deep experience of terror, powerlessness and hopelessness upon pro-independence supporters.'[16] Recommendation 4 duly sets out a wide range of measures to secure justice for Timorese women. Several of these recommendations reference international law, such as 4.1.3 which recommends that crimes against humanity and war crimes committed in Timor Leste that involved sexual violence against women and girls are excluded from any amnesty provisions, in accordance with UN Security Council Resolution 1325 on Women, Peace and Security (Par. 11, S/Res/1325 2000). Recommendation 4.1.8 calls for harmonisation of Timor Leste laws with the United Nations Convention on the Elimination of All Forms of Discrimination Against Women (CEDAW).[17]

Overall, the CAVR recommends a range of measures to secure justice for past atrocities, including renewing the mandate of the Special Panels, but, in line with a legalist approach, also requests that:

> The United Nations and its relevant organs, in particular the Security Council, remains seized of the matter of justice for crimes against humanity in Timor Leste for as long as necessary, and be prepared to institute an International Tribunal pursuant to Chapter VII of the UN Charter should other measures be deemed to have failed to deliver a sufficient measure of justice and Indonesia persists in the obstruction of justice.[18]

6.2 Representation of women in CAVR processes

Was the focus on women in the Final Report achieved by meaningful representation of women in its processes? The CAVR process made a conscious attempt to be inclusive of women from its inception. As John Braithwaite states, '[f]or informal justice to be restorative justice, it has to be about restoring victims, restoring offenders, and restoring communities as a result of participation of a plurality of stakeholders'.[19]

The initial Steering Committee held extensive public consultations and reported that many women survivors of rape supported the idea of a commission with a truth-seeking function.[20] Section 4 of Regulation 2001/10 provided for the Transitional Administrator to appoint between five and seven National Commissioners, at least 30 per cent of whom should be women, on the advice of a Selection Panel that included representatives of the major political parties and civil society groups. Two of the seven National Commissioners, (Maria Olandina Isabel Caeiro Alves and Isabel Amaral Guterres) and ten of the 29 Regional Commissioners were women. Internal recruitment staff policies provided that a minimum of 30 per cent of positions must be filled by women. The CAVR actively tried to recruit women as statement takers and victim support staff, to ensure that nationally women had equal access to the CAVR's work and to acknowledge women's experiences during the conflict. Finally, the Mission Statement for the CAVR also included the principle that:

> ...acknowledged the importance of ensuring that women played a major role in the reconciliation process. This entailed that women should be recruited to the Commission and that female community members should be able to participate in its activities. The Commission recognised the existence of practical, cultural and economic barriers to women's participation, which it would strive to overcome.[21]

However, the Final Report states that despite this commitment the Commission did not succeed in reaching its recruitment targets for women. Only two of the eight members of the Senior Management Team were women. Just one of the six Regional Coordinators was a woman and all 13 District Team Coordinators were men.

The Report states:

> Cultural norms that were particularly strong in regional and rural Timor Leste made it difficult to recruit the desired proportion of women into district teams. The need for staff members to live away from home during the three-month period of field activities in subdistricts other than their own posed particular difficulties for women who had family responsibilities.[22]

'Cultural barriers' included being confined to the home, and being too shy to speak, especially about their own experience: '[m]any men came forward to give statements about human rights violations against female family members, but many women testified about what had happened to their fathers, brothers, husbands or sons during the conflict.'[23] In fact, the majority of violations reported by women related to extrajudicial killings of their male relatives and the impact this made on their lives.[24] The CAVR developed a number of creative methods to try to overcome these barriers, other than the recruitment drive described.[25] For example, the process included many sessions at the community level where women could have the opportunity to speak to female workers in women-only sessions.[26] In organising the household mortality survey, the CAVR included at least one woman in each team who conducted an interview with at least one adult female in the household, in order to try to 'triangulate' findings on gender persecution.[27]

However, despite these efforts the CAVR collected only 1,642 statements from women from an overall total of 7,668 statement from witnesses or victims of human rights violations, representing 21.4 per cent of all statements gathered during the 18 months of operations.[28] Additionally, 260 statements regarding violations reported by women were received as a submission from a women's NGO.[29] A total of 3,482 men and 1,384 women were involved in village-level participatory discussions on human rights violations held in 284 villages in more than 60 sub-districts. Sessions held specifically for women were conducted in 22 of these villages. The Commission's research team conducted more than 200 interviews with witnesses and victims of sexual violence.[30] In comparison, 28 per cent of deponents to the Sierra Leone Truth Commission were women, and 54.8 per cent of deponents to the South African Truth Commission were women.[31] But this does represent a qualitatively higher proportion of women participants than the tiny number involved in the prosecution processes in the Dili and Jakarta trials.

6.3 Women and reparations at the CAVR

In their testimony at the 'Women and Conflict National Public Hearing' in April 2003, Timorese women implored:

> Don't just drive around in your big new cars, or fly around the world. In villages in all thirteen districts there are so many widows and orphans. I ask you to do something to help them in their daily lives.[32]

This was a plea for the CAVR to do more than 'change the curtains', even if the victimhood of women was better recognised than in the Dili and Jakarta trials. The Urgent Reparations Program and final recommendation for a gender-focus in official reparations at least represented an attempt to address the inadequacy of international legal remedies that provide long-term, financial and practical assistance for women, and in many ways were quite innovative.[33]

In its Urgent Reparations Program, the CAVR identified killing, disappearance, detention, torture, rape and other forms of sexual violence as harms or crimes to be addressed by special assistance because of their severity and the longevity of their impact.[34] The Program provided monetary compensation to victims, actively referred victims to existing services, conducted healing workshops, provided funds to local organisations to provide services to these persons and, as a pilot study, implemented a collective reparations programme delivered in conjunction with three NGOs. In total, approximately US$160,000, or approximately 3 per cent of the CAVR's total three-year operational budget, was earmarked for the programme. By the end of its operations, the CAVR had provided urgent reparations in the form of cash grants of US$200 each to 516 men (73%) and 196 women (23%); 322 of these men (77%) and 95 of these women (23%) also received home visits and care by local NGOs; 156 victims – 82 women (52%) and 74 men (47%) – also participated in a total of six healing workshops.[35]

The percentage of women identified as beneficiaries of the Urgent Reparations Program (23%) was consistent with the rate of women's participation in the statement-taking process (21.4%). Wandita and collaborators conclude that because potential beneficiaries were initially identified by statement-takers, the obstacles women faced in accessing the statement-taking process were the same as the problems they faced in accessing the Urgent Reparations Program.[36] These included the cultural barriers described above, limited access to information regarding the CAVR's activities, and the common notion that the men already represented the families' experiences of the conflict.[37] But for at least 196 women then, a Timorese transitional justice mechanism at last provided a material benefit.

The CAVR also proposed a national reparations programme for Timor Leste in its overall recommendations. This proposal, included as Recommendation 12 of the CAVR's Final Report, was presented by the President to Parliament on 28 November 2005. The CAVR urged the Parliament to interpret Article 11 of the Constitution ('valorisation of resistance') to assist all those who contributed to independence and their dependents to include victims of past atrocities on all sides of the conflict and recommended a gender quota stating that '[a]t least 50% of resources in this program shall be earmarked for female beneficiaries'.[38]

The recommendation specifically includes single mothers. Wandita *et al.* explain that without forcing women to identify the group to which they belonged, this designation covered all mothers who were not legally married, whose partner was killed or disappeared, or who were victims of sexual violence and bore children out of the rape. Single mothers would be provided with a scholarship for their school-aged children until they turn 18 years old which acts as an incentive for access to other services such as counselling, peer support, livelihood skills training, and access to micro-credit for livelihood activities.[39]

While this recommendation is welcome and represents a creative attempt to address the material situation of women, the next section examines why the reparations recommendation from the CAVR report may not be accepted by the Timorese Government and therefore be of only symbolic significance. It also does little to change the role of women from victims to heroes. Finally, dealing with forced maternity only as a consequence of crime shows limitations in the categorisation impact of international law. The question of why forced maternity should be seen as a crime itself is examined in the third section.

6.4 Women and the Community Reconciliation Process

The CAVR Community Reconciliation Process (CRP) programme began in August 2002 and ran until March 2004.[40] The CRP represented an attempt to use traditional justice methods to mediate between returnees and communities where there were no serious crimes involved. People involved in 'serious crimes' had to be referred to the SCIU (see Chapter Five). In total, 1,371 minor offenders completed the CRP process. The SCIU considered 1,542 statements from deponents wishing to participate in the CRP and decided to exercise its jurisdiction in respect of 90 suspects. Eighteen of these 90 persons eventually were indicted. Five suspects were referred back to the CRP. Sixty-seven suspects were not indicted or were referred back to the CRP.[41] The International Center for Transitional Justice noted that 'These persons were declared to be ineligible to participate in a CRP under the regulations, but they ultimately were left outside the serious crimes regime as a result of "time and resource constraints"'.[42] This may in time impact on the acceptance of the CAVR processes, which were always designed to be in tandem with the serious crimes process.[43] JSMP reported that '[t]he perception is that those most responsible live comfortably, and with impunity, whether in West Timor or in Timor-Leste'.[44]

The CRP represents a credible effort to include and strengthen the indigenous justice system (*adat* in Bahasa or *lisan* in Tetum) still extant in Timor after the occupation.[45] This is an emerging trend in transitional justice processes and has much to recommend it in terms of speed, expense and legitimacy.[46] However, the vast majority of both deponents and victims in the CRP process were male.[47] The predominant reason given for this was that there was not time in the process to overcome the various barriers to women's participation.[48] Even if women had participated, the CRP process may not have offered much to women. Timorese women leaders have suggested that traditional justice processes are so discriminatory in their practice and outcomes in relation to disputes such as domestic violence that they deserved to be rejected.[49] This criticism is explored further below in relation to the use of *adat* in domestic violence disputes.

NEGATIVE ASPECTS OF THE CAVR PROCESS FOR WOMEN

Many of the negative aspects of the CAVR process for women that I identify in this section flow not from its processes per se but the politics around the Commission which were beyond its control. The three main issues of concern that I identify are the political decision to expedite returnees from West Timor, the failure of the serious crimes process and the lack of political acceptance of the final report. In these processes we can see the exclusion of women from the decision-making processes and little consideration of the impact of the decisions on women and children.

6.5 The 'reception' function of the CAVR

A novel aspect of the CAVR mandate compared to most truth commissions was to focus on the reception of up to 85 thousand refugees from West Timor (part of Indonesia), displaced or forcibly deported during the 1999 violence, especially during the month of September. The UN found that most of these refugees were forcibly evacuated by armed militia and Indonesian troops. The approximately

250,000 refugees who fled or were forcibly evacuated to West Timor were accommodated in several large refugee camps, such as Noelbaki, Tuapukan and Naibonat in Kupang, two camps in Kefamenanu as well as about 200 other smaller camps or shelters. They represented about one-third of East Timor's population at the time.[50]

The UN refugee agency UNHCR had a presence in Kupang from May 1999 to try to provide emergency relief and protection to the refugees, and coordinate returnees to East Timor.[51] UNHCR's efforts were hampered by Indonesian soldiers and East Timorese militia, who tightly controlled the refugees' movement in and out of these camps, as well as their access to humanitarian aid.[52] Conditions in the camps were very difficult, both in terms of living standards and human rights standards.[53] Refugees returned to East Timor in phases, with 60,000 still remaining when the CAVR began its mandate in 2002. Many had been supporters of integration before the Popular Consultation and some had been active members of the militia in their communities.

After the referendum violence, then President Xanana Gusmão felt that the first priority should be securing East Timor's stability and literally rebuilding the new nation, which required the majority of the population in the West Timor camps (including the former militia leaders) to return. Gusmão believed the former militias would pose less of a threat back in Timor.[54] While there were debates about this strategy, in the end militia were encouraged to return with the understanding that those responsible for serious crimes would be prosecuted at a later date once the judicial system was up and running. UNTAET's Chief of Staff, in close cooperation with Xanana Gusmão, and with the full endorsement of the Special Representative of the Secretary General, took the lead on pursuing this approach from October 2000 onwards. Some of Gusmão's strategies, notably the 'wining and dining' of militia leaders in expensive Dili restaurants, were controversial within various parts of the UN mission.[55]

The problem was that some of these militia were almost certainly involved with violence and forced deportations during 1999 and ongoing violations of women and children in West Timor camps. The head of the UNHCR office Bernard Kerblat informed the world that refugees were in 'a hostage-like situation, with women and children tightly controlled by extremist elements'.[56] The most well-known example of a person in this situation was Juliana dos Santos, kidnapped as a 'war prize' at age 16 by Egidio Manek, the deputy leader of the notorious Laksaur militia after a massacre in the Suai church. Under the 1951 Refugee Convention, persons who fulfil the definition of a refugee under Article 1A can be excluded from that status if there are serious reasons that person could be found 'not deserving of international protection' under Article 1F. These reasons include having committed war crimes or crimes against humanity, serious non-political crimes, or acts contrary to the purposes and principles of the UN.[57] Armed combatants are meant to be separated from civilian asylum-seekers.[58]

However, one of the reasons the full extent of the treatment of women in the camps is not known, not even by the CAVR process, is due to this political policy of encouraging returns, even of excludable militia. Even where protection interviews were undertaken, UNHCR focused on a very gendered idea of 'protection needs'. As the guidelines for the reception of returnees from West Timor indicated,

> Persons who might face protection problems are: those suspected of past criminal militia activities, those formerly affiliated to militia groups, persons who were active in the pro-autonomy movement, former TNI, former POLRI, former civil servants, persons belong to an ethnic or religious minority group or persons married to such a person.[59] [*sic*]

Most of these criteria were assumed to apply principally to men, and there were relatively few female interviewers.[60]

The UNHCR evaluation report states:

> The structure of the assessment forms and the assumptions which framed them, the gender of the interviewers and their lack of training all meant that a number of issues relating to women's and children's needs and vulnerabilities – which would have been much more relevant to the majority of returnees – were not picked up in any systematic fashion. This was despite reports that sexual violence was a serious concern in the camps in West Timor. 'The emphasis on identifying such militia involvement in the assessment process thus seems disproportionate'.[61]

The *Chega! Report* is almost silent on this larger context, but adds that the attitudes of female refugees to voluntary return and reconciliation issues were also not well known.

At paragraphs 71–72 of Part 10, the *Chega! Report* states:

> Women were especially constrained in their freedom to engage with the NGO Coalition by the power structures that existed within the camps. The positions women took on reconciliation and repatriation were almost entirely determined by their husbands, fathers and uncles who had brought them to West Timor. They were economically and physically dependent on these male figures, who often both intimidated them and acted as their ultimate protection from other men.
>
> …The NGO Coalition thought that there were several factors explaining women's limited participation. One was East Timorese patriarchal culture, in which the woman's role does not extend beyond the family. Reconciliation was seen as a political issue to be dealt with by men. Women also generally had lower levels of education and poorer health than men, as well as often being the victims of physical and psychological abuse.[62]

The combination of the political imperative to receive refugees back from West Timor by the Timorese leadership, with the gendered application of protection needs by UNHCR, mean that the violence perpetrated against women in West

Timor is still little known. This context is not acknowledged by the Final Report in its summary of the 'reception' function of the CAVR, although some examples of women returning from West Timor are included in the reconciliation hearings:

> The young woman asked the gathering if she could present her one-year-old baby. The audience cried out, 'Yes, please!' and her one-year-old child was brought on stage by her aunt. Named after a former UN High Commissioner for Human Rights, who visited the young woman and other Suai women survivors in 2000, her child is truly a symbol of healing and human rights in Timor-Leste.[63]

The discussion of the *Kasa* case in Chapter Five clearly shows how this silence was compounded by the finding that the serious crimes process had no jurisdiction over crimes committed in West Timor. The situation of refugees in West Timor represents almost a complete failure of international protection.[64] Why was this failure allowed to occur?

Partly it is because where there has been significant displacement of the population, in theory, states should tailor their transitional justice processes to reflect the needs of that population, but this has rarely occurred and did not occur in Timor.[65] UNHCR does take an interest in rule of law and transitional justice issues but they are not part of its core mandate of refugee protection.[66] UNHCR also attempts to focus on protecting female refugees from gender-based violence.[67] In concert with a UN Transitional Administration, one would expect that this part of the UNHCR mandate would have been easier to fulfil. For a series of complex operational and political reasons, it was not possible. The UN itself became a victim in West Timor when several UNHCR staff were murdered in Atambua in September 2000, leading to the complete withdrawal of humanitarian actors.[68]

6.6 Political distance from the Timorese Government

The second realist challenge faced by the CAVR process was the less than enthusiastic response the Final Report received from the Timorese leadership. The factual findings of the *Chega! Report* do not seem to be problematic or shocking to the Timorese. East Timor's Ambassador to the UN, José Luis Guterres, stated that the allegations are not surprising: 'It's well known and it was, during the time, it was already used by resistance leaders to explain about the situation in East Timor and so it's nothing for the entire population, it is not new.'[69]

Two key recommendations of the report however, led to long delays in the release of the report, and as of June 2009, no detailed debate in the Timorese Parliament.[70] The report was leaked to media outlets in January 2006 and termed a 'grenade lobbed into a flammable international arena'.[71] First, as mentioned above, the CAVR calls for a formal reparations programme, funded by both Indonesia and the Government of East Timor for victims of torture, rape and violence perpetrated by Indonesia from its invasion in 1975 to its withdrawal in 1999.

When tabling the report, then President Gusmão told the Parliament that the Commissioners possessed 'grandiose idealism' and that the recommendation on reparations was 'seriously concerning' because it 'does not take into account the situation of political anarchy and social chaos that could easily erupt if we decided to bring to court every crime committed since 1975'.[72]

Second, the *Chega! Report* calls on countries that supported Indonesia's 1975 invasion to compensate the victims. The Government of Timor has also rejected the CAVR recommendation that Australia, Britain and the United States pay compensation for their part in Indonesia's 24-year occupation of East Timor. José Ramos-Horta, East Timor's then foreign minister stated:

> For me, and for my President, and my government as a whole, it's out of the question that we would even raise this issue with these countries – we will not. It would be undiplomatic, it would not be fair, it would be showing a lack of gratitude, lack of statesmanship, a lack of maturity.[73]

The CAVR, itself, has tried to remain impartial. The commission's president Aniceto Guterres stated publicly: 'I just would like to say that the report was from everybody involved in the CAVR process. So the most important thing is that the report returns to all East Timorese. But CAVR itself is not insisting it.'[74]

The momentum for fulfilling the recommendations of the *Chega! Report* has to some extent been overtaken by the Joint Truth and Friendship Commission with Indonesia, although it is widely seen as a sham. The Timorese National Parliament was supposed to hold an extraordinary plenary session in October 2008 to debate these two important reports. A Timorese Parliamentary Committee presented two resolutions to the Parliament that according to the Committee's press release 'recognize the achievements of both Commissions, acknowledge their findings, and propose implementation of their recommendations'. The proposed resolutions highlighted CAVR and CTF recommendations in the areas of victim reparations, a commission for disappeared persons, justice, education and the establishment of an independent institution to oversee implementation efforts.

The formal reaction of the Parliament when the debate finally came on was reduced to a vote to postpone the debate, perhaps indefinitely. Interviewed on Televizaun Timor-Leste on 9 October, President José Ramos-Horta said 'recommendations are only recommendations and are not obligations for the Government and the Parliament to follow them'.[75]

6.7 Failure of the serious crimes process

Women did not participate in the CAVR processes expecting them to be the only justice mechanism ever made available to them. The snapshot of 50 women's views examined by Wandita and their collaborators on possible recommendations for the CAVR report showed an almost unanimous support for judicial proceedings against perpetrators.[76] This aspect of the CAVR is examined in detail in Chapter Six.

FORCED MATERNITY IN EAST TIMOR: A FAILURE OF CATEGORISATION

The CAVR process became the only transitional justice mechanism to mention the issue of forced maternity. Given the events of 1999, the forcible deportation of women and the allegations of rape in the camps of West Timor, the issue of gender-based violence as part of genocidal intent deserves to be properly explored. I argue forced maternity should be seen as a violation in its own right, with the woman as subject, but also with knowledge it may also be a violation with genocidal aspects. Judith Gardam's theoretical ideas that the feminist categorisation project in relation to international humanitarian law should not be considered closed has been borne out by this examination of forced maternity. The proper analysis of the number, situation and rights of children born of rape in Timor is also important to assess as a transitional justice issue.

Forced maternity is the act of a forcibly impregnated woman giving birth to a child of rape.[77] Although the *Chega! Report* as a whole focuses on economic, social and cultural rights in a comprehensive manner, the chapter on women retains the limited script of sexual violence. Corey Levine describes this narrow focus of the women's hearing in Chapter 7.7.

> [D]uring the Women and Conflict Public Hearing process not one woman was asked to speak about all the other suffering that the women experienced because of their gender – their culturally assigned roles, responsibilities and their unequal access to economic survival, political participation and the basic necessities of survival. The hearing never heard from women amputees who lost a limb to a landmine while scouring the neighbourhood for fuel and the fallout from that experience. No women shared their stories of the forced displacement they endured while being solely responsible for the survival of their children, their sick relatives and their elderly parents. No woman spoke of the daily beatings she suffered at the hands of her husband because of the heightened tensions and violence that existed in their community and which was then replicated in the home. No woman spoke of how she was denied sanitary products when she was detained in prison and how degrading this was to her. No woman spoke of how she was not able to access medical care due to checkpoints, harassment, lack of documentation, lack of money, lack of childcare and so lost the baby she was carrying.[78]

Even within the focus of sexual violence, the unfinished feminist categorisation project of international law means that some issues receive the wrong emphasis. Although the report deals with forced maternity and forced abortions, these are seen as consequences of the crime of sexual violence, not as violations of international law in their own right. This section will examine the evidence of forced maternity in East Timor and assess the outcomes in the post-independence period for women survivors. The analysis of forced maternity is important for three main reasons. The first reason relates to the well-being of the subjects of the *Chega! Report*. It is crucial for the women involved that their situation be acknowledged even if their personal privacy is protected, as they have suffered at least three times – first from the initial violation of rape, second from the forced pregnancy, and third from their ostracism or discrimination by their communities, which leaves them vulnerable to further abuse. For example, women and children in this situation could be vulnerable to forced prostitution and trafficking.[79] It is a crucial inquiry for the child, who requires financial support, a name, extended family, an identity and sense of belonging to a community and citizenship rights. Finally it is important research for East Timor, to avoid any generational conflict, integrate the families into Timorese society again and find a transitional justice process that is durable and inclusive. In the end, it could be that by giving status to these women and children the Government will be better able to achieve its goal of economic survival in a sustainable manner.

6.8 Evidence of forced maternity and forced birth control

If conclusive statistical data on rape in East Timor is difficult to find even in the *Chega! Report*, there is no data at all on how many children have been born of rape, or how many 'orphans' there are in East Timor at the present time.[80] However, anecdotal evidence points to perhaps hundreds or even thousands of 'war babies' who have been kept and raised by their mothers, despite stigmatisation and the rejection of these women and children by their families or villages. Some individual examples of forced maternity in Timor can be cited, one of the earliest being contained in a report to the UN Special Rapporteur in 1997,[81] but a full study has never been undertaken. As in the cases of sexual slavery of East Timorese women during the period 1975–99, children were born to women raped during or after the forced displacement. Sian Powell gives an example from the camps in an article entitled 'East Timor's Children of the Enemy' published in *The Weekend Australian* on 10 March 2001.

> His mother is Lorenca Martins, now 23, a wistful East Timorese woman with eyes only for her child. His father is Maximu, a militia thug and rapist. Maximu raped Martins in a refugee camp near Atambua, over the border in West Timor, where she was exiled for six months. A member of the notorious Besi Merah Putih gang (Red and White Iron), he first violated her on December 8, 1999, in broad daylight, in the jungle. 'It happened to many women (in the camps),' she says. 'If they saw a beautiful woman, they just took her.'…A child of the new nation of East Timor, five-month-old Rai, is much loved by his mother. He is one of the first generation born free, yet his past will imprison him.[82]

Rai is one of an unverifiable number of children born as a result of both the systematic sexual slavery and forced marriage of women under the occupation, as well as the mass rapes of the 1999 post referendum violence.[83]

Although no systematic attention has been given to their status and rights relative to other children affected by the political violence in East Timor, anecdotal evidence suggests such children are both at risk of abandonment to orphanages, and likely to experience ostracism and impoverishment if kept by their mothers, due to the mothers' low social status in post-independence East Timorese society. There may also have been children born from consensual relationships between Indonesian soldiers and East Timorese women – it is not known whether these women and their children suffer ostracism as a result. There is contradictory evidence regarding the relative likelihood of child abandonment due to forced maternity in East Timor.[84] The article by Powell suggests that 'No one who works with raped women in East Timor can recall a single instance of a woman abandoning a child because it is the product of rape',[85] but there is one example given in the *Chega! Report*.[86] There is anecdotal evidence of close identification with, and loving acceptance of, the children by their mothers, despite the extremely traumatic circumstances of conception.[87]

To give one example from the *Chega! Report*, the Indonesian military routinely targeted the wives of guerrilla leaders to monitor any communications with the husbands in the mountains and to compromise the women as 'unfaithful' wives, thereby isolating them from community support.[88] This is described in the report as 'proxy violence'. Even the first wife of Xanana Gusmão, Emilia Baptista Gusmão bore a child by an Indonesian army officer after one of the many interrogations she was put through to try to influence Gusmão to surrender. The child died and even after she had been forced to flee Timor for Australia and her relationship with Gusmão had broken down, Emilia said publicly that she would carry the grief of the dead child all her life 'because that child was my child'.[89]

This willingness and ability to attach to children conceived under such circumstances, rather than to define them as 'of the enemy', may be explained by the low status of Timorese women and the fact that status may only proceed from motherhood in some circumstances.[90] However, comparative work should establish how representative these anecdotes are of the population and to what extent they reflect instead the particular media framing of this conflict.

Despite some East Timorese survivors' preference for keeping their babies born of rape, it is nonetheless clear that numerous children of rape have been abandoned by their mothers. A nun, Sister Maria, is quoted whispering to a journalist 'a truth openly voiced in East Timorese society', that in a Catholic orphanage: '[m]ost of the children are mixed race, the babies of women raped by Indonesian soldiers.' She notes that in the early years following the Indonesian invasion, orphanages were filled with 'genuine' orphans: so many adults had been killed in military operations. Another complicating factor is that 'genuine' orphans (the children of dead Timorese parents) generally are not treated well by ordinary Timorese; for example, many families take one on to work as a house slave. Now, most are children of rape. 'One young woman I knew had four babies, I kept asking her why this had happened again and she just said there was nothing she could do.'[91]

6.9 Impact of forced maternity

The *Chega! Report* is particularly good at detailing the gendered consequences of the sexual violence in the occupation, leading to stigmatisation and ostracism.[92] This builds on the finding of the UN Special Rapporteurs' report in 1999:

> Many of the women who were raped as virgins are single mothers who have suffered stigma in their communities after giving birth to children of Indonesian soldiers...Some of these children are the result of rapes, others are the product of a situation that resembles sexual slavery and some are the result of consensual sex...The women are having a very difficult time, not only because of poverty, but because the sight of these children often reminds them of rape.[93]

Coomaraswamy's report concluded that the Indonesian state should take responsibility for these children but no action has been taken to this end.[94] This has resulted in a conceptual gap in the transitional justice mechanisms in East Timor, as well as a lack of appropriate programming attention by civil society actors.

Media reports confirm that the 'victims of militia rape and sex slavery continue to bear the scars of post-ballot violence in East Timor, facing ostracism on their return home'.[95] Abuelda Alves of the Timorese NGO FOKUPERS said bluntly of the women who are able to return home, often with babies who are the product of rape: 'They are viewed as rubbish. Their families are embarrassed. Women who were already married, their husbands reject them.'.[96] In this context, the extremely low level of reporting rates by Timorese women, especially those returning from forced deportation to the West Timor camps is unsurprising.[97] Generally women will only speak to nuns or priests, or as lawyers assisting Timorese asylum-seekers have noted, they will not speak to anyone at all.[98]

The pervasiveness of the stigma against rape survivors and their children in East Timorese society is demonstrated by the euphemistic language associated with the issue. According to the translator's notes for the book *Buibere*, Timorese people 'speak in hints' and there is not a clear Timorese word for rape. When used regarding women, the Portuguese words *violacáo* (violation) or *estraga* (damaged or destroyed) are used. The implication is that 'victims of rape have had their whole sexuality, their "womanhood" damaged, and they will never be the same again'.[99]

Karen Campbell-Nelson's interpretation of the situation for Beatriz in Case Study Two above points to a complicated matrix of sacrificing the individual for the protection of the group and scapegoating by her peers:

> Politically-motivated violence became so distorted that a beating or being shot at was interpreted, correctly it seems, as a soldier's interest in a Timorese woman. Such was the distortion that Beatriz's own community treated her as the village's scapegoat, turning her into a sexual sacrifice to mitigate violence against the larger community. The community logic seemed to be that if military violence could be limited to the women they abused (to Beatriz) it would not so easily spill over into broader attacks on the residents of Lalerek Mutin.

> But once Beatriz 'fell' she became more vulnerable, not only to repeated incidents of forced marriage, but also to community perceptions that this was her fate.
>
> The tendency to blame the victim is nothing new. However, in the context of political violence in Lalerek Mutin this tendency was used to explain away the disappearance of Beatriz's husband as well as to accept her forced marriages as judgment for her simply being alive. They knew Beatriz suffered. Yet they saw her suffering as fate or divine judgment rather than a violation of her rights and in this way deflected blame from themselves and others who did not rally to Beatriz's defense, but indeed pressured her to accept the violations.[100]

The picture that emerges then, is that survivors of militia rape in East Timor and children brought to term as a result are experiencing a degree of hardship specifically related to society's construction of the sexual violence and its sequelae. The physical, economic and psychosocial situation of the children is intricately bound up with the social status of their mothers, and vice versa.

In part, the stigma against survivors of rape and sexual slavery in East Timor derives from the unwarranted or misunderstood association with prostitution, deeply stigmatised in Timorese society. During the occupation East Timorese girls and women were perceived to have become 'prostitutes' as a consequence of rape by Indonesian soldiers, high levels of unemployment and the need to support themselves and their children, often in the absence of their men who were away fighting or had been killed.[101] These women are treated as prostitutes in terms of status, but they are called 'wives'. This characterisation also holds deeper meanings for a strongly Catholic society. As evidenced above, another euphemism commonly used in Timor is that of 'orphan' to refer to a child born of rape. It is difficult to determine whether such obfuscation and use of euphemism is a strategy of denial, benevolent protection against the stigmatisation of illegitimacy or a genuine belief that marriage is not meant to be consensual.

It may be the loyalty of these women to East Timor which is in question, the assumption being that a woman's first loyalty will be to her 'husband' no matter what the circumstances. A Timorese women's NGO took pains to inform the UN Security Council that women who bore Indonesian children remained loyal to the independence movement:

> We know that colonialism leaves vestiges where it passes; the same thing has happened in East Timor where many children have been left without a father. Children have often been born as a result of rape but the mothers have raised the children to oppose the Indonesian administration and become part of the resistance.[10]

Given the Indonesian policy of population control in East Timor preventing Timorese births, it is easy to see why a statement like this was made to the UN. Indeed, loyalty to East Timor seems to have been a coping mechanism for many women. As Beatriz says 'Okay. I'll cut myself in half. The lower half I'll give to him, but the upper half is for my land, the land of Timor'.[103]

Apart from isolated examples such as the book *Buibere* and the CAVR 'Women and Conflict' hearing, women have not spoken out in public about their experiences. As Commissioner of the Indonesian National Commission on Violence against Women (Komnas Perempuan) Samsidar puts it: 'In this situation, women don't feel themselves to be part of humanity anymore. What has been violated is their sense of who they are and their possibility of living without fear.'[104] As explained by Katherine M. Franke, even where women are provided with some level of recognition within transitional justice processes, there may not be a redistribution of shame.[105] This is why a new approach, thinking of non-combatants as veterans may be necessary. Maria Dominggas Alves of FOKUPERS, captures a crucial feminist quandary of international criminal law: 'Why is it that men who are tortured by the military forces are seen as heroes, whereas women who are tortured (including rape) are seen as traitors? Doesn't this show there is a double standard for women?'[106]

6.10 Uncertain recognition of forced maternity as a crime under international law

The focus of the previous analysis has been on rape as a crime under international law with forced maternity as a consequence. This has affected the way women's experience of conflict has been portrayed in the CAVR processes and displays some of the limitations of the legalist approach. Despite the fact that widespread and systematic sexual violence has finally been acknowledged as prevalent in recent conflicts such as Bosnia, Rwanda and the Sudan, even as evidence of genocidal intent, there has never been a prosecution under international law for the offence of forced maternity on behalf of the mother, or any offence on the part of the child.[107]

According to Articles 7 and 8 of the Rome Statute and Sections 5 and 6 of UNTAET Regulation 2000/15, the Dili court is entitled to prosecute the war crimes and crimes against humanity of rape, sexual slavery, enforced prostitution, forced pregnancy, enforced sterilisation or any other form of sexual violence of comparable gravity. Forced pregnancy was listed for the first time as an international crime in the Rome Statute, and copied by the UNTAET Regulation.[108] It is defined as 'the unlawful confinement of a woman forcibly made pregnant, with the intent of affecting the ethnic composition of any population or carrying out grave violations of international law'. This definition is based on the practice of Bosnian Serbs forcibly raping then detaining Muslim and Croat women so they would bear Serbian children.[109] Barbara Bedont and Katherine Hall Martinez comment that the forced pregnancy provisions were the most contentious part of the state negotiations around what should be included as an offence in the Rome Statute.[110]

There are problems with prosecuting forced maternity under the Rome Statute for Timorese women. Kelly Askin argues that the phrase 'other violations of international law' could include the intent to persecute, discriminate against, or torture the victim,[111] but she does not elaborate on the requirement of unlawful confinement. It is clear in assessing the patterns of sexual violence in Timor that rape was not a personal, sexual crime committed by individuals in an opportunistic manner. There is substantial evidence of an intent to commit grave violations of law in the form of the intent to persecute, discriminate against, or torture Timorese female victims. However, the element of unlawful confinement is more difficult. In the case of Beatriz Guterres, she was not confined in a detention facility (although many Timorese women were raped while in detention), but she was also not free to leave.

Forced maternity was also not an afterthought or unintended consequence. However, proving intent under the test required under the Rome Statute may be very problematic for women unless overtly genocidal intent is present.[112] The requisite intent to harm the group would be difficult to prove in a court. One UK official noted: 'There are reports of women and children being forced into trucks to be taken to West Timor while men and boys are left behind. We know and we fear – from Kosovo – what that may mean.'[113] But overt genocidal intent is more difficult to prove in the Timorese context than other conflicts.

Miranda Sissons wrote a careful examination of human rights abuses perpetrated through the implementation of the Indonesian national population control programme, *Program Keluarga Berencana* (the 'KB program').[114] Her report alleged that the Indonesian government targeted indigenous Timorese in particular for 'reproductive oppression' and that these practices might constitute a breach of the Convention on the Prevention and Punishment of the Crime of Genocide, which prohibits intentional limitation of births within a specific national, ethnic, religious or racial group. The report states that the first phase began from the time of the Indonesian invasion and extended through the mid-1980s. The report alleges that Indonesian soldiers raped and impregnated East Timorese women and girls, mutilated pregnant women, and covertly sterilised them. The second phase, which extended to the late 1990s, saw further covert sterilisation and coerced contraception of East Timorese women through the World Bank-funded population control KB programme.[115]

Sissons concluded in 1997 that due to lack of access by human rights NGOs during the occupation period, she could find insufficient evidence to allege genocidal intent by the Indonesian Government under Article II(d) of the Genocide Convention. The CAVR also received very scarce evidence about this practice. She could conclude that there were consistent violations of the reproductive and health rights of the women of East Timor and noted that the majority of Timorese people perceived the KB programme as intended to control the population of Timor.[116]

As Hilary Charlesworth notes: 'the players in international law crises are almost exclusively male…The lives of women are considered part of a crisis only when they are harmed in a way that is seen to demean the whole of their social group.'117 Prosecuting forced maternity only as genocide or where some other violation that harms the group is present diminishes the fact that the violation is against the woman herself, first and foremost.[118] For example, Mario Carrascalão, former Governor of East Timor was asked by the Chair of the CAVR National Public Hearing on Women and Conflict what he thought the objective of violence against women was. He replied simply: 'The aim of this violence against women was to reduce the power of the resistance.'[119] But the violence was also directed against women as powerful individuals. Even if there was a wider political aim meant to be achieved by means of the violence, people, including women, are not merely pawns to be used as a means to an end. Human rights emphasises the inherent dignity of each individual.

In summary, the *Chega! Report* has succeeded in documenting important aspects of the involvement of women in the East Timor conflict, by focusing on human rights violations against women during and after the conflict period that have implications for transitional justice outcomes and the way in which the gendered experience of women in conflict is acknowledged (or not).

CHEGA! AND DOMESTIC VIOLENCE AGAINST WOMEN IN POST-INDEPENDENCE EAST TIMOR

The final point I wish to explore is the linkage between post-conflict justice and domestic violence. Feminist scholars such as Rhonda Copelon have marshalled the psychological and conceptual evidence to stress the link between torture and domestic violence in the light of international legal understanding of what constitutes torture, cruelty, inhuman and degrading treatment. Copelon's argument is that the context, whether torture is committed in domestic context or inflicted officially, does not reduce its intensity of violence, nor does it demand different standards of judgments and actions on the part of the state.[120] She therefore underlines the need for rethinking official instruments such as the ICCPR, and the UN Convention Against Torture (CAT). In this section I examine some of these ideas in the context of transitional justice, arguing that domestic violence occurs in a continuum from armed conflict to 'peace', and that women are particularly vulnerable in states in which a general culture of hate, fear and instability prevails.

Women in East Timor have endured a severe increase in domestic violence and other types of crimes.[121] The *Chega! Report* is particularly groundbreaking because the recommendation on women encompasses action to prevent domestic violence and links the experience to the period of the armed conflict:

> Through its interaction with victims and their families, the Commission observed that domestic violence was a common occurrence in the current lives of many victims. For example, some male survivors of detention and torture told the Commission that they had fallen into a pattern of violent behaviour. The incidence of domestic violence and sexual assault in Timor Leste remains high. A national commitment to the elimination of violence against women, in both the public and private domains, is essential to break the cycle of violence and fear that characterises the lives of many women and girls. This programme of action must also promote the development of a culture of equality because discrimination against women is a key contributing factor to violence against women.[122]

Until the *Chega! Report,* the rise in domestic violence in Timor had not been linked to the armed conflict until recently in a 2005 UNFPA publication.[123] This confirms the idea that women may be only experiencing a change in the curtains, as their men seek to put women back in their box. The post-independence Timorese baby boom may also be evidence of men taking control of women's sexuality.[124] This section will compare women's experience of the formal justice sector inside and outside the serious crimes process, for example for crimes committed after independence. The most pressing issues have been domestic violence and sexual assault, and how these are dealt with in the formal court system and traditional justice processes.

6.11 Evidence of domestic violence

The issue of sexual violence in the home remains the key priority for Timorese women and NGOs, with frightening levels of domestic violence reported in every District,[125] although there have been some recent high profile court cases, such as the case of Dr Sergio Lobo, detailed later. The Timorese legal NGO Judicial System Monitoring Programme (JSMP) stated in June 2003:

> Domestic violence accounts for approximately 40% of all cases before the Criminal Division of the District Court system – yet the justice system continues to undervalue the seriousness of such offences. Local communities, police investigators and prosecutors continue to treat many such offences inappropriately by referring them to mediation for resolution. Further concerns arise as to a substantial number of cases which are dealt with by the traditional justice system with reportedly highly varied, and, for the victim, unsatisfactory outcomes. Inadequate community education, together with a lack of support and counselling services for victims of domestic violence continue to mean that such offences often go unreported and/or inadequately managed.[126]

A 2004 study by the International Rescue Committee (IRC) has given us greater insights into domestic violence.[127] Disturbingly, the report found that family disputes and violence perpetrated by a husband against his wife are considered a 'normal' yet very private occurrence within the family.

Women's own attitudes to domestic violence are disheartening, especially in relation to domestic violence campaigns that have taken place in East Timor and the drafting of the Domestic Violence Legislation in 2005–6.[128] Over half (51%) of those surveyed in the 'IRC Prevalence of GBV Study' published in 2003 strongly agreed that 'a man has good reason to hit his wife if she disobeys him'.[129] Therefore, motivations for seeking assistance for violence are weak. In this study, 44.84 per cent of respondents strongly agreed with the statement that 'family problems should only be discussed with people in the family', and 51 per cent of women felt that the best way to cope was with support from their family. Most women who did seek help for domestic violence went to their family (32%), 5 per cent went to 'traditional justice', 3 per cent went to the police, and 9 per cent tried to forget about it.[130]

Timorese women experience this current violence in a particular context – they have not received the services they need to heal as survivors of gender-based violence in armed conflict. The relationship to the conflict and the tensions of transitional justice period may make dealing with issues of domestic violence even more confronting than usual, especially if the Timorese Government does not treat it as a part of the transition, but a private circumstance. Angelina Saramento, an activist from the Timorese NGO KSI explains this reticence in the following terms:

> From 1975 up to now, women are the ones who suffer more than the men. For example their husbands stay in the jungle, the women stay alone. Then the military came and asked them, where is your husband and they take control of other person's wife, so this is a kind of violation against women. This kind of thing happened all over East Timor so I think women are the ones who really suffered. In order to see how the women can get justice is hard – because in our culture the women sometimes keep quiet, doesn't talk too much, so it is hard for women to give their aspirations or talk in public – to the adat, the court, Truth Commission.[131]

6.12 Legal principles and resources

This situation is made much more complex by the lack of clear legal principles and resources to prosecute violations. In November 2002, work began on domestic violence legislation, and the draft was promulgated in late 2003.[132] As of June 2009 it had not passed, but was closer. The legislation is desperately needed. UNTAET introduced some important rights for victims of violence in its criminal procedure regulation; for example, an investigating judge has the power to prevent a perpetrator who has been arrested for domestic violence from living in the family home while the case is investigated and prosecuted; and when convicting a perpetrator of a crime of violence, the judge may order the payment of compensation to the victim.[133]

However, pursuant to UNTAET Regulation 1, Indonesian law in operation prior to the referendum continued to apply in East Timor, except to the extent that it was inconsistent with specified international human rights standards, including the United Nations Convention on the Elimination of All Forms of Discrimination Against Women (CEDAW). Section 9 makes international law directly implemented into Timor's domestic legal system. Section 37 of the Timorese Constitution states that police can enter homes uninvited if there is reasonable suspicion of threat to life or serious physical injury. In contrast, under the Indonesian Criminal Code, domestic violence is not a specific offence. Prosecutors must rely on the crimes of maltreatment and torture. There is no prohibition against threats of violence, attempted assault or rape within marriage.[134]

The incorporation of CEDAW into Timorese law may be less helpful than one would expect, because there are two main silences in international law in relation to domestic violence. First, there is no specific treaty dealing with it as a criminal violation. Second, the doctrine of state responsibility distinguishes public acts by actors linked to the state for which the state can be held accountable, as opposed to private actors.[135] This explains the anomalous situation whereby violence inflicted on a woman by an enemy soldier in a conflict may be considered a crime under international law, but the same level of violence inflicted by a husband in the home may not, unless the state does not respond appropriately. This is a contrast regularly raised by feminist international lawyers to show the operation of the public/private distinction.[136]

Notwithstanding numerous strengths of CEDAW, including its extension to private actors and its aim to eliminate harmful customary practices,[137] one of the most glaring shortcomings of the Convention is the omission of violence from its terms. The UN Committee monitoring CEDAW has endeavoured to rectify this deficiency through its Recommendation 19, which specifies gender-based violence as a form of discrimination prohibited by the treaty.[138] The adoption of the Declaration for the Elimination of All Forms of Violence against Women by the UN General Assembly has also responded to this gap.[139]

The doctrine of state responsibility in relation to private actors has been under challenge in some recent cases in regional human rights courts, particularly in relation to asylum claims which feature domestic violence.[140] A 'due diligence' test which emerged from the 1988 Inter-American Court of Human Rights case of *Velasquez Rodriguez v. Honduras* holds:

> An illegal act which violates human rights and which is initially not directly imputable to the State (for example, because it is the act of a private person or because the person responsible has not been identified) can lead to international responsibility of the State, not because of the act itself but because of the lack of due diligence to prevent the violation or to respond to it as required by the Convention.[141]

Rebecca Cook has argued that state responsibility could be expanded to include 'private' harms against women if links can be established between systemic discrimination against women and the exercise of power by a state.[142]

6.13 Closing the curtains on domestic violence

As the previous section on forced maternity demonstrates, the situation of women during the occupation has enormous impact on the well-being of women in an independent East Timor and their ability to cope with changed family relationships and the justice system. In order to open the curtains, it is arguably important to successfully prosecute domestic violence attacks. This is particularly true when the traditional justice mechanisms reflect traditional views of the role of women. For example, even if the victim involves the police in the first instance, and most cases still go unreported, she will often relent, as the imprisonment/humiliation of her bread-winner is not in her long-term interests. A church worker in Viqueque reported to the International Rescue Committee:

> In one case, a wife was beaten by her husband and injured badly. They really needed our help to resolve their situation, but when we were ready to send the case to court, the wife refused and wanted to resolve the situation in a traditional way. She told us that this was because there would be no one to take care of the children or provide support for the family if the man went to jail...[143]

This outcome is not just an East Timorese phenomenon. But village communities are still inclined to settle domestic incidents through *adat*, whereby the offended male relatives of the female victim are compensated by the perpetrator with gifts of livestock or other goods. Sometimes the female victims still take the matter to court because they do not feel that *adat* has compensated them personally for their injury/humiliation.[144]

The traditional justice mechanisms reflect traditional views. IRC research revealed that many men still regard their wives as their possessions because they have paid a bride-price for them. Their study revealed that bride prices could reach $1,900, and that coupled with male perceptions of female insubordination could be enough to spark beatings in itself.[145] IRC quote a case where a man who had recently beaten his wife tried to have her arrested for disobedience and was horrified to find that CIVPOL arrested him instead.[146] The IRC report on domestic violence concluded that in East Timor:

> In consideration of international standards, it is evident that women's rights are not given adequate consideration in their search for justice, especially in local justice proceedings. Local beliefs systems stipulate the power which individuals may possess, and women are not attributed any of this power, especially in regard to the decision making power in local justice settings. According to the cultural systems this research approached, women have never had and can never possess such power – in this way the possibility of them receiving equal participation and hearing within justice processes is minimal. The systems are inherently biased towards women's status, decision making capabilities and their roles within their communities.[147]

In the absence of faith in the formal legal sector, women may be completely reliant on traditional justice mechanisms. There is still little clarity around how the country's legal system will cope with harmonising its existing Indonesian-based legal system with international legal norms and treaties, and how customary law, or *adat*, which has regulated local disputes for centuries, will relate to either.[148]

One outcome of the delay in legislation in Timor has been the use of *adat*, traditional justice mechanisms at the village level, to deal with domestic violence cases. There are several concerns with these mechanisms – they are not uniform or consistent, they have been used for cases of serious criminal violence, including murder and rape, and only men can be traditional law judges and so patriarchal attitudes are reinforced.[149] Local NGOs have reported cases where victims have been pressured to accept resolution by traditional means against their will and where suspects have been denied the right to fair trial.

Timor's foremost feminist leader and former UNTAET Gender Adviser Micato states that there is a need to stop all forms of traditional justice and create formal mechanisms based on the law and on women's rights: 'It sends the wrong message to perpetrators and communities – the reliance on traditional justice is not better than nothing, it makes the situation much worse because it limits attempts to develop judicial institutions and undermines the establishment of law and order'.[150]

Even in the formal legal sector, the judiciary too, is not good at dealing with domestic violence. The inexperience of East Timor's fledgling judiciary can be illustrated by the notorious case in 2000 involving one of East Timor's only surgeons, Dr Sergio Lobo, who was arrested after a serious assault on his wife and a nun.

6.14 Dr Lobo – the public man with the private crime

The case of Dr Lobo illustrates well the obstacles facing women seeking justice in East Timor: senior figures are perceived to be above the law and cultural traditions are invoked to defend men's 'disciplining' of their wives. Moreover, in a transitional society, skills such as Dr Lobo's are very important. The case was instrumental in dispelling the preconception established under the Indonesian occupation that some people are above the law. It was also critically important in establishing the seriousness of domestic violence as an unacceptable criminal act.

Dr Sergio Lobo was detained in Dili on 10 July 2001 for physically assaulting his wife at a hotel. He is the former Minister for Health, a prominent surgeon at Dili hospital, former Chairman of the Department of Health for ETTA (East Timor Transitional Authority), the number three candidate for the UDT (Timorese Democratic Union) ticket in the 2000 elections and one of the few qualified East Timorese medical professionals. The case has generated considerable controversy and has become a focal point for women's organisations that have mounted a strong support campaign for Mrs Lobo.

There had been strong criticism from Timorese women's and human rights groups when the court gave Dr Lobo an unconditional release after his arrest in February 2001. The judge turned down the prosecutor's request for a 30-day detention warrant despite being informed of the long history of escalating violence against his wife. CIVPOL expressed concern about their ability to enforce the terms of his conditional release and reported that the judge had been visibly intimidated.

The terms of Lobo's release included bi-weekly reporting to CIVPOL. Within a month, the defendant had failed to fulfil this and spent weeks abroad with the President of CNRT. On that occasion he had been accused of beating his wife with a stick and injecting a sedative into her arm with a syringe he had brought for this purpose. She had gone into hiding in a convent; and several witnesses claimed that he hunted her down, attacked her in the convent with the syringe and also beat up a nun.[151]

Complicating the story even further is the Javanese ethnicity of the doctor's wife. Within East Timor, stereotypes about the promiscuity of Javanese women exist, fuelled by the presence of Javanese prostitutes during the Indonesian occupation. The doctor has exploited these ethnic stereotypes in defending his own behaviour.

No action was taken against the suspect for breaking the terms of release and the victim remained in hiding.[152] When she emerged to begin work in a Dili hotel, the doctor found her out and beat her again. He was arrested again and this time detained.

In spite of having inflicted severe injuries on his wife, Dr. Lobo was released from Becora prison and exonerated by the all male panel of judges who stated that 'the cultural situation in East Timor allows a man to control the actions of his wife'.[153] This decision was widely criticised, both domestically and internationally, and considered dangerous in two respects. First, the message was that East Timor's courts condone domestic violence. Second, the impression was given that people holding prominent positions are able to influence the impartiality of the judges.

CIVPOL spokesperson Luis Carrilho stated publicly during the trial process:

> All people are equal in the eyes of the law and no one is above it, regardless of whether he or she is a renowned public figure...I understand that he [Dr Sergio Lobo] is an intellectual and a medical doctor. But I stress that no one is above the law and the same applies in Timor Lorosa'e...The judiciary is independent and it will not bow to pressure from any institution or influential people.[154]

Dr Lobo appealed against the detention, arguing that according to East Timorese culture, he had an entitlement to know where his wife was and control her. The appeal was upheld by the Judge on the grounds that the offender was needed by his community and that the victim was violating East Timorese cultural norms by working without permission from her husband. In addition, the defendant was granted custody of the couple's children. Lobo was conditionally released, pending trial.[155]

At the hearing, Dr Lobo told the presiding judge that his case was 'sensationalised' by the NGOs in order to get more funding for their work. He said cases like his were common in the country, but previously they were not 'blown up by women's groups', and he 'questioned their motives' now.[156] FOKUPERS was forced to publicly announce that it was not using Dr Lobo's case for its own campaigning purposes to seek more donor money for its domestic violence work.[157]

Dr Lobo's wife lived in a FOKUPERS domestic-violence safe house, and Lobo claimed FOKUPERS was breaking up his home. He refused his wife a divorce. FOKUPERS had previously supported a woman in her divorce proceedings, successfully arguing that her husband had not provided for the family, still the strongest ground for divorce in East Timor.[158] Commentators report that as a result of its support for the divorce, FOKUPERS 'suffers the wrath of the Church, a wrath made tangible through the great political power it holds'.[159]

Dr Lobo's case is illustrative of numerous practical problems in a transitional justice system, as well as gender problems throughout that system. According to JSMP, the manifold difficulties experienced by actors in the justice sector include: the existence of only a small number of legally qualified East Timorese nationals, few of whom are women; delays in the appointments of judges; long absences of judges while attending training in Portugal; more difficulty in making skills transfers from international advisers than had been expected; contracts of short duration for international judges; incomplete legislation; legislation that frequently does not correspond to the realities existing in East Timor, including the realities faced by women; and a lack of administrative skills and poor planning in the judicial sector.[160]

In an analysis of all cases involving women and children victims in East Timor between June 2004 and March 2005 undertaken by JSMP, the monitoring body concluded that 'sexual assault crimes are not being punished as severely as they should be':

> This has ramifications for all women and children victims in Timor Leste. As it is, only a small proportion of cases of violence against women or children are reported to the police, a smaller proportion ever make it to trial, and an even smaller proportion of cases ever reach a final decision. If in those cases which do manage to reach a final decision in the court, a decision is rendered which does not reflect the seriousness of the crime (for example, a one and a half year penalty delivered for a case of rape of a three-year-old) then victims will have little incentive to bother to report their crime to the police or pursue their case through the courts. The short sentences being delivered in these cases would not give the victims much faith in the formal justice system, or provide incentive for future victims to endure the difficulties associated with a trial in the formal justice system.[161]

Is the Lobo case a fair illustration? The content of the responsibility of a transitional state or a UN transitional administration to prevent post-conflict domestic violence has not been ascertained and remains an urgent area for further research. It is at least arguable that as women were most vulnerable to violence in a transitional state, it was most important that efforts to restore the formal legal sector were responsive to women's needs. After several years of a United Nations administered justice system and now under the Government of East Timor, the justice sector in East Timor is widely regarded as weak.[162] Gender-based violence continues in Timor in different forms, one of the most extreme being the January 2007 killing of three Liquiça women as 'witches'.[163]

Given that neither international law nor Timorese legal processes have been able to offer Timorese women the promise of justice that they should, I conclude with some lessons to be adopted by the UN in post-conflict states in the future. The goal should be to open the curtains for women, not just change them, especially not when they are merely cut from the same cloth as before.

CONCLUSION: FROM TRAITORS TO HEROES

Beatriz Guterres cut herself in half for her country, but her sacrifice has not been rewarded in the post-conflict period. However, telling her story has allowed the CAVR process to be successful in including women's stories in the truth-seeking and truth-telling part of its mandate. One of the key obstacles Timorese faced in claiming their rights was that of proper documentation and acknowledgement. A quotation from Bishop Belo is paradigmatic: Belo wrote in 2000 of 'the path to freedom' and asked the international community to take heed of 'the legacy of the past' when watching Timor struggle towards a democratic society 'founded on the values enshrined in the Universal Declaration of Human Rights'.[164] He wrote: 'Up to 3,000 died in 1999, untold numbers of women were raped and 500,000 persons displaced – 100,000 are yet to return.'[165] The phrase 'untold numbers of women' is poignant, and literal – the story of women's experience before, during and after the

1999 violence remains largely untold despite the extraordinary efforts of Timorese women advocates. The *Chega! Report* is an important step forward in finding out both the numbers and the women behind the numbers.

Lack of monitoring and supportive documentation by the UN or NGOs during the conflict put added pressures on women such as Beatriz Guterres to recount their experiences in public to combat the perception that they were collaborators. Few women have been prepared to bear the shame and horror of recounting their appalling experiences, and the fourteen women who did find that courage before the CAVR's national hearing on women were both brave and exceptional. For the same reasons, the ability of East Timorese victims of gender-based violence in its many forms to gain justice remains low.

This chapter sought to address two particular issues which have critical implications for the rights and well-being of Timorese women in the newly independent state. One is the situation of women who bore children from forced maternity. The other was the drastic situation of domestic violence and assault in Timorese society since 1999. The CAVR was the only mechanism to recognise these issues as transitional justice issues, actually consult women about their experience of the conflict and their expectations of justice, even if its capacity to deliver on those expectations is low due to political factors outside its control.

The chapter outlined the position of Timorese women under the legal system in the post-conflict period, noting the serious problems with legislation, traditional justice mechanisms (*adat*) and treatment by the courts. The experience of women in the trials set up for transitional justice purposes will have a direct impact on their faith in the legal system to provide redress for domestic violence in the post-conflict era, and vice versa. The response to rape survivors and their children in East Timor has ranged from denial and silence to efforts to respond to their acute survival needs on the basis of a welfare paradigm that has reproduced conservative cultural conceptions of mothering and domesticity. Domestic violence and sexual assault has been met with patchy legal responses and inadequate policy from the state, and lack of recognition by existing transitional justice mechanisms. Despite the advances in the interpretation of CEDAW provisions, international criminal law appears have little relevance except in the characterisation of the rape that leads to forced maternity as a war crime or crime against humanity in particular circumstances.[166]

The image of Beatriz raising her voice and telling her story at the CAVR hearing gives cause for hope. Resistance during the occupation seems to have given Timorese women a taste for advocacy, which has been obvious in the post-independence period.[167] A story reported from a 'women to women' visit from 23 June to 1 July 1999 of the World Council of Churches and the Christian Conference of Asia details a horrific set of rapes, assaults, destruction of property and constant fear for the wife of a Falintil soldier, and then notes:

> Fortunately her husband understands that it was not her fault. He told her that they all face risks for the sake of freedom, and that she too, as a woman, needs to face risks.
>
> What she said sounded like a theological statement:

> 'This experience has given me a new perception of my womanhood and my power. I know that almost every other woman in my village has had a similar experience of violence. I am determined to fight for the life of other women. Men may fight with guns, but as a woman I will fight with the power that I have gained out of my suffering, by raising my voice.'[168]

The position of the women of East Timor is not static and there are some causes for optimism, but more could have been done by the CAVR process to move Timorese women from victim status to a situation where both their material well-being and their contribution to liberation are rewarded. While in many ways East Timor remains a patriarchal and traditional society, there are social forces that suggest that women could start to play a greater role in post-conflict reconstruction and governance. The question is whether the society can shed the euphemistic veil that lies over a substantial social and moral issue in East Timor – that of the reintegration and acceptance of women who have suffered human rights violations and the right of their children to a future free from violence.

7 Conclusion: 'Operation Love'

Figure 2 Photograph of East Timorese President Xanana Gusmão meeting Indonesian Presidential candidate, former General Wiranto, in Badung, Bali on 29 May 2004, © Dadang Tri, /Reuters/Picture Media.

This photograph, taken on 29 May 2004, shows Timor President Xanana Gusmão and Indonesian Presidential candidate General Wiranto in a friendly embrace in Bali. The picture belies a dramatic background. The Serious Crimes Investigation Unit (SCIU) in Dili indicted General Wiranto on 24 February 2003. The indictment alleged that Wiranto, at that time Minister of Defence and Security and Commander of the Indonesian Armed Forces, was responsible under international law for the crimes against humanity of murder, deportation and persecution. This was based on failing to punish or prevent crimes committed by his subordinates or those acting under his effective control in the period before and after the 1999 popular consultation in East Timor.

The Special Panel for Serious Crimes (SPSC) issued a warrant for the arrest of Wiranto on 10 May 2004 after declining a public hearing. General Wiranto was then a leading candidate in the Indonesian Presidential elections, as he is again in the 2009 elections. Several days later Wiranto was pictured above hugging President Xanana Gusmão on the anniversary of Timorese independence. The photograph was published widely in the Timorese and Indonesian press. Gusmão was met when he returned home to Dili with demonstrations and the sound of hundreds of women weeping.[1] This embrace has become a potent symbol of the complex dilemmas faced by Timor's transitional justice process.

From a realist point of view, Gusmão was given little choice but to reconcile with Wiranto. The February 2003 indictment caused a strong reaction from the Indonesian government. Indonesia blamed the UN for what they saw as a 'politically motivated case'.[2] UNMISET issued a public statement subtly disavowing the action, declaring that the indictment was issued through the prosecution service of Timor Leste and not by the UN.[3] The International Center for Transitional Justice states that the UN statement 'provoked the dismay of those in the Timorese leadership who had expected the UN to show a clear commitment to the justice process and strengthened the view that the UN's support for justice could not be taken for granted'.[4] The Timorese government then countered with a public declaration that the indictment was the work of the UN and not of East Timor.[5] The government also declined offers of overseas aid for the funding and staffing of the serious crimes process.[6]

It was in this context that President Xanana Gusmão met the then Indonesian President Megawati Sukarnoputri in May 2004. They agreed that outstanding human rights issues between the countries would not be solved judicially but through a reconciliatory approach.[7] President Gusmão praised the Jakarta trials in his Independence Day national address, and then met personally with General Wiranto to hug him as an act of reconciliation.[8]

After the photo was taken, General Wiranto chatted to the press. He said the discussion was 'nostalgic':

> Before, we were the same in the forest, the mountains, in positions opposing each other. To see us now, it's quite funny. I think now we have become friends. We are two people who understand that war and battles are not good.[9]

President Gusmão left without comment. However, later that month he told a conference in Berlin that his stance was pragmatic:

> We fought for 24 years and during the struggle we followed many other conflicts, some of them ended, some of them are on the way to [an] end. Two and a half years after independence we are ahead of Guinea Bissau, a former Portuguese colony which was the first to start its independence struggle, and they still face human rights abuses and poverty. With our policy we have security, stability and progress. We have good relations with our big neighbour. NGOs say, on behalf of victims there must be justice. For our process, real

> justice was that the international community recognized our independence and helped to achieve it. For all the sacrifices of our people, our obligation is to bring them real independence, meaning social justice and development. East Timor should not live in the past, but look towards the future.[10]

Then President Xanana Gusmão's reconciliation attempts reached their apex with 'Operasaun Domin' (Operation Love), which collected $77,000 from Timor Leste people for tsunami victims, and then presented it as a personal gift to President Susilo Bambang Yudhoyono.[11] The smiling embrace can therefore be read as a broader symbol of the complex interactions between law and politics, common to studies of transitional justice, which have been explored in this book.

THE FUTURE OF JUSTICE FOR EAST TIMOR

In 1999, Mary Robinson, then UN High Commissioner for Human Rights said of the violence in East Timor: 'To end the century and the millennium tolerating impunity for those guilty of these shocking violations would be a betrayal of everything the United Nations stands for regarding the universal protection and promotion of human rights.'[12]

In 2009, a decade since the ballot, the outcomes of the transitional justice processes set in place by the UN and Indonesia are cause for deep concern in terms of their inadequacy. Not one Indonesian perpetrator has been punished. The prospect of an international tribunal seems dim. As journalist Sian Powell stated: 'Justice for the thousands of East Timorese who were murdered, raped, assaulted and forcibly exiled in 1999 has been slowly but surely buried in an avalanche of paperwork churned out by tribunals, commissions, panels and committees.'[13]

There is no doubt that justice for the victims of the crimes committed in East Timor still has to be done. A full analysis of the reasons is necessary, if a more effective formula is to be found. The general view of commentators and human rights groups has been that the trials within East Timor were well intentioned but massively under-resourced, hamstrung by jurisdiction and lack of access to indictees, and that they ran out of time. The trials in Indonesia have roundly been dismissed as a 'sham' and accused of deliberate design by a politicised Attorney-General's office to avoid successful prosecutions of military commanders.

This book has shown that these conclusions are broadly correct. The failure of both processes can be traced squarely to dwindling political will on behalf of the main actors, the Governments of Timor, Indonesia and key Member States of the UN.[14] In Indonesia, the pressures of democratic and economic reform influenced the political will in the executive and the legislative sectors. In East Timor, the priority for dealing with these crimes was shared with other, formidable priorities. In other words, the political will at the national level in both States was not up to the level required to see the machinery of justice put into effect.

At the international level, the political will, despite the expressions of outrage and condemnation, and the cogent reports of the UN Commission on Human

Rights, simply was not sufficiently strong to bring about the kind of consensus that led to the establishment of ICTY and ICTR. The procedure for convening the extraordinary session of the Commission on Human Rights in September 1999, and the complications surrounding that session, provided clear evidence of the absence of international consensus to handle the crimes through international action. By 2005, the Security Council in Resolution 1599 (2005), acknowledges the improvement of relations between Indonesia and Timor Leste, including the agreement to establish the CTF. The Council also slightly softened its position on the judicial process regarding serious human rights violations in East Timor in 1999, by only reaffirming the need for credible accountability, instead of reaffirming the fight against impunity mentioned in the Resolution 1573 adopted in 2004.

Whether justice will be done for East Timor in the future is unclear. The Special Representative of the Secretary-General in East Timor, Dr Hasegawa, stated that with many competing opinions and interests for Timor, one option would be 'call it a partial victory and close the curtain' when the UN mission finally departs. He thought the only other option was a full international tribunal costing much more than has been invested in the process so far.[15]

The Timorese Government has placed its faith in the bilateral Truth and Friendship Commission established in Bali with the Indonesian Government. East Timor's Ambassador to the United Nations, José Luis Guterres outlined:

> I don't believe that the Government of East Timor will again try to prosecute any of the military figures in Indonesia because of the past human rights violation in East Timor.
>
> The reasons are, as you know, there is the Government has the present determination to first, consolidate the process of democracy, freedom and justice in East Timor. Second, to maintain the good relations with Indonesia. At the same time, also giving the opportunity to the Indonesian system of democracy and freedom to be consolidated in that region.[16]

The Government will still be under pressure from the CAVR report and its own citizens to pursue justice.

New President José Ramos-Horta has responded to an alleged recommendation of the CAVR report to pursue indictments of Indonesian military in the following manner:

> Well, these are very high-sounding statements, but the United Nations were here, from 99 to 2003, with the massive peacekeeping force. They didn't do that. So why should the East Timorese, with our own priorities and concerns, to continue to consolidate peace, reconciliation, creating jobs for our people, reducing poverty – should pretend to be a sort of Don Quixote de la Mancha of justice, in fighting the mighty Indonesian army?[17]

Contemplating the incongruous picture of a smiling President Gusmão hugging General Wiranto forces introspection from an international lawyer. A warrant to arrest Wiranto had been issued only days earlier for crimes against humanity inflicted on the Timorese people in 1999. But in May 2004 when the picture was taken, Wiranto could have also become President of Indonesia, thereby in a position to wield enormous power over the fragile new State of East Timor. The UN had disavowed the actions of the Special Panel that issued his arrest warrant, a court the UN had itself created. The photograph is a reminder that leaders of post-conflict societies must sometimes make heart-breaking choices.

In examinations of transitional justice processes, in theoretical discussions of the role of international law, the political consequences of decisions for leaders and citizens in new states must not be lost. The goal of accountability for *jus cogens* crimes is not unrealistic, but is more difficult than setting up a UN court by decree. It is therefore very important that international lawyers, when advocating for the implementation of the minimum accountability requirements for *jus cogens* crimes required by international law, pay more attention to the practical realities faced by states in an international relations context. This does not mean that accountability is not possible or realistic, but it does mean that international lawyers must be more strategic and cautious in their push for immediate trials after a conflict. The realist challenge to the obligation to punish imposed by international law must be fully reckoned with.

A proper grasp of political challenges is even more of an imperative for a strategic feminist legalist attempting to assist the promotion of gender-inclusive transitional justice processes and the restoration of a rule of law that protects women. It is tempting to analyse the transitional justice processes as an overall failure, and accede some ground to the realist viewpoint. This would merely accord with the pragmatism on transitional justice matters from the Timorese leadership, and there is no guarantee this view has afforded Timorese women a positive future. Many Timorese women who were herded as refugees into West Timor in 1999 are living as internally displaced persons in their own country in 2009. Many women are among the 20,000 still living trapped and in poverty on the Indonesian border as the tenth anniversary of the ballot passed.[18] Within the overall failure of the transitional justice process, it is still crucial to consider how transitional justice processes will have a gendered impact. It is even more crucial to start thinking creatively how to gain material benefit for women in a post-conflict state. It is in this light I propose a veteran strategy.

WOMEN BECOME VETERANS?

This book has argued that the well-being and ability of women to claim their rights in a transitional justice setting is related to their status socially and legally, and this status needs to be addressed in post-conflict states. Within Timor, there is an ambivalence about the idea of women as contributors to independence during the occupation, even though women made up more than 60 per cent of the clandestine movement. One simple but perhaps far-reaching proposal is to expand the definition of veteran in the Veterans Law of East Timor, in order to re-characterise female survivors of violence and their children as 'veterans' of the conflict, with the same status as the former Falantil guerrillas. This would serve the purpose of both providing a pension and acknowledging the status and contribution these women made through their bravery to independence. It would also have the effect of putting the situation of these families squarely into current transitional justice debates in Timor.

Such a proposal, if implemented, could work to counter the prevailing inertia and patriarchal attitudes that account for much of the hardship these survivors and their babies face, while drawing strategically on other nationalist imagery currently at a premium in post-independence East Timor. In part, the reluctance to incorporate a concern with gender-based violence into existing mechanisms for legal redress in East Timor is due to the ambivalence about the idea of women as fighters for independence during the occupation, with special discomfiture reserved for those seen as 'wives' of Indonesian military. The language still used to describe these women is filled with euphemism and the assumption of consent through formal rituals such as 'marriage' and 'wives' – even more pronounced than terms like 'comfort women'. Likewise, the language used to describe the offspring of these unions is, at worst, one that invokes shame and illegitimacy, and at best one that evokes pity for their status as 'orphans' despite the fact that they may be in the custody of their mothers.

The issue of proper support for veterans and the question of who is a veteran has been hotly debated in Timor since independence and is enshrined in Section 11 of the Constitution. The main source of tension is that the UN Mission did not convert the majority of Falantil veterans into the new standing army or reserve. Instead, the East Timor Defense Force (ETDF) is small but well trained, consisting of 1,500 regulars (31 of whom are women) and 1,500 reservists. Over 7,000 people applied for the last round of 428 places, leaving many disgruntled veterans without a position.[19] Women veterans indicate that they are generally highly regarded in their communities,[20] and Maria Paixão, an ex-fighter, is a member of Parliament. However, no female combatants have been included in any formal Disarmament, Demobilisation and Reintegration (DDR) programmes.[21] Gusmão's biographer Sara Niner reports that even today, Gusmão is unable to admit that women bore arms in the struggle. She also notes that the Timorese Resistance Archive and Museum appears to overlook women's involvement in the conflict, focusing instead on elite men.[22]

On 8 June 2004, then President Gusmão formally presented to the National Parliament the report of the Veterans Commission, which recommended forms of recognition and material benefits to the veterans identified through a long registration process. More than 37,000 people have been registered as having fought for independence during the occupation, and are nearly all male combatants. Tensions about the long process led to a demonstration that was dispelled by tear gas outside the Parliament by 120 veterans led by Cornelio Gama (known as L7) on 19 July 2004.[23] An August 2004 interview with President Gusmão shows a Government willing to empathise and negotiate with this group:

> GUSMAO: 'I can understand the position of those former veterans, you know they previously were very clear about who the enemy was, it was the Indonesian military. They had a role as heroes in fighting against that enemy. Nowadays who are they? You know they haven't been given any special recognition from government, they're not clear about what their role is in determining the future of their country. So I think it's very understandable that they are feeling marginalised now and disgruntled with the government and expressing that through demonstrations.'
>
> [INTERVIEWER] WERDEN: 'Well what do you think the government should do with people like L-7?'
>
> GUSMAO: 'I think it's really important that the government sit down and listen to what they're saying and really make a special effort to respond in some way, either with training or employment opportunities for these people, not just because they have the potential to disrupt stability in the future, but because they really are genuinely deserving of attention and special support.'[24]

The situation for veterans is still fraught. In April 2006, more than one-third of the country's armed forces had been discharged over a mutiny linked to claims of poor service conditions and biased promotion.[25] Violent riots ensued, particularly in Dili as explained in Chapter Three. Despite repeated attempts at appeasement, there was an assassination attempt on Ramos-Horta in 2008. This group of veterans is a credible threat, has links with the leadership and the ability to make itself heard,[26] but women survivors and their war babies do not. And yet, why should the needs of ex-combatants necessarily be prioritised over these women and children? Too many Timorese women went from being refugees herded over the border into West Timor in 1999 to internally displaced within their own country in 2007, only now in 2009 returning home.

Policy proposals that would reconstruct women as wartime veterans, rather than current labels that produce shame and stigma, will not resolve their situation overnight. However it may provide a language and a framework in which women's groups and progressive elements within Timorese civil society can engage in work to promote greater social inclusion for these families, and such terminology may be validating to the survivors and their children themselves.

FINDINGS

When Natércia Godinho-Adams addressed the UN Security Council on behalf of Timorese women's networks, she pointed out that while the Indonesian occupation had been a tragedy for the women of East Timor, the crisis had also created a number of new opportunities for them:

> Men's and women's roles changed substantially during the years of conflict and social disruption since 1974. A significant number of women assumed active roles in the clandestine liberation front and the armed resistance. They

> were soldiers, they smuggled medication, food, armament, and information to the resistance movement hiding in the mountains. [...] East Timorese women want to build a society that will respect their newly acquired post-conflict roles, and will not force them to return to traditional powerless roles.[27]

Debate should continue about post-conflict justice being a space for emancipation or retrenchment for women.

Transitional justice processes are meant to assist a nation to come to terms with a violent past and decide what to do with the perpetrators of the violence. However, I have shown that the supposedly gender-neutral processes in East Timor did not address the experience and contribution of women to the independence struggle and are not designed to assist their situation in post-independent East Timor.

In Chapter Two, I considered theoretical debates regarding the impact of international law on transitional justice choices for modern post-conflict states, and noted that the role of law is often controversial, and estimations of any impact are usually lacking an evidentiary basis. I argued that international law can impact on transitional justice mechanisms in three primary ways, categorisation, obligation to punish and prosecution strategies. The first impact is normative, in that international law seeks to categorise what behaviour can be considered a crime under international law. The second impact, consequent on the *categorisation* of certain behaviours into crimes, is that international law imposes an *obligation* to prosecute and punish certain crimes and designates individual responsibility for those crimes, although the site of where that obligation falls is contested. The third impact, again consequential, is that the categorisation of offences influences what is tried and with what priority, or *prosecution* strategies.

Feminist scholarship has mainly focused on the first and third impacts, namely categorisation and prosecution of crimes as they have featured in international criminal trials, aiming for the global acceptance of gender-persecution as crimes under international law. I argued that focusing on the Timor experience shows us that a feminist analysis is also needed of the second impact within the emerging field of transitional justice studies, the obligation to punish as laid down by international law. I have presented a case that trials cannot be assumed to benefit women in post-conflict settings. An approach that I termed *strategic legal feminism* is necessary.

Transitional justice models may have moved on slightly from the crude *realpolitik* position of openly bartering justice for peace, but the substantive outcomes of justice mechanisms are still extremely selective and have substantial flaws in terms of competence and fairness.[28] Generally, my research on East Timor suggests the political debates around transitional justice still reflect differing *Realpolitik* versus anti-impunity views regarding the 'trade-ability' of justice outcomes, the selective gaze and resources of the international community for justice outcomes, and questions over who is the key audience for those outcomes.

A close analysis of the Serious Crimes process in Dili and the Jakarta ad hoc human rights trials through a gendered lens in Chapters Four and Five showed that women were poorly represented, and poorly treated in the court room. Timorese women's gendered experience of conflict was ignored in court or only acknowledged as an afterthought. Worse still, their experience of sexual violence and forced maternity was seen as a source of stigmatisation and marginalisation in an independent Timor. The trials did nothing to counter that perception. Women could lose faith in the courts to deal with violence against them under international law, just as their need to be protected by domestic law from domestic violence dramatically increases.

Chapter Four examined the role, operation and jurisprudence of the Jakarta Court, the most controversial of the transitional justice mechanisms established to date to deal with international crimes in East Timor. The first section presented an analysis of the political circumstances in which the Court came to be established. My analysis showed that the obligation to punish under international law may be realised in such a fashion as to render it meaningless. The gendered analysis highlighted the official silence in the indictments on gender-persecution, the intimidating courtroom atmosphere, ill-treatment of female witnesses and judges, and the reaction of Timorese women's groups to the trials. The trials showcased the military, masculine voice shouting down feminised justice, women victims and the UN (which is also feminised).

In Chapter Five I analysed the Serious Crimes cases, including the *Leonardus Kasa* and *Lolotoe* cases, and concluded that justice for women during the period of Indonesian occupation was not achieved through the Dili court. In the *Kasa* case, the Special Panel of the Dili District Court declared that it held no jurisdiction on the case as the rape had been perpetrated in West Timor, thereby precluding all further cases of women who had been forcibly removed from East to West Timor from being tried.[29] Indeed, many of the initial cases were addressed by domestic rather than international law, therefore leading to narrow court decisions, and the exclusion of pioneering case precedents from the international stage. Even with the one successful prosecution for rape as a crime against humanity, it is unlikely that the judgment would result in the type of integration and financial outcomes that might be required for these families. This one jurisprudential breakthrough in the Dili trials does not outweigh the overall failure of the serious crimes process to meet the needs of female survivors. The narrative of the trials does not do justice in any way to the suffering of Timorese women under the occupation and withdrawal of Indonesia. The Dili trials offered an opportunity at least to show Timorese a fair trial process and engage in capacity-building activities, and this opportunity was mostly squandered.

The image of Beatriz raising her voice and telling her story at the CAVR hearing in Chapter Six gives cause for hope. Even though the CAVR was designed to be a companion for justice, not a substitute for it, generally it was the mechanism that offered the most benefit to Timorese women, in terms of both recognition and redistribution. The CAVR Report stressed that the position of women is fluid. While in many ways East Timor remains a patriarchal and traditional society, the Report allowed public space for the suggestion that women could start to play a greater role in post-conflict reconstruction and governance. As one survivor told the CAVR:

> I will not…hold office like these important men who once fought together with us. All I ask for is my right to a decent life as the family member of a fighter. I got this way because my husband and children disappeared. The important men are not permitted to forget us [just because they] now have a strong chair stuck on the ground. In the past, when their positions were not yet certain, we fought together.[30]

The question is whether Timorese society can shed the euphemistic veil that lies over a substantial social and moral issue in East Timor – that of the reintegration and acceptance of women who have suffered human rights violations and the right of their children to a future free from violence.

Chapter Six also outlined the position of Timorese women under the legal system in the post-conflict period, noting the serious problems with legislation, traditional justice mechanisms (*adat*) and treatment by the courts. The experience of women in the trials set up for transitional justice purposes may have a direct impact on their faith in the legal system to provide redress for domestic violence in the post-conflict era, and vice versa.

CONCLUSION: OPENING THE CURTAINS

I have argued that narrow scholarship in the area of international law may be leading to failures of imagination in responding to the complexities of transitional justice processes. International lawyers need to move beyond the concept of 'trial as endgame', and be more responsive to both the political realities faced by a new state and the situation of women in that state when advocating and designing particular mechanisms. Legalist scholarship has centred on the appropriate forum for prosecuting war criminals and the implications of war crime tribunals for the further development of international humanitarian law and, more generally, of the international criminal justice system. The risk is that if the trials are not well designed and well executed, they may fail and undermine the establishment of the rule of law in the longer peace-building effort. The benefit of Bassiouni's model of minimum accountability for women lies in the fact that a new state or the UN cannot 'trade' the rights of the least powerful for the benefit of the most powerful or vocal in the new state.

Those feminist international lawyers who accept a role for international law in post-conflict societies may need to move beyond improving the content and application of international criminal law in trials to a broader quest for justice for women in post-conflict states. The development of jurisprudence is an important endeavour, but it may not be the sole or even be the primary endeavour in a context where the trials themselves are badly designed or executed. For the reasons explained in this book, holding trials in the wrong circumstances may prove worse for women than doing nothing at all in the early periods of transition. Strategic legal feminists should focus on accountability, certainly, but also on gaining the full participation of women in decisions about transitional justice processes, preserving evidence and acquiring data in relation to international crimes for the day when fair trials can be held, proposing the idea of women as veterans, and stressing the links between conflict and post-conflict spikes in domestic violence. The operation of international law alone may not be enough to turn victims into veterans, indeed it may only act as confirmation of victim status.

The words of Yugoslav Nobel-Prize winning author Ivo Andrić prefaced this book. Andrić notes both the destructive force of war and its transformative potential for gender relations once the 'last mask of humanity' has been stripped away. However, the situation for East Timorese women in 2009 reflects what I termed the 'changing the curtains' phenomena – that fundamental changes in the sovereignty of the state in the form of independence may mean that the basic conditions of women's lives, or their potential to claim their rights, does not change in any meaningful sense. Recognition is flawed and partial and there has been no redistribution of the benefits of peace, not even redistribution of shame.[31] The Timorese adage has not been sufficiently challenged by international interventions: *Feto hakat klot; mane hakat luan (*a woman is born for narrow steps while a man is born for wide steps).[32]

Recognising the economic, social and cultural rights of women in the post-conflict period should be an endeavour of transitional justice. Reconceptualising veteran status is an example of this thinking, but in my view this book calls for a much broader and bolder research agenda focusing on new frontiers for transitional justice. Rama Mani has described the 'thorny' questions facing transitional justice studies, confirmed by this book's analysis of gender equality in post-conflict Timor:

> …Can transitional justice (TJ) today afford not to concern itself directly with social injustice and patterns of inequality, discrimination and marginalization that were underlying causes of a conflict and that inflicted major suffering and victimization on vast swathes of a population? How can (or should) TJ have a more direct impact on reducing social and economic inequality?… How can TJ deliver on its objective of deterrence and create the space for delivery of substantive development to victims of past and present violence?[33]

Unless international law can confront and make itself relevant to that potential for gender justice in a post-conflict setting, not only may opportunities for the betterment of women's situation be lost, but the interventions may worsen their situation. To the call by Sister Maria de Lourdes Martins Cruz of '*a luta continua*' (the fight continues), international law should respond to violations against women with a resounding '*chega*' (enough).

Notes

Chapter 1

1 The correct term for East Timor since independence is the *Democratic Republic of Timor-Leste* (Portuguese) or *Timor Lorosa'e* ('Timor of the rising sun' in Tetum). The term East Timor is used throughout this book because of its popular currency within the English-speaking world.

2 This book relies on the definition of sexual violence in the *Akayesu* case in the ICTR as 'a physical invasion of a sexual nature committed on a person under circumstances which are coercive' at paras 6.4 and 7.7. *Prosecutor v. Jean-Paul Akayesu*, Judgment, Case No. ICTR-96-4-T, 2 September 1998, at para. 598.

3 Rebecca Winters (ed.). *Buibere: Voice of East Timorese Women*. Darwin, NT: East Timor International Support Center, 1999.

4 Amnesty International. *Women in Indonesia and East Timor*. AI Index ASA 21/51/1995. London: Amnesty International, 1995; Miranda E. Sissons, *From One Day to Another: Violations of Women's Reproductive and Sexual Rights in East Timor*, Melbourne: East Timor Human Rights Centre, 1997; George J. Aditjondro, *Violence by the State against Women in East Timor: A Report to the UN Rapporteur on Violence Against Women, including its Causes and Consequences*. Newcastle: East Timor Human Rights Centre, 1997; and Catherine Scott. 'The Feminine Face of Resistance'. Torben Retbøll (ed). *East Timor: Occupation and Resistance*, Copenhagen: International Work Group for Indigenous Affairs, 1998.

5 FOKUPERS, an acronym for 'Forum Komunikasi Untuk Perempuan Loro Sae' (East Timorese Women's Communication Forum), was founded in 1997 and focuses on political victims and gives counselling and other forms of assistance to women victims of violations, including ex political prisoners, war widows and wives of political prisoners.

6 Curt Gabrielson. 'East Timorese Women's Fight Against Violence'. *International Council World Affairs Newsletter*, 1 January 2002.

7 For example, the first Justice Minister was a woman (Ana Pessoa). The most prominent international General Prosecutor for the tribunal in Dili was a woman (Siri Frigaard). There was a female Timorese public defender, Lisete Quintão. The Timorese member of the Appeals court for the Special Panels is a woman (the Hon. Judge Jacinta Correia da Costa who operated the Appeals Court for one year by herself during the transitional justice period). The other most influential Timorese judge on the Special Panels was a woman (Judge Maria Natércia Perreira Gusmão S.H., now President of the Dili District Court, and was herself a survivor of the 1999 violence).

8 Gender refers to 'the economic, social, political and cultural attributes and opportunities associated with being male and female'. Development Assistance Committee (DAC) Guidelines for Gender Equality and Women's Empowerment in Development Co-operation. Paris: OECD, 1998. Gender-based violence is also defined by the United Nations in the 1993 *UN Declaration on the Elimination of Violence against Women*.

9 The World Health Organisation supports the hypothesis that where there is war, post-war or other social upheaval there is an increased incidence of domestic violence. See G. Krug, Dahlberg L, Mercy J, Zwi A and Lozano R (eds). *World Report on Violence and Health*, Geneva: World Health Organisation, 2002. See also Mary O'Kane. 'East Timor: Return of the Revolutionaries'. *The Guardian*, London, 15 January 2001; and Elizabeth Colson. 'War and Domestic Violence' (1995) *Cultural Survival Quarterly* 19 (Spring): 35–38.

10 Women make up 49.4% of the population of East Timor. In the May 2007 Parliamentary elections, it was required of parties that one out of every four candidates on their candidate lists be for women, although the women were mostly placed fourth. Polling data was disaggregated by gender for the first time; 27.69% or 18 women were successful from a total number of 65 seats. Eight candidates stood for election as President, including Lucia Lobato as the one woman candidate. See further Manuela Leong Pereira and Jill Sternberg, 'Women's Involvement in Timor-Leste's Presidential Elections', *1325 Peacewomen E-News*, Issue 89, 24 May 2007.

11 See further Asian Development Bank and UNIFEM, *Gender and Nation Building in Timor-Leste: Country Gender Assessment*, Manila: Asian Development Bank, November 2005; and United Nations Development Programme, *Human Development Report 2006 Timor-Leste: The Path out of Poverty, Integrated Rural Development.* Dili: UNDP, 2006.

12 United Nations Population Fund, *Gender-based Violence in Timor-Leste: A Case Study*. New York: UNFPA, 2005; Vijaya Joshi, 'Building Opportunities: Women's Organizing, Militarism and the United Nations Transitional Administration in East Timor'. PhD thesis, Clarke University, Ann Arbor, Michigan, 2006; and Simi Daniel Schroeter, 'Senses of Violence and the Education of Senses: Gender, Body and Violence in the Independent East Timor' (2006) *Lusotopie* 13(2): 155–72.

13 Mary B. Anderson, *Do No Harm: How Aid can Support Peace – or War*. Boulder: Lynne Rienner Publishers, February 1999.

14 Katherine M. Franke. 'Gendered Subjects of Transitional Justice' (2006) *Columbia Journal of Gender and Law* 15(3): 813–28 at p. 823.

15 Franke, *ibid.*

16 Commission for Reception, Truth and Reconciliation (CAVR). 'Women and the Conflict: National public hearing 28–29 April 2003'. Audiensi Publik Nasional: Balide, East Timor, 2005. See also the Women's Charter of Rights at Appendix A of my SJD thesis, available at http://cigj.anu.edu.au/cigj/people/staff/harris_rimmer.php.

17 'Any assessment of the effect of armed conflict on women requires consideration of a wide variety of factors, the relevance and impact of which differ considerably between cultures and individual women in those cultures. Many factors such as race, ethnicity, age, class, disability and sexuality, in addition to gender, will affect a woman's experience of armed conflict.' Judith G. Gardam and Michelle J. Jarvis. *Women, Armed Conflict and International Law*, The Hague and Boston, MA: Kluwer Law International, 2001, at p. 19.

18 See for example, Cynthia Enloe's question 'Where are the women in international politics?': *Bananas, Beaches and Bases: Making Feminist Sense of International Politics*. London: Pandora, 1990 at p. 11.

19 The aim of this book is not prescriptive in the sense of presenting policy solutions for post-conflict states. It does not represent an attempt to 'ventriloquise' what the women of East Timor might wish for in terms of justice, even if they could be identified as a homogenous group.

20 See further Hilary Charlesworth 'Symposium on Method in International Law: Feminist Methods in International Law' (1999) *American Journal of International Law* 93: 379.

21 Judith Butler. 'Preface'. *Gender Trouble: Feminism and the Subversion of Identity*. New York: Routledge, 1999, pp. vii–xxvi, note 191.

22 For a full survey of the inclusion of gender concerns in Timor's vibrant civil society, see further Anna Trembath and Damian Grenfell, *Mapping the Pursuit of Gender Equality: Non-Government and International Agency Activity in Timor-Leste.* Melbourne: Globalism Institute, RMIT University, and Irish Aid, August 2007.
23 See further the Media Publications section of my Bibliography.
24 Susan Harris Rimmer, 'The Roman Catholic Church and the Rights of East Timorese Women', Carolyn Evans and Amanda Whiting (eds). *Mixed Blessings: Laws, Religions and Women's Rights in the Asia-Pacific Region.* The Hague: Brill, 2006.
25 Trembath and Grenfell, *ibid.*
26 Lisa Palmer, Sara Niner, and Lia Kent. 'Forum Proceedings: Exploring the Tensions of Nation Building in Timor-Leste, Held on 15 September 2006 at Melbourne University'. Monica Minnegal (ed). *School of Social and Environmental Enquiry Research Paper No. 1.* Melbourne: University of Melbourne, 2007.
27 Trembath and Grenfell, *ibid.*
28 See Corey Levine, *Gender and Transitional Justice: A Case Study of East Timor*, Vancouver: Canadian Consortium on Human Security, 2004; Galuh Wandita, Karen Campbell-Nelson, and Manuela Leong Pereira. 'Gender and Reparations in Timor-Leste', Ruth Rubio-Marin (ed), *Engendering Reparations: Recognising and Compensating Women Victims of Human Rights Violations.* New York: International Center for Transitional Justice, 2006; and Hayli Millar. 'Facilitating Women's Voices in Truth Recovery: An Assessment of Women's Participation and the Integration of a Gender Perspective in Truth Commissions'. Helen Durham and Tracey Gurd (eds). *Listening to the Silences: Women and War*, Leiden, Boston: Martinus Nijhoff, 2005: 171–222. See also Elizabeth Stanley, *Torture, Truth and Justice: The Case of Timor Leste*, NY and London: Routledge, 2009.
29 Jack Snyder and Leslie Vinjamuri, 'Advocacy and Scholarship in the Study of International War Crime Tribunals and Transitional Justice' (2004) *Annual Review of Political Science* 7: 345–62.
30 See especially Priscilla B. Hayner, *Unspeakable Truths: Confronting State Terror and Atrocity.* New York: Routledge, 2001; Martha Minow, *Between Vengeance and Forgiveness: Facing History After Genocide and Mass Violence*, Boston: Beacon Press, 1998; and Ruti G. Teitel, *Transitional Justice.* New York: Oxford University Press, 2000.
31 M. Cherif Bassiouni (ed.), 'Accountability for Violations of International Humanitarian Law', *Post-Conflict Justice,* Transnational Publishers: New York. 2002, at p. 27.
32 Kieran McEvoy and Lorna McGregor (eds), *Transitional Justice From Below: Grassroots Activism and the Struggle for Change.* London: Hart Publishing, 2008.
33 Hugo van der Merwe, Victoria Baxter and Audrey Chapman (eds), *Assessing the Impact of Transitional Justice: Challenges for Empirical Research.* Washington: United States Institute for Peace Press, 2009.
34 For an excellent overview and analysis of the claims made for truth in transitional justice settings, see David Mendeloff, 'Truth-seeking, Truth-telling, and Post-conflict Peacebuilding: Curb the Enthusiasm?' (2004) *International Studies Review* 6: 355–80.
35 Michael Ignatieff. 'Articles of Faith'. (1996) *Index on Censorship* 5, at p. 11.
36 '…these are not so much assumptions of epistemology as articles of faith about human nature: the truth is one and if we know it, it will make us free'. Michael Ignatieff, 'Articles of Faith', (1996) *Index on Censorship* 5, at p. 1. See also Rosalind Shaw 'Rethinking Truth and Reconciliation Commissions: Lessons from Sierra Leone', *United States Institute of Peace Special Report No 130*, February 2005.
37 Ariel Dorfman, 'Afterword', *Death and the Maiden.* London: Nick Hern Books and Royal Court Theatre, 1992, p.59.
38 See for example Geoffery Best, *Humanity in Warfare: The Modern History of the International Law of Armed Conflict.* London: Weidenfeld and Nicholson, 1980.

39 The exception to this is the important collection M. Cherif Bassiouni (ed.) *Post-Conflict Justice*. New York: Transnational Publishers, 2002.

40 See further Naomi Roht-Arriaza and Javier Mariezcurrena (eds). *Transitional Justice in the Twenty-First Century: Beyond Truth versus Justice*, Cambridge: Cambridge University Press, 2006.

41 Miriam Aukerman describes this as the 'prosecution preference': 'Extraordinary Evil, Ordinary Crime: A Framework for Understanding Transitional Justice' (2002) 15 *Harvard Human Rights Journal* 39, at p. 47..

42 Secretary General, United Nations. *Report to the Security Council, on the Rule of Law and Transitional Justice in Conflict and Post-Conflict Societies.* United Nations Doc S/2004/616, 23 August 2004.

43 See further Andreas O'Shea, *Amnesty for crime in international law and practice.* The Hague; London: Kluwer Law International, 2002.

44 Diane E. Orentlicher, 'Settling Accounts: The Duty to Prosecute Human Rights Violations of a Prior Regime' (1991) 100 *Yale Law Journal* 2537. See also Geoffrey Robertson, *Crimes Against Humanity: The Struggle for Global Justice*, London, NY: New Press, 2000, see particularly his discussion of amnesties at p. 263.

45 For example, Jodi Halpern and Harvey Weinstein critique the exclusive focus of transitional scholars on states: 'Much of the literature on peace building or stabilization focuses at the level of the state – particularly the creation of institutions, legal and electoral reform, security, economic development, and the return of displaced people. Despite work showing the unique harms inflicted by ethnic conflicts in which neighbours kill neighbours, relatively little attention has been paid to the fact that these people must now learn to live together on a daily basis…This paper suggests that it is the interpersonal ruins, rather than ruined buildings and institutions, that pose the greatest challenge for rebuilding society'. 'Rehumanizing the Other: Empathy and Reconciliation' (2004) *Human Rights Quarterly* 26: 561–83 at pp. 562–63.

46 See further Miriam Aukerman, 'Extraordinary Evil, Ordinary Crime: A Framework for Understanding Transitional Justice' (2002) 15 *Harvard Human Rights Journal* 39, at p. 47.

47 Louise Arbour, United Nations High Commissioner for Human Rights, 'Economic and Social Justice for Societies in Transition'. Paper presented at the Second Annual Transitional Justice Lecture, New York University School of Law, New York, 25 October 2006.

48 See also Susanne Karstedt, 'Coming to terms with the Past in Germany after 1945 and 1989: Public Judgements on Procedures and Justice' (1998) *Law and Policy* 20(1): 15–56.

49 Rama Mani, *Beyond Retribution: Seeking Justice in the Shadows of War*. Cambridge, Polity, 2002.

50 Mani, *ibid*., at p. 53.

51 Mani, *ibid*., at p. 78.

52 Mani, *ibid*., p. 174.

53 See further Laurel Fletcher and Harvey M. Weinstein, 'Violence and Social Repair: Rethinking the Contribution of Justice to Reconciliation', (2002) *Human Rights Quarterly*. 24(3): pp 573–639.

54 See further John Braithwaite, *Crime, Shame and Reintegration*. Cambridge; Sydney: Cambridge University Press, 1989.

55 See further Charles Villa-Vicencio, 'The Reek of Cruelty and the Quest for Healing – Where Retributive and Restorative Justice Meet' (1999/2000) *Journal of Law and Religion* 14: 165–87.

56 See especially Nicola Henry, 'Disclosure, Sexual Violence and International Jurisprudence: A Therapeutic Approach'. PhD dissertation, University of Melbourne, 2005.

57 Note Articles 75, 79 and 43.6 in the Rome Statute.

58 See General Assembly Resolution 60/147 of 16 December 2005, A/RES/60/147; 13 IHRR 907 (2006).

59 Rama Mani, 'Balancing peace with justice in the aftermath of violent conflict' (2005) *Development* 48(3):25–34 at p. 27.

60 Never Again (Hebrew: בוש אל םלועל, *L'vlim la suv*), is a common phrase used in relation to The Holocaust, coined by Rabbi Meir Kahane.

61 Ruti G. Teitel, *Transitional Justice*. Oxford; New York: Oxford University Press, 2000, at p. 6.

62 Teitel, *ibid*. See also Bronwyn Leebaw, 'Book Review: Transitional Justice by Ruti Teitel' (2001) *49 American Journal of Comparative Law* 363, at p. 364.

63 See further *The Responsibility to Protect Report* of the International Commission on Intervention and State Sovereignty, December 2001, at p. 42.

64 M. Cherif Bassiouni, 'Searching for Peace and Achieving Justice: the Need for Accountability', (1996) 59(4) *Law and Contemporary Problems* 9, at p. 23.

65 See further Vesna Nikolic-Ristanovic, 'Sexual violence, international law and restorative justice'. Doris Buss and Ambreena Manji (eds). *International Law: Modern Feminist Approaches*, Oxford and Portland Oregon, Hart Publishing, 2005: 273–94.

66 Human Rights Watch, *Justice Denied for East Timor*. New York, 2004; Amnesty International and JSMP. *Justice for Timor-Leste – the way forward*. Dili, April 2004; David Cohen, *Intended to Fail: The Trials before the Ad Hoc Human Rights Court in Jakarta*. New York: International Center for Transitional Justice, 2003; United Nations Commission of Experts. *Report to the UN Secretary-General of the Commission of Experts to Review the Prosecutions of Serious Violations of Human Rights in Timor Leste (then East Timor) in 1999*. S/2005/458, 15 July 2005 (hereafter cited as the 'Commission of Experts Report'); and the International Crisis Group, *Indonesia: Impunity versus accountability for gross human rights violations* Brussels, 2001.

67 Laura Grenfell, 'Legal Pluralism and the Rule of Law in Timor Leste' (2006) *Leiden Journal of International Law* 19: 305–37.

68 Sven Gunnar Simonsen, 'The Authoritarian Temptation in East Timor: Nation-building and the Need for Inclusive Governance' (2006) *Asian Survey* 46(4): 575–96.

69 Simon Chesterman, *Justice under International Administration: Kosovo, East Timor and Afghanistan*. The International Peace Academy: New York, 2002; Henriette Sachse, 'East Timor: Is the Country Back on Track?' *Asian Analysis*, December 2006.

70 Jeffrey Kingston, 'Balancing justice and reconciliation in East Timor' (2006) *Critical Asian Studies*, 38(3): 271–302; Taina Järvinen, *Human Rights and Post-conflict Transitional Justice in East Timor*. UPI Working Papers. Helsinki: Finnish Institute of International Affairs, 2004.

71 Hilary Charlesworth, 'What Are Women's International Human Rights?' Rebecca Cook (ed.), *Human Rights of Women: National and International Perspectives*, Philadelphia: Pennsylvania University Press, 1994: 58–84 at p. 67.

72 See especially Judith Gardam, 'Women and Armed Conflict: The Response of International Law'. Helen Durham and Tracey Gurd (eds). *Listening to the Silences: Women and War*, Leiden, Boston: Martinus Nijhoff, 2005: 109–24; and Hilary Charlesworth and Christine Chinkin, *The Boundaries of International Law: A Feminist Analysis*, Chapter 6, Manchester; Manchester University Press, 2000.

73 See especially Rhonda Copelon, 'Surfacing Gender: Reconceptualizing Crimes Against Women in Bosnia-Herzegovina', Alexandra Stiglmayer (ed.), *Mass Rape: The War Against Women in Bosnia-Herzegovinia*, Lincoln: University of Nebraska Press, 1994: 197–218.

74 See however Christine Bell and Catherine O'Rourke, 'Does feminism need a theory of transitional justice?' (2007) *International Journal of Transitional Justice* 1: 23–44; and Katherine M. Franke, 'Gendered Subjects of Transitional Justice' (2006) *Columbia Journal of Gender and Law* 15 (3): 813–28. Both these articles have been crucial in the development of this book. See also the December 2007 Special Issue on

Gender and Transitional Justice of the *International Journal of Transitional Justice*, with Judge Navanethem Pillay as guest editor (Issue 3). The recent scholarship of Fionnuala Ni Aolain is also groundbreaking in this field, for example. 'Gender and the Rule of Law in Transitional Societies', *Minnesota Legal Studies Research Paper No. 09–12; Transitional Justice Institute Research Paper No. 09–02*, March 2009 (with Michael Hamilton).

75 Christine Bell and Catherine O'Rourke, 'Does feminism need a theory of transitional justice?', (2007) *International Journal of Transitional Justice* 1: 23–44.

76 See especially Susan Brownmiller, *Against Our Will: Men, Women and Rape*, London: Penguin Books, 1975; Elizabeth Rehn, and Ellen Johnson Sirleaf, *Women, War and Peace: Independent Experts Assessment on the Impact of Armed Conflict on Women and Women's Role in Peace-building*. New York: UNIFEM 2002; and International Committee of the Red Cross (ICRC), *Woman and War Special Report*, ICRC, Geneva, 2003.

77 See further the collected writings of Cynthia Enloe.

78 The most comprehensive is by Brigitte Sorensen, 'Women and post-conflict reconstruction: issues and sources'. *The War-Torn Societies Project Occasional Paper no. 3*, Geneva: UN Research Institute for Social Development, June 1998.

79 Security Council Resolution 1325 was passed unanimously on 31 October 2000 and addresses the impact of war on women, and women's contributions to conflict resolution and sustainable peace.

80 See Kelly Dawn Askin, *War Crimes Against Women: Prosecution in International War Crimes Tribunals*, The Hague: Martinus Nijhoff Publishers, 1997.

81 See further Gabrielle Kirk McDonald, 'Crimes of Sexual Violence: The Experience of the International Criminal Tribunal' (2000) *Columbia Journal of Transnational Law* 39(1): 1–17.

82 Kelly Dawn Askin, *ibid.*, at p. 374.

83 See further Helen Durham, 'International Humanitarian Law and the Protection of Women'. Helen Durham and Tracey Gurd (eds), *Listening to the Silences: Women and War*, Leiden, Boston: Martinus Nijhoff, 2005: 95–108.

84 See especially Nicola Henry, 'Disclosure, Sexual Violence and International Jurisprudence: A Therapeutic Approach'. PhD dissertation, University of Melbourne, 2005; and David B. Wexler and Bruce J. Winnick, *Law in a Therapeutic Key*. Durham, North Carolina; Carolina Academic Press, 1996.

85 See further Chapter 6 – Hilary Charlesworth and Christine Chinkin, *The Boundaries of International Law: A Feminist Analysis*. Manchester: Manchester University Press, 2000.

86 See further Fionnuala Ni Aolain, 'Radical Rules: The Effects of Evidential and Procedural Rules on the Regulation of Sexual Violence in War' (1997) *Albany Law Review* 60(3): 883–905.

87 See for example Doris Buss, 'Prosecuting Mass Rape: Prosecutor v. Dragoljub Kunarac, Radomir Kovac and Zoran Vukovic' (2002) *Feminist Legal Studies* 10(1): 91–99.

88 See in particular Hayli Millar, 'Facilitating Women's Voices in Truth Recovery: An assessment of women's participation and the integration of a gender perspective in truth commissions', Helen Durham and Tracey Gurd (eds.) *Listening to the Silences: Women and War*, Boston, Leiden: Martinus Nijhoff, 2005: 171–222; and Vasuki Nesiah, *Gender and Truth Commission Mandates*. International Center for Transitional Justice, New York, 2006.

89 Fleming Terrell, 'Unofficial Accountability: A Proposal for the Permanent Women's Tribunal on Sexual Violence in Armed Conflict' (2005) *Texas Journal of Women and the Law* 15(1): 107.

90 Laura Grenfell, 'Harnessing Local Law in the Post-Conflict State: The case of Timor-Leste', *Timor-Leste: Challenges for Justice and Human Rights in the Shadow of the Past*. William Binchy (ed). Dublin: Clarus Press, 2009: 81–110.

91 Ruth Rubio-Marin (ed.). *What Happened to the Women? Gender and Reparations for Human Rights Violations*, New York: International Center for Transitional Justice, 2006. Christine Chinkin and Hilary Charlesworth have also assessed economic, social and cultural rights in the context of peace-building processes: 'The failure to prioritise economic, social and cultural rights also assigns the economic and social imperatives of post-conflict reconstruction to international financial institutions, which have limited interest in a human rights framework'; see 'Building Women into Peace' (2006) *Third World Quarterly* 27(5): 937–57 at p. 946.

92 See especially Karen Engle, 'Feminism and its (Dis)contents: Criminalizing Wartime Rape in Bosnia and Herzegovina' (2005) *The American Journal of International Law* 99(4): 778–816.

93 Katherine M. Franke, *ibid.*

94 Karen Engle, *ibid.*, at p. 778.

95 See further Julie Mertus, 'Shouting from the Bottom of the Well: The Impact of International Trials for Wartime Rape on Women's Agency' (2004) *International Feminist Journal of Politics* 6(1): 110–28. Mertus concludes that 'tribunals alone do not serve [victims'] need for creating a record, achieving justice, remembering or forgetting' and that alternative and complementary processes are needed to facilitate the empowerment of women in the aftermath of war.

96 Judith G. Gardam and Michelle J. Jarvis, *Women, Armed Conflict and International Law*, The Hague: Kluwer Law International, 2001, at p.184.

97 See further Judith Gardam, 'Women and Armed Conflict: The response of international law', Helen Durham and Tracey Gurd (eds). *Listening to the Silences: Women and War*, Leiden, Boston: Martinus Nijhoff, 2005: 1009–1124.

98 Christine Bell and Catherine O'Rourke, *ibid.*

99 Katherine M. Franke, *ibid.*, at p. 813.

100 Katherine M. Franke, *ibid.*

101 Fionnuala Ni Aolain, and Michael Hamilton. *ibid.*, at p. 102.

102 Fionnuala Ni Aolain, 'Women, Security and the Patriarchy of Internationalized Transitional Justice', *Minnesota Legal Studies Research Paper No. 08–40*, October 2008.

103 See further, Hilary Charlesworth, 'Saddam Hussein: My Part in his Downfall' (2005) *Wisconsin International Law Journal* 27: 127–43.

104 'Gendered and feminist analysis [of international relations] reveal that the state is in almost all cases male-dominated, and is in different ways a masculinist construct. It is simply not possible to explain state power without explaining women's systematic exclusion from it'. Jan Jindy Pettman. *Worlding Women: A Feminist International Politics*. St. Leonards, NSW: Allen and Unwin, 1996 at p. 5.

105 See especially Karen Engle, *ibid.*

106 Rebecca Winters (ed.), *ibid.*

107 See for example, the Magna Carta concerning Freedoms, Rights, Duties and Guarantees for the People of East Timor adopted by the National Council of East Timorese Resistance (CNRT), Peniche, Portugal, 25 April 1998.

108 See Irena Cristalis and Catherine Scott, *Independent Women. The Story of Women's Activism in East Timor*. Progressio: London, 2005.

109 See further Organização Popular da Mulher Timor (OPMT – The Popular Organisation of East Timorese Women, or Fretilin women's arm), 'Letter to the editor: Response to Kirsty Sword Gusmão's opinion in *The Australian* newspaper dated 7 July 2006', published 8 July 2006.

110 Susan Harris Rimmer. 'Untold Numbers: East Timorese Women and Transitional Justice'. Sharon Pickering and Caroline Lambert (eds). *Global Issues, Women and Justice*. Sydney: Federation Press, 2004: 335–66.

111 Security Council media release, 'United Nations Determined not to Abandon Timor-Leste at Critical Time of Need,' SC/8745 13 June 2006.

112 Joint Truth and Friendship Commission, *Per Memoriam ad Spem (From Memory to Hope): Final Report*, May 2008. Possibly more useful is the report by David Cohen. 'Seeking Truth and Responsibility: Report of the Special Advisor to the CTF'. Berkeley War Crimes Studies Centre, April 2007. See also Tom Hyland, 'Indonesia was behind Timor Atrocities, Says Report', *The Age*, 11 July 2008, Tom Hyland 'Amid the Major Flaws, a Minor Act of Courage', *The Age*, 11 July 2008.

113 See further International Center for Transitional Justice, *Report: Too Much Friendship, Too Little Truth: Report on the Commission of Truth and Friendship in Indonesia and Timor-Leste*, January 2008; and International Center for Transitional Justice. *An Unfinished Truth: An Analysis of the Commission of Truth and Friendship's Final Report on the 1999 Atrocities in East Timor*, 2009.

114 Associated Press, 'Revenge is Low on the List of Priorities', *The Weekend Australian*, 18–19 May 2002, p. 15.

115 Associated Press, *ibid.*

116 Antjie Krog. *Country of My Skull: Guilt, Sorrow and the Limits of Forgiveness in the New South Africa*. Johannesburg: Vintage Press, 1999.

Chapter 2

1 Christine Chinkin, Hilary Charlesworth, and Shelley Wright, 'Feminist approaches to international law: reflections from another century', Doris Buss and Ambreena Manji (eds). *International Law: Modern Feminist Approaches*. Oxford and Portland, Oregon: Hart Publishing, 2005, at p. 44.

2 Martin Luther King Junior (ed.), 'Letter from Birmingham Jail', *Why We Can't Wait*, New York: Harper & Row, 1963 at pp. 77–100.

3 Quoted by Oxfam Community Aid Abroad, 'Women Fight for Freedom: The Struggle for Human Rights and Independence in East Timor', May 1999.

4 Mani, Rama. 'Editorial: Dilemmas of Expanding Transitional Justice, or Forging the Nexus between Transitional Justice and Development' (2009) *International Journal of Transitional Justice* (Special issue on transitional justice and development) 2: 253–65.

5 See further Johan Galtung, *Peace, Research, Education, Action*, Copenhagen: Christian Ejlers, 1975 at pp. 122–30, and p. 135. Galtung is cited as inspiration by two pieces of cutting-edge scholarship in this area: Fionnuala Ni Aolain in her article 'Women, Security and the Patriarchy of Internationalized Transitional Justice' *Minnesota Legal Studies Research Paper No. 08–40,* October 2008, and by Zinaida Miller in 'Effects of invisibility: In search of the 'economic' in transitional justice', (2009) *International Journal of Transitional Justice* (Special issue on transitional justice and development) 2: 266–91.

6 See for example, Gita Sen and Caren Grown, *Development, Crises and Alternative Visions: Third World Women Perspectives*. New York: Monthly Review, 1987.

7 See especially Hayli Millar, 'Facilitating Women's Voices in Truth Recovery: An assessment of women's participation and the integration of a gender perspective in truth commissions', Helen Durham and Tracey Gurd (eds). *Listening to the Silences: Women and War*. Boston, Leiden: Martinus Nijhoff, 2005 at pp. 171–222.

8 'Gendered and feminist analysis [of international relations] reveal that the state is in almost all cases male-dominated, and is in different ways a masculinist construct. It is simply not possible to explain state power without explaining women's systematic exclusion from it.' Jan Jindy Pettman, *Worlding Women: A Feminist International Politics*. St. Leonards, NSW: Allen & Unwin, 1996 at p. 5.

9 See especially Karen Engle, 'Feminism and Its (Dis)contents: Criminalizing Wartime Rape in Bosnia and Herzegovina' (2005) *The American Journal of International Law* 99(4): 778–816.

10 Dianne Otto, 'Disconcerting "Masculinities": reinventing the gendered subject(s) of international human rights law', Doris Buss and Ambreena Manji (eds). *International*

Law: Modern Feminist Approaches. Oxford and Portland, Oregon: Hart Publishing, 2005 at p. 128.

11 Article II of the *Convention on the Prevention and Punishment of the Crime of Genocide 1951* ('Genocide Convention').

12 Article 7 of the Rome Statute.

13 For example, Article 4 of the *International Covenant on Civil and Political Rights 1966*

14 For example, Article 1 of Additional Protocols I and II of the *Geneva Conventions 1949*, plus Common Article 3. See further B. De Schutter and C. Van De Wyngaert, 'Non-international armed conflicts: The borderline between national and international law' (1983) *Georgia Journal of International and Comparative Law* 13: 279.

15 Common Article 2 of the *Geneva Conventions 1949.*

16 For example, Security Council Resolution 1264 (1999).

17 For example, see further the Office of the Prosecutor, 'Informal expert paper: the principle of complementarity in practice', International Criminal Court, The Hague, 2003 and Mireille Delmas-Marty, 'Interactions between National and International Criminal Law in the Preliminary Phase of Trial at the ICC' (2006) *Journal of International Criminal Justice* 4(1): 2–11.

18 For example, see the *Rules of Procedure and Evidence of International Criminal Tribunal for the Former Yugoslavia* (February 1994). See further Sanford Levinson, 'Responsibility for Crimes of War' (1973) *Philosophy and Public Affairs* 2(3): 244–73.

19 See further *'Testimony from the International Center for Transitional Justice to the Constitutional Court of Indonesia by ICTJ staff and colleagues'*, New York: International Center for Transitional Justice, July 2006.

20 *United Nations General Assembly Resolution 60/147 Annex,* adopted 16 December 2005, UN Doc. A/RES/60/147, 21 March 2006.

21 *Report of the Independent Expert to Update the Set of Principles to Combat Impunity*, Addendum, UN Doc. E/CN.4/2005/102/Add.1, 8 February 2005.

22 Mozambique has taken this course, as an example. Certain conflicts with very low political value to the international community can be left completely unaddressed, such as Ethiopia, despite over one million casualties under the Mengitsu regime.

23 United Nations, '*High Commissioner for Human Rights reports on the situation in East Timor as the Commission on Human Rights considers holding special meeting'*, media release, HR/99/90, 17 September 1999.

24 The growth in calls for accountability has been influenced by the changing nature of news media, the rise of the human rights NGO sector, precedents in international criminal law, and the changing nature of conflict to mainly civil wars with high civilian causalities: Neil J. Kritz, 'Progress and Humility: The Ongoing Search for Post-Conflict Justice' M. Cherif Bassiouni (ed.). *Post-Conflict Justice.* Transnational Publishers: New York. 2002 at p. 56.

25 See M. Cherif Bassiouni, 'International Crimes: *Jus Cogens* and *Obligatio Erga Omnes*' (1996) 59 *Law and Contemporary Problems* 63, at p. 67. For a contrary view to Bassiouni from a realist, state-practice based viewpoint, see further Alfred P. Rubin, '*Actio Popularis, Jus Cogens* and Offenses *Erga Omnes*?' (2001) *New England Law Review* 35(2): 265–80.

26 *Barcelona Traction, Light and Power Co. Ltd* (*Spain v Belgium*) (*Second Phase*) [1970] ICJ Rep 3, paras 33–34. See further Article 53 of the 1969 Vienna Convention on the Law of Treaties. Note also M. Cherif Bassiouni (ed.), 'Accountability for Violations of International Law.' *Post-Conflict Justice*. Transnational Publishers: New York. 2002, at p. 20, fn 85.

27 Yoram Dinstein, 'Human Rights in Armed Conflict: International Humanitarian Law'. Theodore Meron (ed.). *Human Rights in International Law: Legal and Policy Issues*. Vol. II. Oxford: Clarendon Press, 1984, pp. 350–54.

28 Paul van Zyl outlines five affirmative state obligations in international law, including the duty firstly to establish the fate of victims and secondly to identify perpetrators, thirdly to provide compensation to victims, fourthly to take affirmative measures to prevent non-repetition, and fifthly to prosecute and punish those found guilty. 'Justice Without Punishment: Guaranteeing Human Rights in Transitional Societies', Charles Villa-Vicencio and Wilhelm Verwoerd (eds), *Looking Back Reaching Forward: Reflections on the Truth and Reconciliation Commission of South Africa*. Cape Town: UCT Press, 2000: 42–53, at p. 49.

29 See further Ben Saul, 'Was the Conflict in East Timor "Genocide" and Why Does it Matter?' (2001) *Melbourne Journal of International Law* 2(2): 477.

30 M. Cherif Bassiouni (ed.). 'Proposed guiding principles for combating impunity for international crimes'. *Post-Conflict Justice*. Transnational Publishers: New York, 2002, at p. 257.

31 Diane Orentlicher, 'Settling accounts: the duty to prosecute human rights violations of a prior regime' (1991) *Yale Law Journal* 100(8): 2537–2615.

32 Aryeh Neier argues that punishment fulfills society's duty 'to honour and redeem the suffering of the individual victim'. Cited by Diane Orentlicher, 'Settling accounts: the duty to prosecute human rights violations of a prior regime' (1991) *Yale Law Journal* 100(8): 2537–2615 at p. 2539. Note contra James O'Connell, 'Gambling with the Psyche: Does Prosecuting Human Rights Violators Console their Victims?' (2005) 46 *Harvard International Law Journal* 295, 340.

33 Ruti Teitel notes that '[o]nly trials are thought to draw a bright line demarcating the normative shift from illegitimate to legitimate rule', but observes that trials have been rarely utilised in practice. *Transitional Justice*. Oxford; New York: Oxford University Press, 2000, at p. 6. See further Jaime Malamud Goti, 'Trying Violations of Human Rights: The Dilemma of Transitional Democratic Governments', *State Crimes, Punishment or Pardon. Papers and Reports of the Conference, November 4–6 1988,* Aspen Institute: Wye Center, Maryland, 1989: 81–82.

34 Theodor Meron has stated '[t]he great hope of tribunal advocates was that the individualization and decollectivisation of guilt…would help bring about peace and reconciliation'. *War Crimes Law Comes of Age: Essays*. Oxford: Oxford University Press 1998, at p. 282.

35 Bassiouni claims that post-conflict or transitional justice strategies should be designed to complement the agenda of political stabilisation, while remaining committed to key human rights principles. M. Cherif Bassiouni (ed.). 'Introduction.' *Post-Conflict Justice*. Transnational Publishers: New York. 2002, at p xv. Similarly, Hannah Arendt in her correspondence with Karl Jaspers after Nuremberg concluded that criminal prosecutions were a necessary but not sufficient response to state-sponsored atrocities. Hannah Arendt,. *Hannah Arendt, Karl Jaspers: Correspondence, 1926–1969*. New York: Harcourt Brace Jovanovich, 1992. Note discussion in Helena Cobban, 'The Legacies of Collective Violence.' (2002) *Boston Review* 27(2): 21–27.

36 M. Cherif Bassiouni (ed.). 'Introduction.' *Post-Conflict Justice*. Transnational Publishers: New York. 2002, at p. xv.

37 See further Shirley Scott, 'International Law as Ideology: Theorizing the Relationship between International Law and International Politics' (1994) *European Journal of International Law* 5: 1–325 at p. 98.

38 Mark A. Drumbl. 'Pluralizing International Criminal Justice' (2005) 106 *Michigan Law Review* 1295, at pp. 1309–11.

39 Samuel Huntington. *The Third Wave: Democratization in the Late Twentieth Century*, Norman: University of Oklahoma Press 1991, at pp. 211–25. Huntington then derives prescriptive 'guidelines for democratizers' at p. 225. Henry Kissinger has also stated that the decision to punish past atrocities in newly democratising states or to forget them is determined by politics, not any legal obligation to punish. See Jack Snyder

and Leslie Vinjamuri, 'Advocacy and Scholarship in the Study of International War Crime Tribunals and Transitional Justice' (2004) *Annual Review of Political Science* 7: 345–62 at p. 354.

40 The Bush Administration's emphasis on 'mixed' tribunals that emphasise local participation is an example of this trend. Jack Snyder and Leslie Vinjamuri, 'Advocacy and Scholarship in the Study of International War Crime Tribunals and Transitional Justice' (2004) *Annual Review of Political Science* 7: 345–62 at p. 354.

41 Agung Yudhawiranata. 'Opinion: RI needs truth commission'. *The Jakarta Post*, 21 October 2003.

42 Simon Chesterman. *Justice under international administration: Kosovo, East Timor and Afghanistan.* NY: International Peace Academy, 2002.

43 Neil Kritz, 'Progress and Humility: The Ongoing Search for Post-Conflict Justice' M. Cherif Bassiouni (ed.). *Post-Conflict Justice*. Transnational Publishers: New York. 2002 at p. 59. See also M. Cherif Bassiouni (ed.), 'Introduction.' *Post-Conflict Justice*. New York: Transnational Publishers. 2002, at p. xv and p. xviii.

44 Neil Kritz, *ibid*., at p. 59.

45 Jack Snyder and Leslie Vinjamuri. 'Advocacy and Scholarship in the Study of International War Crime Tribunals and Transitional Justice' (2004) *Annual Review of Political. Science* 7: 345–62 at p. 361.

46 Carlos Nino, *Radical Evil on Trial*. New Haven: Yale University Press, 1996, at p. 112.

47 Carlos Nino, *ibid*., at p. 131.

48 Laurel Fletcher and Harvey M. Weinstein. 'Violence and Social Repair: Rethinking the Contribution of Justice to Reconciliation', (2002) *Human Rights Quarterly* 24(3): 573–639.

49 Laurel Fletcher and Harvey M. Weinstein, *ibid*., at p. 579.

50 Miriam Aukerman. 'Extraordinary Evil, Ordinary Crime: A Framework for Understanding Transitional Justice', (2002) 15 *Harvard Human Rights Journal* 39, at p. 47.

51 Miriam Aukerman, *ibid*.

52 Laurel Fletcher and Harvey M. Weinstein, *ibid*., at p. 573.

53 Laurel Fletcher and Harvey M. Weinstein, at p. 574.

54 Vasuki Nesiah. *Truth Commissions and Gender: Principles, Policies and Procedures*. Gender Justice Series. International Centre for Transitional Justice: New York, July 2006.

55 Ruti G. Teitel. *Transitional Justice*. Oxford; New York: Oxford University Press, 2000, at p. 6.

56 Fionnuala Ni Aolain and Catherine Turner. 'Gender, Truth and Transition', (2007) *UCLA Women's Law Journal* 16: 229 at p. 240.

57 The feminist concept of the public/private distinction holds that the law only seeks to regulate and protect those acts that are considered 'public' and will not enter into the 'private' realm of the family and domestic life, or enforce those parts of the law which do. What is considered to be objectively public appears to fall along gender lines, and therefore 'cripples women's citizenship'. The 'lie' of the dichotomy is that it 'invokes closure, presupposes there are certain spheres that are naturally "unchangeable" or "beyond the mandate"'. Finally, this construction of the law does not recognise that women can be powerless in both the public and private spheres. The theory is based on commonality of women's experiences and is therefore contingent rather than essentialist. Hilary Charlesworth. 'What are women's international human rights?' Rebecca Cook (ed.). *Human Rights of Women: National and International Perspectives*, Philadelphia: Pennsylvania University Press, 1994 pp: 58–84 at p. 69.

58 Patricia Viseur-Sellers challenges a simplistic view of the public/private distinction in the case of sexual violence, 'Individual(s') liability for collective sexual violence'. Karen Knop (ed.). *Gender and Human Rights.* Oxford; Oxford UP, 2004; and Karen

Engle, 'After the Collapse of the Public/Private Distinction: Strategizing Women's Rights', Dorinda Dallmeyer (ed.). *Reconceiving Reality: Women and International Law*, Washington: American Society of International Law, 1993, at p. 143.

59 See further Cynthia Cockburn. *The Space Between Us: Negotiating Gender and National Identities in Conflict.* London: Zed Books, 1998; and Alexandra Stiglmayer (ed.), *Mass Rape: The War Against Women in Bosnia-Herzegovina.* Lincoln: University of Nebraska Press, 1993.

60 See for example, Judith Gardam and Michelle Jarvis. *Women, Armed Conflict and International Law*, The Hague: Kluwer Law International, 2001 at p.173; and Ratna Kapur, 'The Tragedy of Victimization Rhetoric: Resurrecting the "Native" Subject in International/Post-Colonial Feminist Legal Politics' (2002) *Harvard Human Rights Journal* 15: 1–37.

61 R. Charli Carpenter. 'Stirring Gender into the Mainstream: Feminism, Constructivism, and the Uses of Theory' (2003) *International Studies Review* 5(3): 287.

62 Hayli Millar. 'Facilitating Women's Voices in Truth Recovery: An assessment of women's participation and the integration of a gender perspective in truth commissions', Helen Durham and Tracey Gurd (eds). *Listening to the Silences: Women and War*, Boston, Leiden: Martinus Nijhoff, 2005: 171–222 at p. 172.

63 Secretary-General, United Nations, *Resolution on Women, Peace and Security*, SC Res 1325, 55 UN SCOR (4213th mtg), UN Doc S/RES/1325 (2000) [para 11].

64 See Secretary General, United Nations, *Women, Peace and Security, Study submitted by the Secretary-General pursuant to Security Council resolution 1325, (2000)*, (2002) [paras 116–61, 343–45].

65 See Elisabeth Rehn and Ellen Johnson Sirleaf, *Women, War and Peace: The Independent Experts' Assessment on the Impact of Armed Conflict on Women and Women's Role in Peacebuilding.* New York: UNIFEM, 2002 at pp. 93–101.

66 Hilary Charlesworth and Christine Chinkin, 'The Gender of Jus Cogens' (1993) *Human Rights Quarterly* 15: 63–76.

67 Neil Kritz, 'Progress and Humility: The Ongoing Search for Post-Conflict Justice' M. Cherif Bassiouni (ed.). *Post-Conflict Justice.* Transnational Publishers: New York, 2002 at p. 59.

68 Ratna Kapur, 'The Tragedy of Victimization Rhetoric: Resurrecting the "Native",' Subject in International/Post-Colonial Feminist Legal Politics' (2002) *Harvard Human Rights Journal* 15: 1–37.

69 Hilary Charlesworth and Christine Chinkin. *The Boundaries of International Law: A Feminist Analysis.* Manchester; Manchester University Press, 2000, pp. 38–46.

70 Christine Chinkin and Hilary Charlesworth, 'Building women into peace' (2006) *Third World Quarterly* 27(5): 937–57 at p. 946.

71 Or as Christine Bell and Catherine O'Rourke write, 'women moving too easily from being "pawns of war" to "pawns of peace"', see 'Does feminism need a theory of transitional justice?' (2007) *International Journal of Transitional Justice* 1: 23–44 at p. 25.

72 Christine Bell and Catherine O'Rourke, *ibid.*, at p. 23.

73 Christine Bell and Catherine O'Rourke, *ibid.*

74 Christine Bell and Catherine O'Rourke, *ibid.*

75 Doris Buss, 'Women at the Borders: Rape and Nationalism in International Law', (1998) *Feminist Legal Studies* 6(2): 171–203; Christine Chinkin, 'Symposium – The Yugoslav Crisis: New International Law Issues, Rape and Sexual Abuse of Women in International Law' (1994) *European Journal of International Law* 5: 326–41.

76 Christine Bell and Catherine O'Rourke, 'Does feminism need a theory of transitional justice?' (2007) *International Journal of Transitional Justice* 1: 23–44 at p. 34.

77 Christine Chinkin, 'Peace Agreements as a Means for Promoting Gender Equality and Ensuring Participation of Women'. Consultant to the Division for the Advancement of Women EGM/PEACE/2003/BP.1 31 October 2003 United Nations Division for

the Advancement of Women (DAW) Expert Group Meeting on 'Peace agreements as a means for promoting gender equality and ensuring participation of women – A framework of model provisions' 10–13 November, Ottawa, Canada, 2003.

78 Christine Chinkin, *ibid.*

79 M. Cherif Bassiouni (ed.). 'The United Nations Commission of Experts on the Former Yugoslavia'. *Post-Conflict Justice*. Transnational Publishers: New York. 2002, at p. 449.

80 Christine Chinkin, *ibid.*, at p. 9. See also the work of Catherine Bell.

81 See further Henry Steiner and Philip Alston. 'An Overview of UN Procedures through the Lens of a Single Case: East Timor', *International Human Rights in Context: Law, Politics, Morals*. Oxford; Oxford University Press, 2000, at pp. 672 – 694.

82 Mario Carrascalão, Former Governor of East Timor. Testimony to the Commission for Reception, Truth and Reconciliation (CAVR) National Public Hearing on Women and Conflict. 28–29 April 2003, Dili.

83 Note the comments of Mr A. Zoller at para 64, 1999 Fourth Special Session of the UN Commission, Summary Record of 2nd meeting, 24 September 1999, UN Doc. E/CN.4/S-4/SR.2(1999) as quoted in 'An Overview of UN Procedures through the Lens of a Single Case: East Timor'. Henry Steiner and Philip Alston, *ibid.*, at p. 688.

84 See further Henry Steiner and Philip Alston, *ibid.*, at pp. 672 – 694.

85 '…[T]he kind of democratic participation that prevails shapes the patterns of social relations and processes that develop, especially those associated with the distribution of resources, both material and symbolic': Toni Schofield and Carol Bacchi, 'Reinventing Gender Equality and the Political', Conference paper, University of Sydney, 29–30 September 2005. See also Commonwealth Secretariat. *Gender Equality and the Judiciary: Using International Standards to Promote the Human Rights of Women and the Girl Child.* London: Commonwealth Secretariat, 1999.

86 See for example Diana Francis, 'Culture, Power Asymmetries and Gender in Conflict Transformation', *Berghof Handbook for Conflict Transformation*. Berghof Research Centre for Constructive Conflict Management, 2001, at p. 9.

87 Note Hilary Charlesworth and Christine Chinkin. *The Boundaries of International Law: A Feminist Analysis.* Manchester; Manchester University Press, 2000, at pp. 310–12.

88 Hayli Millar, 'Facilitating Women's Voices in Truth Recovery: An assessment of women's participation and the integration of a gender perspective in truth commissions', Helen Durham and Tracey Gurd (eds). *Listening to the Silences: Women and War*, Boston, Leiden: Martinus Nijhoff, 2005, at p.176.

89 Hayli Millar, *ibid.*, at p. 186.

90 Fionnuala Ni Aolain and Catherine Turner, 'Gender, Truth and Transition' (2007) *UCLA Women's Law Journal* 16: 229–79 at pp. 257–60.

91 Fionnuala Ni Aolain and Catherine Turner, *ibid.*, at pp. 260–62.

92 Fionnuala Ni Aolain and Catherine Turner, *ibid.*, at pp. 262–65.

93 Hayli Millar, *ibid.*, at p. 186. Millar also notes that in South Africa, for instance, entitlement to reparations is limited to those formally declared victims by the Truth and Reconciliation Commission. In view of their reluctance to disclose victimisation or speak about direct victimisation, women either will be ineligible or must rely on their secondary status as the 'relatives or dependents' of formally recognised victims to seek reparations.

94 Fionnuala Ni Aolain and Catherine Turner, 'Gender, Truth and Transition' *ibid*, at p. 273.

95 Jan Jindy Pettman, *Worlding Women: A Feminist International Politics,* St Leonards, NSW: Allen & Unwin, 1996 at p. 8.

96 Chilla Bulbeck, 'Book Reviews' (2005) *International Feminist Journal of Politics*, 7(1): 157–69, at p. 158.

97 See further Kirsten Campbell, 'The Gender of Transitional Justice: Law, Sexual Violence and the International Criminal Tribunal for the Former Yugoslavia' 1 (2007*) International Journal of Transitional Justice* 3: 411–32.

98 *Prosecutor v. Jean-Paul Akayesu*, 2 September 1999, ICTR-96-4-T.

99 *Prosecutor v Dragoljub Kunarac, Radomir Kovac and Zoran Vukovic*, Judgement, Case No. IT-96-23/1-T, 22 February 2001, *Prosecutor v. Anto Furundzija*, 10 December 1998, ICTY-95-17/1-T.

100 (1996) 1 Butterworths Human Rights Cases 229. See Hilary Charlesworth and Christine Chinkin. *The Boundaries of International Law: A Feminist Analysis.* Manchester; Manchester University Press, 2000, at pp. 330–32.

101 Hilary Charlesworth and Christine Chinkin, *ibid.*, at p. 330.

102 Hilary Charlesworth and Christine Chinkin, *ibid.*

103 Hilary Charlesworth and Christine Chinkin, *ibid.* See also Ngaire Naffine, 'Sexing the Subject (of Law)', Margaret Thornton (ed.). *Public and Private: Feminist Legal Debates.* Oxford: Oxford University Press, 1995, at pp. 18, 20 and 32; and Catherine MacKinnon, *Feminism Unmodified: Discourses on Life and Law.* Boston: Harvard University Press, 1987.

104 Christine Chinkin, 'Symposium – The Yugoslav Crisis: New International Law Issues, Rape and Sexual Abuse of Women in International Law' (1994) *European Journal of International Law* 5: 326–41.

105 See for example, Alice Edwards, 'The 'Feminizing' of Torture under International Human Rights Law' (2006) *Leiden Journal of International Law* 19(2): 349–91.

106 Note that forced maternity arising out of rape in Bosnia did receive considerable global attention and contributed to the provisions in the Rome Statute as discussed further in Chapter Five.

107 My thanks to Dianne Otto for prompting this insight.

108 See for example, Catherine MacKinnon, *Are Women Human? And Other International Dialogues.* Cambridge: Belknap Press of Harvard University Press, 2006.

109 See further Judith Gardam, 'Women and Armed Conflict: The Response of International Law', *Listening to the Silences: Women and War*, Helen Durham and Tracey Gurd (eds), Leiden, Boston: Martinus Nijhoff, 2005.

110 Jan Jindy Pettman, *Worlding Women: A Feminist International Politics*, St Leonards, NSW: Allen & Unwin, 1996 at p. 100.

111 International Committee of the Red Cross (ICRC), *Woman Facing War*, ICRC, Geneva, 2001, at pp. 8–9.

112 International Committee of the Red Cross (ICRC), *ibid.*, at p. 10.

113 Helen Durham and Tracy Gurd (eds), 'Preface', *Listening to the Silences: Women and War*, Martinus Nijhoff, Leiden: Boston, 2005, at p. 3.

114 Rhonda Copelon, 'Women and War Crimes' (1995) *St John's Law Review* 69: 61 at p. 65.

115 Hilary Charlesworth and Christine Chinkin. *The Boundaries of International Law: A Feminist Analysis*. Manchester; Manchester University Press, 2000, at p. 333.

116 Hilary Charlesworth and Christine Chinkin, *ibid.*, at p.219.

117 '[T]here is a two-tiered hierarchy in the determination of whether the harms associated with armed conflict are addressed…First, [the] experiences must be regarded as sufficiently "serious" to constitute an international crime. Secondly, crimes committed in armed conflict must "shock the conscience of mankind" before they will be prosecuted. Gender is a factor in determining how seriously an act is viewed and whether resources will be devoted to prosecuting [the act].' Judith Gardam and Michelle Jarvis, *Women, Armed Conflict and International Law*, The Hague: Kluwer Law International, 2001 at pp. 181–82.

118 Elisabeth Rehn and Ellen Johnson Sirleaf, *Women, War and Peace: The Independent Experts' Assessment on the Impact of Armed Conflict on Women and Women's Role in Peacebuilding*, New York: UNIFEM, 2002 at p. 99.

119 Note Susan Opotow, 'Psychology of Impunity and Injustice: Implications for Societal Reconciliation.' M. Cherif Bassiouni (ed.). *Post-Conflict Justice.* Transnational Publishers: New York. 2002, at p. 206.

120 Julie Mertus, 'Truth in a Box: The Limits of Justice through Judicial Mechanisms', I. Amadiume and A. An-Na'im (eds). *The Politics of Memory: Truth, Healing and Social Justice.* New York: Zed Books, 2000.

121 In other words, witnesses are prevented from telling their stories in their own words, due to interrogation from opposing counsel.

122 Nicola Henry, 'Secrecy, Silence and Sexual Violence in International Criminal Proceedings'. Paper read at Activating Human Rights and Diversity, 1–4 July 2003, Byron Bay.

123 Nicola Henry, 'Disclosure, Sexual violence and international jurisprudence: a therapeutic approach'. PhD dissertation, University of Melbourne, 2005.

124 Michelle Staggs Kelsall and Shanee Stepakoff. '"When We Wanted to Talk about Rape": Silencing Sexual Violence at the Special Court for Sierra Leone' 1 (2007) *International Journal of Transitional Justice* 3: 355–74.

125 Judith Herman. *Trauma and Recovery: The Aftermath of Violence from Domestic Abuse to Political Terror.* New York: Basic Books, 1992.

126 See the Kosovo Rehabilitation Centre for Torture Victims (KRCT) study concerning witnesses from the Kosovo population regarding the possibility of their retraumatisation during the trial process of Milosevic in The Hague: Sci Enver Çesko, Melita Kallaba, Vjosa Devaja, Agim Selimi, Shaban Jashari and Merita Emini, *Study with the Clients Treated at the KRCT, from the Witnesses and the Kosovo Population Regarding the Possibility of their Re-Traumatization during the Trial Process of Milosevic in The Hague.* Kosovo Rehabilitation Centre for Torture Victims, 2002, pp. 1–9.

127 Elizabeth Stanley, *Torture, Truth and Justice: The Case of Timor Leste*, NY and London: Routledge, 2009. For these reasons, Rosalind Dixon has proposed an international civil tribunal for war crimes against women. See further Rosalind Dixon, 'Rape as a Crime in International Humanitarian Law: Where to from Here?' (2002) *European Journal of International Law* 13(3): 697–719.

128 Fionnuala Ni Aolain and Catherine Turner, 'Gender, Truth and Transition' (2007) *UCLA Women's Law Journal* 16: 229–79, at p. 233.

129 Katherine M. Franke, 'Gendered Subjects of Transitional Justice' (2006) *Columbia Journal of Gender and Law* 15 (3): 813–28 at p. 820.

130 Anne-Marie L.M. De Brouwer. *Supranational Criminal Prosecution of Sexual Violence: The ICC and the Practice of the ICTY and the ICTR.* Antwerpen, Intersentia 2005.

131 Christine Bell and Catherine O'Rourke, 'Does Feminism Need a Theory of Transitional Justice?' (2007) *International Journal of Transitional Justice* 1: 23–44 at p. 23.

132 There is a long-standing cultural feminist criticism of rights discourse as aggressive or shrill, obsessed with individualism and not an ethic of care, symbolic only, prone to counter-rights claims. Carol Smart (ed.). 'The Problem of Rights', *Feminism and the Power of Law.* London/New York: Taylor and Francis, 1989, pp. 138–59 at p. 159.

133 Criticism of trials could flow naturally from the gap between law and justice, inevitable because rights have a 'symbolic valance' that can never be realised by the laws on the books. Sundhya Pahuja, 'Rights as regulation: The integration of development and human rights', Paper delivered at 15th Annual ANZSIL Conference, Canberra, 29 June 2007.

134 Laurel Fletcher and Harvey M. Weinstein. 'Violence and Social Repair: Rethinking the Contribution of Justice to Reconciliation' (2002), *Human Rights Quarterly* 24(3): 573–639.

135 Christine Bell and Catherine O'Rourke, 'Does feminism need a theory of transitional justice?' (2007) *International Journal of Transitional Justice* 1: 23–44 at p. 35.
136 Christine Bell and Catherine O'Rourke, *ibid.*, at pp. 36–44.
137 Christine Bell and Catherine O'Rourke, *ibid.*, at p. 44.
138 John Braithwaite, 'Rape, Shame and Pride', Address to Stockholm Criminology Symposium, 16 June, 2006.
139 Silva Meznaric, 'Gender as an Ethno-marker: Rape, War and Identity Politics in the Former Yugoslavia', Valentine M. Moghadam (ed.), *Identity, Politics and Women: Cultural Reassertions and Feminisms in International Perspective.* Oxford: Westview Press, 1994 quoted by Cynthia Cockburn. 'Gender, Armed Conflict and Political Violence: Background Paper', The World Bank, Washington DC, June 10th & 11th 1999.
140 Ruth Seifert, 'War and Rape: A Preliminary Analysis', Alexandra Stiglmayer (ed.), *Mass Rape: The War Against Women in Bosnia-Herzegovina.* Lincoln and London: University of Nebraska Press, 1995: 54–72.
141 Elisabeth Rehn and Ellen Johnson Sirleaf, *Women, War and Peace: The Independent Experts' Assessment on the Impact of Armed Conflict on Women and Women's Role in Peacebuilding*, New York: UNIFEM, 2002.
142 Amnesty International, *Broken Bodies, Shattered Minds, Torture and Ill-Treatment of Women*, Alden Press, United Kingdom, 2001, at p. 50.
143 Hilary Charlesworth and Christine Chinkin. *The Boundaries of International Law: A Feminist Analysis.* Manchester; Manchester University Press, 2000, at p. 334.
144 Cynthia Cockburn. 'Gender, Armed Conflict and Political Violence: Background Paper'. The World Bank, Washington DC, June 10th & 11th 1999, p. 11 and 12.
145 Noelle Quenivet, *Sexual Offences in Armed Conflict & International Law*, Transnational Publishers, New York, 2005, at p. 120.
146 Noelle Quenivet, *ibid.*
147 Fionnuala Ni Aolain and Catherine Turner, 'Gender, Truth and Transition' (2007) *UCLA Women's Law Journal* 16: 229–79, at p. 262.
148 Christine Chinkin, Consultant to the Division for the Advancement of Women, 'Peace Agreements as a Means for Promoting Gender Equality and Ensuring Participation of Women' EGM/PEACE/2003/BP.1, 31 October 2003 United Nations Division for the Advancement of Women (DAW) Expert Group Meeting on 'Peace agreements as a means for promoting gender equality and ensuring participation of women – A framework of model provisions' 10–13 November 2003 Ottawa, Canada, at p. 9.
149 Katherine M. Franke, 'Gendered Subjects of Transitional Justice' (2006) *Columbia Journal of Gender and Law* 15(3): 813–28 at p. 823.
150 Katherine M. Franke, *ibid.*, at p. 814.
151 See further Emily Rosser. 'Depoliticised Speech and Sexed Visibility: Women, Gender and Sexual Violence in the 1999 Guatemalan Comisión para el Esclarecimiento Histórico Report' 1 (2007) *International Journal of Transitional Justice* 3: 391–410.
152 Sierra Leone's Truth and Reconciliation Commission, *Witness to Truth: Report of the Sierra Leone Truth and Reconciliation Commission*, 2004, at p. 87.
153 Sierra Leone's Truth and Reconciliation Commission, *ibid.*
154 Cynthia Enloe, *Bananas, Beaches and Bases: Making Sense of Feminist Politics*, Berkeley: University of California Press, 1989, at p. 3.
155 Ruth Seifert, 'War and Rape: A Preliminary Analysis'. Alexandra Stiglmayer (ed.). *Mass Rape: The War Against Women in Bosnia-Herzegovina.* Lincoln, University of Nebraska Press, 1994, at p. 66.
156 Elisabeth Rehn and Ellen Johnson Sirleaf, *Women, War and Peace: The Independent Experts' Assessment on the Impact of Armed Conflict on Women and Women's Role in Peacebuilding*, New York: UNIFEM, 2002 at p. 18.
157 Piers Pigou, *Crying without Tears: In Pursuit of Justice and Reconciliation in East Timor Leste: Community Perspectives and Expectations,* International Center for Transitional Justice: New York, 2003.

158 Jennifer Robinson, 'Dealing with *Memoria Passionis* in Papua', Honours dissertation, Australian National University, 2005: '…there is a lively debate within the transitional justice literature as to whether trials or truth commissions are more effective in dealing with the past. However, scant attention is given to the fact that both mechanisms can be equally susceptible to manipulation.'
159 Second Women's Congress National Action Plan July 2004, Dili. See further Galuh Wandita, Karen Campbell-Nelson, and Manuela Leong Pereira. 'Gender and Reparations in Timor-Leste', Ruth Rubio-Marin (ed.). *Engendering Reparations: Recognising and Compensating Women Victims of Human Rights Violations*. New York: International Center for Transitional Justice, 2006.
160 See further Jane Hearn and Susan Harris, 'Debating the relationship between human rights and aid in Australia', (2002) *Development Bulletin,* Development Studies Network 59: 77–81.
161 Second Women's Congress National Action Plan July 2004, Dili.
162 'We have grappled with the dilemma of describing the atrocities experienced by women in war in a way that will not [only] ascribe to women the characteristics of passivity and helplessness. Women are everything but that. But as with all groups facing discrimination, violence and marginalization, the causes and consequences of their victimization must be addressed. If not, how will preventive measures ever focus on women? How will the resources and means to protect women be put in place? How will the UN system, governments and NGOs be mobilized to support women? [It is important to keep writing about the ways women experience conflict as marginalized because] so far, not enough has been done.' Elisabeth Rehn and Ellen Johnson Sirleaf, *Women, War and Peace: The Independent Experts' Assessment on the Impact of Armed Conflict on Women and Women's Role in Peacebuilding*, New York: UNIFEM, 2002 at p. 2.
163 Katherine M. Franke, 'Gendered Subjects of Transitional Justice' (2006) *Columbia Journal of Gender and Law* 15(3): 813–28 at p. 823.
164 Katherine M. Franke, *ibid*., at p. 824.
165 Sheila Meintjes, 'War and Post-War Shifts in Gender Relations'. S. Meintjes, M. Turshen, and A. Pillay (eds). *The Aftermath: Women in Post-Conflict Transitio*n, London: Zed Press, 2001, at p. 64.
166 Fionnuala Ni Aolain, and Michael Hamilton. 'Gender and the Rule of Law in Transitional Societies', *Minnesota Legal Studies Research Paper No. 09–12; Transitional Justice Institute Research Paper No. 09–02,* March 2009, at p. 102.
167 Fionnuala Ni Aolain and Catherine Turner, 'Gender, Truth and Transition' (2007) *UCLA Women's Law Journal* 16: 229–79, at p. 239.
168 R. Charli Carpenter, *'Innocent Women and Children': Gender, Norms and the Protection of Civilians*, Ashgate: Hampshire, 2006, at p. 2–3. See also Brandon Hamber, 'Masculinity and Transitional Justice: An Exploratory Essay' 1 (2007) *International Journal of Transitional Justice* 3: 375–90.
169 Katherine M. Franke, 'Gendered Subjects of Transitional Justice' (2006) *Columbia Journal of Gender and Law* 15(3): 813–28 at p. 822.
170 Marita Sturken, 'The Wall, the Screen, and the Image: The Vietnam Veterans Memorial' (1991) *Representations*, No. 35, Special Issue: Monumental Histories (Summer), pp. 118–42. Most of the literature around veterans is medical in nature or historical description. See for example Matthew J. Friedman, 'Veterans' Mental Health in the Wake of War' (2005) *New England Journal of Medicine* 352(13): 1287–90.
171 Christine Chinkin and Hilary Charlesworth, 'Building women into peace' (2006) *Third World Quarterly*, 27(5): 937–57 at p. 946.
172 Jan Jindy Pettman, *Worlding Women: A Feminist International Politics,* St. Leonards, NSW: Allen & Unwin, 1996 at p. 49.
173 Jan Jindy Pettman, *ibid.*

174 Fionnuala Ni Aolain, 'Rethinking the Concept of Harm and Legal Categorisations of Sexual Violence During War' (2000) *Theoretical Inquiries in Law* 1(2): 1.
175 Jan Jindy Pettman, *Worlding Women: A Feminist International Politics,* St. Leonards, NSW: Allen & Unwin, 1996 at p. 51.
176 For example, the International Criminal Court Trust Fund for Victims or the UNIFEM Trust Fund in Support of Actions to Eliminate Violence Against Women.
177 Catharine MacKinnon, 'Crimes of War, Crimes of Peace', S. Shute and S. Hurley (eds). *On Human Rights. The Oxford Amnesty Lectures.* London: Basic Books, 1993 at p. 93.
178 C.M. de Vos, 'What price truth? South Africa's Truth and Reconciliation Commission in Critical Perspective' (2002) 29 *Politikon* 209 at p. 225. See also Jeremy Sarkin and Erin Daly, 'Too Many Questions, Too Few Answers: Reconciliation in Transitional Societies' (2004) 35 *Colombia Human Rights Law Review* 661, at p. 664; Reed Brody, 'Justice: The First Casualty of Truth' (2002) 272 *The Nation* 25, at pp. 28–29 and Neil J. Kritz, 'Book Review: War Crimes, Brutality, Genocide, Terror and the Struggle for Justice' (1999) 93 *American Journal of International Law* 98.
179 Martha Minow, *Between Vengeance and Forgiveness: Facing History after Genocide and Mass Violence,* Boston: Beacon Press: 1998, at p. 5. For another account of the limitations of legal responses see Carlos Nino, *Radical Evil on Trial* New Haven: Yale University Press, 1996, at pp. 104–85. See further Jennifer Robinson, 'Dealing with *Memoria Passionis* in Papua', Honours dissertation, Australian National University, 2005.
180 Robert L. Rothstein, cited by Wendy Lambourne, 'Post-Conflict Peacebuilding: Meeting human needs for justice and reconciliation' (2004) *Peace, Conflict and Development* 4, at p. 2.
181 Bronwyn Leebaw, 'Book Review: Transitional Justice by Ruti Teitel' (2001) 49 *American Journal of Comparative Law* 363, 364.
182 My thanks to James Hathaway for this suggestion.
183 Christine Bell and Catherine O'Rourke, 'Does feminism need a theory of transitional justice?' (2007) *International Journal of Transitional Justice* 1: 23–44 at p. 44.
184 Mark Drumbl, 'Pluralizing International Criminal Justice (Review Essay)' (2005) *Michigan Law Review* 103, at p. 10.

Chapter 3

1 Sonny Inbaraj, 'Human Rights Day: East Timor Invasion Leaves Haunting Legacy', *Inter-Press Service*, Dili, 10 December 2005.
2 Sonny Inbaraj, *ibid.* See also Commission for Reception, Truth and Reconciliation (CAVR). 'Chapter 7.3 Forced displacement and famine'. *Chega! Final Report of the Commission for Reception, Truth and Reconciliation.* Dili: Commission for Reception, Truth and Reconciliation, 2005.
3 See UN General Assembly Resolution 1542(XV) of 16 December 1960.
4 An excellent summary of the history of East Timor is contained in the International Commission of Inquiry on East Timor, *Report of the International Commission of Inquiry on East Timor to the Secretary-General.* UN Document A/54/726. 31 January, 2000, at paras. 18–36.
5 The 100,000 figure is cited in Hamish McDonald, Desmond Ball, James Dunn, Gerry van Klinken, David Bourchier, Douglas Kammen, and Richard Tanter (eds). *Masters of Terror: Indonesia's Military and Violence in East Timor in 1999.* Strategic and Defence Studies Centre Canberra Paper #145. Canberra: Australian National University, 2002, at p. 215.
6 There was arguably de facto acceptance by other nations. See *Case Concerning East Timor (Portugal v. Australia)* International Court of Justice General List No. 84, 1995 I.C.J. 90 (1995).

7 William Burr and Michael L. Evans (eds), *Ford and Kissinger Gave Green Light to Indonesia's Invasion of East Timor, 1975: New Documents Detail Conversations with Suharto.* National Security Archive Electronic Briefing Book No. 62, 6 December 2001.

8 James Dunn, *East Timor: A Rough Passage to Independence.* (3rd edn). Double Bay, NSW: Longueville Books, 2003.

9 Adam Schwarz, *A Nation in Waiting: Indonesia's Search for Stability.* Boulder: Westview Press, 2000, at p. 205.

10 See John Taylor's chronology, 'East Timor: Contemporary History,' P. Carey and G. Carter Bentley (eds), *East Timor at the Crossroads: The Forging of a Nation.* London: Cassell, 1995, at p. 240.

11 See Amnesty International, '200,000 Dead. Enough is Enough.' *New York Times* (advertisement), 23 September 1999.

12 *ABC Radio Asia-Pacific.* 'East Timor: Indonesia's Actions "Genocide" says Expert.' 29 August 2001.

13 Commission for Reception, Truth and Reconciliation (CAVR). *Chega! Final Report of the Commission for Reception, Truth and Reconciliation.* Dili: Commission for Reception, Truth and Reconciliation, 2005.

14 Mark Forbes, 'Indonesian Rule Led to 100,000 East Timor Dead', *Sydney Morning Herald*, 20 December 2005: John McBeth, 'Commentary: Juggling Pragmatic Politics with Bloody Past', *The Straits Times* (Singapore), 19 December 2005.

15 Commission for Reception, Truth and Reconciliation (CAVR). 'Chapter 7.3 Forced displacement and famine', *Chega! Final Report of the Commission for Reception, Truth and Reconciliation.* Dili: Commission for Reception, Truth and Reconciliation, 2005.

16 Henry J. Steiner & Philip Alston, *International Human Rights in Context: Law, Politics, Morals: Text and Materials*, (2nd edn), Oxford: Oxford University Press, 2000, pp. 672–94.

17 Hilmar Farid and Rikardo Simarmata, 'The Struggle for Truth and Justice: A Survey of Transitional Justice Initiatives Throughout Indonesia', *International Center for Transitional Justice Occasional Paper Series*, January 2004, at p. 20. See also Mary S. Zuburchen, 'History, Memory and the "1965 Incident" in Indonesia' (2002) 42 *Asian Survey* 564, at p. 564; and M.N. Djuli and Robert Jereski, 'Prospects for Indonesia's Survival', (2002) 11 *The Brown Journal of World Affairs* 35: 38–39, at p. 40.

18 Between the Republic of Indonesia and the Portuguese Republic on the Question of East Timor (5 May Agreements), Annex 1, Article 3.

19 See further Hamish McDonald *et al.* (eds) *Masters of Terror: Indonesia's Military and Violence in East Timor in 1999*, Canberra Papers on Strategy & Defence No. 145, Canberra, Australian National University, 2002.

20 KPP HAM, *Full Report of the Investigative Commission into Human Rights Violations in East Timor* (KPP HAM)', in Hamish McDonald *et al.* (eds) *Masters of Terror: Indonesia's Military and Violence in East Timor in 1999*, Canberra Papers on Strategy & Defence No. 145, Canberra, Australian National University, 2002 at p. 16.

21 KPP HAM, *ibid.*, at p.17.

22 Deputy British Representative to the United Nations Stewart Eldon, statement to the Security Council, 11 September 1999. See also Matthew Jardine, *East Timor: Genocide in Paradise*. Tuscon, AZ: Odonian Press, 1995, at p. 62.

23 Emily Roynestad, *Are Women Included or Excluded in Post-Conflict Reconstruction: A Case Study from Timor-Leste.* United Nations Division for the Advancement of Women (DAW) Expert Group Meeting on 'Peace agreements as a means for promoting gender equality and ensuring participation of women – A framework of model provisions' EGM/PEACE/2003/BP.1 31. Ottawa, Canada, 10–13 November 2003.

24 David Hicks, *Tetum Ghosts and Kin: Fertility and Gender in East Timor* (2nd edn). Waveland Press: USA, 2004.

25 See further Alexis Dudden, 'We came to tell the truth: Reflections of the Tokyo Women's Tribunal', (2001) *Critical Asian Studies* 33(4): 591–602.

26 Special Rapporteurs, United Nations. *Report on the Joint Mission to East Timor Undertaken by the Special Rapporteur on Extrajudicial, Summary or Arbitrary Executions, the Special Rapporteur on the Question of Torture, and the Special Rapporteur on Violence against Women, Its Causes and Consequences. Situation of Human Rights in East Timor.* Based on visit between 4–10 November 1999. UN Document A/54/660, Geneva: United Nations, 10 December 1999.

27 See especially the *Report of the International Commission of Inquiry on East Timor to the Secretary-General.* UN Document A/54/726. 31 January, 2000. *Report of the Security Council Mission to Jakarta and Dili*, S/1999/976, 14 September 1999. *Report of UN Special Rapporteurs: Situation of Human Rights in East Timor.* Based on visit between 4–10 November 1999. UN Document A/54/660, 10 December 1999.

28 Amnesty International. *East Timor Justice – Past, Present and Future.* AI Index ASA 57/001/2001. London, 27 July 2001.

29 KPP HAM. *Full Report of the Investigative Commission into Human Rights Violations in East Timor.* Jakarta: KPP HAM, 2000.

30 Hamish McDonald, Desmond Ball, James Dunn, Gerry van Klinken, David Bourchier, Douglas Kammen and Richard Tanter (eds). *Masters of Terror: Indonesia's Military and Violence in East Timor in 1999.* Strategic and Defence Studies Centre, Australian National University Canberra Paper No. 145, 2002.

31 See generally N. Godinho, 'UN Security Council "Arria formula" meeting on the implementation of Security Council Resolution 1325', 30 October 2001 and FOKUPERS, *Gender-based Human Rights Abuses during the Pre and Post-Ballot Violence in East Timor*, 2000.

32 Commission for Reception, Truth and Reconciliation (CAVR). 'Chapter 7.7 Sexual Violence', *Chega! Final Report of the Commission for Reception, Truth and Reconciliation.* Dili: Commission for Reception, Truth and Reconciliation, 2005.

33 Commission for Reception, Truth and Reconciliation (CAVR), *ibid.*

34 M Hynes, J Ward, K Robertson and C Crouse, 'A Determination of the Prevalence of Gender-based Violence among Conflict-Affected Populations in East Timor' (2004) *Disasters* 28(3): 294–321.

35 Agence France Presse, 'Scars of Vote Violence Remain Real for Many East Timor Women', 2000.

36 Tim Kemanusiaan Timor Barat, 'Violence against IDP/refugee women – Report of TKTB (Tim Kemanusiaan Timor Barat) findings in IDP/Refugee Camps in West Timor', August 2000.

37 Diane Farsetta, 'East Timorese Refugees in Militia-Controlled Camps'. M. H. C. Pus (ed.). *The Devastating Impact of Small Arms & Light Weapons on the Lives of Women: A Collection of Testimonies*, WILPF for International Action Network on Small Arms (IANSA) Women's Caucus, 2001. Note the case of 15-year-old Juliana dos Santos in particular.

38 Special Rapporteurs, United Nations. *Report on the Joint Mission to East Timor Undertaken by the Special Rapporteur on Extrajudicial, Summary or Arbitrary Executions, the Special Rapporteur on the Question of Torture, and the Special Rapporteur on Violence against Women, Its Causes and Consequences. Situation of Human Rights in East Timor.* Based on visit between 4–10 November 1999. UN Document A/54/660, Geneva: United Nations, 10 December 1999.

39 Report of UN Special Rapporteurs, *ibid.*

40 Tim Eaton, 'Raping the Future', *Mother Jones Magazine*, San Francisco, 26 August 1999.

41 Miranda Sissons, *From One Day to Another Violations of Women's Reproductive and Sexual Rights in East Timor.* East Timor Human Rights Centre, Melbourne, 1997.

42 Miranda Sissons, *ibid.*

43 UN Doc. S/Res/1264 (1999).

44 UN Doc. S/Res/1272 (1999)

45 Report of the International Commission of Inquiry on East Timor to the Secretary-General, January 2000. UN Doc. A/54/726 and S/2000/59, 31 January 2000.
46 KPP HAM. *Full Report of the Investigative Commission into Human Rights Violations in East Timor*. Jakarta: KPP HAM, 2000.
47 Kofi Annan, Identical letters dated 31 January 2000 from the Secretary-General to the President of the General Assembly, the President of the Security Council and the Chairperson of the Commission on Human Rights. New York, United Nations General Assembly. UN Doc. A/54/726, 2000.
48 Traci Hukill, *UN Wire*. Dili, 4 May 2004.
49 Security Council, 'Security Council Establishes One-Year Political Mission in Timor-Leste, Unanimously Adopting Resolution 1599 (2005). UN Office Will Remain until 20 May 2006, Supporting Development of Police, Border Patrol, Other Critical Institutions'. *Press Release* SC/8371, New York, 2005.
50 Report of the Secretary-General on Timor-Leste pursuant to Security Council Resolution 1690 (2006), S/2006/628, 8 August 2006.
51 Report of the United Nations Independent Special Commission of Inquiry for Timor-Leste, Geneva, 2 October 2006, para.136.
52 Jill Jolliffe, 'Suffer the Children Caught in Timor Crossfire', *Canberra Times*, 24 August 2007.
53 International Crisis Group. 'Timor-Leste: No Time for Complacency', *Asia Briefing No. 87*, Brussels: International Crisis Group, 9 February 2009.
54 See Resolutions S/2006/923 and S/2006/924.
55 UNMIT 'Facts and Figures', available at http://unmit.unmissions.org/ (accessed 22 June 2009).
56 Ranked 163 in the world out of 193. United States Central Intelligence Agency (CIA), *The World Factbook*, 20 March 2008.
57 United Nations Development Programme. 'The Path out of Poverty', *Timor Leste Human Development Report 2006*, Dili, 2006.
58 World Health Organisation, *WHO's Contribution to Health Sector Development in East Timo*r, WHO: Dili, July 2001, p. 10. Note also Manuela Leong Pereira, 'Domestic Violence: A Part of Women's Daily Lives in East Timor,' *La'o Hamutu*k *Bulletin*, Vol. 2, No. 5, August 2001, a special issue about women.
59 United Nations Development Programme, 'More women die in childbirth in East Timor than anywhere in East Asia.' Press release for International Women's Day. Dili, 8 March 2002.
60 Sophie Boudre, 'A Cruel History for East-Timorese Women', *Voices Unabridged* E-Magazine No 1 Jan–March 2004, 19 January 2004.
61 For a graphic account of the plight of women in camps due to the riots and ongoing violence see Christine Kearney, 'What it feels like to have to run', *Eureka Street* 17:1, 23 January 2007.
62 Report of the Secretary-General on Timor-Leste pursuant to Security Council resolution 1690 (2006), S/2006/628, 8 August 2006 at para. 99.
63 Agence France Presse, 'East Timor ends era of camps', Dili, 17 June 2009.
64 M. Cherif Bassiouni (ed.), 'Introduction.' *Post-Conflict Justice*. Transnational Publishers: New York. 2002, at p. xv. See however the *Human Security Report 2005*, New York, Oxford: Oxford UP 2005, on the complexity of such data.
65 Jennifer Balint, 'The Place of Law in Addressing Internal Regime Conflicts', (1996) *Law and Contemporary Problems* 59: 103.
66 Leslie Vinjamuri and Jack L. Snyder, 'Advocacy and Scholarship in the Study of International War Crime Tribunals and Transitional Justice' (2004) *Annual Review of Political. Science* 7: 345–62 at p. 345.
67 Xanana Gusmão, 'Notes on comments by Xanana Gusmão and José Ramos-Horta on dealing with past human rights violations made during a Panel Discussion'. Paper

read at German Council on Foreign Relations (Deutsche Gesellschaft für Auswaertige Politik, DGAP), Berlin, *Watch Indonesia*, 20 October 2004.

68 John Magro, 'Is there Justification for an International Criminal Tribunal for East Timor?' (2000) *Murdoch University Electronic Journal of Law* 7:3.

69 UN Doc. UNTAET/REG/2000/15, 6 June 2000.

70 Hansjoerg Strohmeyer, 'Collapse and Reconstruction of a Judicial System: The United Nations Missions in Kosovo and East Timor', (2001) *American Journal of International Law* 95, Symposium: State Reconstruction After Civil Conflict): 43–63 at p. 55.

71 The ICJ has ruled in the *Yeroda* case that sitting officials are immune from domestic prosecutions by third states – *Case Concerning the Arrest Warrant of April 11, 2000*, (Democratic Republic of Congo v. Belgium), International Court of Justice Reports, 2002.

72 Universal jurisdiction is a complex area and this book will not explore the issue in detail. Readers are directed to Roger O'Keefe, 'Universal Jurisdiction-Clarifying the Basic Concept' (2004) *Journal of International Criminal Justice* 2(3): 735–60.

73 See further Ruti Teitel, 'The alien tort and the global rule of law' (2005) *International Social Science Journal* 57(185): 551–560.

74 *Doe v. Lumintang*, (D.D.C. CV0064) (Filed March 28, 2000; Judgment Sept. 10, 2001). See further Richard Tanter, 'Practical Justice in Doe v. Lumintang : the Successful Use of Civil Remedies against 'an Enemy of All Mankind', Hamish McDonald, Richard Tanter, Gerry van Klinken MD Lanham and Desmond Ball (eds), *Masters of Terror: Indonesia's Military and Violence in East Timor*, Rowman and Littlefield, 2006: 157–75.

75 See ETAN, 'East Timor Action Network Hails $66 Million Judgment in Rights Lawsuit Against Indonesian General', *ETAN media release*, 2000.

76 Randolph Ryan, 'Indonesia aide told to pay $14m in suit over death', *The Boston Globe*, 28 October 1994.

77 *Todd v. Panjaitan* (No. 92–12255, slip op. (D. Mass. Oct. 26, 1994)).

78 Mark Byrne and Kath Gibson, 'Chasing Shadows: Indonesian War Criminals and Australian Law', *UNIYA Occasional Paper no.13*, Sydney NSW, May 2007. See further Jill Jolliffe, *Cover-Up: The Inside Story of the Balibo Five*. Carlton North, Vic.: Scribe, 2001.

79 *AFP*, 'US can work with a future president Wiranto, ambassador says', 22 April 2004: The United States can work with former military chief Wiranto if he wins the Indonesian presidency despite his indictment for crimes against humanity, US ambassador Ralph Boyce says. 'We can work with anybody that comes out of a free (election) process,' Boyce told reporters.

80 See Priscilla Hayner, *Unspeakable Truths: Confronting State Terror and Atrocity*, New York; London: Routledge, 2001, at p. 14, p. 23 fn 26, and pp. 32–71.

81 Ruti G. Teitel, *Transitional Justice*. Oxford; New York: Oxford University Press, 2000.

82 UNTAET Regulation No. 2001/10.

83 See Lia Kent, 'Community Views on CAVR's Community Reconciliation Process', Dili: Judicial System Monitoring Programme, 2004.

84 H.E. Kay Rala Xanana. 'Gusmão Challenges for Peace and Stability: Address by President Gusmão on the occasion of the Chancellor's Human Rights Lecture', University of Melbourne, Australia 7 April 2003.

85 Sarah Boyd, 'Timor justice slow but sure', *Asia Intelligence Wire*, 29 July 2004.

86 Law No. 27/2004 concerning the Truth and Reconciliation Commission [Undang-Undang Republik Indonesia Nomor 24. Tahun 2004 tentang Komisi Kebenaran dan Rekonsiliasi].

87 . M. S. 'Saraswati, Commission Could Be "Whitewash Machine"', *The Jakarta Post*. Jakarta, 2004.

88 See further Jennifer Robinson. 'Dealing with Memoria Passionis in Papua', Honours thesis, Australian National University, 2005.

89 Associated Press, 'Indonesian Court Rules Truth Commission Illegal, Casts Doubt on Justice For Suharto Abuses', 7 December 2006.

90 Note adverse comments on the JTFC made by the United Nations Commission of Experts, Report to the Secretary-General of the Commission of Experts to Review the Prosecution of Serious Violations of Human Rights in Timor-Leste (then East Timor) in 1999 (UN Commission of Experts Report), 26 May 2005, S/2005/458, 81–88. See also Ellen Nakashima, 'For Survivors of East Timor Massacres, Justice Still Elusive', *Washington Post* (Washington), 18 September 2005 and 'Indonesia Attempts to Avert Tribunal to Probe East Timor', *Washington Post* (Washington), 16 July 2005; Robin Perry and Eleanor Taylor Nicholson, 'Australia Must Help Timor Find Justice', *The Age*, 26 August 2005; and Ramesh Thakur, 'East Timor: When Peace and Justice Collide', *International Herald Tribune* (Hong Kong), 31 August 2005.

91 Agence France Presse, 'Timor Truth Commission to Question Indonesian Generals over 1999 Violence', Jakarta, 20 November 2006.

92 M. Taufiqurrahman, 'Amnesties OK for Timor Leste Rights Violators, Says Body', *Jakarta Post*, 17 January, Jakarta; UNMIT Daily Briefing, 'MPs Rejects CVA Recommendations', Dili 16 January 2007.

93 President José Ramos-Horta, Prime Minister Xanana Gusmão and Armed Forces Commander Taur Matan Ruak testified in the fifth hearings in Dili on 24–27 September 2007.

94 Joint Truth and Friendship Commission, *Per Memoriam ad Spem (From Memory to Hope): Final Report*, May 2008..

95 International Center for Transitional Justice. *An Unfinished Truth: An Analysis of the Commission of Truth and Friendship's Final Report on the 1999 Atrocities in East Timor*, New York: International Center for Transitional Justice, 2009.

96 Commission of Experts. *Report to the Secretary-General of the Commission of Experts to Review the Prosecution of Serious Violations of Human Rights in Timor-Leste (the Then East Timor) in 1999*. New York: United Nations, 2005.

97 Jill Jolliffe, 'Jakarta's Timor Trials "A Sham"'. *The Age*, Darwin, 19 June 2005.

98 *Report of the Secretary-General on Justice and Reconciliation for Timor-Leste*, S/2006/580, 26 July 2006.

99 Sonny Inbaraj, 'Human Rights Day: East Timor Invasion Leaves Haunting Legacy', *Inter-Press Service*, Dili, 10 December 2005.

Chapter 4

1 On 6 September 1999 several hundred persons had sought refuge in the Suai church and were attacked by the Laksuar Merah Putih and Mahidi militias and members of the TNI and POLRI. At least 40 and up to 200 people were killed. Accounts of the militia and TNI removing the bodies of those killed in the church were corroborated by the exhumation in West Timor of 26 bodies from Oeluli beach, Kobalima district, approximately 3 kilometres inside West Timor. The exhumations were undertaken at the direction of the Indonesian National Inquiry Commission on East Timor (KPP Ham). The forensic expert who accompanied the International Commission of Inquiry examined the bodies and concluded that the remains were of three priests, 12 males, eight females and three bodies of undetermined sex. One was a child, two in their teens, six in their teens to mid-20s, 12 were middle-aged and two elderly. *Report of the International Commission of Inquiry on East Timor to the Secretary-General* (ICIET Report) UN Doc A/54/726 and S/2000/59, 31 January 2000 at paras 72–82. Thirty men were indicted by the SCUI (Egidio Manek *et al.*, case no. 9/2003 and the Second Coalima cases 14/2003) and remain at large in Indonesia. Militia member Miguel da Silva was sentenced to 9 years prison on 26 November 2003.

2 Amnesty International and Judicial System Monitoring Programme, *Indonesia: Justice for Timor-Leste: The Way Forward*. AI Index: ASA 21/006/2004, April 2004, at pp. 42–43.
3 Jennifer Robinson, 'Dealing with *Memoria Passionis* in Papua'. Honours Thesis, Australian National University, 2005.
4 See further, Office of the Prosecutor, 'Informal expert paper: the principle of complementarity in practice', International Criminal Court, The Hague, 2003; and Mireille Delmas-Marty, 'Interactions between National and International Criminal Law in the Preliminary Phase of Trial at the ICC' (2006) *Journal of International Criminal Justice* 4(1): 2–11.
5 Note in particular David Cohen, *Intended to Fail: The Trials before the Ad Hoc Human Rights Court in Jakarta*. International Center for Transitional Justice, 2003; United Nations Commission of Experts, *Report to the UN Secretary-General of the Commission of Experts to Review the Prosecutions of Serious Violations of Human Rights in Timor Leste (then East Timor) in 1999*. S/2005/458, 15 July 2005 ('Commission of Experts Report') and the International Crisis Group, *Indonesia: Impunity Versus Accountability for Gross Human Rights Violations*, Brussels, 2001.
6 Cynthia Enloe, *The Curious Feminist: Searching for Women in a New Age of Empire*, Berkeley: University of California Press 2004, at p. 196.
7 Commission of Experts Report, *ibid*.
8 See further, Susan Harris Rimmer, 'Untold Numbers: East Timorese Women and Transitional Justice', *Global Issues, Women and Justice*. Caroline Lambert and Sharon Pickering (eds), Sydney: Federation Press, 2004: 335–66.
9 International Crisis Group, *Indonesia: Impunity versus Accountability for Gross Human Rights Violations*. Brussels, International Crisis Group, 2001 at p. 1.
10 Galuh Wandita, 'Healing the Past Atrocities against Women', *Jakarta Post*, Jakarta, 30 March 2007.
11 Fionnuala Ni Aolain. 'Women, Security and the Patriarchy of Internationalized Transitional Justice', *Minnesota Legal Studies Research Paper No. 08–40*, October 2008.
12 UN Security Council Resolution 1264 of 1999.
13 *Jakarta Post*. 'Indonesia Vows to Avoid War Crimes Court', Jakarta, 8 December 1999.
14 *Indonesia Observer*, Jakarta, 26 January 2000.
15 *Indonesia Observer*, *ibid*.
16 Letter dated 26 January 2000 from the Minister for Foreign Affairs of Indonesia to the Secretary-General. UN Doc. A/54/727 and S/2000/65, January 2000.
17 *Komisi Nasional Hak Asasi Manusia*. After the fall of Soeharto, Indonesia claimed to have Komnas HAM independent investigation powers pursuant to the Law No. 39 of 1999 concerning Human Rights. In 1999 Komnas HAM had a well-deserved reputation for independence in Indonesia according to Human Rights Watch. They cite as an example that in January 1995, Komnas sent a team to East Timor after soldiers shot and killed six civilians in the district of Liquiça. Komnas found that the six had been tortured before being killed and that the army had tried to prevent the families from finding out how their relatives had died. As a result of the investigation, two soldiers were tried and sentenced to four years and four years and six months respectively for violating procedures. Human Rights Watch, 'Strong Independent Commission of Inquiry Urged for East Timor', media release, New York, 27 September 1999. Indonesian NGOs often refer to Komnas HAM as a 'chained watchdog'. See further Suzannah Linton, 'Accounting for Atrocities in Indonesia', (2006) *Singapore Year Book of International Law* 10: 1–33.
18 *CNN International Diplomatic License*. 'Indonesia and East Timor Welcome Kofi Annan'. 19 February 2000.
19 *CNN International Diplomatic License*, 'Indonesia and East Timor Welcome Kofi Annan.' 19 February 2000.

20 *Antara*, 'RI Needs to Remain Alert about Possibility of International Tribunal', 16 February 2000.
21 *CNN*, 'UN Chief Says International Court Possible for East Timor'. Dili, 18 February 2000.
22 Mark Riley, 'UN Scorn at Jakarta Justice for Timor', *Sydney Morning Herald*, 2 February 2000.
23 This was confirmed by comments from China foreign ministry spokesperson Zhu Bangzao – see *Jakarta Post*, 'East Timor inquiry impresses global community', 2 February 2000.
24 *Deutsche Presse-Agentur*, 'Senior U.N. Official Fears Indonesian Human Rights Commission will not Work', 3 February 2000.
25 Mark Riley, 'UN Scorn at Jakarta Justice for Timor', *Sydney Morning Herald*, 2 February 2000.
26 Komisi Penyelidik Pelanggaran Hak Asasi Manusia di Timor Timur.
27 KPP HAM, 'Executive Summary', *Full Report of the Investigative Commission into Human Rights Violations in East Timor.* Jakarta: KPP HAM, 2000, at p. 3. ('KPP HAM Report')
28 *Report to the UN Secretary-General of the Commission of Experts to Review the Prosecutions of Serious Violations of Human Rights in Timor Leste (then East Timor) in 1999*. S/2005/458, 15 July 2005 ('Commission of Experts Report'), at para. [39].
29 Human Rights Watch reported that the Timorese would not accept a KPP HAM inquiry as impartial: Human Rights Watch, 'Strong Independent Commission of Inquiry Urged for East Timor'. New York, 27 September 1999.
30 Commission on Human Rights resolution 1999/S-4/1 of 27 September 1999, as endorsed by the Economic and Social Council in its decision 1999/293 of 15 November 1999.
31 Commission on Human Rights resolution 1999/S-4/1 of 27 September 1999, *ibid*.
32 Report of the International Commission of Inquiry on East Timor to the Secretary-General, January 2000. UN Doc A/54/726 and S/2000/59, 31 January 2000.
33 Report on the joint mission on East Timor undertaken by the Special Rapporteur of the Commission on Human Rights on extrajudicial, summary or arbitrary executions, the Special Rapporteur of the Commission on the question of torture and the Special Rapporteur of the Commission on violence against women, its causes and consequences, in accordance with Commission resolution 1999/S-4/1 of 27 September 1999. UN Document A/54/60, 10 December 1999.
34 Report of the International Commission of Inquiry on East Timor to the Secretary-General, January 2000. UN Doc A/54/726 and S/2000/59, 31 January 2000 at [153].
35 Report on the joint mission to East Timor undertaken by the Special Rapporteur on extrajudicial, summary or arbitrary executions, the Special Rapporteur on the question of torture, and the Special Rapporteur on violence against women, its causes and consequences. Situation of Human Rights in East Timor. Geneva, United Nations. UN Doc. A/54/660, 10 December 1999.
36 KPP HAM, 'Executive Summary', *Full Report of the Investigative Commission into Human Rights Violations in East Timor.* Jakarta: KPP HAM, 2000, at p. 3. ('KPP HAM Report')
37 KPP HAM report, *ibid*.
38 The report is reprinted in full in an appendix to Hamish McDonald *et al.* (eds), *Masters of Terror: Indonesia's Military and Violence in East Timor in 1999*: Paper 3 – Full Report of the Investigative Commission into Human Rights Violations in East Timor KPP- HAM (pages 15–59, 262–64), Canberra Papers on Strategy and Defence No. 145. Canberra: Strategic and Defence Studies Centre, Australian National University, 2002.
39 Tapol, *Ending the Cycle of Impunity: Can the East Timor Investigations Pave the Way?* Surrey: Tapol, the Indonesia Human Rights Campaign, 2000.
40 Tapol, *ibid*.

41 *Business Times*, Singapore, 2 February 2000. Notably Indonesia has had positive experiences of fact-finding committees in the post-Suharto era to investigate past crimes. There have been five such official committees that have investigated the following incidents: the violence in Aceh during the period when the province was called a Military Operation Area (1989–98); the Jakarta riots of 13–15 May 1998; the massacre in Tanjung Priok in 1984; the violence in East Timor during the referendum process in 1999, and the killing of students during demonstrations in Jakarta at Trisakti University and the Semanggi cloverleaf in 1998–99. The government established the first two commissions while the latter three were formed by Komnas HAM.

42 The most thorough examination of gender violence is contained in the UN Special Rapporteurs report, as examined in Chapters One and Five: see further Report of UN Special Rapporteurs: Situation of Human Rights in East Timor. Based on visit between 4–10 November 1999. UN Document A/54/660, 10 December 1999.

43 KPP HAM, 'Executive Summary', *Full Report of the Investigative Commission into Human Rights Violations in East Timor*. Jakarta: KPP HAM, 2000, at p. 3. ('KPP HAM Report')

44 *Report of the International Commission of Inquiry on East Timor to the Secretary-General* (ICIET Report) UN Doc A/54/726 and S/2000/59, 31 January 2000 at paras 72–82.

45 See further, Susan Harris Rimmer, 'Untold Numbers: East Timorese Women and Transitional Justice', Caroline Lambert and Sharon Pickering (eds). *Global Issues, Women and Justice*. Sydney: Federation Press, 2004: 335–66.

46 International Crisis Group, *Indonesia: Impunity Versus Accountability for Gross Human Rights Violations*. Brussels, International Crisis Group, 2001 at p. 15.

47 Law No. 26/2000 concerning the Human Rights Courts, enacted 23 November 2000 (Undang-Undang Republik Indonesia Nomor 26 Tahun 2000 tentang Pengadilan Hak Asasi Manusia ('UU No. 26/2000')).

48 Suzannah Linton, 'Accounting for Atrocities in Indonesia', (2006) *Singapore Year Book of International Law* 10: 1–33, at p. 13.

49 Clause 42.

50 The International Crisis Group reports that when the Human Rights Courts bill was taken to the DPR in June 2000, its possible retroactivity was criticised particularly by the military and Golkar representatives who had been most identified with the New Order regime. The majority, however, accepted that without retroactive prosecution of 'crimes of omission' it would be at least extremely difficult to convict those most responsible for human rights violations in East Timor and elsewhere and to persuade the international community that Indonesia was making a serious effort to hold those responsible for gross violations accountable. International Crisis Group, *Indonesia: Impunity versus accountability for gross human rights violations*. Brussels, International Crisis Group, 2001, at p. 15, quoting Kompas, 16 June 2000.

51 Note Articles 14 and 15 of the International Covenant on Civil and Political Rights.

52 The KKR Law finally passed into law in September 2004 but was struck down as unconstitutional in December 2006. Law No. 27/2004 concerning the Truth and Reconciliation Commission [Undang-Undang Republik Indonesia Nomor 24. Tahun 2004 tentang Komisi Kebenaran dan Rekonsiliasi].

53 International Crisis Group, *Indonesia: Impunity Versus Accountability for Gross Human Rights Violations*. Brussels, International Crisis Group, 2001 at p. 1.

54 Tapol, *Ending the Cycle of Impunity: Can the East Timor Investigations Pave the Way?* Surrey, Tapol, the Indonesia Human Rights Campaign, 2000.

55 Tapol, *ibid*.

56 The Justice Initiative and the Coalition for International Justice, *Unfulfilled Promises: Justice in East Timor*, November 2004, at p. 22.

57 KPP HAM, 'Executive Summary', *Full Report of the Investigative Commission into Human Rights Violations in East Timor*. Jakarta: KPP HAM, 2000, at p. 3. ('KPP HAM Report')

58 A list of 23 senior military figures who should be indicted is contained in the report of James Dunn, written as a consultant to the UNTAET Prosecutor General Mr Mohamed Othman, entitled 'Crimes Against Humanity in East Timor, January to October 1999: Their Nature and Causes', 14 February 2001 which was leaked to the press: Associated Press, 'UN Distances Itself from Report on East Timor War Crimes', 20 April 2001.
59 *The Deputy General Prosecutor against Wiranto, Zacky Anwar Makarim, Kiki Syahnakri, Adam.* From unofficial transcripts compiled by Judicial System Monitoring Programme's trial observer. Suhartono Suratman, Mohammad Noer Muis, Yayat Sudrajat and Abilio José Osorio Soares, 22 February 2003.
60 See further David Cohen, *Intended to Fail: The Trials before the Ad Hoc Human Rights Court in Jakarta.* International Center for Transitional Justice, 2003.
61 *Report to the UN Secretary-General of the Commission of Experts to Review the Prosecutions of Serious Violations of Human Rights in Timor Leste (then East Timor) in 1999.* S/2005/458, 15 July 2005 ('Commission of Experts Report'), at para [211].
62 Commission of Experts Report, *ibid.*
63 Commission of Experts Report, *ibid.*
64 M. MacGregor, 'East Timor: Last Indonesian governor is first jailed over violence.' *Asia Pacific.* Sydney, Asia Pacific/Radio Australia, 2004.
65 *Laksamana.Net.* '18 Tried, 16 Acquitted', 9 August 2004.
66 The Justice Initiative and the Coalition for International Justice, *Unfulfilled Promises: Justice in East Timor*, November 2004, at p. 23, see Askin *et al.* 2004.
67 *Ibid.*, at p. 40.
68 Ian Timberlake, 'We did all we could to keep peace – Wiranto', *The Sydney Morning Herald*, Sydney, 5 April 2002, p. 9.
69 Tiarma Siboro and Tertiani Z. Simanjuntak, 'Indonesian Government Unveils Names of Rights Tribunal Judges', *The Jakarta Post*, Jakarta, 2002.
70 Tiarma Siboro and Tertiani Z. Simanjuntak, *ibid.*
71 *Report to the UN Secretary-General of the Commission of Experts to Review the Prosecutions of Serious Violations of Human Rights in Timor Leste (then East Timor) in 1999.* S/2005/458, 15 July 2005 ('Commission of Experts Report'), at para [18].
72 Leila Nadya Sadat, 'The Legacy of the ICTY: The International Criminal Court' (2002) *New England Law Review* 37(4): 1073–80 at p. 1077.
73 Dieter Magsam, 'Coming to Terms with Genocide in Rwanda: The Role of International and National Justice' Wolfgang Kaleck, Michael Ratner, Tobias Singelnstein and Peter Weiss (eds). *International Prosecution of Human Rights Crimes.* Springer: Berlin, 2007, at p. 101.
74 Don Greenlees, 'Human Rights are on Trial, and so is the Court', *The Australian*, Sydney, 25 November 2002, at p. 12.
75 Don Greenlees, *ibid.*
76 M. N. Kurniawan, 'No Hope of Punishment Military, Police in Rights Cases', *Jakarta Post*, Jakarta, December 2002.
77 Tiarma Siboro, 'Rights abusers Should Be Executed: East Timor Leader'. *Jakarta Post*, Jakarta, 2000.
78 *Report to the UN Secretary-General of the Commission of Experts to review the prosecutions of serious violations of human rights in Timor Leste (then East Timor) in 1999.* S/2005/458, 15 July 2005 ('Commission of Experts Report'), at para [17].
79 *Report to the UN Secretary-General of the Commission of Experts to review the prosecutions of serious violations of human rights in Timor Leste (then East Timor) in 1999.* S/2005/458, 15 July 2005 ('Commission of Experts Report'), at para [211].
80 Judicial System Monitoring Programme case update, 'Eurico Guterres', Dili, 2002.
81 The Manuel Carrascalão House Massacre occurred April 17, 1999 in Dili, East Timor, at the house of prominent East Timor independence leader Manuel Carrascalão. The massacre

consisted of the murder of 12 people. It was conducted by the well-known Aitarak militia, then commanded by Eurico Guterres. The bodies of the victims were transported after they were killed to the village of Maubara, the headquarters of the Besi Merah Putih militia. There, the bodies were buried, in coffins, with personal possessions and identification. The bodies were exhumed later, in 2000, by the UNTAET Crime Scene Detachment.

82 'Observing three main cases of Adam Damiri, Tono Suratman and Eurico Gutteres', Institute For Policy Research and Advocacy (ELSAM) Monitoring Report on Ad Hoc Human Rights Court Against Gross Human Rights Violations in East Timor, *Report No. 6*, Jakarta, Indonesia, 2002.

83 See further AFP, 'Gusmão Regrets Jailing of Former East Timor Governor', 19 July 2004; and M. Davis, 'Abilio Soares – The Man in the Middle', *SBS Dateline*, Melbourne, SBS, July 2004.

84 At least three pieces of evidence which could have been used by the judges to secure a conviction in the Liquiça trial, including a priest eyewitness, an Indonesian military investigator and an Australian embassy report. See Don Greenlees, 'Smiles, but Still No Justice', *The Australian*. Sydney, 2 December 2002, at p. 12.

85 Don Greenlees, *ibid.*

86 Tiarma Siboro, 'SBY Told to Summon AG over General's East Timor Acquittal.' *The Jakarta Post*. Jakarta, 2005.

87 M. Taufiqurrahman, 'Reopening East Timor Cases Possible, Says AGO.' *The Jakarta Post*, Jakarta, 10 November 2004.

88 Hamish McDonald, 'Australia's bloody East Timor secret,' *Sydney Morning Herald*, 14 March 2002; 'Editorial: Silence over a Crime against Humanity', *Sydney Morning Herald*, 14 March 2002.

89 *Lusa*, 'Jakarta court acquittals 'scandalous': Ramos-Horta'. Jakarta, 1 December 2002. Notably, the Australian Foreign Minister, Alexander Downer, however, still expressed faith in the process..He said the Guterres sentence was 'welcome and appropriate', and 'shows that the ad hoc tribunal process in Indonesia is now starting to work and work well'. Hamish Mcdonald, 'Guterres: The One that Didn't Get Away.' *The Age*, Melbourne, 30 November 2002, at p. 3.

90 Agence France Presse, 'Gusmão Regrets Jailing of Former East Timor Governor', 19 July 2004.

91 Linda LoPresti, 'Critics Say Guterres Sentence Is Meaningless', *Radio Australia*. Sydney, 2 December 2002.

92 *Associated Press*, 'East Timor's Foreign Minister Opposes Rights Tribunal'. Jakarta, July 2004.

93 James Balowski, 'TNI Let Off the Hook Again', *Green Left Weekly*, Issue 519, 4 December 2002.

94 *Voice of America News*, 'Voice of America Editorial'. *Radio Scripts – Editorial 0–11521*, 2004.

95 Declaration by the Presidency on behalf of the European Union on the ad hoc Human Rights Tribunal for crimes committed in East Timor, 6 August 2003.

96 Associated Press, 'Indonesia Stung over US Criticism of Timor Acquittals'. Jakarta, July 2004.

97 Associated Press, *ibid.*

98 Agence France Presse, 'Indonesian ministers tell Washington to keep quiet on Timor verdicts' Jakarta, 12 August 2004.

99 'Indonesia is gambling that the war on terrorism will save them': David Cohen, 'Indonesia's Show Trials and Seeking Justice on the Cheap in East Timor', *East West Center media release*, Honolulu, 23 August 2002.

100 *Report to the UN Secretary-General of the Commission of Experts to review the prosecutions of serious violations of human rights in Timor Leste (then East Timor) in 1999*. S/2005/458, 15 July 2005 ('Commission of Experts Report'), at para [224].

101 Jill Jolliffe, 'Jakarta's Timor Trials "A Sham"', *The Age*, Darwin, 19 June 2005.
102 *Report to the UN Secretary-General of the Commission of Experts to review the prosecutions of serious violations of human rights in Timor Leste (then East Timor) in 1999*. S/2005/458, 15 July 2005 ('Commission of Experts Report'), at para [224].
103 Nine out of ten CTF commissioners are male. Olandina, a National Commissioner from the CAVR is the sole female commissioner. They have so far heard one female witness/victim Bertha dos Santos in March 2007. Olandina led a silent protest when the Chair did not allow dos Santos to answer one of Olandina's questions. 'Silent protest won't happen again, says Timor commission member', *The Jakarta Post*, Jakarta, 9 May 2007.
104 Report of the Secretary-General on Justice and Reconciliation for Timor-Leste, S/2006/580, 26 July 2006. Report of the Secretary-General on Timor-Leste pursuant to Security Council Resolution 1690 (2006), S/2006/628, 8 August 2006.
105 M. Rizal Maslan, 'Rights Activists want Truth and Reconciliation Commission Disbanded', *Detik.com*, Jakarta, 28 August, 2006. Suzannah Linton states that it 'represents the worst in truth commissions, with none of the positive attributes', Suzannah Linton, 'Accounting for Atrocities in Indonesia', (2006) *Singapore Year Book of International Law* 10: 1–33, at p. 25.
106 Article 14, International Covenant on Civil and Political Rights (ICCPR) 1971, 'everyone shall be entitled to a fair and public hearing by a competent, independent and impartial tribunal established by law'.
107 Commission on Human Rights, Sergio Vieira de Mello, 'Situation of Human Rights in Timor Leste, Report of the United Nations High Commissioner for Human Rights', UN Doc. E/CN.4/2003/37, 4 March 2003, para. 52.
108 Anastasia Vrachnos, 'A Long March Home', *AsiaWeek*, 26(43), 3 November 2000, p. 3.
109 Ian Timberlake, 'We Did All We Could to Keep Peace – Wiranto', *The Sydney Morning Herald*, Sydney, 5 April 2002, p. 9.
110 Cathy Munro, 'East Timor Atrocities Set for Human Rights Court', *The Canberra Times*, Canberra, 23 August 2001, at p. 10.
111 Amanda Morgan, 'The State and International Law'. Interview with Professor Hilary Charlesworth. Australian National University, Canberra 2003.
112 Amanda. Morgan, *ibid.*
113 Carol Cohn, 'War, Wimps, and Women: Talking Gender and Thinking War.' M. Cooke and A. Woollacott (eds). *Gendering War Talk.* Princeton, Princeton University Press, 1993: 227–46 at p. 230.
114 S. Sunindyo, 'When the Earth is Female and the Nation is Mother: Gender, the Armed Forces and Nationalism in Indonesia' (1998) *Feminist Review* 58(1): 1–21.
115 Jan Jindy Pettman, *Worlding Women: A Feminist International Politics*. St. Leonards, NSW: Allen & Unwin, 1996 at p. 5. See also the collected writings of Cynthia Enloe.
116 Amnesty International and Judicial System Monitoring Programme, *Indonesia: Justice for Timor-Leste: The Way Forward*. AI Index: ASA 21/006/2004, April 2004, at pp. 42–43.
117 Amnesty International and Judicial System Monitoring Programme, *ibid.*, at p. 42. See further Agence France Presse, 'East Timor Massacre Survivors Shun Jakarta Trial Over Safety Fears', 4 June 2002. At least 13 witnesses told UN officials they are too scared to come to Jakarta; Associated Press, 'East Timor Trial Verdicts Expected; Will Justice Be Done?', 11 August 2002; and Human Rights Watch interview with ELSAM trial monitor, Jakarta, 12 November 2002.
118 *Report to the UN Secretary-General of the Commission of Experts to Review the Prosecutions of Serious Violations of Human Rights in Timor Leste (then East Timor) in 1999*. S/2005/458, 15 July 2005 ('Commission of Experts Report'), at para [261].
119 Commission of Experts Report, *ibid.*

120 Note in contrast the witness protection provisions of the International Criminal Court detailed in the Rules of Procedure and Evidence detail the functions of the Victims and Witnesses Unit.
121 The presence of an interpreter, provided by UNTAET, had previously been agreed between UNTAET and the Attorney General's Office. However, at the hearing the judge refused to allow the interpreter to appear on the grounds that he did not have 'official accreditation' and because, in his view, the witness was fluent in Bahasa Indonesia and an interpreter was therefore not required. See further Amnesty International and Judicial System Monitoring Programme, *Indonesia: Justice for Timor-Leste: The Way Forward*. AI Index: ASA 21/006/2004, April 2004, at p. 43.
122 Amnesty International and Judicial System Monitoring Programme, *ibid*., at pp. 42–43.
123 Amnesty International and Judicial System Monitoring Programme, *ibid*., p. 43.
124 Amnesty International and Judicial System Monitoring Programme, *ibid*., at pp. 42–43.
125 Alison Young, 'The Wasteland of the Law, The Wordless Song of the Rape Victim' (1998) 22 *Melbourne University Law Review* 442 at 456, extracted in Regina Graycar and Jenny Morgan (eds), *The Hidden Gender of Law* (2nd edn), Annandale: Federation Press, 2002, pp. 356–57.
126 Alison Young, *ibid*.
127 Rate Laek, '"Widows"' group demands international tribunal', 24 August 2002.
128 Hilmar Farid and Rikardo Simarmata, *The Struggle for Truth and Justice: A Survey of Transitional Justice Initiatives Throughout Indonesia*. International Center for Transitional Justice Occasional Paper Series, January 2004, p. 24.
129 Tiarma Siboro and Tertiani Z. Simanjuntak, 'Indonesian Government Unveils Names of Rights Tribunal Judges', *The Jakarta Post*, Jakarta, 2002.
130 Amnesty International and Judicial System Monitoring Programme, *Indonesia: Justice for Timor-Leste: The Way Forward*. AI Index: ASA 21/006/2004, April 2004.
131 David Cohen, *Intended to Fail: The Trials before the Ad Hoc Human Rights Court in Jakarta*. International Center for Transitional Justice, 2003.
132 'Preface' by Ian Martin, David Cohen, *Intended to Fail: The Trials before the Ad Hoc Human Rights Court in Jakarta*. International Center for Transitional Justice, 2003, at p. iii.
133 See also Suzannah Linton, 'Accounting for Atrocities in Indonesia', (2006) *Singapore Year Book of International Law* 10: 1–33, at p. 31.
134 David Cohen, *Intended to Fail: The Trials before the Ad Hoc Human Rights Court in Jakarta*. International Center for Transitional Justice, 2003.
135 In November 2006, the Indonesian Film Censorship Institute (LSF) banned the screening of five films, three on East Timor, one on the 2002 Bail bombings and one about Aceh province, at the 8th international Jakarta film festival (JiFFest).
136 Ian Martin, who supervised the UN-organised independence ballot, has said that the court was accepting a 'mythical version' of events – that troops and police were powerless to halt violence between pro-integration and pro-independence East Timorese factions. In reality, Martin said, the army had created the militias, which waged a campaign of terror and coercion against pro-independence leaders and supporters; Agence France Presse, 'Rights Court Acquits Former Dili Military Chief', 29 November 2002.
137 Cynthia Enloe, *The Curious Feminist: Searching for Women in a New Age of Empire*, Berkeley: University of California Press 2004, at p. 214.
138 Agence France Presse, 'Rights Court Acquits Former Dili Military Chief', 29 November 2002.
139 For an analysis of the judgment see further International Center for Transitional Justice, Indonesia: 'A Case of Impunity', 30 June 2008.

Chapter 5

1 Xanana Gusmão, 'Notes on comments by Xanana Gusmão and José Ramos-Horta on dealing with past human rights violations made during a Panel Discussion'. Paper read at German Council on Foreign Relations (Deutsche Gesellschaft für Auswaertige Politik, DGAP), Berlin: Watch Indonesia, 20 October 2004.

2 Joao Ferreira, 'Judge Rapoza Reflects on East Timor Tribunal', *The Standard Times*, 12 November 2005, p. A1.

3 Christine Bell and Catherine O'Rourke, 'Does feminism need a theory of transitional justice?' (2007) *International Journal of Transitional Justice* 1: 23–44 at p. 23 and Katherine M. Franke, 'Gendered Subjects of Transitional Justice' (2006) *Columbia Journal of Gender and Law* 15(3): 813–28.

4 Katherine M. Franke, *ibid.*, p. 813.

5 Franke, *ibid.*

6 Franke, *ibid.*

7 The term 'justice judgments' refers to the acceptance of the outcomes of the prosecution process and the legitimacy of the court in the minds of the general public: Suzanne Karstedt 'Coming to Terms with the Past in Germany after 1945 and 1989: Public Judgments on Procedures and Justice' (1998) *Law & Policy* 20(1): 15–56.

8 Miriam Aukerman, 'Extraordinary Evil, Ordinary Crime: A Framework for Understanding Transitional Justice' (2002) 15 *Harvard Human Rights Journal* 39, at p. 47.

9 Definition taken from Suzanne Katzenstein, 'Hybrid Tribunals: Searching for Justice in East Timor', (2000) *Harvard Human Rights Journal* 16(6): 245–78 at p. 245.

10 Suzannah Linton, 'Prosecuting Atrocities at the District Court of Dili' (2001) 2 *Melbourne Journal of International Law* 414 at p. 416.

11 Laurel Fletcher and Harvey M. Weinstein, 'Violence and Social Repair: Rethinking the Contribution of Justice to Reconciliation' (2002) *Human Rights Quarterly* 24(3): 573–639.

12 Theodor Meron, *War Crimes Law Comes of Age: Essays*. Oxford, UK: Oxford University Press, 1998, at p. 282.

13 Suzannah Linton, *ibid.*, at p. 458.

14 2187 U.N.T.S. 90, entered into force July 1, 2002.

15 Definition taken from Suzanne Katzenstein, *ibid.*, at p. 245.

16 Katherine M. Franke, *ibid.*, at p. 820.

17 Hans Strohmeyer, 'Collapse and Reconstruction of a Judicial System: The United Nations Missions in Kosovo and East Timor' (2001) *American Journal of International Law* 95 (Symposium: State Reconstruction after Civil Conflict): 43–63 at p. 48.

18 For example, Hans Strohmeyer, *ibid.*

19 UNDP, *East Timor Human Development Report 2002*, 13 May 2002.

20 See further Hilmar Farid and Rikardo Simarmata, 'The Struggle for Truth and Justice: A Survey of Transitional Justice Initiatives throughout Indonesia', International Center for Transitional Justice *Occasional Paper Series*, January 2004, especially at p. vi.

21 Laura Grenfell makes the point that this view is overly focused on the formal legal sector, 'Harnessing Local Law in the Post-Conflict State: The case of Timor-Leste', *The Role of International Law in Rebuilding Societies after Conflict: Great Expectations*, B. Bowden, H. Charlesworth and J. Farrall (eds), Cambridge: Cambridge University Press, 2009.

22 *Report of the International Commission of Inquiry on East Timor to the Secretary-General* (ICIET Report), January 2000. UN Doc A/54/726 and S/2000/59, 31 January 2000 at [153].

23 ICIET Report, *ibid.*, at [136].

24 ICIET Report, *ibid.*, at [147].

25 *Report of United Nations Special Rapporteurs: Situation of Human Rights in East Timor*. Based on visit between 4–10 November 1999. UN Document A/54/660, 10 December 1999.

26 KPP HAM. *Full Report of the Investigative Commission into Human Rights Violations in East Timor*. Jakarta: KPP HAM, 2000. This background is examined further in Chapter Three.

27 Amnesty International and JSMP (AI and JSMP). *Indonesia: Justice for Timor-Leste: The Way Forward*. Dili, 2004.

28 There was one outreach session by the SCIU in April 2005. See further on this point Reiger and Wierda, *ibid*., at pp. 31–34.

29 UN Doc. S/RES/1264 (1999).

30 In fact, Tanja Hohe has convincingly argued that the UN administration was autocratic in most aspects of its functioning and created 'feudal democracy'. Tanja Hohe, 'Building Feudal Democracy in East Timor', Edward Newman and Roland Rich (eds), *The UN Role in Promoting Democracy: Between Ideals and Reality*, UNU Press: Tokyo, 1994, 302–15 at p. 302.

31 In contrast, the Afghanistan Independent Human Rights Commission (AIHRC) conducted a survey of more than 6,000 Afghans from 32 provinces and refugee camps. The overwhelming preference was for lustration measures. See AIHRC, *A call for Justice: Conclusion of National Consultation on Transitional Justice in Afghanistan*, Kabul, January 2005

32 UN Doc. UNTAET/REG/2000/15.

33 Section 5, UNTAET Regulation 2000/11, UN Doc. UNTAET/REG/2000/11.

34 Strohmeyer has noted that in practice, this requirement of reconciling Indonesian law with international human rights laws proved to be difficult to apply in East Timor: *ibid*., at p. 59.

35 Judicial System Monitoring Programme (JSMP), *Report on the Court of Appeal decision on the Applicable Subsidiary Law in Timor-Leste*. Dili, 2003: 1–14.

36 Note the Court of Appeal decision on 15 July 2003: *Public Prosecutor v. Armando dos Santos* Court of Appeal, (15 July 2003) which decided the applicable law in East Timor was the Law of Portugal, rather than Indonesia.

37 Democratic Republic Of East Timor Law No. 2/02 Interpretation of Applicable Law on 19 May 2002.

38 The confusion arises from language in United Nations regulations 2000/11, paragraph 10.2 and regulation 2000/15, paragraph 2.3 which provide exclusive jurisdiction to the Special Panels of the District Court in Dili for the crimes of rape and murder committed between 1 January 1999 and 25 October 1999. See further JSMP, *The Future of the Serious Crimes Unit*. Dili, 2004: 1–15 at pp. 4–5.

39 Suzannah Linton, *ibid*., at p. 416.

40 Convention on the Prevention and Punishment of the Crime of Genocide, 78 U.N.T.S. 277, entered into force Jan. 12, 1951, Article 2.

41 In the *Akayesu* case, the ICTR found Jean-Paul Akayesu guilty of genocide. The tribunal's decision was based in part on evidence that he had witnessed and encouraged rapes and sexual mutilation of women in the course of a genocidal campaign against the Tutsi population while he was a communal leader. In dicta in the Akayesu decision, the ICTR described a situation in which a rapist might deliberately impregnate his victim with the intent to force her to give birth to a child who would, because of patrilineal social conventions, not belong to its mother's group. The tribunal noted that such an act might be a constitutive element of genocide. *Prosecutor v. Jean-Paul Akayesu*, 2 September 1999, ICTR-96-4-T.

42 In the *Akayesu* decision, the ICTR found the defendant guilty of crimes against humanity based on evidence that he had witnessed and encouraged rapes of Tutsi women while he was a communal leader. The tribunal found that the rapes were both systematic and carried out on a massive scale. *Prosecutor v. Jean-Paul Akayesu*, 2 September 1999, ICTR-96-4-T.

43 This formula reflects a distillation of Common Article 3 of the Geneva Conventions and Article 4(2)(e) of Protocol II, and has been further interpreted by ICTY and ICTR jurisprudence.

44 In the *Furundzija* decision, the ICTY found Anto Furundzija, a local Bosnian Croat military commander, guilty of aiding and abetting a war crime, the rape of a Bosnian Muslim woman. Furundzija was found to have provided 'assistance, encouragement, or moral support which ha[d] a substantial effect on the perpetration of the crime' when his subordinate orally, anally and vaginally raped a Bosnian Muslim woman Furundzija was interrogating. *Prosecutor v. Anto Furundzija*, 10 December 1998, ICTY-95-17/1-T.

45 This definition of forced pregnancy is considered at length in Chapter Five.

46 Various international authorities have recognised rape to constitute a form of torture, as defined by the Torture Convention, when it is used in order to obtain information or confession, or for any reason based on discrimination, or to punish, coerce or intimidate, and is performed by state agents or with their acquiescence. In the *Celebici* case, the ICTY characterised the rape of Bosnian Serb women prisoners at the Celebici prison camp as acts of torture. *Prosecutor v. Dragoljub Kunarac, Radomir Kovac and Zoran Vukovic*, Judgment, Case No. IT-96-23/1-T, 22 February 2001.

47 10 Dec. 1984, 1465 U.N.T.S. 85.

48 Establishment of Panels with Exclusive Jurisdiction over Serious Criminal Offences. UNTAET/REG/2000/15, 6 June 2000.

49 Gordon Renouf, *Some Features of the Legal System in East Timor*. East Timor Legal Coordination Symposium, Darwin, 2002, at p.2.

50 Suzannah Linton, 'Rising from the Ashes: The Creation of a Viable Criminal Justice System in East Timor'. (2001) *Melbourne University Law Review* 25 at p. 217.

51 *Report of the International Commission of Inquiry on East Timor to the Secretary-General*, January 2000. UN Doc A/54/726 and S/2000/59, 31 January 2000.

52 Nelson Belo and Christian Ranheim, 'Prosecuting Serious Crimes in East Timor', *Justice and Accountability in East Timor: International Tribunals and Other Options: Report of a One-day Seminar in Dili, East Timor*, JSMP, 16 October 2001.

53 Serious Crimes Unit Update, 4 February 2004

54 By comparison, the death toll from the whole occupation period is estimated at 183,000 by the CAVR. The number of people killed in the war in Bosnia-Herzegovina was around 102,000, according to research done by the ICTY. The ICTR was investigating from 500,000 up to 910,000 deaths in the Rwanda conflict.

55 Megan Hirst and Howard Varney, *Justice Abandoned: An Assessment of the Serious Crimes Process in East Timor*. International Center for Transitional Justice Occasional Paper Series, June 2005, at p. 7.

56 Carl de Faria, 'East Timor's Quest for Justice: The Serious Crimes File', paper presented at the *UNMISET International Symposium on United Nations Peacekeeping Operations in Post-conflict Timor-Leste: Accomplishments and Lessons Learned*, April 28, 2005, at p. 2. See further JSMP, *Torture Survivors: Their Experiences of Violation, Truth and Justice*, Dili, April 2007, at p. 17.

57 See discussion of *Prosecutor v. Marcelino Soares*, Special Panel Case No. 11/2003, 11 December 2003 by Martin Clutterbuck, 'Crimes against Humanity Trials on our Doorstep' (2005) *Law Institute Journal* 79(12): 63.

58 Martin Clutterbuck, *ibid.*

59 Lisa Clausen, 'Slow Road to Justice', *Time Magazine*, 17 March 2003.

60 Lisa Clausen, *ibid.*

61 See Suzanne Katzenstein, *ibid.*, at p. 251.

62 *Report to the United Nations Secretary-General of the Commission of Experts to Review the Prosecutions of Serious Violations Of Human Rights in Timor Leste (then East Timor) in 1999*. S/2005/458, 15 July 2005.

63 JSMP, *The Role, Practice and Procedure of the Court of Appeal*, Dili, 28 July 2005.

64 See further JSMP, *The Right to Appeal in East Timor*. Dili, 2002, 1–24 at p. 10.

65 Quoted by JSMP, *ibid*., at p. 1.
66 JSMP, *Overview of the Jurisprudence of the Court of Appeal in its First Operation since East Timor's Independence*, Dili, August 2004.
67 International Crisis Group, 'Resolving Timor-Leste's Crisis', *Asia Report No.120*, 10 October 2006, at p. 18.
68 JSMP, 'Justice Update: Leadership Crisis in the Judicial Organs of Timor Leste', Dili, March 2009.
69 David Cohen, 'Seeking Justice on the Cheap: Is the East Timor Tribunal Really a Model for the Future?' (2002) *East West Centre Paper No. 61*, at p. 3.
70 JSMP, *The Future of the Serious Crimes Unit*. Dili, 2004, p. 14. JSMP cite Radio Australia broadcast, 'Concern over Future of Serious Crimes Unit', 29 April 2003.
71 *Report to the Secretary General of the Commission of Experts to Review the Prosecution of Serious Violations of Human Rights in Timor-Leste (the then East Timor) in 1999*, 26 May 2005, para. 99.
72 Commission of Experts report, *ibid*.
73 Hilary Charlesworth and Christine Chinkin, *The Boundaries of International Law: A Feminist Analysis*, Manchester; Manchester UP, 2000 at pp. 310–12.
74 Seth Mydans, 'Modest Beginnings for East Timor's Justice System', *New York Times*, 4 March 2001.
75 See further Hilary Charlesworth and Mary Wood. 'Women and Human Rights in the Rebuilding of East Timor' (2002) *Nordic Journal of International Law* 71: 325–48.
76 2187 U.N.T.S. 90, entered into force July 1, 2002.
77 Megan Hirst and Howard Varney, *ibid*., at p. 7.
78 Address by Siri Frigaard at the conference, 'Domestic Prosecutions and Transitional Justice', organised by ICTJ and the Foundation for Human Rights on May 18, 2005, in Johannesburg, South Africa. Although as Wandita *et al*. have observed '[t]he CAVR has demonstrated that, given the right conditions, Timorese women will speak out about the violations they have experienced': Galuh Wandita, Karen Campbell-Nelson, and Manuela Leong Pereira, 'Learning to Engender Reparations in Timor-Leste: Reaching Out to Female Victims', *What Happened to the Women?: Gender and Reparations for Human Rights Violations*, Ruth Rubio-Marín (ed.), New York: Social Science Research Council, 2006, at p.316.
79 *The General Prosecutor of the United Nations Transitional Administration in East Timor v. Leonardus Kasa*. Dili District Court Special Panel for Serious Crimes Case no. 11/CG/2000, 9 May 2001.
80 *The General Prosecutor of the United Nations Transitional Administration in East Timor v. Joao Franca Da Silva alias Jhoni Franca, José Cardoso Fereira alias Mouzinho and Sabino Gouvia Leite*. Dili District Court Special Panel for Serious Crimes Case no. 4/CG/2000. (The Lolotoe Trial).
81 *The General Prosecutor of the United Nations Transitional Administration in East Timor v. Francisco Soares*. Dili District Court Special Panel for Serious Crimes Case no. 14/2001.
82 Kasa case, *ibid*.
83 Indictment.
84 JSMP, 'Dili Court Increases Pressure on Indonesia', 10 May 2001.
85 Seth Mydans, 'Sexual Violence as Tool of War: Pattern Emerging in East Timor', *New York Times*, 1 March 2001.
86 'Establishment of Panels with Exclusive Jurisdiction over Serious Criminal Offences'. UNTAET/REG/2000/15, 6 June 2000
87 Note Suzannah Linton, 'Experiments in International Justice' (2001) *Criminal Law Forum* 12: 210–11. The ICTR defined rape in the *Akayesu* case as 'a physical invasion of a sexual nature committed on a person under circumstances which are coercive' at paras 6.4 and 7.7.
88 Kasa Judgment, 2001, at p. 3.

89 A Latin legal term meaning 'making the necessary changes'.
90 Kasa Judgment, 2001, at p. 4.
91 Kasa Judgment, *ibid.*
92 Kasa Judgment, *ibid.*, at p. 5.
93 Kasa Judgment, *ibid.*, at p. 6.
94 JSMP, 'Dili Court Increases Pressure on Indonesia', 10 May 2001
95 See further International Law Association Committee on Human Rights Law and Practice, 'Final Report on the Exercise of Universal Jurisdiction in Respect of Gross Human Rights Violations', *Report of the Sixty-Ninth Conference*, London 2000, at pp. 403–31.
96 Section 5, UNTAET Regulation 2000/11.
97 Judge Pillay asked the Prosecution to amend the indictment and undertake further investigation in the *Akayesu* case before the ICTR, leading to the first judgment of rape as a crime against humanity: Bill Berkely, 'Judgment Day', *Washington Post Magazine*, 11 October 1998, at p. W10.
98 Section 5, UNTAET Regulation 2000/11.
99 *Prosecutor v. Anto Furundzija*, ICTY-95-17/1-T, Judgment 10 December 1998. See further Hilary Charlesworth and Christine Chinkin, *ibid.*, at pp. 322–23.
100 JSMP has raised concerns over the training and experience of both local and international public defenders in the Los Palos case. *A JSMP Trial Report The General Prosecutor v. John Marques and 9 Others (The Los Palos Case)*, Dili, 2002, at pp 23–24.
101 In the Los Palos case, eight people, mostly nuns and deacons who had gone to distribute food and medicine to refugees, were gunned down by the road in September 1999. The judgment in the first Crimes Against Humanity trial, the Los Palos case, was delivered on 11 December 2001 and convicted ten suspects of committing Crimes Against Humanity. The case focused on 13 charges of murder, torture and the forcible transfer of civilian population in Lautem district between April and September 1999. The sentences ranged from four years to 33 years and four months. An eleventh suspect, the former second-in-command of the Indonesian Kopassus Special Forces in Lautem district, appeared on the indictment but is still at large. UNTAET Fact Sheet 7, April 2002.
102 JSMP, *A JSMP Trial Report The General Prosecutor v. Joni Marques and 9 Others (The Los Palos Case)*, Dili, 2002, at p. 30.
103 *General Prosecutor v. Joao Fernandes*, Case No. 001/00.CG.2000 (25 January 2000). *General Prosecutor v. Julio Fernandes*, Case No. 002/00C.G.2000 (1 March 2000).
104 Suzannah Linton, 'Prosecuting Atrocities at the District Court of Dili' (2001) 2 *Melbourne Journal of International Law* 414.
105 The Maliana massacre in September 1999 was one of the worst in East Timor, in which 47 civilians were hacked to death with machetes while seeking refuge at a police station.
106 Suzannah Linton, *ibid.*
107 Suzannah Linton, *ibid.*, at fn 30.
108 Suzannah Linton, *ibid.*, at p. 422.
109 Hilary Charlesworth and Christine Chinkin, *ibid.*, at p. 19.
110 *The General Prosecutor of the United Nations Transitional Administration in East Timor v. Joao Franca Da Silva alias Jhoni Franca, José Cardoso Fereira alias Mouzinho and Sabino Gouvia Leite*. Dili District Court Special Panel for Serious Crimes Case no. 4/CG/2000. (The Lolotoe Trial)
111 UNTAET Daily Briefing 7 May 2002 'Lolotoe Trial Begins Phase Of Hearing Witnesses'.
112 JSMP Report, *The Lolotoe Case: A Small Step Forward*, Dili, July 2004.

113 JSMP Report, *ibid.*, at p. 2.
114 As of June 2009. See further JSMP, *Digest of the Jurisprudence of the Special Panels for Serious Crimes*, Dili, April 2007, p. 14.
115 Indictment, 4/2001.
116 *Prosecutor v Dragoljub Kunarac, Radomir Kovac and Zoran Vukovic*, Judgement, Case No. IT-96-23/1-T, 22 February 2001.
117 JSMP Report, *The Lolotoe Case: A Small Step Forward* Dili, July 2004.
118 JSMP Report, *ibid.*, at p.15.
119 JSMP Report, *ibid.*
120 *José Cardoso*, 4c/2001, Judgment, 5 April 2003.
121 *José Cardoso*, 4c/2001, Judgment, 5 April 2003.
122 José Cardoso, Final Statement of the Prosecutors. 1 April 2003, pp. 37–46.
123 José Cardoso, 4c/2001, Judgment, 5 April 2003, at [274], citing M. Cherif Bassiouni, 'Crimes against Humanity', *International Criminal Law*, (2nd edn) Cambridge MA: Kluwer Law International, 1999 at p. 344.
124 *Prosecutor v. Dragoljub Kunarac et al.* (Judgment) IT-96-23-T & IT-96-23/I-T, 22 February 2001.
125 José Cardoso Judgment at 128, quoted in JSMP Report, *The Lolotoe Case: A Small Step Forward*, July 2004 at p. 6.
126 Kelly Askin, 'The Jurisprudence of the International War Crimes Tribunals', Helen Durham and Tracey Gurd (eds). *Listening to the Silences: Women and War*. Leiden: Boston: Martinus Nijhoff, 2005 at p. 132.
127 JSMP Report, *The Lolotoe Case: A Small Step Forward*, Dili, July 2004 at pp. 30–31.
128 *Prosecutor v Furundzija*, Case IT-95-17/1-T, Judgment, 10 December 1998.
129 *Prosecutor v Aleksovski*, Case IT-95-14/1-T, Judgment 25 June 1999: Appeal Judgment, 24 March 2002.
130 José Cardoso Judgment at 458 quoted in JSMP (JSMP) Report, *The Lolotoe Case: A Small Step Forward*, Dili, July 2004 at p. 31.
131 JSMP Report, *ibid.*, at p. 32.
132 JSMP Report, *ibid.*, at pp. 33–34.
133 See JSMP Report, *ibid.*, at p. 33.
134 JSMP unofficial transcript of Lolotoe trial 2 April 2003, quoted in JSMP Report, *ibid.*, at p. 15.
135 JSMP Report, *ibid.*, at p. 25.
136 JSMP Report, *ibid.*
137 JSMP Report, *ibid.*
138 JSMP Report, *ibid.*
139 JSMP Report, *ibid.*, noting the unofficial transcript of Lolotoe trial 14 November 2002.
140 Alexander Zahar, 'Commentary on Trial Judgments of the East Timor Special Panels in the Cases of José Cardoso Ferreira and Agustinho Atolan' (1 December 2008). *Annotated Leading Cases Of International Criminal Tribunals*, Vol. 13: Timor Leste: The Special Panels For Serious Crimes, 2001–3, André Klip and Göran Sluiter, eds., Intersentia, 2008, pp. 762–65 at 765.
141 CEDAW Committee General Comment 19 on Article 16 (and article 5), Violence against women: 29/01/92, A/47/38 designates rape within marriage a crime.
142 JSMP, 'Timor Serious Crimes Panel Hands Down First Rape Conviction', 12 September 2002.
143 Case Number: 8/2002.
144 Serious Crimes Unit 'Information Release. Crimes Against Humanity Rape Charges For Five TNI Soldiers', 10 April 2003.
145 Diane Farsetta, 'East Timorese Refugees in Militia-Controlled Camps', M. H. C. Pus (ed.), *The Devastating Impact of Small Arms & Light Weapons on the Lives of Women: A Collection of Testimonies*, WILPF for International Action Network on Small Arms (IANSA) Women's Caucus, 2001.

146 Kirsty Sword Gusmão, 'The Case of Ms Juliana Dos Santos', *Alola Foundation Report*, Dili, October 2001.
147 Mark Dodd, 'A Family in East Timor Grieves for a Daughter', *International Herald Tribune*, 22 December 2000.
148 *Report to the United Nations Secretary-General of the Commission of Experts to review the prosecutions of serious violations of human rights in Timor Leste (then East Timor) in 1999.* S/2005/458, 15 July 2005.
149 *Report to the United Nations Secretary-General of the Commission of Experts, ibid.*
150 JSMP. *The Future of the Serious Crimes Unit.* Dili, 2004, at p. 14.
151 Report of the Secretary-General on Justice and Reconciliation for Timor-Leste, S/2006/580, 26 July 2006.
152 Megan Hirst and Howard Varney, *ibid.*, at p. 7.
153 Report of the Secretary-General on Justice and Reconciliation for Timor-Leste, S/2006/580, 26 July 2006.
154 For descriptions of the difficulties in building the judicial system in East Timor, see Hansjörg Strohmeyer *ibid.*, and Suzannah Linton, 'Rising from the Ashes: The Creation of a Viable Criminal Justice System in East Timor' (2001) *Melbourne University Law Review* 25.
155 Seth Mydans, 'Modest Beginnings for East Timor's Justice System', *New York Times*, New York, USA, 4 March 2001, at p. 10.
156 Megan Hirst and Howard Varney, *ibid.*, at p. 7.
157 AI and JSMP. *Indonesia: Justice for Timor-Leste: The Way Forward.* AI Index: ASA 21/006/2004, April 2004.
158 Reiger and Wierda, *ibid.*, at pp. 14–15.
159 David Cohen, *ibid.*, at p. 5. See also Suzanne Katzenstein, *ibid.*, at pp. 262–64.
160 Mark Dodd, 'Massacres Go Unpunished as UN Crimes Unit Heads for Collapse.' *Sydney Morning Herald.* 1 May 2001.
161 Dodd, *ibid.*
162 Dodd, *ibid.* Mohamed Othman, the first United Nations chief prosecutor in East Timor, a Tanzanian judge with experience at the International Criminal Tribunal for Rwanda, admitted in 2001 that there was a shortage of competent investigators.
163 John Martinkus, 'Beyond Justice'. *The Bulletin*, 2002, at p. 34.
164 Maryanne Keady, 'Concern over Future of Serious Crimes Unit'. ABC Radio Australia. 2003.
165 JSMP. *The Future of the Serious Crimes Unit* at p. 7.
166 JSMP, *ibid.*, at p. 6.
167 Suzannah Linton, 'Prosecuting Atrocities at the District Court of Dili' (2001) 2 *Melbourne Journal of International Law* 414 at p. 458.
168 David Cohen, *ibid.*, at p. 7.
169 John Martinkus, 'Beyond Justice'. *The Bulletin*, 2002, at p. 34.
170 Suzannah Linton, 'Rising from the Ashes: The Creation of a Viable Criminal Justice System in East Timor' (2001) *Melbourne University Law Review* 25 at p. 217. This article is a seminal piece on transitional justice issues in East Timor.
171 Serious Crimes Unit Update VII/03, 5 August 2003.
172 See Detik Com, 'Indonesian Politicians React to UN Move to Indict Senior Military',26 February 2003; and Associated Press, 'Indonesia Will Ignore Indictments of Ex-Officials', 25 February 2003.
173 Associated Press, 'Indonesia Will Ignore Indictments of Ex-Officials', 25 February 2003.
174 It may be that the legal basis of the extradition process was itself flawed: see further Anton Girginov, 'Extradition from Indonesia to East Timor and the serious crimes process in East Timor (1999–2005)' (2006) *East Timor Law Journal* 2.
175 See AI and JSMP, *ibid.*

176 Joint Truth and Friendship Commission, *Per Memoriam ad Spem (From Memory to Hope): Final Report*, May 2008.
177 JSMP. *The Lolotoe Case: A Small Step Forward*. July 2004 at p. 33.
178 Report of the United Nations Independent Special Commission of Inquiry for Timor-Leste, Geneva, 2 October 2006.
179 Unconfirmed reports say that the files were all returned in exchange for a refrigerator. Lisa Palmer, Sara Niner and Lia Kent. 'Forum Proceedings: Exploring the Tensions of Nation Building in Timor-Leste, Held on 15 September 2006 at Melbourne University.' *School of Social and Environmental Enquiry Research Paper No. 1*, Monica Minnegal (ed.), Melbourne: University of Melbourne, 2007.
180 Report of the Secretary-General on Justice and Reconciliation for Timor-Leste, S/2006/580, 26 July 2006.
181 Interview with Ms. Eliza da Silva Dos Santos, the chief of Rate Laek Victim's Group, 16 January 2004, quoted by JSMP, *The Future of the Serious Crimes Unit*, Dili, 2004 at p. 9.
182 JSMP, *ibid.*
183 Bureau of Democracy, Human Rights and Labor. *US Government: Country Reports on Human Rights Practices 2003.*Washington, 25 February 2004.
184 Maryanne Keady, 'Concern over Future of Serious Crimes Unit'. ABC Radio Australia. 2003.
185 JSMP, *Justice Update: Legal Perspectives on Clemency*, June 2008.
186 Keady, *ibid.*
187 Keady, *ibid.*
188 Suzanne Katzenstein, *ibid.*, at p. 277.
189 Mohamed Othman, 'East Timor: A Critique of the Model of Accountability for Serious Human Rights and International Humanitarian Law Violations', (2003) *Nordic Journal of International Law* 72(4): 449–82.
190 Hansjörg Strohmeyer, *ibid.*, at p. 60.
191 Strohmeyer, *ibid.*, at pp. 60–61.
192 Strohmeyer, *ibid.*, at p. 61.
193 See Elisabeth Rehn and Ellen Johnson Sirleaf, *Women, War and Peace: The Independent Experts' Assessment on the Impact of Armed Conflict on Women and Women's Role in Peacebuilding*, UNIFEM, 2002, at pp. 93–101.
194 Rehn and Johnson Sirleaf, *ibid.*
195 In a World Bank report released in November 2002, justice was ranked eleventh out of the twelve sectors evaluated for progress in the transition to independence, beating out only the power sector for the wooden spoon. Klaus Rohland and Sarah Cliffe, 'The East Timor Reconstruction Program: Successes, Problems and Tradeoffs' *Conflict Prevention and Reconstruction Unit Working Paper No.2*, World Bank Group, November 2002, at p. 11.
196 Laura Grenfell, 'Legal Pluralism and the Rule of Law in Timor Leste' (2006) *Leiden Journal of International Law* 19: 305–37.
197 Suzanne Katzenstein, *ibid.*, at p. 245.
198 Katzenstein, *ibid.*, at p. 246.
199 Katzenstein, *ibid.*, at p. 278.

Chapter 6

1 Galuh Wandita, Karen Campbell-Nelson, and Manuela Leong Pereira, 'Learning to Engender Reparations in Timor-Leste: Reaching Out to Female Victims.' Ruth Rubio-Marín (ed.), *What Happened to the Women? Gender and Reparations for Human Rights Violations*, New York: Social Science Research Council, 2006, at p. 295.
2 Commission for Reception, Truth-seeking, and Reconciliation (CAVR), 'Women and the Conflict: National Public Hearing 28–29 April 2003', Audiensi Publik Nasional: Balide, East Timor, 2005.

3 Extract from Karen Campbell-Nelson, Researcher, Commission for Reception, Truth-seeking, and Reconciliation (CAVR), Dili, East Timor. 'East Timor Women Must Tell of Atrocities by Indonesians', *The Jakarta Post*, 9–10 June 2003.
4 CAVR, 'Women and the Conflict', *ibid.*
5 CAVR, *Chega! Final Report of the Commission for Reception, Truth and Reconciliation.* Dili: Commission for Reception, Truth and Reconciliation, 2005.
6 1951 Convention relating to the Status of Refugees, 189 U.N.T.S. 150, entered into force April 22, 1954, as amended by the 1967 Protocol 606 U.N.T.S. 267.
7 Vasuki Nesiah, 'Gender and Truth Commission Mandates', International Centre for Transitional Justice, New York, 2006 at p. 1.
8 Fionnuala Ni Aolain and Catherine Turner, 'Gender, Truth and Transition' (2007) *UCLA Women's Law Journal* 16: 229–79 at pp. 257–60.
9 Ni Aolain and Turner, *ibid.*, at pp. 262–65.
10 Ni Aolain and Turner, *ibid.*, pp. 260–62.
11 Hayli Millar, 'Facilitating Women's Voices in Truth Recovery: An Assessment Of Women's Participation and The Integration of a Gender Perspective in Truth Commissions', Helen Durham and Tracey Gurd (eds). *Listening to the Silences: Women and War.* Boston, Leiden: Martinus Nijhoff, 2005: 171–222, at p. 186.
12 Ni Aolain and Turner, *ibid.*, at p. 273.
13 CAVR. *Chega!*, *ibid.*, at p. 25.
14 CAVR. *Chega!*, *ibid.*, at p. 24.
15 Based on the authority of *Prosecutor v Anto Furundzija*, ICTY Case No IT-95-17/1-T, Trial Chamber Judgment, 10 December 1998, para 168.
16 CAVR. *Chega!*, *ibid.*, Chapter 7.7 at p.108, para 25. This finding was picked up by international media, see Sian Powell, 'UN verdict on East Timor', *The Australian*, 19 January 2006.
17 18 Dec. 1979, 1249 U.N.T.S. 513.
18 CAVR. *Chega!*, *ibid.*, Chapter 11, p. 26, recommendation 7.2.
19 John Braithwaite, 'Restorative Justice: Assessing Optimistic and Pessimistic Accounts', (1999) *Crime and Justice* 25: 1–127 at 1.
20 CAVR. *Chega!*, *ibid.*, Part 1: Introduction, p. 11, para. 42, point 6.
21 CAVR. *Chega!*, *ibid.*, Part 1: Introduction, 'Gender and staffing', pp. 40–42.
22 CAVR. *Chega!*, *ibid.*, 'Part 1: Introduction', p. 40.
23 CAVR. *Chega!*, *ibid.*, at p. 42.
24 Galuh Wandita *et al.*, *ibid.*, at p. 291.
25 CAVR. *Chega!*, *ibid.*, Chapter 7.7, p. 4.
26 CAVR. *Chega!*, *ibid.*
27 Vasuki Nesiah, *et al.*, *ibid.*, at p. 19.
28 CAVR. *Chega!*, *ibid.*, Chapter 7.7, p. 4.
29 CAVR, *ibid.*
30 CAVR, *ibid.*
31 Vasuki Nesiah *et al.*, *ibid.*, at p. 18.
32 CAVR, Women and Conflict: National Public Hearing, *ibid.*
33 Hilary Charlesworth and Christine Chinkin, *The Boundaries of International Law: A Feminist Analysis.* Manchester: Manchester University Press, 2000, at p. 334.
34 CAVR, *Chega!*, *ibid.*, 'Part 10: *Acolhimento* and Victim Support', 10.3.4, pp. 38–46.
35 CAVR *ibid.*, p. 41.
36 Galuh Wandita, *et al.*, *ibid.*, at p. 312.
37 CAVR, *Chega!*, *ibid.*
38 CAVR, *Chega!*, *ibid.*, Recommendation 12, p. 39 and 41.
39 Galuh Wandita *et al.*, *ibid.*, at p. 312. The broad definition of victims of sexual violence covers not only women and girls, but also men and boys who were subjected to acts such as rape, sexual slavery, forced marriage or 'other forms of sexual violence'.

40 The process is outlined at length in Part 9 of the Chega report.
41 Megan Hirst and Howard Varney, *Justice Abandoned: An Assessment of the Serious Crimes Process in East Timor*. International Center for Transitional Justice Occasional Paper Series, June 2005, at p. 11.
42 Megan Hirst and Howard Varney, *ibid.*, at p. 31.
43 See further Caitlin Reiger and Marieke Wierda, 'The Serious Crimes Process in Timor-Leste: In Retrospect', *Prosecution Case Studies Series*, New York: International Center for Transitional Justice, March 2006, at pp. 34–35.
44 Judicial System Monitoring Programme, Lia Kent, *Unfulfilled Expectations: Community Views on CAVR's Community Reconciliation Process*, Dili, August 2004, at p. 15.
45 Laura Grenfell, 'Legal Pluralism and the Rule of Law in Timor Leste' (2006) *Leiden Journal of International Law* 19: 305–37.
46 Laura Grenfell, *ibid.*
47 Lia Kent, *ibid.*, at p. 39.
48 *Ibid.*, at p. 40.
49 Tanja Hohe and Rod Nixon. *Report on Reconciling Justice 'Traditional' Law and State Judiciary in East Timor*, January 2003. See further Laura Grenfell, 'Harnessing Local Law in the Post-Conflict State: The Case of Timor-Leste', *Timor-Leste: Challenges for Justice and Human Rights in the Shadow of the Past*. William Binchy (ed.). Dublin: Clarus Press, 2009: 81–110.
50 Chris Dolan, Judith Large and Naoko Obi, Evaluation *of UNHCR's Repatriation and Reintegration Programme in East Timor,1999–2003*, EPAU/2004/02, February 2004, p. 1 and 88.
51 United Nations High Commissioner for Human Rights, 'UNHCR News, Timor Emergency Update', 25 November 1999. Of the 110,000 initial returns in late 1999, over 65,000 were reportedly spontaneous, the rest assisted by UNHCR. The mandate of UNHCR is contained in the Statute of the Office of the United Nations High Commissioner for Refugees, Annex to UNGA Res. 428(V), 14 Dec. 1950.
52 Extracted from CAVR *Chega! ibid.*, Part 10, p. 6. See also 'Indonesia: UNHCR Asks Government to Control Militias', *Refugees Daily*, 10 November 1999.
53 Human Rights Watch, *Indonesia/ East Timor: Forced Expulsions to West Timor and the Refugee Crisis* Vol. 11, No. 7 (c), December 1999.
54 Fabrizio Hochschild, '"It is Better to Leave, We Can't Protect You": Flight in the First Months of the United Nations Transitional Administrations in Kosovo and East Timor', (2004) *Journal of Refugee Studies* 17 (3): 286–300.
55 Chris Dolan *et al.*, *ibid.*, at pp. 1 and 88.
56 Victoria Brittain, 'Traumatised Timorese Women', *The Guardian*, Dili, 30 July 2001.
57 UNHCR Guidelines on International Protection: Application of the Exclusion Clauses: Article 1F of the 1951 Convention relating to the Status of Refugees, HCR/GIP/03/05, 4 September 2003.
58 According to international standards governing the protection and assistance for refugees, the strictly civilian and humanitarian nature of refugee camps and settlements must be upheld in order to preserve the peaceful character of asylum.
59 Chris Dolan *et al.*, *ibid.*, at p. 32.
60 Chris Dolan *et al.*, *ibid.*, at p. 1 and p. 88.
61 Chris Dolan *et al.*, *ibid.*
62 CAVR, *Chega!*, *ibid.*, Part 10, p. 17.
63 CAVR, *Chega!*, *ibid.*, Part 10, p. 23.
64 *The La'o Hamutuk Bulletin*, 'Editorial: The United Nations: Aiding or Undermining a Resolution of the Refugee Crisis?' Vol. 2, No. 4: July 2001.
65 See in contrast the Afghanistan Independent Human Rights Commission. *A Call for Justice: Conclusion of National Consultation on Transitional Justice in Afghanistan*. Kabul: Afghanistan Independent Human Rights Commission, 2005.

66 Steven Wolfson, 'Refugees and Transitional Justice.' (2005) *Refugee Survey Quarterly* 24(4): 55–59. Senior UNHCR official Erika Feller stated in 2006 that UNHCR has shifted to a 'responsibility to protect' framework, replacing the idea of right of humanitarian intervention in the 1990s: '[r]esponsibility should lie on need, not mandates or artificial legal categorisations'.
67 See further Alice Edwards, 'Overview of International Standards and Policy on Gender Violence and Refugees: Progress, Gaps and Continuing Challenges for NGO Advocacy and Campaigning'. Paper delivered at the Canadian Refugee Council International Refugee Rights Conference, Toronto, Canada, 17–19 June 2006. Amnesty International, AI Index: POL/33/004/2006.
68 ABC TV, 'UN Aid Workers Killed in West Timor', *Lateline*, 6 September 2000.
69 Tom Iggulden, 'East Timor Plays Down Damning UN Report', *ABC Radio National AM*, 19 January 2006.
70 International Center for Transitional Justice, 'Timorese Parliament Should Release Truth Commission Report Immediately', *media release*, New York, 28 November 2005.
71 Sian Powell, 'Leaders Favour Silence on Horrors with Indonesia', *The Australian*, 19 January 2006.
72 Sonny Inbaraj, 'Human Rights Day: East Timor Invasion Leaves Haunting Legacy', *Inter-Press Service*, Dili, 10 December 2005.
73 Sen Lam, 'Timor: No Compensation Wanted for Occupation', *Radio Australia*, 1 December 2005.
74 Sonny Inbaraj, *ibid*.
75 Susan Harris Rimmer, 'Struggle Continues for Timor Occupation Survivors', Opinion Editorial, *The Canberra Times*, 3 November 2008.
76 Galuh Wandita *et al*., *ibid*., at p. 300.
77 Robyn Charli Carpenter, 'Forced Maternity, Children's Rights and the Genocide Convention: A Theoretical Analysis' (2000) *Journal of Genocide Research* 2(2): 213–44.
78 Corey Levine, *Gender and Transitional Justice: A Case Study of East Timor*, Canadian Consortium on Human Security, Vancouver, 2004 at pp. 29–30.
79 United Nations Population Fund, *Gender-based Violence in Timor-Leste: A Case Study*. New York: UNFPA, 2005, at pp. 18–19.
80 Mario Carrascalão, former Governor of East Timor stated in his testimony to the Commission for Reception, Truth and Reconciliation (CAVR) National Public Hearing on Women and Conflict that in 1985, there were 40,000 orphans in Timor, 28–29 April 2003, Dili.
81 Dr George J. Aditjondro, *Violence By The State Against Women In East Timor – A Report to the UN Special Rapporteur on Violence Against Women, Including its Causes and Consequences*, East Timor Human Rights Centre, Newcastle University, Australia, 7 November 1997.
82 Sian Powell, 'East Timor's Children of The Enemy'. *The Weekend Australian*, 10 March 2001, at p. 3.
83 The children of female fighters in the Falintil are also termed 'orphans': 'The usual practice was for women guerrillas to place their new-borns in the gardens of village convents. If they died, it was bad luck. If they survived until morning and were found by the sisters, they would be adopted and cared for in orphanages.' Irena Cristalis and Catherine Scott, *Independent Women. The Story of Women's Activism in East Timor*, London: Progressio, 2005, Ch. 2.
84 Joana Daniel, 'No Man's Child: The War Rape Orphans'. Masters thesis, Ludwig Boltzmann Institute of Human Rights, University of Vienna: Vienna, 2002.
85 Sian Powell, 'East Timor's Children of The Enemy', *The Weekend Australian*, 10 March 2 001, at p. 3.
86 CAVR, *Chega!*, *ibid*.,Chapter 7.7, p. 95.

87 This is in contrast to some testimonies from women in other contexts such as Bosnia, where survivors routinely expressed a desire to kill or abandon their children of rape. Joana Daniel, 'No Man's Child: The War Rape Orphans', *ibid.*

88 CAVR. *Chega!*, *ibid.*, Chapter 7.7, p. 11.

89 George J. Aditjondro, *Violence By The State Against Women In East Timor – A, Report to the UN Special Rapporteur on Violence Against Women, Including its Causes and Consequences* East Timor Human Rights Centre, Newcastle University, Australia, 7 November 1997, at p. 12.

90 See Miranda Sissons, *From One Day to Another: Violations of Women's Reproductive and Sexual Rights in East Timor.* East Timor Human Rights Centre, Melbourne, 1997 at p. 8. Note the comment by a young refugee woman that 'Women are always second. Women are trusted only to have children and feed them.'

91 Louise Williams and Leonie Lamont, 'Rape Used Over and Over as a Systematic Torture' *The Sydney Morning Herald*, 11 September 1999.

92 CAVR. *Chega!*, *ibid.*, Chapter 7.7, pp. 93–103.

93 Report of UN Special Rapporteurs: Situation of Human Rights in East Timor. Based on visit between 4–10 November 1999, UN Document A/54/660, 10 December 1999.

94 Radhika Coomaraswamy, 'Report of the Special Rapporteur on Violence against Women, Its Causes and Consequences, Ms. Radhika Coomaraswamy, Submitted in Accordance with Commission on Human Rights Resolution 2000/45 Violence against Women Perpetrated and/or Condoned by the State During Times of Armed Conflict (1997–2000)'. Geneva: United Nations Commission on Human Rights, 2001. Article 24 of the Fourth Geneva Convention relative to the Protection of Civilian Persons in Time of War (Fourth Geneva Convention) provides protection, maintenance and education for orphans or children separated from their family under the age of 15.

95 Agence France Presse, 'Scars of Vote Violence Remain Real for Many East Timor Women' 19 November 2000.

96 Agence France Presse, *ibid.*

97 Note comments by UNHCR quoted by Sian Powell, 'East Timor's Children of The Enemy', *The Weekend Australian*, 10 March 2001.

98 George J. Aditjondro, *ibid.*, at p. 2.

99 Rebecca Winters (ed.), *Buibere: Voices of East Timorese Women.* East Timor International Support Centre, Darwin, 1999, at p. 36.

100 Karen Campbell-Nelson. Researcher, Commission for Reception, Truth-seeking, and Reconciliation (CAVR), Dili, East Timor. 'East Timor Women Must Tell of Atrocities by Indonesians', *The Jakarta Post*, June 9–10, 2003.

101 George J. Aditjondro, *ibid.*

102 Rede Feto Timor Lorosae, 'Women, Peace and Security in East Timor.' Presentation by a network of East Timorese women and women's organisations on the occasion of the United Nations Security Council special session on the Role of Women in Maintaining International Peace and Security, Dili, 24 October 2000.

103 Testimony to the Commission for Reception, Truth and Reconciliation (CAVR) National Public Hearing on Women and Conflict. 28–29 April 2003, Dili.

104 Testimony, *ibid.*

105 Katherine M. Franke, 'Gendered Subjects of Transitional Justice' (2006) *Columbia Journal of Gender and Law* 15(3):813–28.

106 Oxfam Community Aid Abroad, 'Women Fight for Freedom: The Struggle for Human Rights and Independence in East Timor', May, 1999.

107 The closest development is that the Special Court for Sierra Leone will be the first transitional justice mechanism to prosecute forced marriage as a crime against humanity. Even in domestic criminal law there are no parallels. There have been cases of 'wrongful life' suits brought against doctors for negligent advice in torts law where a sterilisation has not been successful, and there is the possibility of pursuing a father who has abandoned a child for maintenance in family law. Anne Tierney

Goldstein, *Recognising Forced Impregnation as a War Crime under International Law*, New York: The Center for Reproductive Law and Policy, 1993.

108 See Chapter 5: 'The Controversy: Gender And Forced Pregnancy': Marlies Glasius, *The International Criminal Court: A Global Civil Society Achievement*, New York, NY: Routledge, 2006.

109 See further Catherine MacKinnon, 'Turning rape into pornography: Post-modern genocide', Alex Stiglmayer (ed.), *Mass Rape: The War against Women in Bosnia-Herzegovina*, Lincoln: University of Nebraska Press, 1994.

110 Barbara Bedont, and Katherine Hall Martinez 'Ending Impunity for Gender Crimes under the International Criminal Court', *The Brown Journal of World Affairs*, Vol. VI, Issue 1: 65–85. 1999.

111 Kelly Askin, 'The jurisprudence of the international war crimes tribunals.' Helen Durham and Tracey Gurd (eds). *Listening to the Silences: Women and War*, Leiden: Boston: Martinus Nijhoff, 2005 at p. 144.

112 While there has been some analysis of genocide in East Timor, there has been very little examination of whether forced maternity practices constituted genocide. See further Roger Clark, 'Does the Genocide Convention Go Far Enough? Some Thoughts on the Nature of Criminal Genocide in the Context of Indonesia's Invasion of East Timor' (1981) 8 *Ohio Northern University Law Review* 321; Ben Kiernan, 'The Demography of Genocide in South-East Asia: The Death Tolls in Cambodia 1975–79 and East Timor, 1975–80' (2003) *Critical Asian Studies* 35(4):585–97 at p. 594; and Ben Saul, 'Was the Conflict in East Timor "Genocide" and Why Does it Matter?' (2001) *Melbourne Journal of International Law* 2(2): 447.

113 Deputy British Representative to the United Nations Stewart Eldon, statement to the Security Council, 11 September 1999.

114 Miranda Sissons, *From One Day to Another: Violations of Women's Reproductive and Sexual Rights in East Timor*, East Timor Human Rights Centre, Melbourne, 1997. For a contrary view, see Ben Saul, *ibid.*, at pp. 477–522.

115 Miranda Sissons, *ibid.*

116 Miranda Sissons, *ibid.*

117 Hilary Charlesworth, 'International Law: A Discipline of Crisis.' (2002) *The Modern Law Review* 65: 377–92 at p. 389.

118 See further Rosalind Dixon, 'Rape as a crime in international humanitarian law: where to from here?' (2002) *European Journal of International Law* 13(3): 697–719 at p. 702.

119 Testimony given 28–29 April 2003, Dili.

120 Rhonda Copelon, 'Intimate Terror: Understanding Domestic Violence as Torture', in Rebecca Cook, (ed.), *Human Rights of Women: National and International Perspectives*, University of Pennsylvania Press, 1994 and 'Recognizing the Egregious in the Everyday: Domestic Violence as Torture', (1994) *Columbia Human Rights Law Review* 25: 291–367.

121 AusAID Office of Development Effectiveness. 'East Timor Country Supplement'. Violence against Women in Melanesia and East Timor: Building on Regional and Global Promising Approaches, Canberra: AusAID, 2008.

122 CAVR. *Chega!*, *ibid.*

123 United Nations Population Fund. Gender-based Violence in Timor-Leste: a Case Study. New York: UNFPA, 2005, pp. 18–19.

124 As a result of the 2004 UNFPA conducted census, there is finally data available on the current population of East Timor and it has revealed a baby boom. 926,000 people were counted using a sophisticated satellite system to track every household, no matter how remote, which found 100,000 more people than expected. Moreover, the fertility rate was found to be the highest in the world, at 8.3 babies per woman. This sudden increase in population means that nutrition and health levels for Timorese children are extremely low and expected to get worse. Professor Terrence Hull, a demographer at

the Australian National University opined that the census result may indicate 'East Timor at the moment is still in a psychology of post-genocidal assumptions'.

125 Manuela Peirera, 'Domestic Violence: A Part of Women's Daily Lives in East Timor', *La'o Hamutuk Bulletin*, 2001.

126 Judicial System Monitoring Programme, *Background Paper on the Justice Sector*. Paper presented at the Timor Leste and Development Partners Meeting, Dili, 6 June 2003.

127 Aisling Swaine, *Traditional Justice and Gender Based Violence Research Report*. International Rescue Committee, Dili, August 2003. See also Michelle Hynes, Jeanne Ward, Kathryn Robertson, Chadd Crouse, 'A Determination of the Prevalence of Gender-based Violence among Conflict-affected Populations in East Timor' (2004) *Disasters* 28(3): 294–321.

128 Aisling Swaine, *Traditional Justice and Gender Based Violence Research Report*. International Rescue Committee, Dili, August 2003.

129 Aisling Swaine, *ibid.*, at p. 17.

130 Aisling Swaine, *ibid.*

131 Interview with author, January 2000.

132 Draft in English available only from the Judicial System Monitoring Programme website: www.jsmp.minihub.org.

133 UNTAET Regulation 30/2000.

134 Note Section 285 of the Indonesian Penal Code.

135 Hilary Charlesworth and Christine Chinkin, *The Boundaries of International Law: A Feminist Analysis*. Manchester: Manchester University Press, 2000, at p. 148.

136 See further Rebecca Cook, 'State Responsibility for Violations of Women's Human Rights' (2004) *Harvard Human Rights Journal* 7:125.

137 See Articles 2 and 5.

138 CEDAW Committee General Comment 19 on Article 16 (and article 5), Violence against Women: 29/01/92, A/47/38.

139 General Assembly resolution 48/104 of 20 December 1993.

140 Alice Edwards, *ibid.*

141 28 ILM 294 (1989), para. 172 (emphasis added). The test of 'due diligence' was expanded in para. 167. See also, D. Shelton, 'Private Violations, Public Wrongs, and the Responsibility of States', (1989) 13 *Fordham International Law Journal* 23.

142 Rebecca Cook, 'State Responsibility for Violations of Women's Human Rights' (1994) *Harvard Human Rights Journal* 7:125.

143 International Rescue Committee Report, *Focus Groups on Gender based Violence*, Dili, 2003.

144 Tanja Hohe and Rod Nixon, *Report on Reconciling Justice 'Traditional' Law and State Judiciary in East Timor*, January 2003.

145 The bride price tradition is an extremely complex one, outside the parameters of this book.

146 Aisling Swaine, *Traditional Justice and Gender Based Violence Research Report*. International Rescue Committee. August 2003.

147 Aisling Swaine, *ibid.*

148 Tanja Hohe and Rod Nixon. *Report on Reconciling Justice 'Traditional' Law and State Judiciary in East Timor*, January 2003.

149 Tanja Hohe and Rod Nixon. *ibid.*

150 Amnesty International. *East Timor Justice – Past, Present and Future*, AI Index ASA 57/001/2001, 27 July 2001

151 La'o Hamutuk Press Release. 'Public Figure Detained Again for Domestic Violence', 12 July 2001.

152 Amnesty International, *ibid.*

153 Judicial System Monitoring Programme, *Judicial System Monitoring Programme Comments to the Sergio Lobo Interlocutory Appeal*, 27 July 2001.

154 *Suara Timor Lorosae*, 'Luis Carrilho: The Law Does not Recognize "Public Figures"', 12 July 2001.

155 See further Judicial System Monitoring Programme, *Judicial System Monitoring Programme Comments to the Sergio Lobo Interlocutory Appeal*, 27 July 2001.
156 Judicial System Monitoring Programme, *ibid.*
157 'Fokupers not using Dr Sergio Lobo's case to seek more funding' Extract from Suara Timor Lorosae, p.1. East Timor Headlines – 20 July 2001.
158 Susan Harris Rimmer, 'The Roman Catholic Church and the Rights of East Timorese Women'. C. Evans and A. Whiting (eds), *Mixed Blessings: Laws, Religions and Women's Rights in the Asia-Pacific Region*, The Hague: Brill. 2006.
159 Gabrielson, Curt, 'The Church in East Timor'. Institute of Current World Affairs Letters. The Crane Rogers Foundation, 1 August 2001.
160 Judicial System Monitoring Programme. *An Analysis of a Sexual Assault Decision from the Dili District Court*. Dili, July 2004, at p. 9.
161 Judicial System Monitoring Programme, *Analysis of Decisions in Cases Involving Women And Children Victims: June 2004 – March 2005*, April 2005, at p. 5.
162 Judicial System Monitoring Programme, *Report on Women in Formal Justice Sector*, 7 April 2004.
163 Agence France Presse, 'Three Suspects Arrested for Killing of Timorese "witches"', 10 January 2007.
164 Bishop Carlos Filipe Ximenes Belo. 'To Forge a Future, Timor Needs Justice for the Past'. The *Sydney Morning Herald*, 28 August 2001.
165 Bishop Carlos Filipe Ximenes Belo, *ibid.*
166 Susan Harris Rimmer,. 'Orphans or Veterans? Justice for Children Born of War in East Timor' in *Born of War: Protecting Children Born to Sexual Violence; Survivors in Conflict Zones*, R. Charli Carpenter (ed.), Bloomfield CT: Kumarian Press, 2007: 53–75.
167 Irena Cristalis and Catherine Scott, Independent Women. *The Story of Women's Activism in East Timor*, London: Progressio, 2005.
168 World Council of Churches (WCC) and Christian Conference of Asia (CCA). *Women to Women: A Solidarity Visit to Indonesia and East Timor*. 23 June – 1 July 1999.

Chapter 7

1 *Lusa*, 'Demonstrators protest Wiranto meeting on Gusmão's return', 31 May 2004. *Tempo Magazine*, 'Xanana and Wiranto meeting reaped condemnations in Timor-Leste', 40: IV, 8–14 June 2004.
2 Megan Hirst and Howard Varney, *Justice Abandoned? An Assessment of the Serious Crimes Process in East Timor*. Occasional Paper Series, International Center for Transitional Justice, New York, June 2005, at p. 25.
3 United Nations News Centre, 'Timor-Leste, not UN, Indicts Indonesian General for War Crimes', 26 February 2003. The International Center for Transitional Justice explains that 'while this is technically correct, it did not acknowledge the work of the prosecution service was carried out by a UN unit and staffed by UN employees'. Megan Hirst and Howard Varney, *ibid.* See also *Catholic Institute International Relations*. 'Church Network Urges UN to Press Ahead with Timor Prosecutions', 18 March 2003; 'East Timor: General Wiranto Said Ready for Dili Video-Conference Atrocity Hearing', *Lusa*, 4 February 2004 and Mark Dodd, 'Massacres Go Unpunished as UN Crimes Unit Heads for Collapse', *Sydney Morning Herald*, 1 May 2001.
4 Megan Hirst and Howard Varney, *Justice Abandoned? An Assessment of the Serious Crimes process in East Timor*. Occasional Paper Series, International Center for Transitional Justice, New York, June 2005, at p. 25.
5 Megan Hirst and Howard Varney, *ibid.*
6 Megan Hirst and Howard Varney, *ibid.*
7 Megan Hirst and Howard Varney, *ibid.*
8 Megan Hirst and Howard Varney, *ibid.*

9 Matthew Moore, 'Lay off Wiranto', *Sydney Morning Herald*, 31 October 2004.
10 Xanana Gusmão, 'Notes on Comments by Xanana Gusmão and José Ramos-Horta on Dealing with Past Human Rights Violations Made during a Panel Discussion'. Paper read at German Council on Foreign Relations (Deutsche Gesellschaft für Auswaertige Politik, DGAP), Berlin, *Watch Indonesia*.20 October 2004.
11 Douglas Keatinge, 'All to Play For in East Timor's Modest Aid Gesture', *The Irish Times*, 31 January 2005.
12 United Nations, 'High Commissioner for Human Rights Reports on the Situation in East Timor as the Commission on Human Rights Considers Holding Special Meeting', media release, HR/99/90, 17 September 1999.
13 Sian Powell, 'East Timor Forgoes Justice for the Rape of A Nation', *The Australian*, Jakarta, 1 August 2005.
14 'Editorial: Indonesia's Generals Take a Back Seat', *Sydney Morning Herald*, Sydney, 2004.
15 Sarah Boyd, 'Timor Justice Slow but Sure', *Asia Intelligence Wire*, 29 July 2004.
16 Tom Iggulden, 'East Timor Plays Down Damning UN Report', *ABC Radio National AM*, 19 January 2006.
17 Sen Lam, 'Timor: No Compensation Wanted for Occupation', *Radio Australia*, 1 December 2005.
18 Miki Perkins. 'Forgotten Victims of East Timor's Independence', *The Age* (Melbourne), 16 June 2009.
19 Joe Havely, 'Timor's Army Marches out of the Jungle', *CNN. Com.* 19 May 2002.
20 Susan Blackburn, 'The Aftermath for Women Warriors: Cambodia and East Timor', IIAS Newsletter 48: Women Warriors, Summer, Leiden, 2008.
21 Sara Niner, 'The Contested Place of Women in Post-Conflict Timor-Leste', unpublished, on file with author, June 2009.
22 Sara Niner, *ibid.*
23 See also the *Progress Report of the Secretary-General on the United Nations Mission of Support in East Timor (29 April to 13 August 2004)* UN Security Council S/2004/669, 13 August 2004, at para 5.
24 ABC Radio Australia Asia-Pacific. 'East Timor: First Lady calls on PM Alkatiri to respond to L-7', Broadcast, 6 August 2004.
25 International Crisis Group, *Resolving Timor Leste's Crisis,* Asia Report No. 120. Brussels: International Crisis Group, 2006.
26 Edward Rees, *Under Pressure: Falintil – Forcas de Defesa de Timor Leste: Three Decades of Defence Force Development in Timor Leste 1975–2004,* April 2004.
27 Natércia Godinho-Adams, 'UN Security Council "Arria Formula" Meeting on the Implementation of Security Council Resolution 1325', 30 October 2001.
28 See further Charles T. Call, 'Is Transitional Justice Really Just?' (2004) *Brown Journal of World Affairs* XI(1): 101–13.
29 Susan Harris Rimmer, 'Untold Numbers: East Timorese Women and Transitional Justice', Sharon Pickering and Caroline Lambert (eds), *Global Issues, Women and Justice.* Sydney: Federation Press, 2004.
30 BK from Fatubessi, quoted by Galuh Wandita, Karen Campbell-Nelson, and Manuela Leong Pereira. 'Learning to Engender Reparations in Timor-Leste: Reaching Out to Female Victims', Ruth Rubio-Marín (ed.), What *Happened to the Women?: Gender and Reparations for Human Rights Violations* New York: Social Science Research Council, 2006, at p. 319.
31 Katherine M. Franke, 'Gendered Subjects of Transitional Justice' (2006) *Columbia Journal of Gender and Law* 15(3): 813–28.
32 Cited by Aurora Ximenes, Prime Ministerial counsellor, 15 March 2007, UCAN.
33 Rama Mani, 'Editorial: Dilemmas of Expanding Transitional Justice, or Forging the Nexus between Transitional Justice and Development' (2009) *International Journal of Transitional Justice* (Special issue on transitional justice and development) 2: 253–65.

Bibliography

Ackerly, Brooke, Maria Stern, and Jacqui True (eds). *Feminist Methodologies for International Relations*. Cambridge: Cambridge University Press, 2006.

Aditjondro, George J. *The Shadow of Mount Ramelau: The Impact of the Occupation of East Timor*. Leiden, The Netherlands: Indonesian Documentation and Information Centre, 1994.

Aditjondro, George J. *Violence by the State against Women in East Timor – a Report to the United Nations Special Rapporteur on Violence against Women, including its Causes and Consequences*. Newcastle: East Timor Human Rights Centre, 1997.

Afghan Independent Human Rights Commission (AIHRC). *A Call for Justice: Conclusion of National Consultation on Transitional Justice in Afghanistan*, Kabul, January 2005.

Alldén, Susanne. 'Internalising the Culture of Human Rights: Securing Women's Rights in Post-Conflict East Timor', (2007) *Asia-Pacific Journal on Human Rights and the Law* 1: 1–23.

Alves, Maria Domingas Fernandes, Laura Soares Abrantes, and Filomena B. Reis. *Written with Blood / Hakerek ho Raan,* Office for Promotion of Equality, Prime Minister's Office, Democratic Republic of Timor-Leste, year of publication unstated (trans. by Noeno Anuno Sarmento and Lucsendar R. Fernandes Alves), 2002.

Amnesty International. *East Timor: Violations of Human Rights: Extrajudicial Executions, 'Disappearances', Torture, and Political Imprisonment, 1975–1984*. London: Amnesty International, 1985.

Amnesty International. *Women in Indonesia and East Timor*. AI Index ASA 21/51/1995. London: Amnesty International, 1995.

Amnesty International. *East Timor: Justice – Past, Present and Future*. AI Index ASA 57/001/2001. London: Amnesty International, 27 July 2001.

Amnesty International. *Broken Bodies, Shattered Minds, Torture and Ill-Treatment of Women*, Alden Press, United Kingdom, 2001, 50.

Amnesty International and Judicial System Monitoring Programme. *Indonesia: Justice for Timor-Leste: The Way Forward*. Dili, 2004.

Anderlini, S.N. 'Peace through Justice or Justice through Peace? Women and Transitional Justice', (2005) *Development* 48(3): 103–10.

Anderson, Mary B. *Do No Harm: How Aid Can Support Peace – or War*. Boulder, CO: Lynne Rienner Publishers, 1999.

Arbour, Louise. 'Economic and Social Justice for Societies in Transition'. Paper presented at the Second Annual Transitional Justice Lecture, New York University School of Law, New York, 25 October 2006.

Arendt, Hannah. *On Violence*. New York: Harcourt Brace and World, 1970.

Arendt, Hannah. *Hannah Arendt, Karl Jaspers: Correspondence, 1926–1969*. New York: Harcourt Brace Jovanovich, 1992.

Asia Foundation. *Law and Justice in East Timor: A Survey of Citizen Awareness and Attitudes Regarding Law and Justice in East Timor*. Dili: Asia Foundation, 2004.

Asia Human Rights News. *East Timor: Sexual Violence Including Rape Was a Deliberate Military Strategy against East Timorese Women*. 2001.

Asia Pacific Centre for Military Law, and Judicial System Monitoring Programme. Report of Proceedings. Paper presented at the *Symposium on Justice for International Crimes Committed in the Territory of East Timor*, January 16–17, Faculty of Law, University of Melbourne, 23 June 2003.

Asian Development Bank and UNIFEM. *Gender and Nation Building in Timor-Leste: Country Gender Assessment*. Manila: Asian Development Bank, November 2005.

Asian Human Rights Defender. *Human Rights in Peace Processes: Timor Leste Crisis Resurfaces Bitter Memories*. 17 January 2007.

Askin, Kelly Dawn. *War Crimes against Women: Prosecution in International War Crimes Tribunals*. The Hague/Cambridge, MA: Martinus Nijhoff Publishers, 1997.

Askin, Kelly Dawn. 'The Jurisprudence of the International War Crimes Tribunals'. Helen Durham and Tracey Gurd (eds). *Listening to the Silences: Women and War*. Leiden, Boston, MA: Martinus Nijhoff, 2005, 125–53.

Askin, Kelly Dawn, Stephanie Frease and Sonja Starr. *Unfulfilled Promises: Justice in East Timor*. New York: Open Society Institute and the Coalition for International Justice, 2004.

Aukerman, Miriam. 'Extraordinary Evil, Ordinary Crime: A Framework for Understanding Transitional Justice', (2002) *Harvard Human Rights Journal* 15: 39.

AusAID Office of Development Effectiveness. 'East Timor Country Supplement'. *Violence against Women in Melanesia and East Timor: Building on Regional and Global Promising Approaches*, Canberra: AusAID, 2008.

Babo-Soares, Dionísio. 'Nahe Biti: The Philosophy and Process of Grassroots Reconciliation (and Justice) in Timor-Leste', (2004) *The Asia Pacific Journal of Anthropology* 5(1): 15–33.

Balint, Jennifer. 'The Place of Law in Addressing Internal Regime Conflicts', (1996) *Law and Contemporary Problems* 59: 103.

Ballington, J. and D. Dahlerup. 'Gender Quotas in Post-Conflict States: East Timor, Afghanistan and Iraq'. D. Dahlerup (ed.). *Women, Quotas and Politics*. London and New York: Routledge, 2006, 249–58.

Bassiouni, M. Cherif. 'International Crimes: *Jus Cogens* and *Obligatio Erga Omnes*' (1996) 59 *Law and Contemporary Problems* 63.

Bassiouni, M. Cherif. 'Searching for Peace and Achieving Justice: the Need for Accountability', (1996) 59(4) *Law and Contemporary Problems* 9: 23.

Bassiouni, M. Cherif. *International Criminal Law* (2nd edn). Ardsley, New York: Transnational Publishers, 1999.

Bassiouni, M. Cherif. 'Crimes against Humanity', *International Criminal Law* (2nd edn). Cambridge, MA: Kluwer Law International, 1999.

Bassiouni, M. Cherif (ed.). *Post-Conflict Justice*. International and Comparative Criminal Law Series. Ardsley, New York: Transnational Publishers, 2002.

Bassiouni, M. Cherif (ed.). 'Accountability for Violations of International Humanitarian Law', *Post-Conflict Justice*. Transnational Publishers: New York, 2002.

Bastick, Megan, Karin Grimm and Rahel Kunz. *Sexual Violence in Armed Conflict: Global Overview and Implications for the Security Sector*. Geneva: The Geneva Centre for the Democratic Control of Armed Forces, 2007.

Beauvais, Joel C. 'Benevolent Despotism: A Critique of United Nations State-building in East Timor', (2001) *International Law and Politics* 33: 1101–78.

Bedont, Barbara and Katherine Hall Martinez. 'Ending Impunity for Gender Crimes under the International Criminal Court', (1999) *The Brown Journal of World Affairs* VI(1): 65–85.

Bell, Christine and Catherine O'Rourke. 'Does Feminism Need a Theory of Transitional Justice? An Introductory Essay', (2007) *International Journal of Transitional Justice* 1: 23–44.

Belo, Bishop Carlos Filipe Ximenes. 'To Forge a Future, Timor Needs Justice for the Past'. *The Sydney Morning Herald.*, 28 August 2001.

Belo, Bishop Carlos Filipe Ximenes and Christian Ranheim. 'Prosecuting Serious Crimes in East Timor', *Justice and Accountability in East Timor: International Tribunals and Other Options: Report of a One-day Seminar in Dili, East Timor*. JSMP, 2001.

Best, Geoffrey. *Humanity in Warfare: The Modern History of the International Law of Armed Conflict*. London: Weidenfeld and Nicholson, 1980.

Binchy, William (ed.). *Timor-Leste: Challenges for Justice and Human Rights in the Shadow of the Past*. Dublin: Clarus Press, 2009.

Blackburn, Susan. 'Gender Violence and the Indonesian Political Transition', (1999) *Asian Studies Review* 23(4): 433–48.

Blackburn, Susan, 'The Aftermath for Women Warriors: Cambodia and East Timor', IIAS Newsletter 48: Women Warriors, Summer, Leiden, 2008.

Boudre, Sophie. 'A Cruel History for East-Timorese Women', *Voices Unabridged* E-Magazine No 1 Jan-March 2004, 19 January 2004.

Braithwaite, John. *Crime, Shame and Reintegration*. Cambridge; Sydney: Cambridge University Press, 1989.

Braithwaite, John. *Restorative Justice and Responsive Regulation*, *Studies in Crime and Public Policy*. Oxford; New York: Oxford University Press, 2002.

Braithwaite, John. 'Rape, Shame and Pride'. Address to Stockholm Criminology Symposium, 16 June, 2006.

Brody, Reed. 'Justice: The First Casualty of Truth', (2002) 272 *The Nation* 25: 28–29.

Brownmiller, Susan. *Against Our Will: Men, Women and Rape*, London: Penguin Books, 1975.

Bulbeck, Chilla. 'Book Reviews' (2005) *International Feminist Journal of Politics*, 7(1): 157–69.

Bureau of Democracy, Human Rights, and Labor. *US Government: Country Reports on Human Rights Practices 2003*. Washington, 2004.

Burgess, Patrick. 'Justice and Reconciliation in East Timor: The Relationship between the Commission for Reception, Truth and Reconciliation and the Courts', (2004) *Criminal Law Forum* 15: 135–58.

Burgess, Patrick. 'A New Approach to Restorative Justice – East Timor's Community Reconciliation Procedure'. Naomi Roht-Arriaza, and Javier Mariezcurrena (eds). *Transitional Justice in the Twenty-First Century: Beyond Truth Versus Justice*. Cambridge: Cambridge University Press, 2006, 176–205.

Burr, William, and Michael L. Evans. 'Ford and Kissinger Gave Green Light to Indonesia's Invasion of East Timor, 1975: New Documents Detail Conversations with Suharto'. *National Security Archive Electronic Briefing Book No. 62*, 2001.

Buss, Doris. 'Women at the Borders: Rape and Nationalism in International Law', (1998) *Feminist Legal Studies* 6(2): 171–203.

Buss, Doris. 'Prosecuting Mass Rape: Prosecutor v. Dragoljub Kunarac, Radomir Kovac and Zoran Vukovic', (2002) *Feminist Legal Studies* 10(1): 91–99.

Buss, Doris and Ambreena Manji (eds). *International Law: Modern Feminist Approaches*. Oxford and Portland, Oregon: Hart Publishing, 2005.

Butler, Judith. 'Preface'. *Gender Trouble: Feminism and the Subversion of Identity*. New York: Routledge, 1999.

Bye, Hanne Hovde. 'The Fight against Domestic Violence in East Timor: Forgetting the Perpetrators', Masters Thesis, University of Tromsø, 2005.

Byrne, Mark and Kath Gibson. 'Chasing Shadows: Indonesian War Criminals and Australian Law', *UNIYA Occasional Paper no.13,* Sydney NSW, May 2007.

Call, Charles. 'Is Transitional Justice Really Just?', (2004) *Brown Journal of World Affairs* XI(1): 101–13.

Campbell, Kirsten. 'The Gender of Transitional Justice: Law, Sexual Violence and the International Criminal Tribunal for the Former Yugoslavia', 1 (2007) *International Journal of Transitional Justice* 3: 411–32.

Campbell-Nelson, Karen. 'East Timor Women Must Tell of Atrocities by Indonesians'. *The Jakarta Post*, 9–10 June 2003.

Campbell-Nelson, Karen. 'Liberia is not Just a Man Thing: Transitional Justice Lessons for Women, Peace and Security'. Brussels: Initiative for Peacebuilding, 2008.

Carey, Peter. 'Dimensions of Domination: Institutionalised Violence against Women During the Indonesian Occupation of East Timor (1975–99)'. Ingrid and Wimhöfer Wessel (eds). *Violence in Indonesia*. Georgia: Abera Verlag Markus Voss, 2001, 185–209.

Carpenter, R. Charli. 'Forced Maternity, Children's Rights and the Genocide Convention: A Theoretical Analysis'. (2000) *Journal of Genocide Research* 2(2): 213–44.

Carpenter, R. Charli. 'Stirring Gender into the Mainstream: Feminism, Constructivism, and the Uses of Theory', (2003) *International Studies Review* 5(3): 287.

Carpenter, R. Charli. *'Innocent Women and Children': Gender, Norms and the Protection of Civilians*, Ashgate: Hampshire, 2006.

Carpenter, R. Charli. *Born of War: Protecting Children of Sexual Violence Survivors in Conflict Zones*. Bloomfield, CT: Kumarian Press, 2007.

Catholic Institute for International Relations and International Platform of Jurists for East Timor. *International Law and the Question of East Timor*. London: CIIR/ IPJET, 1995.

Catholic Institute for International Relations and International Platform of Jurists for East Timor. 'Church Network Urges UN to Press Ahead with Timor Prosecutions'. 18 March 2003.

Çesko, Sci Enver, Melita Kallaba, Vjosa Devaja, Agim Selimi, Shaban Jashari and Merita Emini. *Study with the Clients Treated at the KRCT, from the Witnesses and the Kosovo Population Regarding the Possibility of their Re-Traumatization during the Trial Process of Milosevic in The Hague*. Kosovo Rehabilitation Centre for Torture Victims, 2002, 1–9.

Charlesworth, Hilary. 'What Are Women's International Human Rights?' Rebecca Cook (ed.). *Human Rights of Women: National and International Perspectives*. Philadelphia: Pennsylvania University Press, 1994. 54–84.

Charlesworth, Hilary. 'International Human Rights Law: Prospects and Problems for Palestinian Women'. S. Bowen (ed.). *Human Rights, Self-Determination and Political Change in the Occupied Palestinian Territories*. The Hague: Kluwer, 1997. 79–91.

Charlesworth, Hilary. 'Symposium on Method in International Law: Feminist Methods in International Law', (1999) *American Journal of International Law* 93: 379.

Charlesworth, Hilary. 'International Law: A Discipline of Crisis', (2002) *The Modern Law Review* 65: 377–92.

Charlesworth, Hilary. 'The Constitution of East Timor', (2003) *International Journal of Constitutional Law* 2: 325–34.

Charlesworth, Hilary. 'Not Waving but Drowning: Gender Mainstreaming and Human Rights in the United Nations', (2005) *Harvard Human Rights Journal* 18: 1–18.

Charlesworth, Hilary. 'Saddam Hussein: My Part in his Downfall', (2005) *Wisconsin International Law Journal* 27: 127–43.

Charlesworth, Hilary. 'Building Democracy and Justice After Conflict'. 2006 Cunningham Lecture, *Occasional Paper 2/2007*, Academy of the Social Sciences in Australia: Canberra, 2007.

Charlesworth, Hilary and Christine Chinkin. 'The Gender of Jus Cogens', (1993) *Human Rights Quarterly* 15: 63–76.

Charlesworth, Hilary, and Christine Chinkin. *The Boundaries of International Law: A Feminist Analysis*. Manchester: Manchester University Press, 2000.

Charlesworth, Hilary, Christine Chinkin, and Shelley Wright. 'Feminist Approaches to International Law', (1991) *American Journal of International Law* 85: 613–45.

Charlesworth, Hilary and Judith Gardam. 'Protection of Women in Armed Conflict', (2000) *Human Rights Quarterly* 22: 148–66.

Charlesworth, Hilary and Mary Wood. 'Gender Mainstreaming: The Case of East Timor', (2001) *Yale Journal of International Law* 26: 313–18.

Charlesworth, Hilary and Mary Wood. 'Women and Human Rights in the Rebuilding of East Timor', (2002) *Nordic Journal of International Law* 71: 325–48.

Chesterman, Simon (ed.). 'No Justice without Peace? International Criminal Law and the Decision to Prosecute'. *Civilians in War*. Boulder, CO: Lynne Rienner Publishers, 2001.

Chesterman, Simon. *Justice under International Administration: Kosovo, East Timor and Afghanistan*. New York: The International Peace Academy, 2002.

Chinkin, Christine. 'Symposium – The Yugoslav Crisis: New International Law Issues, Rape and Sexual Abuse of Women in International Law' (1994) *European Journal of International Law* 5: 326–41.

Chinkin, Christine. 'Peace Agreements as a Means for Promoting Gender Equality and Ensuring Participation of Women'. Prepared as consultant to the Division for the Advancement of Women EGM/PEACE/2003/BP.1, 31 October 2003. United Nations Division for the Advancement of Women (DAW) Expert Group Meeting on 'Peace agreements as a means for promoting gender equality and ensuring participation of women – A framework of model provisions', 10–13 November, Ottawa, Canada, 2003.

Chinkin, Christine. 'Feminist Reflections on International Criminal Law'. Andreas Zimmermann (ed.). *International Criminal Law and the Current Development of Public International Law*. Berlin; Duncker and Humblot, 2003.

Chinkin, Christine, and Hilary Charlesworth. 'Building Women into Peace: The International Legal Framework', (2006) *Third World Quarterly* 27: 951–71.

Chinkin, Christine, Hilary Charlesworth and Shelley Wright. 'Feminist Approaches to International Law: Reflections from Another Century'. Doris Buss and Ambreena Manji (eds). *International Law: Modern Feminist Approaches*. Oxford and Portland, Oregon: Hart Publishing, 2005. 19–23.

Chomsky, Noam. *A New Generation Draws the Line: Kosovo, East Timor and the Standards of the West*. London; New York: Verso, 2000.

Chopra, Jarat. 'Building State Failure in East Timor', (2002) *Development and Change* 33(5): 979–1000.

Clark, Roger. 'Does the Genocide Convention Go Far Enough? Some Thoughts on the Nature of Criminal Genocide in the Context of Indonesia's Invasion of East Timor',

(1981) 8 *Ohio Northern University Law Review* 321.

Clutterbuck, Martin. 'Crimes against Humanity Trials on our Doorstep', (2005) *Law Institute Journal* 79(12): 63.

Coakley, Victoria. 'Towards Justice and Reconciliation in East Timor' (2001), *Alternative Law Journal* 28(5): 229–41.

Cobban, Helena. 'The Legacies of Collective Violence', (2002) *Boston Review* 27(2): 21–27.

Cockburn, Cynthia. *The Space between Us: Negotiating Gender and National Identities in Conflict.* London: Zed Books, 1998.

Cockburn, Cynthia. 'Gender, Armed Conflict and Political Violence: Background Paper'. The World Bank, Washington DC, 10–11 June 1999.

Cohen, David. *Seeking Justice on the Cheap: Is the East Timor Tribunal Really a Model for the Future?* Honolulu: East West Centre, 2002.

Cohen, David. *Intended to Fail: The Trials before the Ad Hoc Human Rights Court in Jakarta.* New York: International Center for Transitional Justice, 2003.

Cohen, David. 'Indifference and Accountability: The United Nations and the Politics of International Justice in East Timor'. *East West Centre Special Reports*. Honolulu: East West Centre, 2006.

Cohen, David. 'Seeking Truth and Responsibility: Report of the Special Advisor to the CTF'. Berkeley War Crimes Studies Centre, April 2007.

Cohn, Carol. 'War, Wimps, and Women: Talking Gender and Thinking War'. M. Cooke and A. Woollacott (eds). *Gendering War Talk.* Princeton: Princeton University Press, 1993. 227–46.

Colson, Elizabeth. 'War and Domestic Violence', (1995) *Cultural Survival Quarterly* 19: 35–38.

Commission for Reception, Truth and Reconciliation (CAVR). '*Chega!* Final Report of the Commission for Reception, Truth and Reconciliation'. Dili: CAVR, 2005.

Commission for Reception, Truth and Reconciliation (CAVR). 'Women and the Conflict: National Public Hearing 28–29 April 2003'. Audiensi Publik Nasional: Balide, East Timor, 2005.

Commission of Experts. *Report to the Secretary-General of the Commission of Experts to Review the Prosecution of Serious Violations of Human Rights in Timor-Leste (the Then East Timor) in 1999.* New York: United Nations, 2005.

Commonwealth Secretariat. *Gender Equality and the Judiciary: Using International Standards to Promote the Human Rights of Women and the Girl Child.* London: Commonwealth Secretariat, 1999.

Conway, Jude. 'Report of Women's Seminar Dili'. Dili: FOKUPERS (Komunikasi Untuk Perempuan Loro Sae – Communication Forum for Women from the East), 25 November 1998.

Cook, Rebecca. 'State Responsibility for Violations of Women's Human Rights', *Harvard* (1994) *Human Rights Journal* 7: 125.

Coomaraswamy, Radhika. *Report of the Special Rapporteur on Violence against Women, Its Causes and Consequences, Ms. Radhika Coomaraswamy, Submitted in Accordance with Commission on Human Rights Resolution 2000/45 Violence against Women Perpetrated and/or Condoned by the State During Times of Armed Conflict (1997–2000).* Geneva: United Nations Commission on Human Rights, 2001.

Copelon, Rhonda. 'Intimate Terror: Understanding Domestic Violence as Torture'. Rebecca Cook (ed.). *Human Rights of Women: National and International Perspectives.* Philadelphia: University of Pennsylvania Press, 1994, 116–51.

Copelon, Rhonda. 'Surfacing Gender: Reconceptualizing Crimes Against Women in Bosnia-Herzegovina'. Alexandra Stiglmayer (ed.). *Mass Rape: The War Against Women in Bosnia-Herzegovinia,* Lincoln: University of Nebraska Press, 1994, 197–218.

Copelon, Rhonda. 'Recognizing the Egregious in the Everyday: Domestic Violence as Torture', (1994) *Columbia Human Rights Law Review* 25: 291–367.

Copelon, Rhonda. 'Women and War Crimes', (1995) *St John's Law Review* 69: 65.

Corcoran-Nantes, Yvette. 'The Politics of Culture and the Culture of Politics – a Case Study of Gender and Politics in Lospalos, Timor-Leste', (2009) *Conflict, Security & Development*: Special Issue: Security, Development and the Nation Building Agenda in Timor-Leste 9(2): 165–87.

Cristalis, Irena. *Bitter Dawn: East Timor, a People's Story*. London; New York: Zed Books: Palgrave, 2002.

Cristalis, Irena and Catherine Scott. *Independent Women. The Story of Women's Activism in East Timor*. London: Progressio, 2005.

Daly, Erin. 'Truth Skepticism: An Inquiry into the Value of Truth in Times of Transition', (2008) *International Journal of Transitional Justice* 2: 23–41.

Daly, Erin and Jeremy Sarkin. *Reconciliation in Divided Societies: Finding Common Ground....* Philadelphia: University of Pennsylvania Press, 2007.

Daniel, Joana. 'No Man's Child: The War Rape Orphan's. Masters thesis, University of Vienna, 2002.

De Brabandere, Eric, *Post-Conflict Administrations in International Law: International Territorial Administration, Transitional Authority and Foreign Occupation in Theory and Practice*. Leiden / Boston: Martinus Nijhoff Publishers, 2009.

De Brouwer, Anne-Marie L.M. *Supranational Criminal Prosecution of Sexual Violence: The ICC and the Practice of the ICTY and the ICTR*. Antwerpen, Intersentia 2005.

de Faria, Carl. 'East Timor's Quest for Justice: The Serious Crimes File', paper presented at the *UNMISET International Symposium on United Nations Peacekeeping Operations in Post-conflict Timor-Leste: Accomplishments and Lessons Learned*, April 28, 2005.

DeLaet, Debra L. 'Gender Justice: A Gendered Assessment of Truth-telling Mechanisms'. Tristan Ann Borer (ed.). *Telling the Truths: Truth Telling and Peace Building in Post-Conflict Societies*. Notre Dame, Indiana: University of Notre Dame Press, 2006. 151–179.

Delmas-Marty, Mireille. 'Interactions between National and International Criminal Law in the Preliminary Phase of Trial at the ICC', (2006) *Journal of International Criminal Justice* 4(1): 2–11.

De Schutter, B. and C. Van De Wyngaert, 'Non-international armed conflicts: The borderline between national and international law', (1983) *Georgia Journal of International and Comparative Law* 13: 279.

de Vos, C.M. 'What price truth? South Africa's Truth and Reconciliation Commission in Critical Perspective', (2002) 29 *Politikon* 209: 225.

DevTech Systems Inc. 'Gender Assessment for US AID/Timor-Leste Country Strategy Plan 2004–9'. Women in Development: US AID, 2004.

Dinstein, Yoram. 'Human Rights in Armed Conflict: International Humanitarian Law'. Theodore Meron (ed.). *Human Rights in International Law: Legal and Policy Issues*. Vol. II. Oxford: Clarendon Press, 1984, 350–54.

Dixon, Rosalind. 'Rape as a Crime in International Humanitarian Law: Where to from Here?' (2002) *European Journal of International Law* 13(3): 697–719.

Djuli, M.N. and Robert Jereski. 'Prospects for Indonesia's Survival', (2002) 11 *The Brown Journal of World Affairs* 35: 38–39.

Dolan, Chris, Judith Large and Naoko Obi. *Evaluation of UNHCR's Repatriation and Reintegration Programme in East Timor 1999–2003*. UNHCR Evaluation and Policy Analysis Unit (EPAU/2004/02). Geneva: UNHCR, 2004.

Dolgopol, Ustinia and Judith Gardam (eds). *The Challenge of Armed Conflict: International Law Responds*. Christopher Greenwood and Tim McCormack (series eds). *International Humanitarian Law Series 13*. Leiden, Boston: Martinus Nijhoff, 2006.

Dorfman, Ariel. 'Afterword', *Death and the Maiden*. London: Nick Hern Books and Royal Court Theatre, 1992.

Drumbl, Mark A. 'Rights, Culture, and Crime: The Role of Rule of Law for the Women of Afghanistan', (2004) *Columbia Journal of Transnational Law* 42: 349.

Drumbl, Mark A. 'Pluralizing International Criminal Justice', (2005) 106 *Michigan Law Review* 1295: 1309–11.

Drumbl, Mark A. *Atrocity, Punishment and International Law*. Cambridge: Cambridge University Press, 2007.

DuBois, Page. *Torture and Truth*. New York: Routledge, 1991.

Dudden, Alexis. 'We Came to Tell the Truth: Reflections of the Tokyo Women's Tribunal', (2001) *Critical Asian Studies* 33(4): 591–602.

Dunn, James. *East Timor: A Rough Passage to Independence* (3rd edn). Double Bay, NSW: Longueville Books, 2003.

Durham, Helen. 'International Humanitarian Law and the Protection of Women'. Helen Durham and Tracey Gurd (eds). *Listening to the Silences: Women and War*, Leiden, Boston: Martinus Nijhoff, 2005, 95–108.

Durham, Helen, and Tracey Gurd (eds). *Listening to the Silences: Women and War*. Leiden, Boston: Martinus Nijhoff, 2005.

Eaton, Tim. 'Raping the Future', *Mother Jones Magazine*, San Francisco, 26 August 1999.

Edwards, Alice. 'The "Feminizing" of Torture under International Human Rights Law', (2006) *Leiden Journal of International Law* 19(2): 349–91.

Edwards, Alice.'Overview of International Standards and Policy on Gender Violence and Refugees: Progress, Gaps and Continuing Challenges for NGO Advocacy and Campaigning'. Paper delivered at the Canadian Refugee Council International Refugee Rights Conference, Toronto, Canada, 17–19 June 2006. Amnesty International, AI Index: POL/33/004/2006.

Elshtain, Jean Bethke. *Women, Militarism, and War: Essays in History, Politics, and Social Theory*. Lanham: Rowman and Littlefield, 1990.

Elshtain, Jean Bethke. *Women and War* (2nd edn). Chicago: University Of Chicago Press, 1995.

Engle, Karen. 'After the Collapse of the Public-private Distinction: Strategizing Women's Rights'. *Reconceiving Reality: Women and International Law*. Edited by Dorinda Dollmeyer. Washington, DC: American Society of International Law, 1993, 143–155.

Engle, Karen. 'Feminism and Its (Dis)contents: Criminalizing Wartime Rape in Bosnia and Herzegovina', (2005) *The American Journal of International Law* 99(4): 778–816.

Enloe, Cynthia. *Bananas, Beaches and Bases: Making Feminist Sense of International Politics*. (1st edn). Berkeley: University of California Press, 1990.

Enloe, Cynthia. *Manoeuvres: The International Politics of Militarizing Women's Lives*. Berkeley: University of California Press, 2000.

Enloe, Cynthia. *Updating the Gendered Empire: Where Are the Women in Occupied Afghanistan and Iraq?* Berkeley: University of California Press, 2004.

Enloe, Cynthia. *The Curious Feminist: Searching for Women in a New Age of Empire*. Berkeley: University of California Press, 2004.

European Union. 'Declaration by the Presidency on Behalf of the European Union on the Ad Hoc Human Rights Tribunal for Crimes Committed in East Timor', 2003.

Fahey, Stephanie. 'The Future of East Timor: Threats and Opportunities for Economic Development of a Small Island State'. Paper presented at the Symposium on East Timor, Indonesia and the Region: Perceptions of History and Prospects for the Future, Lisbon, 10–15 July 2000.

Farid, Hilmar, and Rikardo Simarmata. *The Struggle for Truth and Justice: A Survey of Transitional Justice Initiatives Throughout Indonesia.* International Center for Transitional Justice Occasional Paper Series. New York: International Center for Transitional Justice, 2004.

Farsetta, Diane. 'East Timorese Refugees in Militia-Controlled Camps'. Magdalene Hsien Chen Pus (ed.). *The Devastating Impact of Small Arms and Light Weapons on the Lives of Women: A Collection of Testimonies.* Washington: Women's International League for Peace and Freedom (WILPF) for International Action Network on Small Arms (IANSA) Women's Caucus, 2001. 4–5.

Feith, Herbert. *The East Timor Issue Since the Capture of Xanana Gusmão*. Fitzroy, Vic.: East Timor Talks Campaign, 1993.

Fitzpatrick, Daniel. *Land Claims in East Timor*. Canberra: Asia Pacific Press, 2002.

Fletcher, Laurel, and Harvey M. Weinstein. 'Violence and Social Repair: Rethinking the Contribution of Justice to Reconciliation'. (2002) *Human Rights Quarterly* 24(3): 573–639.

FOKUPERS (Komunikasi Untuk Perempuan Loro Sae – Communication Forum for Women from the East). *The End of the Dry Season: Efforts by East Timorese women to end violence, a beginning*. (Pamphlet). Dili: Fokupers, 1999.

FOKUPERS (Komunikasi Untuk Perempuan Loro Sae – Communication Forum for Women from the East). *Gender-based Human Rights Abuses during the Pre and Post-Ballot Violence in East Timor*. Dili: Fokupers, 2000.

Foucault, Michel. *Discipline and Punish: The Birth of the Prison*. Alan Sheridan (trans.). New York. Pantheon Books, 1975.

Fox, James J. and Dionisio Babo-Soares. *Out of the Ashes: Destruction and Reconstruction of East Timor*. Adelaide, SA: Crawford House, 2000.

Fox, James J., Anthony J. Regan, Michael Maley and Dionisio Babo-Soares. *Elections and Constitution Making in East Timor*. Canberra: State Society and Governance in Melanesia Project, The Australian National University, 2003.

Francis, Diana 'Culture, Power Asymmetries and Gender in Conflict Transformation', *Berghof Handbook for Conflict Transformation*. Berghof Research Centre for Constructive Conflict Management, 2001.

Franke, Katherine M. 'Gendered Subjects of Transitional Justice' (2006) *Columbia Journal of Gender and Law* 15(3): 813–28.

Friedman, Matthew J. 'Veterans' Mental Health in the Wake of War' (2005) *New England Journal of Medicine* 352(13): 1287–90.

Furusawa, Kiyoko and Jean Inglis. 'Violence against Women in East Timor under the Indonesian Occupation'. Indai Lourdes Sajor (ed.). *Common Grounds: Violence against Women in War and Armed Conflict Situations*. Quezon City, Philippines: Asian Centre for Women's Human Rights, 1998. 349–355.

Gabrielson, Curt. 'The Church in East Timor'. *Institute of Current World Affairs Letters,* Dili, 1 August 2001.

Gabrielson, Curt. 'East Timorese Women's Fight against Violence'. *International Council World Affairs Newsletter,* 2002.

Galtung, Johan. *Peace, Research, Education, Action*. Copenhagen: Christian Ejlers, 1975.

Gardam, Judith. 'Women and Armed Conflict: The Response of International Law'. Helen Durham and Tracey Gurd (eds). *Listening to the Silences: Women and War*. Leiden, Boston: Martinus Nijhoff, 2005, 109–24.

Gardam, Judith and Michelle Jarvis. 'Women and Armed Conflict: The International Response to the Beijing Platform for Action', (2000) *Columbia Human Rights Law Review* 32(1): 1–65.

Gardam, Judith, and Michelle Jarvis. *Women, Armed Conflict and International Law*. The Hague and Boston, MA: Kluwer Law International, 2001.

Girginov, A. 'Extradition from Indonesia to East Timor and the serious crimes process in East Timor (1999–2005)', (2006) *East Timor Law Journal* 2: 1–2.

Glasius, Marlies. *The International Criminal Court: A Global Civil Society Achievement*. New York, NY: Routledge, 2006.

Godinho, N. 'United Nations Security Council "Arria Formula" Meeting on the Implementation of Security Council Resolution 1325'. New York: United Nations, 2001.

Goldblatt, Beth and Sheila Meintjes. *Gender and the Truth and Reconciliation Commission: A Submission to the Truth and Reconciliation Commission*. Johannesburg: South African Truth and Reconciliation Commission, 1996.

Goldstein, Anne Tierney. *Recognizing Enforced Impregnation as a War Crime Under International Law*. New York: The Centre for Reproductive Law and Policy, 1993.

Goti, Jaime Malamud. 'Trying Violations of Human Rights: The Dilemma of Transitional Democratic Governments'. *State Crimes, Punishment or Pardon. Papers and Reports of the Conference, November 4–6 1988*. Aspen Institute: Wye Center, Maryland, 1989, 81–82.

Graycar, Regina and Jenny Morgan (eds), *The Hidden Gender of Law* (2nd edn), Annandale: Federation Press, 2002.

Grenfell, Damian. 'Reconstituting the Nation: Reconciliation and the national community in Timor-Leste'. *Occasional Papers in Justice and International Studies*. Melbourne: School of International Studies, RMIT University, 2006.

Grenfell, Damian, Anna Trembath and Chris Scanlon. *Challenges and Possibilities: International Organisations and Women in Timor-Leste*. Melbourne: Globalism Institute, RMIT University, 2005

Grenfell, Laura. 'Legal Pluralism and the Rule of Law in Timor Leste'. (2006) *Leiden Journal of International Law* 19: 305–37.

Grenfell, Laura. 'Harnessing Local Law in the Post-Conflict State: The case of Timor-Leste'. *Timor-Leste: Challenges for Justice and Human Rights in the Shadow of the Past*. William Binchy (ed.). Dublin: Clarus Press, 2009, 81–110.

Grenfell, Laura. 'Legal Pluralism and the Challenge of Building the Rule of Law in Post-Conflict States: A Case-Study of Timor-Leste' *The Role of International Law in Rebuilding Societies after Conflict: Great Expectations*, B. Bowden, H. Charlesworth & J. Farrall (eds.), Cambridge: Cambridge University Press, 2009, 124–140.

Gusmão, H.E. Kay Rala Xanana. 'Challenges for Peace and Stability: Address by President Gusmão on the occasion of the Chancellor's Human Rights Lecture', University of Melbourne, Australia, 7 April 2003.

Gusmão, H.E. Kay Rala Xanana. Opening Address by H.E. Kay Rala Xanana Gusmão, President of the Democratic Republic of Timor-Leste on the Occasion of the 3rd National Dialogue on Justice. Paper presented at the 3rd National Dialogue on Justice, Dili, 5 March 2004.

Gusmão, H.E. Kay Rala Xanana. 'Notes on Comments by Xanana Gusmão and José Ramos-Horta on Dealing with Past Human Rights Violations Made During a Panel Discussion'. Paper presented at the German Council on Foreign Relations (Deutsche Gesellschaft für Auswaertige Politik, DGAP), Berlin. *Watch Indonesia*, 20 October 2004.

Gusmão, Kirsty Sword. 'The Case of Ms Juliana Dos Santos'. *Alola Foundation Report*. Dili, October 2001.

Gusmão, Kirsty Sword. *A Woman of Independence*. Sydney: Pan Macmillan, 2003.

Guterres, Francisco da Costa. 'Elites and Prospects of Democracy in East Timor'. PhD thesis, Griffith University, 2006.

Hamber, Brandon. 'Masculinity and Transitional Justice: An Exploratory Essay', (2007) *International Journal of Transitional Justice* 1(3): 375–90.

Halpern, Jodi and Harvey Weinstein. 'Rehumanizing the Other: Empathy and Reconciliation', (2004) *Human Rights Quarterly* 26: 561–83.

Hamber, Brandon. 'Masculinity and Transitional Justice: An Exploratory Essay', (2007) *International Journal of Transitional Justice* 1(3): 375–90.

Harrington, Andrew. 'The Commission of Truth and Friendship Indonesia-Timor Leste: Competing Concepts of Justice', (2007) *East Timor Law Journal* 7. 1–29

Harris Rimmer, Susan. 'Untold Numbers: East Timorese Women and Transitional Justice'. Sharon Pickering and Caroline Lambert (eds). *Global Issues, Women and Justice*. Sydney: Federation Press, 2004, 335–66.

Harris Rimmer, Susan. 'The Roman Catholic Church and the Rights of East Timorese Women'. Carolyn Evans and Amanda Whiting (eds). *Mixed Blessings: Laws, Religions and Women's Rights in the Asia-Pacific Region*, The Hague: Brill, 2006, 654–701.

Harris Rimmer, Susan. '"Orphans" or Veterans? Justice for Children Born of War in East Timor', (2007) *Texas International Law Journal* 42(2): 323–44.

Harris Rimmer, Susan. 'Beloved Madam: Gender Issues at the Indonesian ad hoc Human Rights Court' *Timor-Leste: Challenges for Justice and Human Rights in the Shadow of the Past*. William Binchy (ed.). Dublin: Clarus Press, 2009, 427–74.

Hayner, Priscilla B. 'Fifteen Truth Commissions – 1974 to 1994: A Comparative Study', (1994) *Human Rights Quarterly* 16(4): 597–655.

Hayner, Priscilla B. *Unspeakable Truths: Confronting State Terror and Atrocity*. New York; London: Routledge, 2001.

Hearn, Jane and Susan Harris, 'Debating the Relationship between Human Rights and Aid in Australia', (2002) *Development Bulletin,* Development Studies Network 59: 77–81.

Henry, Nicola. 'Secrecy, Silence and Sexual Violence in International Criminal Proceedings'. Paper read at Activating Human Rights and Diversity, 1–4 July 2003, Byron Bay.

Henry, Nicola. 'Disclosure, Sexual Violence and International Jurisprudence: A Therapeutic Approach'. PhD thesis. University of Melbourne, 2005.

Herman, Judith. *Trauma and Recovery: The Aftermath of Violence from Domestic Abuse to Political Terror*. New York: Basic Books, 1992.

Hicks, David. *Tetum Ghosts and Kin: Fertility and Gender in East Timor* (2nd edn). USA: Waveland Press, 2004.

Hirst, Megan, and Howard Varney. 'Justice Abandoned? An Assessment of the Serious Crimes Process in East Timor'. *ICTJ Occasional Paper Series*. New York: International Center for Transitional Justice, 2005.

Hite, Katherine. 'Panel 6: Amnesty and Truth Commissions'. *Accounting for Atrocities: Prosecuting War Crimes 50 Years after Nuremberg: Proceedings of the Conference 5–6 October 1998*. Bard College Annandale-on-Hudson, New York, 1998.

Hochschild, Fabrizio. '"It Is Better to Leave, We Can't Protect You": Flight in the First Months of the United Nations Transitional Administrations in Kosovo and East Timor', (2004) *Journal of Refugee Studies* 17(3): 286–300.

Hofmann, Bjoern. 'Are Hybrid Political Orders an Appropriate Concept for State Formation? Timor-Leste Revisited. A Response by Bjoern Hofmann', Berghof Research Center for Constructive Conflict Management, April 2009, at http://www.berghof-handbook.net/uploads/download/dialogue8_hofmann_comm.pdf.

Hohe, Tanja. 'Building Feudal Democracy in East Timor'. Edward Newman and Roland Rich (eds). The *United Nations Role in Promoting Democracy: Between Ideals and Reality*, UNU Press: Tokyo, 2004. 302–319

Hohe, Tanja and Rod Nixon. *Report on Reconciling Justice, 'Traditional' Law and State Judiciary in East Timo*. Washington, DC: United States Institute for Peace, January 2003.

Huckerby, Jayne. *Transitional Justice and Treatment of Refugee Returnees Suspected of Criminal Offenses: East Timor and Beyond.* New York University: Center for Human Rights and Global Justice Working Paper No. 9, 2004.

Human Rights Watch. 'Remembering History in East Timor: The Trial of Xanana Gusmão and a Follow-up to the Dili Massacre'. *Human Rights Watch/Asia 5(8)*. New York: Human Rights Watch, 1993.

Human Rights Watch. *The Limits of Openness: Human Rights in Indonesia and East Timor*. New York: Human Rights Watch, 1994.

Human Rights Watch. *Strong Independent Commission of Inquiry Urged for East Timor.* New York: Human Rights Watch, 27 September 1999.

Human Rights Watch. *Indonesia/East Timor: Forced Expulsions to West Timor and the Refugee Crisis*. New York: Human Rights Watch, December 1999.

Human Rights Watch. *Unfinished Business: Justice for East Timor.* New York: Human Rights Watch, 2000.

Human Rights Watch. *Indonesia: Courts Sanction Impunity for East Timor Abuses*. New York: Human Rights Watch, 2004.

Human Rights Watch. *Justice Denied for East Timor.* New York: Human Rights Watch, 2004.

Human Rights Watch. *Tortured Beginnings: Police Violence and the Beginnings of Impunity in East Timor.* New York: Human Rights Watch, 2006.

Human Security Report 2005, New York, Oxford: Oxford UP 2005.

Huntington, Samuel. *The Third Wave: Democratization in the Late Twentieth Century*, Norman: University of Oklahoma Press, 1991, 211–25.

Hynes M., J. Ward, K. Robertson and C. Crouse. 'A Determination of the Prevalence of Gender-based Violence Among Conflict-Affected Populations in East Timor', (2004) *Disasters* 28(3): 294–321.

Ignatieff, Michael. 'Articles of Faith'. (1996) *Index on Censorship* 5: 1.

Institute For Policy Research and Advocacy (ELSAM). 'Observing three main cases of Adam Damiri, Tono Suratman and Eurico Gutteres', Institute For Policy Research and Advocacy (ELSAM) Monitoring Report on Ad Hoc Human Rights Court Against Gross Human Rights Violations in East Timor, *Report No. 6*, Jakarta, Indonesia, 2002.

International Center for Transitional Justice. 'Timorese Parliament Should Release Truth Commission Report Immediately', *media release*, New York, 28 November 2005.

International Center for Transitional Justice. '*Testimony from the International Center for Transitional Justice to the Constitutional Court of Indonesia by ICTJ staff and colleagues*', New York, July 2006.

International Center for Transitional Justice, *Report: Too Much Friendship, Too Little Truth: Report on the Commission of Truth and Friendship in Indonesia and Timor-Leste* New York: International Center for Transitional Justice, January 2008.

International Center for Transitional Justice *Feature: Indonesia: A Case of Impunity*, New York: International Center for Transitional Justice, 30 June 2008.

International Center for Transitional Justice. *An Unfinished Truth: An Analysis of the Commission of Truth and Friendship's Final Report on the 1999 Atrocities in East Timor*. New York: International Center for Transitional Justice, 2009.

International Commission of Inquiry on East Timor. *Report of the International Commission of Inquiry on East Timor to the Secretary-General*. UN Document A/54/726. S/2000/59, 31 January, 2000.

International Commission on Intervention and State Sovereignty. *The Responsibility to Protect Report*. Toronto, December 2001.

International Committee of the Red Cross (ICRC). *Woman Facing War*. Geneva: ICRC, 2001.

International Committee of the Red Cross (ICRC). *Woman and War Special Report*. Geneva: ICRC, 2003.

International Crisis Group. *Indonesia: Impunity Versus Accountability for Gross Human Rights Violations*. Jakarta/Brussels: International Crisis Group, 2001.

International Crisis Group. *Afghanistan: Judicial Reform and Transitional Justice*. Kabul: International Crisis Group, 2003.

International Crisis Group. 'Resolving Timor Leste's Crisis', *Asia Report No. 120*. Brussels: International Crisis Group, 2006.

International Crisis Group. Timor-Leste's Parliamentary Elections, *Asia Briefing No. 6*., Brussels: International Crisis Group, 12 June 2007.

International Crisis Group. Timor-Leste: Security Sector Reform, *Asia Report No. 143*. Brussels: International Crisis Group, 17 January 2008.

International Crisis Group. Timor-Leste's Displacement Crisis, *Asia Report No. 148*. Brussels: International Crisis Group, 31 March 2008.

International Crisis Group. Timor-Leste: No Time for Complacency, *Asia Briefing No. 87*. Brussels: International Crisis Group, 9 February 2009.

International Development Research Center. *Gender and Reparations: Opportunities for Transitional Democracies?* Toronto: IDRC, 2004.

International Law Association Committee on Human Rights Law and Practice, 'Final Report on the Exercise of Universal Jurisdiction in Respect of Gross Human Rights Violations'. *Report of the Sixty-Ninth Conference*, London, 2000.

International Rescue Committee Report. Focus Groups on Gender based Violence, Dili, 2003

Ishizuka, Katsumi. 'Diplomatic and Judicial Response to the Human Rights Violations in East Timor, 1999 to Present'. Paper presented at the 17th meeting of the Academic Council on the United Nations System (ACUNS), Geneva, Switzerland, 30 June – 2 July 2004.

Jardine, Matthew. *East Timor: Genocide in Paradise*. Tuscon, AZ: Odonian Press, 1995.

Järvinen, Taina. 'Human Rights and Post-Conflict Transitional Justice in East Timor'. *UPI Working Papers*. Helsinki: Finnish Institute of International Affairs, 2004.

Joint Truth and Friendship Commission. *Per Memoriam ad Spem (From Memory to Hope): Final Report*. May 2008.

Jolliffe, Jill. *Cover-Up: The Inside Story of the Balibo Five*. Carlton North, VIC: Scribe, 2001.

Jones, Sidney. *Injustice, Persecution, Eviction: A Human Rights Update on Indonesia and East Timor, March 1990*. New York: Asia Watch, 1990.

Joshi, Vijaya. Building Opportunities: Women's Organizing, Militarism and the United Nations Transitional Administration in East Timor. PhD thesis. Clarke University, 2006.

Judicial System Monitoring Programme. *Justice in Practice: Human Rights in Court Administration.* Dili, 2001.

Judicial System Monitoring Programme. 'Dili Court Increases Pressure on Indonesia'. Dili, 2001.

Judicial System Monitoring Programme. *Judicial System Monitoring Programme Comments to the Sergio Lobo Interlocutory Appeal.* 27 July 2001.

Judicial System Monitoring Programme. *Findings and Recommendations: Workshop on Formal and Local Justice Systems in East Timor.* Dili, 2002.

Judicial System Monitoring Programme. *The Right to Appeal in East Timor.* Dili, 2002.

Judicial System Monitoring Programme. 'Timor Serious Crimes Panel Hands Down First Rape Conviction'. Dili, 2002.

Judicial System Monitoring Programme. *Report on the Court of Appeal Decision on the Applicable Subsidiary Law in Timor-Leste.* Dili, 2003.

Judicial System Monitoring Programme. *Background Paper on the Justice Sector.* Dili: Timor-Leste and Development Partners Meeting. 2003.

Judicial System Monitoring Programme. *Briefing to Donors: The Justice System in East Timor.* Dili, 2004.

Judicial System Monitoring Programme. *Women in the Formal Justice Sector.* Dili, 2004.

Judicial System Monitoring Programme. 'Dili District Court Releases Detention Decision in Rape Case against PNTL Officers'. *Media Release.* Dili, 2004.

Judicial System Monitoring Programme. *The Future of the Serious Crimes Unit.* Dili, 2004.

Judicial System Monitoring Programme. *The Lolotoe Case: A Small Step Forward.* Dili, 2004.

Judicial System Monitoring Programme. *Overview of the Jurisprudence of the Court of Appeal in its First Operation since East Timor's Independence*, Dili, 2004.

Judicial System Monitoring Programme. *Report on Women in Formal Justice Sector.* 7 April 2004.

Judicial System Monitoring Programme. *An Analysis of a Sexual Assault Decision from the Dili District Court.* Dili, July 2004.

Judicial System Monitoring Programme. *Analysis of Decisions in Cases Involving Women And Children Victims: June 2004 – March 2005*, April 2005.

Judicial System Monitoring Programme. *Police Treatment of Women in Timor-Leste.* Dili, 2005.

Judicial System Monitoring Programme. *The Role, Practice and Procedure of the Court of Appeal* Dili, July 2005.

Judicial System Monitoring Programme. *Torture Survivors: Their Experiences of Violation, Truth and Justice.* Dili, April 2007.

Judicial System Monitoring Programme. *Digest of the Jurisprudence of the Special Panels for Serious Crimes*, Dili, April 2007.

Judicial System Monitoring Programme. *Justice Update: Legal Perspectives on Clemency*, June 2008.

Judicial System Monitoring Programme. 'Justice Update: Leadership Crisis in the Judicial Organs of Timor Leste'. Dili, March 2009.

Judicial System Monitoring Programme. 'Trial of Railos and others: Step forward in case of attack on the F-FDTL HQ', media release. Dili, May 2009.

Kapur, Ratna. 'The Tragedy of Victimization Rhetoric: Resurrecting the 'Native' Subject in International/Post-Colonial Feminist Legal Politics', (2002) *Harvard Human Rights Journal* 15: 1–37.

Karstedt, Susanne. 'Coming to Terms with the Past in Germany after 1945 and 1989: Public Judgments on Procedures and Justice', (1998) *Law and Policy* 20(1): 15–56.

Katzenstein, S. 'Hybrid Tribunals: Searching for Justice in East Timor', (2003) *Harvard Human Rights Journal* 16(6): 245–78.

Kelsall, Michelle Staggs and Shanee Stepakoff. 'When We Wanted to Talk about Rape: Silencing Sexual Violence at the Special Court for Sierra Leone' 1 (2007) *International Journal of Transitional Justice* 3: 355–74.

Kent, Lia. *Community Views on CAVR's Community Reconciliation Process*. Dili: Judicial System Monitoring Programme, 2004.

Kiernan, Ben. 'The Demography of Genocide in South-East Asia: The Death Tolls in Cambodia 1975–79 and East Timor, 1975–80', (2003) *Critical Asian Studies* 35(4): 585–97.

King, Martin Luther Jr (ed.). 'Letter from Birmingham Jail'. *Why We Can't Wait*. New York: Harper and Row, 1963.

Kingsbury, Damien. *East Timor: The Price of Liberty*. New York: Palgrave, 2009.

Kingsbury, Damien and Monash Asia Institute. *Guns and Ballot Boxes: East Timor's Vote for Independence. Monash Papers on Southeast Asia No. 54*. Melbourne: Monash Asia Institute, 2000.

Kingston, Jeffrey. 'Balancing Justice and Reconciliation in East Timor'. (2006) *Critical Asian Studies* 38(3): 271–302.

Kohen, Arnold S. *From the Place of the Dead: Bishop Belo and the Struggle for East Timor*. (1st edn). Oxford, UK: Lion, 1999.

KPP HAM. 'Full Report of the Investigative Commission into Human Rights Violations in East Timor'. Jakarta: KPP HAM, 2000.

Kritz, Neil J. 'Book Review: War Crimes, Brutality, Genocide, Terror and the Struggle for Justice', (1999) 93 *American Journal of International Law* 98.

Kritz, Neil J. 'Progress and Humility: The Ongoing Search for Post-Conflict Justice', M. Cherif Bassiouni (ed.). *Post-Conflict Justice*. New York: Transnational Publishers, 2002: 55–87.

Krog, Antjie. *Country of My Skull: Guilt, Sorrow and the Limits of Forgiveness in the New South Africa*. Johannesburg: Vintage Press, 1999.

Krug, G., Dahlberg L., Mercy J., Zwi A. and Lozano R. (eds). *World Report on Violence and Health*. Geneva: World Health Organisation, 2002.

Laakso, Jennifer, 'Pursuit of Truth, Justices and Reconciliation: The Truth Commissions of East Timor and South Africa', (2003) *Social Alternatives* 22(2): 48–54.

Laakso, Jennifer. 'Justice, Order and Peacebuilding in Timor-Leste', PhD Thesis. University of Queensland, 2008.

Laek, Rate. '"Widows"' group demands international tribunal', La'o Hamutuk Bulletin, 24 August 2002.

Lambourne, Wendy. 'Post-Conflict Peacebuilding: Meeting Human Needs for Justice and Reconciliation'. (2004) *Peace, Conflict and Development* 4. 1–24.

Lambourne, Wendy. 'Transitional Justice and Peacebuilding after Mass Violence', (2009) *International Journal of Transitional Justice*, 3(1): 28–48.

Law, David M. 'The Post-Conflict Security Sector'. *Geneva Centre for the Armed Forces (DCAF) Policy Paper*. Geneva: Geneva Centre for the Armed Forces (DCAF), 2006.

Leebaw, Bronwyn. 'Book Review: Transitional Justice by Ruti Teitel', (2001) *American Journal of Comparative Law* 49: 363.

Levine, Corey. *Gender and Transitional Justice: A Case Study of East Timor*. Vancouver: Canadian Consortium on Human Security, 2004.

Levinson, Sanford. 'Responsibility for Crimes of War', (1973) *Philosophy and Public Affairs* 2(3): 244–73.

Lindsey, Charlotte. *Women Facing War: ICRC Study of the Impact of Armed Conflict on Women*. Geneva: International Committee of the Red Cross (ICRC), 2001.

Linton, Suzannah. 'Cambodia, East Timor and Sierra Leone: Experiments in International Justice'. (2001) *Criminal Law Forum* 12: 185–246.

Linton, Suzannah. 'Prosecuting Atrocities at the District Court of Dili', (2001) *Melbourne Journal of International Law* 2(2): 414–58.

Linton, Suzannah. 'Rising from the Ashes: The Creation of a Viable Criminal Justice System in East Timor', (2001) *Melbourne University Law Review* 25.

Linton, Suzannah. 'Experiments in International Justice' (2001) *Criminal Law Forum* 12: 210–11.

Linton, Suzannah. 'New Approaches to International Justice in Cambodia and East Timor' (2002) *International Review of the Red Cross* 845: 93–119.

Linton, Suzannah. 'Unravelling the First Three Trials at Indonesia's Ad Hoc Court for Human Rights Violations in East Timor' (2004) *Leiden Journal of International Law* 17(2): 303–61:

Linton, Suzannah. 'Putting Things into Perspective: The Realities of Accountability in East Timor, Indonesia and Cambodia'. *Maryland Series in Contemporary Asian Studies* 3, 2005.

Linton, Suzannah. 'Accounting for Atrocities in Indonesia', (2006) *Singapore Year Book of International Law* X: 199–231.

Linton, Suzannah and Caitlin Reiger. 'The Evolving Jurisprudence of East Timor's Special Panel for Serious Crimes on Admissions of Guilt, Duress and Superior Orders', (2004) *Yearbook of International Humanitarian Law* IV:167–213.

Logan, William and Keir Reeves. *Places of Pain and Shame: Dealing with 'Difficult Heritage'*, Key Issues in Cultural Heritage Series, Milton Park, New York: Routledge, 2009.

McCormack, Timothy. 'War Crimes and the Milosevic Trial. Paper presented at the Centre for International and Public Law Seminar'. Australian National University, Canberra, 12 August 2004. 319–338.

McCormack, Timothy. 'The Importance of Effective Enforcement of International Humanitarian Law'. Johanna van Sambeek Liesbeth Ljinzaad and Bahia Tahzib-Lie (eds). *Making the Voice of Humanity Heard: Essays on Humanitarian Assistance and International Humanitarian Law in Honour of HRH Princess Margriet of the Netherlands*. Leiden: Martinus Nijhoff Publishers, 2004.

McDonald, Gabrielle Kirk. 'Crimes of Sexual Violence: The Experience of the International Criminal Tribunal', (2000) *Columbia Journal of Transnational Law* 39(1): 1–17.

McDonald, Hamish, Desmond Ball, James Dunn, Gerry van Klinken, David Bourchier, Douglas Kammen, and Richard Tanter (eds). *Masters of Terror: Indonesia's Military and Violence in East Timor in 1999*. Strategic and Defence Studies Centre Canberra Paper No. 145. Canberra: The Australian National University, 2002.

McEvoy, Kieran and Lorna McGregor (eds). *Transitional Justice From Below: Grassroots Activism and the Struggle for Change*. London: Hart Publishing, 2008.

MacKinnon, Catharine. *Feminism Unmodified: Discourses on Life and Law*. Boston: Harvard University Press, 1987.

MacKinnon, Catharine. 'Crimes of War, Crimes of Peace', S. Shute and S. Hurley (eds). *On Human Rights. The Oxford Amnesty Lectures*. London: Basic Books, 1993, 93.

MacKinnon, Catharine. 'Turning Rape into Pornography: Post-modern Genocide'. Alex Stiglmayer (ed.). *Mass Rape: The War against Women in Bosnia-Herzegovina*, Lincoln: University of Nebraska Press, 1994. 170–174

MacKinnon, Catharine. 'Women's September 11th: Rethinking the International Law of Conflict', (2006) *Harvard International Law Journal* 47(1): 1–31.

MacKinnon, Catharine. *Are Women Human? And Other International Dialogues.* Cambridge: Belknap Press of Harvard University Press, 2006.

McWilliam, Andrew and Angie Bexley, 'Performing Politics: The 2007 Parliamentary Elections in Timor Leste', (2008) *The Asia Pacific Journal of Anthropology* 9(1): 66–82.

Magro, John. 'Is there Justification for an International Criminal Tribunal for East Timor?' (2000) *Murdoch University Electronic Journal of Law* 7:3.

Magsam, Dieter. 'Coming to Terms with Genocide in Rwanda: The Role of International and National Justice'. Wolfgang Kaleck, Michael Ratner, Tobias Singelnstein and Peter Weiss (eds). *International Prosecution of Human Rights Crimes.* Springer: Berlin, 2007. 159–168.

Mahoney, K. and P. Mahoney (eds). *Human Rights in the Twenty-First Century: A Global Challenge.* Dordrecht: Martinus Nijhoff, 1993.

Mani, Rama. *Beyond Retribution: Seeking Justice in the Shadows of War.* Cambridge: Polity, 2002.

Mani, Rama. 'Balancing Peace with Justice in the Aftermath of Violent Conflict', (2005) *Development* 48(3): 25–34.

Mani, Rama. 'Editorial: Dilemmas of Expanding Transitional Justice, or Forging the Nexus between Transitional Justice and Development', (2009) *International Journal of Transitional Justice* (Special Issue on Transitional Justice and Development) 2: 253–65.

Martin, Ian. *Self-Determination in East Timor: The United Nations, the Ballot, and International Intervention.* International Peace Academy Occasional Paper Series. Boulder, Colorado: Lynne Rienner Publishers, 2001.

Martinkus, John. *A Dirty Little War.* Milsons Point, NSW: Random House, 2001.

Mason, Christine, 'Women, Violence and Non-Violent Resistance in East Timor', (2005) *Journal of Peace Research*, London 42(6): 737–49.

Mearns, David (ed.). *Democratic Governance in Timor-Leste: Reconciling the Local and the National.* Darwin: CDU Press, 2008.

Meintjes, Sheila. 'War and Post-War Shifts in Gender Relations'. S. Meintjes, M. Turshen and A. Pillay (eds). *The Aftermath: Women in Post-Conflict Transitio*n, London: Zed Press, 2001, 95–108.

Mello, Sergio Vieira de. 'Situation of Human Rights in Timor Leste, Report of the United Nations High Commissioner for Human Rights'. Paper presented at the Commission on Human Rights, Geneva, 4 March 2003.

Mendeloff, David. 'Truth-seeking, Truth-telling, and Post-conflict Peace Building: Curb the Enthusiasm?', (2004) *International Studies Review* 6: 355–80.

Meron, Theodor. 'Rape as a Crime under International Humanitarian Law', (1993) *American Journal of International Law* 87(3): 424–26.

Meron, Theodor. *War Crimes Law Comes of Age: Essays.* Oxford: Oxford University Press 1998.

Mertus, Julie. 'Truth in a Box: The Limits of Justice through Judicial Mechanisms'. I. Amadiume and A. An-Na'im (ed.). *The Politics of Memory: Truth, Healing and Social Justice.* New York: Zed Books, 2000. 142–150.

Mertus, Julie. 'Shouting from the Bottom of the Well: The Impact of International Trials for Wartime Rape on Women's Agency', (2004) *International Feminist Journal of Politics* 6(1): 110–28.

Mertus, Julie and Judy A. Benjamin. *War's Offensive on Women: The Humanitarian Challenge in Bosnia, Kosovo, and Afghanistan.* Bloomfield, Conn.: Kumarian Press, 2000.

Mertus, Julie and Jeffrey W. Helsing (eds). *Human Rights and Conflict: Exploring the Links between Rights, Law, and Peacebuilding*. Washington, DC: United States Institute of Peace Press, 2006.

van der Merwe, Hugo, Victoria Baxter and Audrey Chapman (eds), *Assessing the Impact of Transitional Justice: Challenges for Empirical Research*. Washington: United States Institute for Peace Press, 2009.

Meznaric, Silva. 'Gender as an Ethno-marker: Rape, War and Identity Politics in the Former Yugoslavia', Valentine M. Moghadam (ed.), *Identity, Politics and Women: Cultural Reassertions and Feminisms in International Perspective*. Oxford: Westview Press, 1994. 76–97.

Millar, Hayli. 'Facilitating Women's Voices in Truth Recovery: An Assessment of Women's Participation and the Integration of a Gender Perspective in Truth Commissions'. Helen Durham and Tracey Gurd (eds). *Listening to the Silences: Women and War*. Leiden, Boston: Martinus Nijhoff, 2005, 171–222.

Miller, Zinaida. 'Effects of Invisibility: In Search of the "Economic" in Transitional Justice', (2009) *International Journal of Transitional Justice* (Special issue on transitional justice and development) 2: 266–91.

Minow, Martha. *Between Vengeance and Forgiveness: Facing History after Genocide and Mass Violence*. Boston: Beacon, 1998.

Mohanty, Chandra Talpade. *Feminism Without Borders: Decolonizing Theory, Practicing Solidarity*. Durham and London: Duke University Press, 2004.

Morgan, Amanda. 'The State and International Law'. Interview with Professor Hilary Charlesworth. Australian National University, Canberra 2003.

Mutua, Makau W. 'Transitional Justice in Sexual and Gender-Based Violence', *Buffalo Legal Studies Research Paper No. 2008–18*, 2008.

Naffine, Ngaire. 'Sexing the Subject of Law)', Margaret Thornton (ed.). *Public and Private: Feminist Legal Debates*. Oxford: Oxford University Press, 1995: 18, 20, 32.

National Council of East Timorese Resistance (CNRT). *Magna Carta concerning Freedoms, Rights, Duties and Guarantees for the People of East Timor,* adopted by the Peniche, Portugal, 25 April 1998.

Nesiah, Vasuki. *Truth Commissions and Gender: Principles, Policies and Procedures*. Gender Justice Series. International Centre for Transitional Justice: New York, July 2006.

Nesiah, Vasuki. *Gender and Truth Commission Mandates*. International Center for Transitional Justice, New York, 2006.

Nevins, Joseph. 'Truth, Lies, and Accountability: Search of Justice for East Timor', (2007) *Boston Review*, January/February, 21–23.

Newman, Edward and Joanne van Selm. *Refugees and Forced Displacement: International Security, Human Vulnerability, and the State*. Tokyo; New York: United Nations University Press, 2003.

Ni Aolain, Fionnuala. 'Radical Rules: The Effects of Evidential and Procedural Rules on the Regulation of Sexual Violence in War' (1997) *Albany Law Review,* 60(3): 883–905.

Ni Aolain, Fionnuala. 'Rethinking the Concept of Harm and Legal Categorisations of Sexual Violence During War' (2000) *Theoretical Inquiries in Law* 1(2): Article 3.

Ni Aolain, Fionnuala. 'Political Violence and Gender in Times of Transition' (2006) *Columbia Journal of Gender and the Law* 15(3): 829–49.

Ni Aolain, Fionnuala. 'Women, Security and the Patriarchy of Internationalized Transitional Justice', *Minnesota Legal Studies Research Paper No. 08–40,* October 2008.

Ni Aolain, Fionnuala and Colm Campbell. 'The Paradox of Transition in Conflicted Democracies' (2005) *Human Rights Quarterly* 27: 172–213.

Ni Aolain, Fionnuala and Michael Hamilton. 'Gender and the Rule of Law in Transitional Societies'. *Minnesota Legal Studies Research Paper No. 09–12; Transitional Justice Institute Research Paper No. 09–02,* March 2009.

Ni Aolain, Fionnuala and Eilish Rooney. 'Under-enforcement and Intersectionality: Gendered Aspects of Transition for Women'. Navanethem Pillay (ed.) (2007) *International Journal of Transitional Justice* (Special Issue: Gender and Transitional Justice) 3: 338–54.

Ni Aolain, Fionnuala and Catherine Turner. 'Gender, Truth and Transition'. (2007) *UCLA Women's Law Journal* 16: 229–79.

Nikolic-Ristanovic, Vesna. 'Sexual Violence: International Law and Restorative Justice'. Doris Buss and Ambreena Manji (eds). *International Law: Modern Feminist Approaches*. Oxford and Portland, Oregon: Hart Publishing, 2005, 273–94.

Niner, Sarah (ed.) *To Resist is to Win: the Autobiography of Xanana Gusmão with selected letters and speeches*. Aurora Books, Melbourne, 2000.

Niner, Sara. 'The Contested Place of Women in Post-conflict Timor-Leste', unpublished, on file with author, June 2009.

Nino, Carlos Santiago. *Radical Evil on Trial*. New Haven: Yale University Press, 1996.

O'Connell, James. 'Gambling with the Psyche: Does Prosecuting Human Rights Violators Console their Victims?' (2005) 46 *Harvard International Law Journal* 295, 340.

Office of the Deputy General Prosecutor for Serious Crimes Timor Leste. *Serious Crimes Unit Update*. 2004.

Office of the High Commissioner for Human Rights. *Report of the High Commissioner for Human Rights on the Human Rights Situation in East Timor*. Geneva: United Nations, 1999.

Office of the High Commissioner for Human Rights. *Report of the International Commission of Inquiry on East Timor to the Secretary-General.* Geneva: United Nations, 2000.

Office of the High Commissioner for Human Rights. *Rule of Law Tools for Post Conflict States: Monitoring Legal Systems.* Geneva: United Nations, 2006.

Office of the Prosecutor for the International Criminal Court. *Informal Expert Paper: the Principle of Complementarity in Practice.* The Hague, 2003.

O'Keefe, Roger. 'Universal Jurisdiction-Clarifying the Basic Concept' (2004) *Journal of International Criminal Justice* **2**(3): 735–60.

Okello, Moses Chrispus and Lucy Hovil. 'Confronting the Reality of Gender-based Violence in Northern Uganda'. (2007) *International Journal of Transitional Justice* 1(3): 433–43.

Open Society Institute. Forum: Gender and Transitional Justice: Pursuing Justice and Accountability in Post-Conflict Situations. OSI-New York, 7 February 2006 (audio file).

Opotow, Susan.'Psychology of Impunity and Injustice: Implications for Societal Reconciliation.' M. Cherif Bassiouni (ed.). *Post-Conflict Justice*. Transnational Publishers: New York. 2002, 206.

Orentlicher, Diane, Human Rights Watch and Asia Watch Committee (US). *Human Rights in Indonesia and East Timor, Asia Watch Report.* New York, New York: Asia Watch Committee, 1989.

Orentlicher, Diane E. 'Settling Accounts: The Duty to Prosecute Human Rights Violations of a Prior Regime', (1991) 100 *Yale Law Journal* 2537.

Orford, Anne. 'Feminism, Imperialism and the Mission of International Law', (2002) 71 *Nordic Journal of International Law* 275–96.

Orford, Anne. 'Commissioning the Truth' (2006), 15 *Columbia Journal of Gender and Law* 851–83.

Orford, Anne. 'What can we do to stop people harming others? Humanitarian intervention in Timor-Leste (East Timor)'. Jenny Edkins and Maja Zehfuss (eds), *Global Politics: A New Introduction*. Oxon: Routledge, 2009, 427–53.

O'Shea, Andreas. *Amnesty for Crime in International Law and Practice*. The Hague; London: Kluwer Law International, 2002.

Othman, Mohamed. 'East Timor: A Critique of the Model of Accountability for Serious Human Rights and International Humanitarian Law Violations', (2003) *Nordic Journal of International Law* 72(4): 449–82.

Otto, Dianne. 'Disconcerting "Masculinities": Reinventing the Gendered Subject(s) of International Human Rights Law'. Doris Buss and Ambreena Manji (eds). *International Law: Modern Feminist Approaches*. Oxford and Portland, Oregon: Hart Publishing, 2005. 105–129.

Oxfam Community Aid Abroad. 'Women Fight for Freedom: The Struggle for Human Rights and Independence in East Timor'. Melbourne, May 1999.

Pahuja, Sundhya. 'Rights as Regulation: The Integration of Development and Human Rights'. Paper delivered at 15th Annual ANZSIL Conference, Canberra, 29 June 2007.

Palmer, Lisa, Sara Niner, and Lia Kent. 'Forum Proceedings: Exploring the Tensions of Nation Building in Timor-Leste, held on 15 September 2006 at Melbourne University'. Monica Minnegal (ed.). *School of Social and Environmental Enquiry Research Paper No. 1*, Melbourne: University of Melbourne, 2007.

Parliament of Australia. *The Human Rights and Conditions of the People of East Timor, September 1983*. Senate Standing Committee on Foreign Affairs and Defence. Canberra: Parliament of the Commonwealth of Australia, 1983.

Pascoe, Daniel C. Justice for Serious Crimes in Timor-Leste. Honours thesis, Asian Studies, Australian National University, 2006.

Paixao de Jesus da Costa, Maria. 'Voices for change{--}women's voices in politics and decision making in post-conflict societies: the voices and experiences of women parliamentarians caucus in promoting gender equality and women's empowerment in the national parliament of Timor-Leste' by the Vice-President of the National Parliament and President of Grupo das Mulherese Parliamentares de Timor-Leste (GMPTL), Paper presented at the 2nd International Women for Peace Conference, Dili, 2009.

Peirera, Manuela Leong. 'Domestic Violence: A Part of Women's Daily Lives in East Timor'. *La'o Hamutuk Bulletin*. Dili, 2001.

Pereira, Manuela Leong and Jill Sternberg. 'Women's Involvement in Timor-Leste's Presidential Elections', *1325 Peacewomen E-News*, Issue 89, 24 May 2007.

Perry, Robin and Eleanor Taylor Nicholson, 'Australia Must Help Timor Find Justice', *The Age*, 26 August 2005.

Pettman, Jan Jindy. *Worlding Women: A Feminist International Politics*. St. Leonards, NSW: Allen and Unwin, 1996.

Pigou, Piers. *Crying without Tears: In Pursuit of Justice and Reconciliation in East Timor Leste: Community Perspectives and Expectations*. International Center for Transitional Justice: New York, 2003.

Pillay, Navanethem (guest ed.). 1 *International Journal of Transitional Justice* (2007) (Special Issue: Gender and Transitional Justice), 3.

Quenivet, Noelle N. R. *Sexual Offenses in Armed Conflict and International Law,* Ardsley, NY: Transnational Publishers, 2005.

Rae, James. 'War Crimes Accountability: Justice and Reconciliation in Cambodia and East Timor?', (2003) *Global Change, Peace and Security* 15(2): 157–78.

Rajagopal, B. *International Law from Below: Developments, Social Movements and Third World Resistance*: Cambridge University Press, 2003.

Ramos-Horta, José. *Towards a Peaceful Solution in East Timor*. (2nd edn). Sydney, NSW: East Timor Relief Association, 1997.

Rede Feto Timor Lorosae. 'Women, Peace and Security in East Timor'. Paper presented at the United Nations Security Council special session on the role of women in maintaining international peace and security. Dili, 24 October 2000.

Rees, Edward. *Under Pressure: Falintil – Forcas de Defesa de Timor Leste: Three Decades of Defence Force Development in Timor Leste 1975–2004,* Working Paper No. 139, Geneva Center for the Democratic Control of Armed Forces, Geneva, April 2004.

Rehn, Elizabeth and Ellen Johnson Sirleaf. *Women, War and Peace: Independent Expert's Assessment on the Impact of Armed Conflict on Women and Women's Role in Peace-Building*. New York: UNIFEM, 2002.

Reiger, Caitlin. 'Hybrid Attempts at Accountability for Serious Crimes in Timor Leste'. Naomi Roht-Arriaza, and Javier Mariezcurrena (eds). *Transitional Justice in the Twenty-First Century: Beyond Truth Versus Justice*. Cambridge: Cambridge University Press, 2006. 143–170.

Reiger, Caitlin and Marieke Wierda. 'The Serious Crimes Process in Timor-Leste: Retrospect'. *Prosecutions Case Studies No. 41*. New York: International Center for Transitional Justice, 2006.

Reilly, Niamh. 'Seeking Gender Justice in Post-Conflict Transitions: Toward a Transformative Human Rights Approach. (2007) *International Journal of Law in Context* 3(2): 155.

Renouf, Gordon. 'Some Features of the Legal System in East Timor'. Paper presented at the East Timor Legal Coordination Symposium, Darwin, 11–12 March 2002.

Retbøll, Torben. *East Timor: The Struggle Continues. IWGIA Document No. 50*. Copenhagen: International Work Group for Indigenous Affairs, 1984.

Retbøll, Torben (ed.) *East Timor: Occupation and Resistance*. Copenhagen: International Work Group for Indigenous Affairs, 1998.

Richards, Esther Joy. '"First I Cry, Then I Fight": Documenting Sexual Violence in Occupied East Timor and Evaluating the Response of Representatives of the Timorese Catholic Church'. Masters Thesis. Department of Theology and Religious Studies, University of Leeds, 2005.

Robertson, Geoffrey. *Crimes Against Humanity: The Struggle for Global Justice*. London, New York: New Press, 2000.

Robertson, Kathryn. *Gender-Based Violence in Timor-Leste: A Case Study*. Dili: UNFPA Women, Peace and Security Technical Division and PRADET Timor Lorosa'e, 2005.

Robinson, Darryl. 'Serving the Interests of Justice: Amnesties, Truth Commissions and the International Criminal Court', (2003) *European Journal of International Law* 14(3): 481–505.

Robinson, Jennifer. 'Dealing with *Memoria Passionis* in Papua'. Honours thesis, Australian National University, 2005.

Rohland, Klaus and Sarah Cliffe. 'The East Timor Reconstruction Program: Successes, Problems and Tradeoffs'. *Conflict Prevention and Reconstruction Unit Working Paper No. 11*, World Bank Group, 2002.

Roht-Arriaza, Naomi. *The Pinochet Effect: Transnational Justice in the Age of Human Rights*. Pennsylvania: Penn Press, 2006.

Roht-Arriaza, Naomi, and Javier Mariezcurrena (eds). *Transitional Justice in the Twenty-First Century: Beyond Truth Versus Justice*. Cambridge: Cambridge University Press, 2006.

Romano, Cesare P.R., André Nollkaemper and Jann K. Kleffner. *Internationalized Criminal Courts: Sierra Leone, East Timor, Kosovo, and Cambodia*. Oxford: Oxford University Press, 2004.

Romany, Celia. 'Women as Aliens: A Feminist Critique of the Public/Private Distinction in International Human Rights Law', (1993) *Harvard Human Rights Journal* 6: 87.

Ross, Fiona. *Bearing Witness: Women and the truth and Reconciliation Commission in South Africa*. London: Pluto Press 2003.

Rosser, Emily. 'Depoliticised Speech and Sexed Visibility: Women, Gender and Sexual Violence in the 1999 Guatemalan Comisión para el Esclarecimiento Histórico Report', 1 (2007) *International Journal of Transitional Justice* 3: 391–410.

Roynestad, Emily. *Are Women Included or Excluded in Post-Conflict Reconstruction: A Case Study from Timor-Leste*. United Nations Division for the Advancement of Women (DAW) Expert Group Meeting on 'Peace Agreements as a Means for Promoting Gender Equality and Ensuring Participation of Women – A Framework of Model Provisions' EGM/PEACE/2003/BP.1 31. Ottawa, Canada, 10–13 November 2003.

Rubio-Marín, Ruth (ed.). *What Happened to the Women? Gender and Reparations for Human Rights Violations*. New York: Social Science Research Council, 2006.

Rubio-Marin, Ruth and Pablo de Grieff. 'Women and Reparations' (2007) *International Journal of Transitional Justice* 1(3): 318–37.

Rubin, Alfred P., '*Actio Popularis, Jus Cogens* and Offenses *Erga Omnes*?' (2001) *New England Law Review* 35(2): 265–80.

Ryan, Alan. *Primary Responsibilities and Primary Risks: Australian Defence Force Participation in the International Force East Timor. Land Warfare Studies Centre Study Paper No. 304*. Duntroon, ACT: Land Warfare Studies Centre, 2000.

Sachse, Henriette. 'East Timor: Is the Country Back on Track?', *Asian Analysis*, December 2006.

Sadat, Leila Nadya. 'The Legacy of the ICTY: The International Criminal Court', (2002) *New England Law Review* 37(4): 1073–80.

Salla, Michael E. 'Promoting Reconciliation in East Timor: Imperatives for Transition to Self-government', (2000) *Pacific Review* 12(1): 33–46.

Sarkin, Jeremy and Erin Daly. 'Too Many Questions, Too Few Answers: Reconciliation in Transitional Societies', (2004) 35 *Colombia Human Rights Law Review* 661: 664.

Saul, Ben. 'Was the Conflict in East Timor "Genocide" and Why Does it Matter?', (2001) 2 *Melbourne Journal of International Law* 2.

Savage, David. *Dancing with the Devil: A Personal Account of Policing the East Timor Vote for Independence. Monash Papers on Southeast Asia No. 57*. Clayton, Vic: Monash Asia Institute, 2002.

Scheiner, Charles. 'Suggestions for the Next United Nations Mission in Timor-Leste'. *La'o Hamutuk: Timor-Leste Institute for Reconstruction Monitoring and Analysis*. Dili, 2006.

Schirmer, Jennifer. 'The Seeking of Truth and the Gendering of Consciousness: The Co-Madres of El Salvador and the Conavigua Widows of Guatemala'. Sarah A. Radcliffe and Sally Westwood (eds). *Viva, Women and Popular Protest in Latin America*. London: Routledge, 1993, 360–64.

Schofield, Toni and Carol Bacchi, 'Reinventing Gender Equality and the Political', Conference paper, University of Sydney, 29–30 September 2005.

Schroeter, Simi Daniel. 'Senses of Violence and the Education of Senses: Gender, Body and Violence in the Independent East Timor', (2006) *Lusotopie* 13(2): 155–72.

Schwarz, Adam. *A Nation in Waiting: Indonesia's Search for Stability*. Boulder, CO: Westview Press, 2000.

Scott, Catherine. 'The Feminine Face of Resistance'. Torben Retbøll (ed.). *East Timor: Occupation and Resistance*. Copenhagen: International Work Group for Indigenous Affairs, 1998, 141–152.

Scott, Shirley. 'International Law as Ideology: Theorizing the Relationship between International Law and International Politics', (1994) *European Journal of International Law* 5(1): 325.

Secretary-General, United Nations. *Identical letters dated 31 January 2000 from the Secretary-General. The President of the General Assembly, the President of the Security Council and the Chairperson of the Commission on Human Rights*. New York: United Nations General Assembly. United Nations Doc. A/54/726, January 2000.

Secretary-General, United Nations. *Women, Peace and Security, Study Submitted by the Secretary-General Pursuant to Security Council Resolution 1325 (2000)*. United Nations Doc S/2002/1154. New York: United Nations, 2002.

Secretary-General, United Nations. *Report to the Security Council, on the Rule of Law and Transitional Justice in Conflict and Post-Conflict Societies*. United Nations Doc S/2004/616, 23 August 2004.

Secretary-General, United Nations. *Report of the Secretary-General on Justice and Reconciliation for Timor-Leste*. New York: United Nations, 2006.

Secretary-General, United Nations. *Report of the Secretary-General on Timor-Leste Pursuant to Security Council Resolution 1690 (2006)*. New York: United Nations, 2006.

Security Council, United Nations. *Report of the Security Council Mission to Jakarta and Dili, 8 to 12 September 1999*. New York, 1999.

Security Council, United Nations. *Resolutions 1264 and 1272*. New York, 1999.

Security Council, United Nations. *Resolution 1325*. New York, 2000.

Security Council, United Nations. 'Timor-Leste Making Steady Progress Towards Self-Sufficiency, but Continued International Assistance Needed, Security Council Told'. New York, 2004.

Security Council, United Nations. 'Security Council Establishes One-Year Political Mission in Timor-Leste, Unanimously Adopting Resolution 1599 (2005). United Nations Office Will Remain until 20 May 2006, Supporting Development of Police, Border Patrol, Other Critical Institutions'. *Press Release SC/8371*. New York, 2005.

Security Council, United Nations. *United Nations Determined Not to Abandon Timor-Leste at Critical Time of Need*. New York, 2006.

Security Council Mission, United Nations. 'Report of the Security Council Mission to Jakarta and Dili'. New York: United Nations, 1999.

Seifert, Ruth. 'War and Rape: A Preliminary Analysis'. Alexandra Stiglmayer (ed.), *Mass Rape: The War Against Women in Bosnia-Herzegovina*. Lincoln and London: University of Nebraska Press, 1995, 54–72.

Sen, Gita and Caren Grown. *Development, Crises and Alternative Visions: Third World Women Perspectives*. New York: Monthly Review, 1987.

Serious Crimes Unit. 'Information Release. Crimes against Humanity Rape Charges for Five TNI Soldiers'. Dili, 2003.

Serious Crimes Unit. 'Information Release. Indonesian Aitarak Militia Commander and Aitarak Militia Member Convicted of Crimes against Humanity, Murder by Special Panel Judges'. Dili, 2004.

Shaw, Rosalind. 'Rethinking Truth and Reconciliation Commissions: Lessons from Sierra Leone'. *United States Institute of Peace Special Report No 130*. Washington DC: United States Institute of Peace, February 2005.

Shelton, D. 'Private Violations, Public Wrongs, and the Responsibility of States', (1989) 13 *Fordham International Law Journal* 23. 1{-]34.

Siapno, Jacqueline. 'Bitter Taste of Victory'. *Inside Indonesia*, Oct–Nov 2006.

Siapno, Jacqueline. 'Whispered Confidences: Articulating the Female in the PNTL (Police) and the F-FDTL (Military) in Timor-Leste', *IIAS Newsletter: Women Warriors* 2008, Leiden, 48: 7–8.

Siapno, Jacqueline. 'Living through Terror: Everyday Resilience in East Timor and Aceh', (2009) *Social Identities*, 15(1): 43–64.

Sierra Leone's Truth and Reconciliation Commission. *Witness to Truth: Report of the Sierra Leone Truth and Reconciliation Commission*. 2004.

Simonsen, Sven Gunnar. 'The Authoritarian Temptation in East Timor: Nation-building and the Need for Inclusive Governance', (2006) *Asian Survey* 46(4): 575–96.

Sissons, Miranda E. *From One Day to Another: Violations of Women's Reproductive and Sexual Rights in East Timor*. Melbourne: East Timor Human Rights Centre, 1997.

Smart, Carol (ed.). 'The Problem of Rights'. *Feminism and the Power of Law*. London/ New York: Taylor and Francis, 1989.

Smith, Michael G. and Moreen Dee. *Peacekeeping in East Timor: The Path to Independence, International Peace Academy Occasional Paper Series*. Boulder, CO: Lynne Rienner Publishers, 2003.

Snyder, Jack and Leslie Vinjamuri. 'Trials and Errors: Principle and Pragmatism in Strategies of International Justice', (2003 – 2004) *International Security* 28(3).

Snyder, Jack and Leslie Vinjamuri. 'Advocacy and Scholarship in the Study of International War Crime Tribunals and Transitional Justice', (2004) *Annual Review of Political Science* 7: 345–62.

Suharto. *Address by His Excellency Suharto, President of the Republic of Indonesia, before the Extraordinary Session of the Regional House of People's Representatives of East Timor, Dili, July 17, 1978*. Jakarta: Departemen Penerangan, 1978.

Sorensen, Brigitte. 'Women and Post-Conflict Reconstruction: Issues and Sources', *The War-Torn Societies Project Occasional Paper no. 3*, Geneva: UN Research Institute for Social Development, June 1998.

Special Rapporteurs, United Nations. *Report on the Joint Mission to East Timor Undertaken by the Special Rapporteur on Extrajudicial, Summary or Arbitrary Executions, the Special Rapporteur on the Question of Torture, and the Special Rapporteur on Violence against Women, its Causes and Consequences. Situation of Human Rights in East Timor*. Geneva: United Nations, 1999.

Stahn, Carsten. 'Accommodating Individual Criminal Responsibility and National Reconciliation: The United Nations Truth Commission for East Timor', (2001) *American Journal of International Law* 95(4): 952–66.

Stanley, Elizabeth. *Torture, Truth and Justice: The Case of Timor Leste*. NY and London: Routledge, 2009.

Steiner, Henry J. and Philip Alston. *International Human Rights in Context: Law, Politics, Morals: Text and Materials*. Oxford New York: Clarendon Press; Oxford University Press, 1996.

Steiner, Henry J. and Philip Alston. 'An Overview of UN Procedures through the Lens of a Single Case: East Timor'. *International Human Rights in Context: Law, Politics, Morals*. Oxford: Oxford University Press, 2000, 672 – 694.

Stiglmayer, Alexandra (ed.). *Mass Rape: The War against Women in Bosnia-Herzegovina*. Lincoln: University of Nebraska Press, 1994.

Strang, Heather and John Braithwaite. *Restorative Justice: Philosophy to Practice.* Aldershot: Dartmouth, 2000.

Strohmeyer, Hansjoerg. 'Building a New Judiciary for East Timor: Challenges of a Fledgling Nation', (2000) *Criminal Law Forum* 11: 259.

Strohmeyer, Hansjoerg. 'Collapse and Reconstruction of a Judicial System: The United Nations Missions in Kosovo and East Timor' (Symposium: State Reconstruction after Civil Conflict) (2001), *American Journal of International Law* 95: 43–63.

Sunindyo, S. 'When the Earth is Female and the Nation is Mother: Gender, the Armed Forces and Nationalism in Indonesia', (1998) *Feminist Review* 58:1–21.

Swaine, Aisling. *Traditional Justice and Gender Based Violence Research Report.* Dili: International Rescue Committee, 2003.

Tanter, Richard. 'Practical Justice in Doe v. Lumintang: the Successful Use of Civil Remedies against "an Enemy of All Mankind"'. Richard Tanter, Gerry van Klinken and Desmond Ball (eds). *Masters of Terror: Indonesia's Military and Violence in East Timor.* Canberra: Rowman and Littlefield, 2006, 157–75.

Tapol. 'The 1987 Indonesian Election in East Timor'. Thornton Heath, Surrey, 1987.

Tapol. 'Ending the Cycle of Impunity: Can the East Timor Investigations Pave the Way?' Thornton Heath, Surrey, 2000.

Tapol and United Nations. General Assembly Special Committee on the Situation With Regard to the Implementation of the Declaration on the Granting of Independence to Colonial Countries and Peoples. *Statement on the Question of East Timor to the United Nations Committee of 24, August 1988. Tapol Occasional Reports No. 9.* Thornton Heath, Surrey, 1988.

Taylor, John. 'East Timor: Contemporary History'. P. Carey and G. Carter Bentley (eds). *East Timor at the Crossroads: The Forging of a Nation.* London: Cassell, 1995: 240.

Taylor, John G. *East Timor: The Price of Freedom.* New York: Zed Books Ltd: Annandale NSW: Pluto Press, 1999.

Teitel, Ruti G. *Transitional Justice.* Oxford; New York: Oxford University Press, 2000.

Teitel Ruti G. 'The Alien Tort and the Global Rule of Law', (2005) *International Social Science Journal* 57(185): 551–560.

Terrell, Fleming. 'Unofficial Accountability: A Proposal for the Permanent Women's Tribunal on Sexual Violence in Armed Conflict', (2005) *Texas Journal of Women and the Law 15(1): 107.*

The Post-CAVR Technical Secretariat. 'Post CAVR Update September–October 2006'. Dili, 2006.

Tim Kemanusiaan Timor Barat. 'Violence against IDP/Refugee Women'. *Report of TKTB (Tim Kemanusiaan Timor Barat) Findings in IDP/Refugee Camps in West Timor.* Jakarta: Tim Kemanusiaan Timor Barat, 2000.

Trembath, Anna and Damian Grenfell. *Mapping the Pursuit of Gender Equality: Non-Government and International Agency Activity in Timor-Leste.* Melbourne: Globalism Institute, RMIT University, and Irish Aid, 2007.

Turshen, M., S. Meintjes and A. Pillay (eds). *The Aftermath: Women in Post-Conflict Transformation.* London, New York: Zed, 2001.

United Nations. *High Commissioner for Human Rights Reports on the Situation in East Timor as the Commission on Human Rights Considers Holding Special Meeting*'. Media release. HR/99/90, Geneva, 17 September 1999.

United Nations. *The United Nations and East Timor: Self-Determination through Popular Consultation.* New York: Dept. of Public Information United Nations, 2000.

United Nations Commission on Human Rights. Sub-Commission on Prevention of Discrimination and Protection of Minorities, Special Rapporteur, Theo Van Boven. *Study Concerning The Right To Restitution, Compensation And Rehabilitation For Victims Of Gross Violations Of Human Rights And Fundamental Freedoms*, U.N. Doc. E/CN.4/Sub.2/1992/8 (interim report); E/CN.4/Sub.2/1993/8 (final report); E/CN.4/sub.2/1996/17 (amended principles), Geneva, 1993.

United Nations Commission on Human Rights. Special Rapporteur on Amnesties, Louis Joinet. *The Administration of Justice and the Human Rights of Detainees,* ESCOR, 48th Sess., Annex II, U.N. Doc. E/CN.4/Sub 2/1996/18, Geneva, 1996.

United Nations Commission on Human Rights. Independent Expert, M. Cherif Bassiouni. *Report on the Right to Restitution, Compensation and Rehabilitation for Victims of Grave Violations of Human Rights and Fundamental Freedoms*. United Nations Doc E/CN.4/2000/62, Geneva, 2000.

United Nations Development Programme. *East Timor National Human Development Report: Ukan Rasik A'an: The Way Ahead.* Dili: United Nations Development Programme, 2002.

United Nations Development Programme, 'More Women Die in Childbirth in East Timor than Anywhere in East Asia'. Press release for International Women's Day. Dili, 8 March 2002.

United Nations Development Programme. *Human Development Report 2006 Timor-Leste: The Path out of Poverty, Integrated Rural Development.* Dili: UNDP, 2006.

United Nations General Assembly. Resolution 1542 (XV). New York, 1960.

United Nations General Assembly. *United Nations Declaration on the Elimination of Violence against Women.* 1993.

United Nations General Assembly. Resolution 60/147 of 16 December 2005, A/RES/60/147; 13 IHRR 907 (2006).

United Nations General Assembly. *Report of the United Nations Independent Special Commission of Inquiry for Timor-Leste.* Geneva: United Nations, 2006.

United Nations High Commissioner for Human Rights. 'UNHCR News, Timor Emergency Update'. 25 November1999.

United Nations International Training and Research Institute for the Advancement of Women (INSTRAW). *Securing Equality, Engendering Peace: A Guide to Policy and Planning on Women, Peace and Security*. Dominican Republic, 2005.

United Nations Mission of International Support for East Timor. 'Progress Report of the Secretary-General on the United Nations Mission of Support in East Timor (29 April to 13 August 2004) United Nations Security Council S/2004/669, 13 August 2004, Para 5'. UNMISET, 2004.

United Nations News Centre. 'Timor-Leste, Not United Nations, Indicts Indonesian General for War Crimes'. Dili, 2003.

United Nations Population Fund. *Gender-Based Violence in Timor-Leste: A Case Study.* New York: UNFPA, 2005.

United Nations Populations Fund. *Global Review of Challenges and Good Practices in Support of Women in Conflict and Post-Conflict Situations.* Hammamet, Tunisia: UNFPA, June 2007.

United States Central Intelligence Agency (CIA), *The World Factbook*, 20 March 2008.

United States Department of State. 'Country Reports on Human Rights Practices – 2003: East Timor'. Washington: Bureau of Democracy, Human Rights and Labor, 2004.

United States Department of State. 'Country Reports on Human Rights Practices – 2004: East Timor'. Washington: Bureau of Democracy, Human Rights and Labour, 2005.

UNTAET Daily Briefing. 'Lolotoe Trial Begins Phase Of Hearing Witnesses', 7 May 2002.

Valji, Nahla. 'Gender, Justice and Reconciliation'. Berlin: Friedrich-Ebert-Stiftung (FES), November 2007.

Villa-Vicencio, Charles. 'The Reek of Cruelty and the Quest for Healing – Where Retributive and Restorative Justice Meet', (1999/2000) *Journal of Law and Religion* 14: 165–87.

Villa-Vicencio, Charles. 'Why Perpetrators Should not Always Be Prosecuted: Where the International Criminal Court and Truth Commissions Meet', (2000) *Emory Law Journal* 49: 205.

Viseur-Sellers, Patricia. 'Individual(s') Liability for Collective Sexual Violence', Karen Knop (ed.). *Gender and Human Rights*. Oxford: Oxford University Press, 2004. 153[-]194.

Walsh, Pat. 'East Timor's Political Parties and Groupings'. *Briefing Notes*. Canberra: Australian Council for Overseas Aid, 2001.

Wandita, Galuh. 'The Tears Have Not Stopped, the Violence Has Not Ended: Political Upheaval, Ethnicity, and Violence against Women in Indonesia', (1998) *Gender and Development* 6(3): 34–41.

Wandita, Galuh, Karen Campbell-Nelson and Manuela Leong Pereira. 'Gender and Reparations in Timor-Leste'. Ruth Rubio-Marin (ed.). *Engendering Reparations: Recognising and Compensating Women Victims of Human Rights Violations*. New York: International Center for Transitional Justice, 2006.

Webb, Phillipa. 'Paths to Peace: Experiments in Post-conflict Justice in East Timor', (2004) *Conflict Resolution Journal* (Columbia University School of International and Public Affairs): 41–64.

Weitekamp, Elmar G. M. and Hans-Jèurgen Kerner. *Restorative Justice in Context: International Practice and Directions*. Cullompton: Willan, 2003.

Wessel, Ingrid and Georgia Wimhöfer. *Violence in Indonesia*. Hamburg: Abera, 2001.

Wexler, David B. and Bruce J. Winnick. *Law in a Therapeutic Key*. Durham, North Carolina; Carolina Academic Press 1996.

Wheeler, Nicholas J. and Timothy Dunne. 'East Timor and the New Humanitarian Interventionism', (2001) *International Affairs* 77(4): 805–27.

White, Ken. *Criado: A Story of East Timor*. Briar Hill, Vic.: Indra Publishing, 2002.

Winters, Rebecca (ed.). *Buibere: Voice of East Timorese Women*. Darwin, NT: East Timor International Support Center, 1999.

Winters, Rebecca and Brian Kelly. *Children of the Resistance: The Current Situation in East Timor as Seen through the Eyes of Two Australian Tourists*. Darwin: Australians for a Free East Timor, 1996.

Wolfson, Steven. 'Refugees and Transitional Justice', (2005) *Refugee Survey Quarterly* 24(4): 55–59.

Women's Caucus for Gender Justice. *War Crimes Draft Text*. New York: Women's Caucus for Gender Justice, 1997.

Women's Commission for Refugee Women and Children. *Displaced Women and Girls at Risk: Risk Factors, Protection Solutions and Resource Tools*. New York, 2006.

World Bank. *Timor Leste at a Glance*. Dili: World Bank, 2003.

World Bank. *Gender, Justice and Truth Commissions*. Washington: World Bank, 2006.

World Council of Churches (WCC), and Christian Conference of Asia (CCA). *Women to Women: A Solidarity Visit to Indonesia and East Timor, 23 June – 1 July 1999*. Geneva: World Council of Churches, 1999.

World Health Organisation, *WHO's Contribution to Health Sector Development in East Timor*, WHO: Dili, July 2001.

Yayasan Hak and Nug Katjasungkana, Solidarity Forum for East Timor in Indonesia (FORTILOS). *The Justice Process in Indonesia Regarding the Prosecution of the Serious Crimes Cases of Human Rights Violation in East Timor in 1999.* Dili, 16 October 2001.

Young, Alison. 'The Wasteland of the Law, the Wordless Song of the Rape Victim', (1998) *Melbourne University Law Review* 22: 442.

Zahar, Alexander. 'Commentary on Trial Judgments of the East Timor Special Panels in the Cases of José Cardoso Ferreira and Agustinho Atolan' (1 December 2008). *Annotated Leading Cases Of International Criminal Tribunals*, Vol. 13: Timor Leste: The Special Panels For Serious Crimes, 2001–3, André Klip and Göran Sluiter (eds), pp. 762–65, Intersentia, 2008. Available at SSRN: http://ssrn.com/abstract = 1358038.

Zuburchen, Mary S. 'History, Memory and the "1965 Incident" in Indonesia', (2002) *Asian Survey* 42: 564.

Zyl, Paul van. 'Justice without Punishment: Guaranteeing Human Rights in Transitional Societies'. Charles Villa-Vicencio and Wilhelm Verwoerd (eds). *Looking Back Reaching Forward: Reflections on the Truth and Reconciliation Commission of South Africa*. Cape Town: UCT Press, 2000: 42–53.

MEDIA PUBLICATIONS

AAP. 'Indonesia Sets up Truth Commission'. *The Age*, 8 September 2004.

AAP. 'Probe on Atrocities'. Jakarta, 7 September 2004.

ABC Radio Asia-Pacific. 'East Timor: Indonesia's Actions "Genocide" says Expert'. 29 August 2001.

ABC Radio Australia. 'Portugal Welcomes Timor into United Nations'. *Radio Australia News*. Sydney, 2002.

ABC Radio Australia. 'East Timor: First Lady Calls on PM Alkatiri to Respond to L-7'. *Asia Pacific*. Australia: ABC, 2004.

ABC Radio Australia. 'East Timor's Population Is on the Rise'. *Asia Pacific*. Sydney: ABC, 2004.

ABC TV, 'United Nations Aid Workers Killed in West Timor', *Lateline*. 6 September 2000.

Agence France Presse. 'Scars of Vote Violence Remain Real for Many East Timor Women'. 19 November 2000.

Agence France Presse, 'East Timor Massacre Survivors Shun Jakarta Trial over Safety Fears'. 4 June 2002.

Agence France Presse. 'Rights Court Acquits Former Dili Military Chief'. 29 November 2002.

Agence France Presse. 'US Can Work with a Future President Wiranto, Ambassador Says'. 22 April 2004.

Agence France Presse.. 'Indonesian Ministers Tell Washington to Keep Quiet on Timor Verdicts'. 12 August 2004.

Agence France Presse. 'Gusmão Regrets Jailing of Former East Timor Governor'. Dili, 2004.

Agence France Presse. 'Timor Truth Commission to Question Indonesian Generals over 1999 Violence'. Jakarta, 20 November 2006.

Agence France Presse. 'Three Suspects Arrested for Killing of Timorese 'Witches'. 10 January 2007.

Agence France Presse. 'East Timor Ends Era of Camps'. Dili, 17 June 2009.

Amnesty International. *Women in Indonesia and East Timor*. AI Index ASA 21/51/1995.

Amnesty International. '200,000 Dead. Enough is Enough'. *New York Times* (advertisement), 23 September 1999.

Antara. 'Annan: No Need for International Tribunal If Republic of Indonesia Itself Can Uphold Justice'. 16 February 2000.

Antara. 'RI Needs to Remain Alert About Possibility of International Tribunal'. 16 February 2000.

Antara. 'RI to Decide What to Do with United Nations Commission of Experts on East Timor'. Jakarta, 10 September 2004.

Antara. 'U.N. Secretary-General Dissatisfied with Indonesia's Ad-Hoc Court for Rights Abuses in East Timor'. New York, 8 September 2004.

Associated Press. 'UN Distances Itself from Report on East Timor War Crimes'. 20 April 2001.

Associated Press. 'Revenge is Low on the List of Priorities'. *The Weekend Australian*, 18–19 May 2002.

Associated Press. 'East Timor Trial Verdicts Expected: Will Justice Be Done?'. 11 August 2002.

Associated Press. 'Indonesia Will Ignore Indictments of Ex-Officials'. Jakarta, 25 February 2003.

Associated Press. 'East Timor Suspect to Run in Indonesia'. Jakarta, 15 December 2004.

Associated Press. 'East Timor's Ex-Governor to Resist Arrest over 1999 Violence'. Jakarta, 2004.

Associated Press. 'East Timor's Foreign Minister Opposes Rights Tribunal'. Jakarta, 2004.

Associated Press. 'Indonesian General's Election Bid Decried'. Jakarta, 2004.

Associated Press. 'Indonesia Stung over US Criticism of Timor Acquittals'. Jakarta, 2004.

Associated Press. 'Indonesian Supreme Court Upholds Timor-Leste Governor Conviction, Acquits Indonesian Military Officer'. Jakarta, 2004.

Associated Press. 'Supreme Court Clears Three Indonesian Officials in Timor Violence'. 2004.

Associated Press. 'Indonesian Court Rules Truth Commission #illegal, Casts Doubt on Justice for Suharto Abuses'. 7 December 2006.

Balowski, James. 'TNI Let off the Hook Again'. *Green Left Weekly*, Issue 519, 4 December 2002.

BBC News. 'Court Slams Belgrade Resistance'. The Hague, 4 May 2004.

BBC News. 'Ex-East Timor Governor Acquitted'. Jakarta, November 2004.

BBC News. 'Timor Governor's Sentence Upheld'. Jakarta, November 2004.

Berkely, Bill. 'Judgment Day'. *Washington Post Magazine*, 11 October 1998.

Boyd, Sarah. 'Timor Justice Slow but Sure'. *Asia Intelligence Wire*, 29 July 2004.

Brittain, Victoria. 'Traumatised Timorese Women'. *The Guardian*, Dili, 30 July 2001.

Clausen, Lisa. 'Slow Road to Justice'. *Time Magazine*, 17 March 2003.

CNN. 'U.N. Chief Says International Court Possible for East Timor'. 18 February 2000.

CNN International Diplomatic License. 'Indonesia and East Timor Welcome Kofi Annan'. Jakarta, 2000.

Cooper, Helen. 'Waiting for their Moment in the Worst Place on Earth to Be a Woman'. *New York Times*, 16 November 2005.

Davis, Mark. *Abilio Soare–the Man in the Middle*. Melbourne: SBS Radio, 2004.

Detik Com. 'Indonesian Politicians React to United Nations Move to Indict Senior Military'. 26 February 2003.

Deutsche Presse-Agentur. 'Senior U.N. official fears Indonesian human rights commission will not work'. 3 February 2000.

Dodd, Mark. 'A Family in East Timor Grieves for a Daughter'. *International Herald Tribune*, 22 December 2000.

Dodd, Mark. 'Massacres Go Unpunished as United Nations Crimes Unit Heads for Collapse'. *Sydney Morning Herald*, 1 May 2001.

ETAN, 'East Timor Action Network Hails $66 Million Judgment in Rights Lawsuit Against Indonesian General', *ETAN media release*, 2000.

ETAN. 'Congress Disappointed with Secretary Rumsfeld's Plans for U.S.-Indonesia Military Ties: Calls for Reconsideration of Bilateral Defense Dialogue'. New York, 2004.

Ferreira, Joao. 'Judge Rapoza Reflects on East Timor Tribunal'. *The Standard Times*, 12 November 2005, p. A1.

Forbes, Mark. 'Indonesian Rule "Led to 100,000 East Timor Dead"'. *Sydney Morning Herald*, 20 December 2005.

Greenlees, Don. 'Human Rights Are on Trial, and So Is the Court'. *The Australian*, 25 November 2002, p. 12.

Greenlees, Don. 'Court Accused of Human Rights Bias'. *The Weekend Australian*, 30 November 2002, p. 15.

Greenlees, Don. 'Smiles, but Still No Justice'. *The Australian*. 2 December 2002, p. 12.

Guilart, Guido. 'Indonesian Military Forced Women to Become Sex Slaves'. Associated Press, 29 April 2003.

Gusmão, Kirsty Sword. 'Opinion: Women Suffering in Silence'. *The Australian*, 7 July 2006.

Harahap, Franz, F. Rumhardjono, and Machmudi Romli. *Newspaper Articles on East Timor*. Jakarta: Department of Information, Republic of Indonesia, 1977.

Havely, Joe. 'Timor's Army Marches out of the Jungle'. CNN.Com, 19 May 2002.

Hukill, Traci. *UN Wire*. Dili, 4 May 2004.

Hyland, Tom. 'Indonesia was behind Timor atrocities, says report'. *The Age*, 11 July 2008.

Hyland, Tom. 'Amid the Major Flaws, a Minor Act of Courage'. *The Age*, 11 July 2008.

Iggulden, Tom. 'East Timor Plays Down Damning UN Report'. ABC Radio National AM, 19 January 2006.

Inbaraj, Sonny. 'East Timor: Pressure for International Tribunal Grows'. Inter Press Service News, 2000.

Inbaraj, Sonny. 'Human Rights Day: East Timor Invasion Leaves Haunting Legacy'. Inter Press Service News, 10 December 2005.

Indonesia Observer. 'RI Opposed to International Tribunal'. 26 January 2000.

Jakarta Post. 'East Timor Inquiry Impresses Global Community'. 2 February 2000.

Jakarta Post. 'Indonesia Vows to Avoid War Crimes Court'. 8 December 1999.

Jakarta Post. ' Abilio to Continue Judicial Process'. Jakarta, 2005.

Jolliffe, Jill. 'Timor's Haunted Women'. *The Age*, 3 November 2001.

Jolliffe, Jill. 'Sex Slaves the Prize for Army, Timor Court Told'. *Sydney Morning Herald*, 2 May 2003.

Jolliffe, Jill. 'Jakarta's Timor Trials "A Sham"'. *The Age*, Darwin, 19 June 2005.

Jolliffe, Jill. 'Suffer the Children Caught in Timor Crossfire'. *Canberra Times*, 24 August 2007.

Keady, Maryanne. 'Concern over Future of Serious Crimes Unit'. *ABC Radio Australia*, 29 April 2003.

Kearney, Christine. 'What It Feels Like to Have to Run'. *Eureka Street*. Melbourne, 23 January 2007.

Keatinge, Douglas. 'All to Play for in East Timor's Modest Aid Gesture'. *The Irish Times*, 31 January 2005.

Khalik, Abdul. 'Indictment of Soldiers Who Murder Civilians Weak: Experts'. *The Jakarta Post*, 23 August 2004.

Kurniawan, M.N. 'Guterres Ready to Carry the Can for Military'. *The Jakarta Post,* 26 November 2002.

Kurniawan, M.N. 'No Hope of Punishment Military, Police in Rights Cases'. *Jakarta Post*, 2 December 2002.

Laksamana.Net. '18 Tried, 16 Acquitted'. 18 July 2004.

Lam, Sen.'Timor: No Compensation Wanted for Occupation'. ABC Radio Australia, 1 December 2005.

La'o Hamutuk Press Release. 'Public Figure Detained Again for Domestic Violence', 12 July 2001.

Lloyd, P. 'Militia Leader Sentenced'. ABC Radio Australia. Sydney, 2002.

LoPresti, L. 'Critics Say Guterres Sentence Is Meaningless'. ABC Radio Australia. Sydney, 2002.

Lusa. 'Jakarta Court Acquittals "Scandalous": Ramos-Horta'. Jakarta, 2002.

Lusa. 'East Timor: PM Alkatiri Wants Amnesty for Crimes of 1999'. Jakarta, 2003.

Lusa. 'East Timor: General Wiranto Said Ready for Dili Video-Conference Atrocity Hearing'. Jalarta, 4 February 2004.

Lusa. 'Demonstrators Protest Wiranto Meeting on Gusmão's Return'. Jakarta, 31 May 2004

MacGregor, Marion. 'East Timor: Last Indonesian Governor is First Jailed over Violence'. *Asia Pacific*. Sydney: Asia Pacific/Radio Australia, 2004.

Martinkus, John. 'Beyond Justice'. *The Bulletin*, 11 June 2002, p. 34.

McBeth, John. 'Commentary: Juggling Pragmatic Politics with Bloody Past'. *The Straits Times*, 19 December 2005.

McDonald, Hamish. 'Australia's Bloody East Timor Secret', *Sydney Morning Herald*, 14 March 2002.

McDonald, Hamish. 'Guterres: The One that Didn't Get Away'. *The Age,* Melbourne, 30 November 2002.

Maslan, M. Rizal. 'Rights Activists Want Truth and Reconciliation Commission Disbanded', *Detik.com*, Jakarta, 28 August 2006.

Montlake, Simon. 'Female Backers of Aceh's Rebels Now Battle to Rebuild Lives', *Christian Science Monitor*. Pidie, 11 January 2007.

Moore, Matthew. 'Militia Leader Guterres Gets 10 Years'. *The Age*, 28 November 2002, p. 17.

Moore, Matthew. 'Lay Off Wiranto, Gusmão Tells Law Man'. *Sydney Morning Herald*, 25 May 2004.

Munro, Cathy. 'East Timor Atrocities Set for Human Rights Court'. *The Canberra Times*, 23 August 2001, p.10.

Murdoch, Lindsay. 'East Timor Tense as Soldiers Desert Barracks'. *Sydney Morning Herald*, 30 March 2006, p.10.

Murdoch, Lindsay. 'East Timor's Soldiers "Treated Like Dogs"'. *The Age*. 30 March 2006, p.12.

Murdoch, Lindsay. 'United Nations Acts to Stamp out Abuse by Staff in East Timor'. *The Age*. 30 August 2006, p. 9.

Mydans, Seth. 'Sexual Violence as Tool of War: Pattern Emerging in East Timor'. *New York Times*, 1 March 2001.

Mydans, Seth. 'Modest Beginnings for East Timor's Justice System'. *New York Times*, 4 March 2001, p.10.

Nakashima, Ellen. 'Indonesia Attempts to Avert Tribunal to Probe East Timor', *Washington Post* (Washington), 16 July 2005.

Nakashima, Ellen. 'For Survivors of East Timor Massacres, Justice Still Elusive', *Washington Post* (Washington), 18 September 2005.

Newsweek. 'Keepers of the Peace'. 14 November 2005.

O'Kane, Mary. 'East Timor: Return of the Revolutionaries'. *The Guardian*, 15 January 2001.

Organização Popular da Mulher Timor (OPMT). 'Letter to the Editor: Response to Kirsty Sword Gusmão's Opinion in the Australian Newspaper Dated 7 July 2006'. *The Australian*, 8 July 2006.

Perkins, Miki. 'Forgotten Victims of East Timor's Independence'. *The Age* (Melbourne), 16 June 2009.

Powell, Sian. 'East Timor's Children of the Enemy'. *The Weekend Australian*, 10 March 2001.

Powell, Sian. 'Ex-Governor Jailed for Timor Carnage'. *The Australian*, 19 July 2004.

Powell, Sian. 'East Timor Forgoes Justice for the Rape of a Nation'. *The Australian*, Jakarta, 1 August 2005.

Powell, Sian. 'UN Verdict on East Timor'. *The Australian*, 19 January 2006.

Powell, Sian.'Leaders Favour Silence on Horrors with Indonesia', *The Australian*, 19 January 2006.

Republika. 'Constitutional Court Rejects Abilio Soares' Proposal'. Jakarta, 2005.

Reuters. 'ICTY Reports to United Nations over Belgrade Resistance'. 6 May 2004.

Riley, Mark.'UN Scorn at Jakarta Justice for Timor', *Sydney Morning Herald,* 2 February 2000.

Rimmer, Susan Harris. 'Struggle Continues for Timor Occupation Survivors', Opinion Editorial, *The Canberra Times*, 3 November 2008.

Ryan, Randolph. 'Indonesia Aide Told to Pay $14m in Suit over Death'. *The Boston Globe*, 28 October 1994.

Saraswati, Muninggar Sri. 'Commission Could Be "Whitewash Machine"'. *The Jakarta Post*, 9 September 2004.

Saunders, Joe. 'Wheels of Justice: Unfinished Business in East Timor'. *Asian Wall Street Journal*, 30 August 2000.

Siboro, Tiarma. 'Rights Abusers Should Be Executed: East Timor Leader'. *The Jakarta Post*, 29 November 2002.

Siboro, Tiarma. 'SBY Told to Summon AG over General's E. Timor Acquittal'. *The Jakarta Post*, 10 March 2005.

Siboro, Tiarma, and Tertiani ZB Simanjuntak. 'Indonesian Government Unveils Names of Rights Tribunal Judges'. *The Jakarta Post*, 15 January 2002.

Simamora, Adianto P. 'RI Rejects Int'l Tribunal for E. Timor Human Rights Abuses'. *The Jakarta Post*, 12 August 2004.

Sipress, Alan. 'East Timorese Struggling for Survival'. *Washington Post*, 8 October 2003.

Sturken, Marita. 'The Wall, the Screen, and the Image: The Vietnam Veterans Memorial' (1991) *Representations*, No. 35, Special Issue: Monumental Histories (Summer), pp. 118–42.

Suara Timor Lorosae. 'Luis Carrilho: The Law Does not Recognize "Public Figures"'. 12 July 2001.

Suara Timor Lorosae. 'Fokupers not Using Dr Sergio Lobo's Case to Seek More Funding'. Dili, 20 July 2001.

Sydney Morning Herald. 'Editorial: Indonesia's Generals Take a Back Seat'. 23 August 2004.

Taufiqurrahman, M. 'Reopening East Timor Cases Possible, Says Ago'. *The Jakarta Post*, 10 November 2004.

Taufiqurrahman, M. 'Amnesties OK for Timor Leste Rights Violators, Says Body', *Jakarta Post*, Jakarta, 17 January 2007.

Tempo Magazine. 'Xanana and Wiranto Meeting Reaped Condemnations in Timor-Leste'. 8–14 June 2004.

Thakur, Ramesh. 'East Timor: When Peace and Justice Collide', *International Herald Tribune* (Hong Kong), 31 August 2005.

The Guardian. 'United Nations Indicts General for East Timor Crimes'. 25 February 2003.

The La'o Hamutuk Bulletin. 'Editorial: Women and the Reconstruction of East Timor'. August 2001.

The La'o Hamutuk Bulletin. 'Chronology of Justice and Accountability for East Timor'. October 2001.

The La'o Hamutuk Bulletin. 'Bilateral Aid to East Timor: An Overview'. Dili, December 2001.

The La'o Hamutuk Bulletin. 'Editorial: The United Nations: Aiding or Undermining a Resolution of the Refugee Crisis?' 2(4): 2001, 1.

Timberlake, Ian. 'We Did All We Could to Keep Peace – Wiranto'. *The Sydney Morning Herald*, 5 April 2002, p. 9.

Timberlake, Ian. 'Acquittals Show Untamed Might of Indonesian Military: Observers'. Agence France Presse, 12 August 2004.

UPI. 'Torture Reported in East Timor Jails'. 23 April 2006.

Vencat, Emily Flynn. 'Keepers of the Peace'. *Newsweek International*, 14 November 2005.

Voice of America News. 'Voice of America Editorial'. Radio Scripts – EDITORIAL 0–11521, 2004.

Vrachnos, Anastasia. 'A Long March Home'. *AsiaWeek*, 26(43), 3 November 2000,

Wandita, Galuh. 'Healing the Past Atrocities against Women'. *The Jakarta Post*, 30 March 2007.

Williams, Louise. 'Papua Braces for Jakarta Onslaught'. *Sydney Morning Herald*, 12 August 2004, 10.

Williams, Louise and Leonie Lamont. 'Rape Used Over and Over as a Systematic Torture'. *The Sydney Morning Herald*, 11 September 1999.

Yudhawiranata, Agung. 'Opinion: RI Needs Truth Commission'. *The Jakarta Post*, 21 October 2003.

LEGISLATION

Treaties

Basic Principles and Guidelines on the Right to a Remedy and Reparation for Gross Violations of International Human Rights Law and Serious Violations of International Humanitarian Law United Nations General Assembly Resolution 60/147 Annex, adopted 16 December 2005, United Nations Doc. A/RES/60/147, 21 March 2006.

1951 Convention Relating to the Status of Refugees, 189 U.N.T.S. 150, entered into force April 22, 1954, as amended by the 1967 Protocol, 606 U.N.T.S. 267.

Convention on the Prevention and Punishment of the Crime of Genocide, 78 U.N.T.S. 277, entered into force Jan. 12, 1951.

Convention on the Elimination of All Forms of Discrimination against Women (CEDAW) 18 Dec. 1979, 1249 U.N.T.S. 513.

Declaration on the Protection of Women and Children in Emergency and Armed Conflict General Assembly resolution 3318 (XXIX) of 14 December 1974.

Declaration on the Elimination of Violence against Women General Assembly resolution 48/104 of 20 December 1993.

Geneva Convention for the Amelioration of the Condition of Wounded, Sick and Shipwrecked Members of Armed Forces at Sea, Aug. 12, 1949, art. 50, 6 U.S.T. 3217, 75 U.N.T.S. 85 [Convention II].

Geneva Convention Relative to the Treatment of Prisoners of War, Aug. 12, 1949, 6 U.S.T. 3316, 75 U.N.T.S. 135 [Convention III].

Geneva Convention Relative to the Protection of Civilian Persons in Time of War, Aug. 12, 1949, 6 U.S.T. 3516, 75 U.N.T.S. 287 [Convention IV].

Geneva Convention for the Amelioration of the Condition of the Wounded and Sick in Armed Forces in the Field, Aug. 12, 1949, art. 49, 6 U.S.T. 3114, 75 U.N.T.S. 31 [Convention I].

International Covenant on Civil and Political Rights, 1966

Optional Protocol to the Convention on the Elimination of All Forms of Discrimination against Women (CEDAW-OP) GA res. 54/4, annex, 54 United Nations GAOR Supp. (No. 49) at 5, United Nations Doc. A/54/49 (Vol. I); 2131 UNTS 83, 6 October 1999.

Princeton Principles on Universal Jurisdiction, 2001.

Rome Statute of the International Criminal Court, 2187 U.N.T.S. 90, entered into force July 1, 2002.

Security Council Resolution 1325 'Women, Peace and Security', 2000.

Statute of the International Criminal Tribunal for the Former Yugoslavia, SecurityCouncil Resolution 808 (1993).

Statute of the International Criminal Tribunal for Rwanda, Security Council Resolution 955 (1994).

Statute of the Office of the United Nations High Commissioner for Refugees, Annex to UNGA Res. 428(V), 14 Dec. 1950.

United Nations Convention against Torture and Other Cruel, Inhuman or Degrading Treatment or Punishment 10 Dec. 1984, 1465 U.N.T.S. 85.

United Nations Commission on Human Rights (now the Human Rights Council), Updated Set of Principles for the Protection and Promotion of Human Rights through Action to Combat Impunity. Report of the Independent Expert to Update the Set of Principles to Combat Impunity, Addendum, United Nations Doc. E/CN.4/2005/102/Add.1, 8 February 2005.

Vienna Convention on the Law of Treaties, May 23, 1969, art. 53, 1155 U.N.T.S. 331.

East Timorese Legislation

Security Council Resolution 1264 (1999).

Security Council Resolution 1272 (25 October 1999) 'East Timor'.

1999/1 Authority of the Transitional Administration (incl. applicable law)

Official Constitution of the Democratic Republic of East Timor, (English).

1999/1 Authority of the Transitional Administration (incl. applicable law).
1999/3 Establishment of the Transitional Judicial Services Commission.
2000/11 Organisation of Courts in East Timor (Amended by Regulation 2001/25).
2000/14 Amendments to Regulation 2000/11.
2000/15 Establishment of Panels with Exclusive Jurisdiction over Serious Criminal Offences. UNTAET/REG/2000/15 6 June 2000.
2000/16 Organisation of the Prosecution Service.
2000/30 Transitional Rules of Criminal Procedure (Amended by Regulation 2001/25).
2001/10 Establishment of a commission for reception, truth and reconciliation in East Timor.
2001/25 Amending Regulations No. 2000/11 and 2000/30.
2001/26 On the amendment of UNTAET Regulation No. 1999/3 on the establishment of a Transitional Judicial Service Commission and on the amendment of UNTAET Regulation No. 2000/16 on the organization of the Public Prosecution Service in East Timor.
Memorandum of Understanding between the Republic of Indonesia and UNTAET regarding cooperation in Legal, Judicial and Human Rights related matters.
Agreement between the Republic of Indonesia and the Portuguese Republic on the Question of East Timor (5 May Agreements), Annex 1, Article 3.
Resolution S/2006/923 (29 November 2006) Letter dated 30 October 2006 from the Secretary-General addressed to the President of the Security Council (Special Representative for Timor-Leste and Head of the United Nations Integrated Mission in Timor-Leste (UNMIT)).
Resolution S/2006/924 (29 November 2006) Letter dated 29 November 2006 from the President of the Security Council to the Secretary-General (Special Representative for Timor-Leste and Head of the United Nations Integrated Mission in Timor-Leste (UNMIT)).

Indonesian Legislation

Law No 26/2000 on the Human Rights Court (Bahasa Indonesia).
Government Regulation on Witness Protection for the Human Rights Court (Bahasa Indonesia).
Government regulation on Compensation, Restitution and Rehabilitation for Victims (Bahasa Indonesia)
Presidential Decree (Keppres) No.53/2001 on the Ad Hoc Human Rights Court (Bahasa Indonesia).
Presidential Decree (Keppres) No.96/2001 on the Ad Hoc Human Rights Court (Bahasa Indonesia).
Treaty between Australia and the Republic of Indonesia on the Zone of Cooperation in an Area between the Indonesian Province of East Timor and Northern Australia (Timor Gap Treaty), (Timor Sea, 11 December 1989) : Entry into Force: 9 February 1991. Australian Treaty Series; 1991 No. 9. Canberra: Australian Govt. Publishing Service, 1991.
UN Doc. A/54/727 and S/2000/65 (26 January 2000) *Letter from the Minister for Foreign Affairs of Indonesia to the Secretary-General.*, January 2000.

CASE LAW

Serious Crimes Court, Dili

The General Prosecutor of the United Nations Transitional Administration in East Timor v. Joao Fernandes, Case No. 001/00.CG.2000 (25 January 2000). (**The Joao Fernandes Case**).

The General Prosecutor of the United Nations Transitional Administration in East Timor v. Julio Fernandes, Case No. 002/00C.G.2000 (1 March 2000) **(The Julio Fernandes Case).**

The General Prosecutor of the United Nations Transitional Administration in East Timor v. Joni Marques, Manuel Da Costa, Joao Da Costa alias Lemorai, Paulo Da Costa, Amelio Da Costa, Hilario Da Silva, Gonsalo Dos Santos, Alarico Fernandes, Mautersa Monis, Gilberto Fernandes and Syaful Anwar. Dili District Court Special Panel for Serious Crimes Case no. 9/CG/2000, 11 December 2001. (**The Los Palos Case**).

The General Prosecutor of the United Nations Transitional Administration in East Timor v. Joao Franca Da Silva alias Jhoni Franca, José Cardoso Fereira alias Mouzinho and Sabino Gouvia Leite. Dili District Court Special Panel for Serious Crimes Case no. 4/CG/2000. (**The Lolotoe Trial**).

The General Prosecutor of the United Nations Transitional Administration in East Timor v. Leonardus Kasa. Dili District Court Special Panel for Serious Crimes Case no. 11/CG/2000, 9 May 2001. (**The Kasa Case**).

The General Prosecutor of the United Nations Transitional Administration in East Timor v. Francisco Soares. Dili District Court Special Panel for Serious Crimes Case no. 14/2001.

Jakarta ad hoc Human Rights Court

Eurico Guterres. Indictment not available in English. JSMP Case Update online: http://www.jsmp.minihub.org/Indonesia/caseupdates/UpdEurico.pdf.

Drs. G.M. Timbul Silaen. Case File No: 01/HAM/TIM-TIM/02/2002. Indictment available online: http://socrates.berkeley.edu/%7Ewarcrime/.

Abilio José Osorio Soares. Case File No. : 02/HAM/TIM-TIM/02/2002. Indictment available online: http://socrates.berkeley.edu/%7Ewarcrime/.

Cases on Universal Criminal Jurisdiction

DPP v. Doot [1973] 1 All E.R. 940, pp. 954–58; [1973] 2 WLR 532, pp. 547–52 (see speech of Lord Salmon).

Joyce v. DPP [1946] AC 347.

Liangsiriprasert v. Govt. of the USA [1990] 2 All E.R. 866; [1990] 3 WLR 606; 85 ILR 109.

United States v. Yunis, 924 F.2d 1086, 1091 (D.C. Cir. 1991).

Doe v. Lumintang, (D.D.C. CV0064) (Filed March 28, 2000; Judgment Sept. 10, 2001).

Regina v. Bow Street Metropolitan Stipendiary Magistrate And Others, Ex Parte Pinochet Ugarte (No. 3), [2000] 1 A.C. 147.

Todd v. Panjaitan (No. 92–12255, slip op. (D. Mass. Oct. 26, 1994)).

International Tribunal for the Former Yugoslavia

Prosecutor v. Dragoljub Kunarac, Radomir Kovac and Zoran Vukovic, IT-96-23/1-T, Judgement 22 February 2001. (**The Celebici camp cases**).

Prosecutor v. Anto Furundzija, ICTY-95-17/1-T, Judgment 10 December 1998.

International Criminal Tribunal for Rwanda

Prosecutor v. Jean-Paul Akayesu, ICTR-96-4-T, Judgment 2 September 1998.

Inter-American Commission of Human Rights

Mejia Egocheaga v. Peru (1996) 1 Butterworths Human Rights Cases 229,1996.

Portugal v. Australia, International Court of Justice General List No. 84, 1995 I.C.J. 90 (1995).

Prosecutor v. Aleksovski, Case IT-95-14/1-T, Judgment 25 June 1999: Appeal Judgment, 24 March 2002.

Public Prosecutor v. Armando dos Santos Court of Appeal,15 July 2003.

Index

For Product Safety Concerns and Information please contact our EU representative GPSR@taylorandfrancis.com
Taylor & Francis Verlag GmbH, Kaufingerstraße 24, 80331 München, Germany

www.ingramcontent.com/pod-product-compliance
Lightning Source LLC
LaVergne TN
LVHW011124300926
849160LV00008B/503
* 9 7 8 0 4 1 5 6 2 6 2 2 4 *